Seaplane Pilot

Seaplane Pilot

Training for the Seaplane Pilot Certificate and Beyond

Dale DeRemer

A Focus Series Book
Aviation Supplies & Academics, Inc.
Newcastle, Washington

Seaplane Pilot: Training for the Seaplane Pilot Certificate and Beyond
by Dale DeRemer

Aviation Supplies & Academics, Inc.
7005 132nd Place SE
Newcastle, Washington 98059 U.S.A.
Website: www.asa2fly.com
Email: asa@asa2fly.com

Published by Aviation Supplies & Academics, Inc., 2003

Printed in the United States of America

2013 2012 2011 2010 2009 9 8 7 6 5 4 3 2

ASA-SPT
ISBN 1-56027-502-2
978-1-56027-502-2

Cover photos: Bill McCarrel and Dale DeRemer

Acknowledgements and credits for Photography: Acknowledgements and photography credits: Thanks to the many contributors of seaplane photography to this book. Many of the photos are by Dale DeRemer—if a photo credit does not appear adjacent to a photo it is by the author; these are on pages ix, xiii, xv, xvi, 2, 5, 6, 12, 17, 19, 22, 23, 35, 38, 42, 44, 45, 47, 52, 54, 56, 58, 73, 77, 92, 101, 198, 205, 206, 208, 209, 210, 211, 213, 215, 219, 220, 223, 228, 230, 231, 260, 264, 276, 280, 288, 291, 316, 336. Other photo credits as follows—p. xiv, EDO corporation; Seaplane Pilots Association (SPA) courtesy Mike Volk, pp. xvii, xix, xx, 1, 12, 33, 74, 84, 102, 110, 123, 156, 166, 259, 272, 301, 318, 332; photos by Burke Mees on pp. 14, 40, 119, 130, 178, 238, 306, 334; p. 28, ASA; photos by Bill McCarrel on pp. 50, 148, 150, 158, 301(bottom); photos by Robert Grant on pp. xii, 248, 256, 258; courtesy Wipaire, Inc., pp. 149, 299; p. 174 by John Lowery; p. 265 by Russ Hewitt; and Super Cub photos courtesy of Dave Bennett on pp. 20, 55, 104, 144, 165.

Library of Congress Cataloging-in-Publication data:

DeRemer, Dale.
Seaplane pilot : training for the seaplane pilot certificate and beyond / by Dale DeRemer. — 1st ed.
p. cm.
Includes bibliographical references and index.
ISBN 1-56027-502-2 (trade paperback)
1. Seaplanes — Piloting — Examinations — Study guides. 2. Air pilots — Licenses — United States. I. Title.

TL684.D3327 2003
629.132'5247—dc21
2003013798

02

Contents

Continued

Section III **Flight Operations**

Section IV **Preflight and Checkride Preparation**

About The Author

Called "the recognized dean of seaplane pilots" by *Vintage Airplane* magazine and "the father of the SEAWINGS national safety program for seaplane pilots" by *Water Flying* magazine, Dr. DeRemer started flying into the Northwest Territories many years ago. In the past 17 years, he has conducted his well known wilderness courses, training hundreds of pilots, one-on-one, in the skills of wilderness seaplane operations from the rain forests and high volcanic lakes of Central America to beyond the Arctic Circle. He is ATP-rated land and sea with more than 20,000 hours flight experience in landplanes, seaplanes and helicopters. He is a Gold Seal Flight Instructor. He has had prestigious recognition as "Seaplane Pilot of the Year" by the Seaplane Pilots Association in 1998, inducted into the EAA-NAFI Flight Instructor Hall of Fame in 1999 and "Professor Emeritus of Aviation" by the University of North Dakota College of Aerospace Sciences in 2000 after 20 years of teaching aviation subjects at the university level. He has flown as charter pilot, agricultural pilot and chief corporate pilot. He is an experienced mariner, well versed in the ways of the water, having lived aboard his 46-foot sailboat for seven years while sailing it over 70,000 miles.

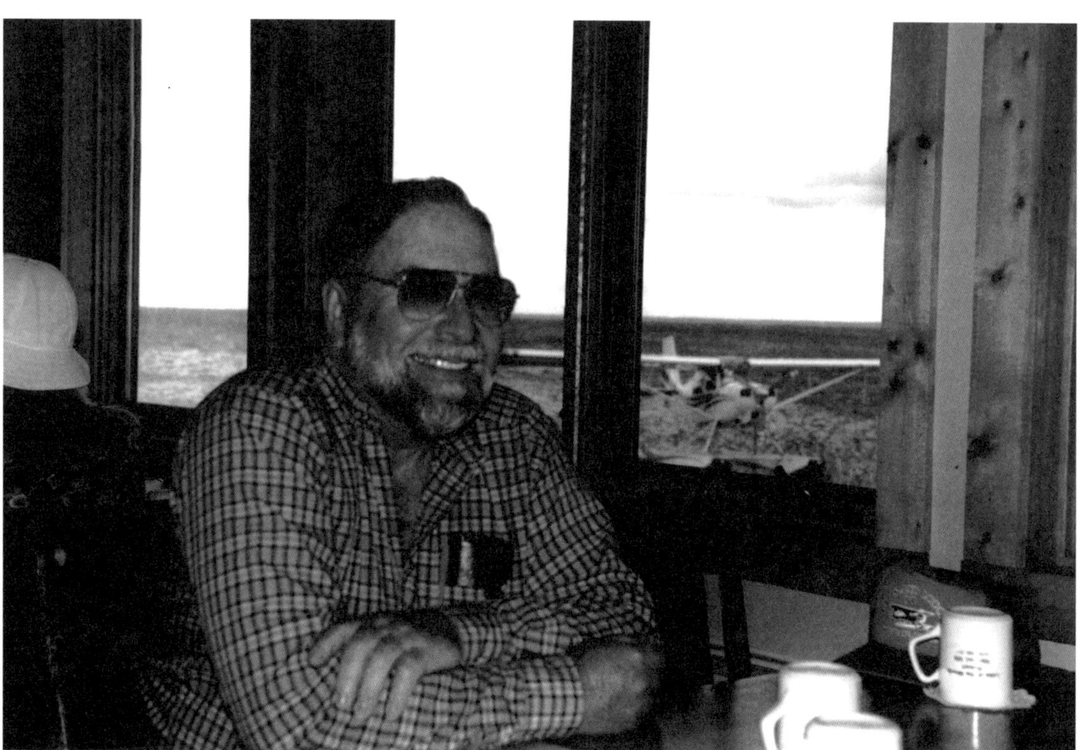

Dr. DeRemer is the author of these other books:

Water Flying Concepts: an advanced text on wilderness water flying, Published by Aviation Supplies & Academics, Inc.

Aircraft Systems for Pilots, Jeppesen Co.

Global Navigation for Pilots: International Flight Techniques and Procedures, Aviation Supplies & Academics, Inc.

Seaplane Operations: basic and advanced techniques for floatplanes, amphibians and flying boats from around the world, Aviation Supplies & Academics, Inc.

The author's website is found at **http://bobcat.aero.und.edu/deremer/**

Acknowledgements

The author is most grateful for the assistance in the writing of this book to the following respected seaplane affectionados:

Robert Curtis, SPA Field Director for Kansas and Missouri and Credit Manager for Cessna Finance Corporation who wrote much of the multi-engine sea chapter, in partial fulfillment of the requirements for a Masters Degree in Aviation at the University of North Dakota, Center for Aerospace Sciences.

Robert Grant, Canadian bush pilot and photographer/writer who provided the Foreword and many photographs throughout the book as well as a critique of many of the chapters.

Bill McCarrell, aviation photographer, for the many fine photos found throughout the book.

Marlan Perhus, FAA Aviation Safety Inspector in the MSP FSDO, who provided a good critique and information for the multi-engine chapter and was a willing and most capable source of information on many topics in this book.

David Wiley, Wiley's Seaplanes, Lake Oswego, Oregon, senior flight instructor and examiner for seaplane and many other pilot ratings, for helping me find many of the oversights in this book.

And to the many pilots, students and clients I have flown with over the years, thank you for what you have taught me. Fly safely!

Foreword

Quite some years ago, I happened to be standing behind several pilots waiting for dinner at a fishing lodge near Brainerd, Minnesota. Tired after a long drive south from Canada to a Seaplane Pilots Association gathering, my only thoughts concerned the plate of steak and potatoes waiting at the end of the buffet line. Someone tapped me on the shoulder.

The tapper introduced himself as Dale DeRemer and immediately launched into an arm-waving, finger-pointing discourse on the pleasures of seaplane flying. The enthusiasm of this big, bearded lumberjack in red and black check shirt and pants wet at the cuffs, proved so contagious that all of us in the steak parade forgot our hunger pangs. By the time I managed to ease the first forkful of filet into my mouth, it occurred to me that perhaps Dale DeRemer was crazy—about seaplanes.

Only later did I learn more about this colorful character. Reflecting back on that pleasant evening in Minnesota sometime in 1983, it took several more get-togethers and chance meetings before appreciating the modesty and humility of Dale DeRemer. He never mentioned his accomplishments as corporate pilot, helicopter pilot or flight instructor nor the fact he'd sailed over 70,000 miles learning to understand winds, currents, tides and a myriad of other nautical knowledge—factors which helped *Vintage Aircraft* magazine declare him the "recognized dean of seaplane pilots."

DeRemer also skipped the part where he'd starved as a graduate teaching assistant earning a skimpy $125 a week while married with two daughters. In that same period, Utah State University awarded him a masters degree in soil chemistry and before long, nonstop plugging and persisting brought in a doctorate. DeRemer's drive—he even aerial sprayed cattle yards at night and along the way, managed a Christmas tree farm—seemed incredible.

In 1989, DeRemer channeled his fervor for seaplanes into his first book, a hardcover. Called *Water Flying Concepts,* this advanced text on wilderness flying came into existence after he realized little had been published for anyone with a recent seaplane rating. It provided a scientific approach to seaplane performance and allowed pilots to flight test their own machines to determine precise performance airspeeds. Frequently, as I docked my government floatplane, people asked if I knew Dr. Dale DeRemer. (He taught for seventeen years at the University of North Dakota's Center for Aerospace Sciences and retired as full professor.) Clearly, much of the keenness the crazy man felt for aviation had leapt from those pages into the minds of thousands of readers.

DeRemer logged plenty of hours sampling North and Central American lakes and rivers with his 1963 Cessna 180 N2125Z and other airplanes belonging to numerous wilderness course students. He found that pilots came with wide varieties of training and standards as if they had absorbed their seaplane understanding by trial and error and passed experiences "father-to-son" or "pilot-to-pilot," similar to the dissemination of tribal knowledge through Indian lore and legends. The system worked, but DeRemer wanted a better way, especially since pioneer pilots were fading from the water flying scene.

Fastidiously kept notes and conversations with high time pilots wherever he went supplemented his own vast experience and led to a considerable store of data, much of which DeRemer incorporated in this book. He also studied accident reports and training syllabi and concluded that seaplane pilots needed continued, recurrent training and thus became the "father" of the FAA's SEAWINGS safety program.

DeRemer, never content to rest on his catalogue of honors and awards, decided to push on to a more detailed textbook. After all, he reasoned, there still weren't enough publications in the pilot world oriented to wheel-trained individuals exploring seaplane flying and for freshly rated or veteran float enthusiasts. This latest work reaches far beyond unwritten "bush" traditions and, when studied, extends common sense based on sound knowledge of basics and "tricks of the trade" to make seaplane flying easier and safer. Readers will get caught up in the passion characterizing the "Dean's" teaching which will take them beyond the delights of a pair of floats kissing a remote lake to the satisfaction of knowing they are doing their job safely.

When readers understand what this book offers, they will understand seaplanes. Hopefully, the time will come for another DeRemer book—one delving into advanced navigation of wilderness terrain and how situations differ closer to the earth's poles and other subjects helpful to all pilots.

Robert S. Grant

Robert S. Grant currently flies DeHavilland Twin Otters in western Africa and previously spent 22 years with Ontario's Ministry of Natural Resources on DeHavilland Turbo-Beavers, single Otters and Twin Otters with wheels, skis and floats as well as Canadair CL-215 water bombers. He previously worked in numerous regions of Canada's north on aircraft from Piper PA-18 Super Cubs to Douglas DC-3s. As a journalist, Grant has produced over 1,500 articles for press releases, newspapers, magazines and journals of six countries. His three books—*Bush Flying: Romance of the North*; *Great Northern Bushplanes*; *Wheels, Skis and Floats*—feature northern flying and pilots. He has logged 15,000 hours and says he expects to fly commercially until age 101.

Introduction

Welcome to the Wonderful World of Seaplane Flying!

Learning

Learning to fly is a new and wonderful experience. I was privileged to be able to learn to fly three times in my life. The first was flying a landplane and I consider myself most privileged that it was in a taildragger. The second time was a helicopter. The third, and most enjoyable, was the seaplane.

If you are already a landplane pilot, getting the seaplane rating is just pure fun. Combine it with a vacation or other trip. Don't get locked into the idea that you must do it near home. The seaplane rating should only take a very few days or maybe only a long weekend if you study well before. Planning such a vacation trip is easy with the Seaplane Pilots Association's National Training Directory, found at **http://www.seaplanes.org**.

Once you have the seaplane pilot rating, you have the entry ticket to a lifetime of enjoyable water flying and learning. You won't ever learn it all. Mark my word, the seaplane rating

A floatplane is an adventuresome way to travel. Seeing the Mississippi River from south to north, passing the St. Louis arch at 500 feet above the water.

itself will give you the experience you need to realize you really know very little yet, of the skills needed to meet all the challenges of Mother Nature and the water She controls. The really good news is that the joy of learning will continue. The seaplane is a magnificent teacher. Always pay attention to what the seaplane is telling you. If you don't understand what the airplane is telling you, seek answers from other sources. Take every opportunity to fly with pilots from other parts of the country as you will learn something new from them every time you go up.

History

History tells us that the first airplane was flown off the water and successfully landed by Henri Fabre in 1910. Just nine years later, in 1919, the first commercial seaplane operation was started in Halifax, Nova Scotia, flying a Curtiss HS-2L, according to *The Bush Pilots* (Time-Life Books). I have always found it to be most remarkable, how quickly this developed! The seaplane did its part to help settle much of North America and other parts of the world. Further evidence was the great hull-type multi-engine seaplanes that pioneered air travel all over the world.

EDO Corporation

In 1934, Mayor LaGuardia spearheaded establishment of New York City's two seaplane facilities on Manhattan which allowed TWA to provide passenger service from Manhattan to the rest of the world. The Ford TriMotor on EDO 43-14060 floats with P&W 450 HP had a range of 400–500 miles.

Enjoying a little cabin built in 1937, on a pristine lake in Ontario, easily accessible only by seaplane.

Freedom

The mystique of the seaplane is that, when it departs, it is like a sailboat sailing out of the harbor… it can go anywhere, which stimulates the imagination about where it might be going. When a land airplane departs, everyone knows it must land at another airport. When a seaplane departs, it can go anywhere there is water. Even in the states that are considered dry there is lots of water and therefore, landing areas. So, there are few restrictions to where that departing seaplane might be headed—a remote lake, a rushing river far from mankind or a beautiful resort on the water somewhere.

Enjoying the out-of-doors

Our modern society shields us from the out-of-doors. We live indoors. Most of us work indoors. Our car surrounds us and keeps us inside, even though we can see out. Even the seaplane protects us from the elements (but gives us a great, close up view of it). Ahh, but when we land and open the window, we are once again a boat on the water, in some beautiful place. That is one of the great attractions of the seaplane.

Access to remote places

There is no place on this continent we can't go with a seaplane. From the shores of the Northwest Passage in the Arctic to the lakes in the rain forest of Guatemala or remote tributaries of the Amazon. Even the great desert southwest has water we can land upon, step ashore and enjoy the desert. Along with this special privilege is the fact that most remote places have little or no services. There is no one to be sure your runway is free of foreign objects, no one to wash your windshield, no guarantee the gasoline, in barrels, is clean or even that there will be gasoline there, when you arrive. When you fly there, you are an adventurer. But it is a whole lot simpler than it was for the seaplane pilot-pioneer. Today we have charts...they had to make their charts as they flew into uncharted territory. We have GPS, but you better still know how to navigate skillfully without it or you will place yourself and others with you at a higher level of risk.

Flying seaplanes into remote places is an advanced skill you can look forward to learning after you master the basics.

The seaplane has many jobs, including saving lives: Loading a stroke victim aboard for the trip from a remote island to the hospital at Ketchikan, AK, under the watchful eye of flying physician Dr. Meloche (left rear).

The water…and the challenge

Some of us are mysteriously attracted to the water. We like to look at it, constantly moving like gazing at a flickering fire, or glassy and mirrored, reflecting some other beauty.

We also are attracted to the challenges of flight. Vast new challenges appear when we fly from water. We do battle with the infinite and ever changing challenges and eventually, as we grow old, enjoyment of the challenges changes to a mixture of confidence, respect for the strength and grandness of the water and the satisfaction of doing something well that very few other people can do.

So, come with me on a learning adventure. There are many lessons in each chapter of this book. Whether you are studying intensely for the oral and checkride or just reviewing your knowledge and skills from the comfort of your easy chair, welcome to this seaplane learning experience!

SPA

A Cub "on the buoy" in safe harbor at the Oshkosh fly-in.

How To Use This Book

So many times I have said, "flying a floatplane is about as much fun as you can have with your clothes on!" In the "Welcome" section you just read, I told you how much fun it was learning to fly seaplanes. Now, as we get into the serious part of learning about seaplanes, let's keep it fun!

Are you a licensed seaplane pilot?

This book is going to be a learning resource for you so let me call your attention to the index which is quite comprehensive, so any time you need to look anything up, I suggest starting there.

If you are already a rated seaplane pilot, Chapter 2 may expand your horizons with seaplane learning resources you aren't currently aware of, as will the rather extensive Bibliography at the back of the book. You are beyond the need for Chapters 1 and 3.

At the beginning of most chapters, I have put a comment about what you, as a licensed seaplane pilot, might expect to learn by reading that chapter. I hope, and suspect, that you will learn something new, or forgotten, from every chapter you read.

Another way to see if there is something interesting for you in a chapter is to read the **Review** at the end of the chapter. It will probably pique your interest in getting into the details of the chapter.

You might want to start with the chapter on sailing (Chapter 8) as it has been my experience that most of us don't do enough sailing to keep proficient. There are some pretty good hints there that might make it easier for you. How good are you at getting an anchor out and having it stick, to keep you from going over a rapids in a river or on the rocks if the engine won't start? Chapter 16 is full of good mooring ideas and information about line, and a few knots you should know.

I put some of the "heavier reading" chapters near the end of the book. They cover seaplane performance and limitations (Chapter 18), water rudder, fuel and amphibian systems (Chapter 19), what you need to know to answer the question, "if the (whatever) is broken in my airplane, am I still safe and legal to fly it?" is in Chapter 20, characteristics of water and seaplanes are covered in Chapter 21, maritime rules and marine aids to navigation are in Chapter 22, and what you need to know about certificates and documents that need to be in your airplane are covered in Chapter 23.

Enjoy!

Multi-Engine Sea?

For those of you who are, or will one day be, interested in a multi-engine seaplane rating, Chapter 17 will take you there.

Are you adding "seaplane" to your current land-restricted pilot's license?

If you are starting to study for your seaplane rating, the next three chapters of Section I, "Getting Started" tell you what goals are ahead of you (Chapter 1), where to find additional information (Chapter 2) and how to find the right flight instructor or flight school (Chapter 3).

As a pilot, I am sure you want to just go down to the floatplane and get started, leaving all the heavier learning for another time when you are more in the mood. So we will do just that in this book, with Chapter 4 about the preflight inspection, then some ideas in Chapter 5 about managing your cockpit, crew and passengers so that everybody has more fun. Then we will get the engine started (Chapter 6). "How can there be a whole chapter about starting the engine?" you ask. There is a lot to learn about seaplanes!

All about taxiing is in Chapter 7, sailing in Chapter 8 (it is amazing how many seaplane pilots haven't had anyone teach them how easy it is to taxi their seaplanes in high winds). What needs to be done just before takeoff, including water rudder management, is in Chapter 9. Some things you need to know when airborne are in Chapter 10. Then we go flying!

The "in-flight" chapters include Chapter 11 about takeoffs, Chapter 12 about how to determine if a water location is safe to land on, and Chapter 13 is all about approaches, landings and go-arounds in seaplanes. After a discussion of slow flight, steep turns, stalls and spin awareness (how to avoid the nasty accidents that can happen to seaplanes), a discussion of emergency operations can be found in Chapter 15.

Then the fun on-the-water topics of the seaplane are covered in Chapter 16 where the secrets of docking, beaching, ramping and securing your seaplane are covered along with in-

SPA

A plow-taxiing Husky on Wipline amphibious floats.

formation about lines (ropes) and a few very useful knots so you can operate confidently like a real mariner.

There is some "heavier reading" toward the back of the book; I did it this way just to avoid dulling your enthusiasm by reading regulations, etc., until you have a real need-to-know. Once you start flying seaplanes, you will quickly develop a need-to-know about seaplane performance and limitations (Chapter 18), plus: operation of seaplane systems like water rudders and special stuff about amphibians (Chapter 19); more about the water itself and characteristics of seaplanes like porpoising and skipping (Chapter 21): how to answer the question "the (whatever) is broken on my airplane, am I still legal and safe to fly it?" (Chapter 20); and then, what you need to know about seaplane bases and aids to marine navigation (Chapter 22).

Finally, Chapter 23 will get you ready for your checkride. This book works closely with the Practical Test Standards (PTS), the FAA document that you, your flight instructor, and the examiner must follow while getting ready for and passing the checkride. The PTS can be found in the appendix, and they're referenced by blue "PTS headings" at the beginning of each chapter, or blue text in the sidebar nearby the related discussion. It is a good idea to read the referenced section in the PTS while reading the chapter.

Just before the checkride, you will want to do a review. At the end of most of the chapters is a **Review**. This section will help you to remember what you read earlier. If you need to, go back into the chapter and read again what your review shows to be a weak area.

Have fun and Good Luck on the checkride! Once that is done, you have only begun to learn! Then, read Chapter 24 that has some answers to the question, "what now?"

SPA

A Lake amphibian landing on glassy water.

Section I
Getting Started

Burke Mees

A pilot preflights her floatplane.

Chapter 1
Qualifying for the Seaplane Rating

How is the Seaplane Rating Obtained?

If you are already a rated seaplane pilot, you should skip ahead and go directly to Chapter 4 now (go to Page 21).

The seaplane pilot rating, called the ASES certificate (Airplane Single Engine Sea) may be obtained as the first pilot rating or, most commonly, as an add-on rating for those pilots who already hold the ASEL (Airplane, Single Engine Land) certificate. Since probably 99% of ASES ratings are add-on, this book will primarily address the topics required for the add-on rating. They just happen to be all the topics directly related to seaplane flying. Since about the same percentage of ratings obtained are done in floatplanes, this book primarily discusses operation of the floatplane. However, the same principles apply to the monohull seaplane.

A table, called the Rating Task Table, will be found near the beginning of the Practical Test Standards (PTS), which is the FAA document that specifies the knowledge and skills you need to know. In appendix 1, the PTS task table is found on Page 354. More about this reference is covered in Chapter 2. This table defines which tasks will be tested, based on the ratings the applicant holds and the sea rating sought. The PTS referred to in this book is reprinted in the appendix.

For an example of this table, *see* Appendix 1, Page 354.

While there are separate PTS's for Private and Commercial sea ratings, close inspection of the two will show that the tasks in each, for the add-on sea rating (adding private/commercial pilot sea to an existing private/commercial pilot land) are essentially the same. However, the examiner will expect a higher level of knowledge and skill from the commercial pilot applicant.

FAA-8081-14AS, *Private Pilot Practical Test Standards for Airplane (SEL and SES)*

For this reason, when discussing the PTS "Tasks," this book does not differentiate between private and commercial.

To qualify for the sea rating, you must pass an oral examination and a flight check with an FAA examiner or designated seaplane examiner, based on the required tasks outlined in the PTS and discussed in detail in this book. The good news is that there is no written examination.

Private or Commercial Sea Rating?

If you hold a commercial pilot land certificate, you may choose to take either the private or commercial checkride. If the private check is selected, your pilot's certificate will read "Commercial pilot–land, private privileges–sea." Since there is little difference between the private and commercial checkrides, my recommendation is definitely to take the commercial sea checkride. Another situation where this issue may come up is the pilot who has the private pilot land and sea rating. Taking the commercial pilot land checkride does not provide commercial pilot sea privileges. Another checkride in the seaplane is necessary to upgrade to commercial sea. So, if possible, acquire the commercial land certificate, *then* get the seaplane rating. That way, only one seaplane checkride is needed.

What Standards Will You be Held To?

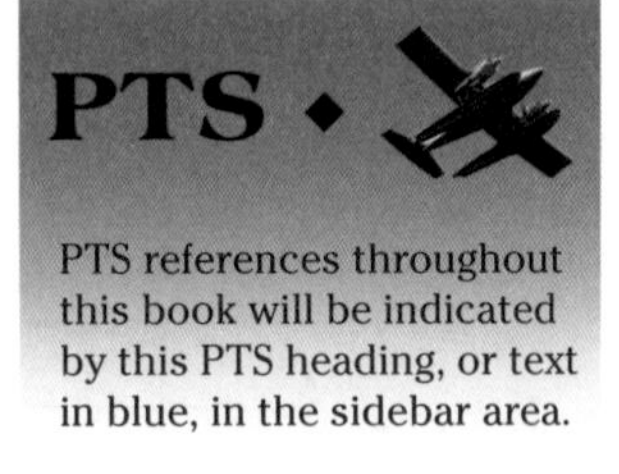

PTS references throughout this book will be indicated by this PTS heading, or text in blue, in the sidebar area.

The standards (topics and tasks to be tested) are spelled out in the PTS. References to the appropriate section are found in the sidebars throughout this book. If there has been a recent update, it is also available in print and on the FAA website. This book takes each topic in the PTS and discusses it in detail. If the reader is familiar with the discussions herein, and has acquired adequate skill in operating the seaplane, passing the examination will be just another fun seaplane experience.

How Much Flying is Required?

Flight time needed to reach proficiency varies from about 4.5 hours to 15 hours. Why this variation? Training time needed is a function of the skill of the pilot (as a pilot and a mariner), the complexity of the aircraft used for learning and testing, and the level of skill required by the flight instructor before the applicant is signed off to take the practical test. Most flight schools and experienced flight instructors can give a good estimate of the time required because, for them, the only unknown is the skill of the pilot. Even that can be approximated by the instructor or school after a quick look at the applicant's logbook. So you should have a good idea of the flight time required before starting the course.

Canadian landplane pilots presently need fly a seaplane for only about five hours and have an endorsement entered in their log-book by a commercial seaplane pilot in order to be certified to fly seaplanes. However, the same knowledge and skills discussed in this book are what seaplane pilots anywhere in the world need to know.

Let's get started!

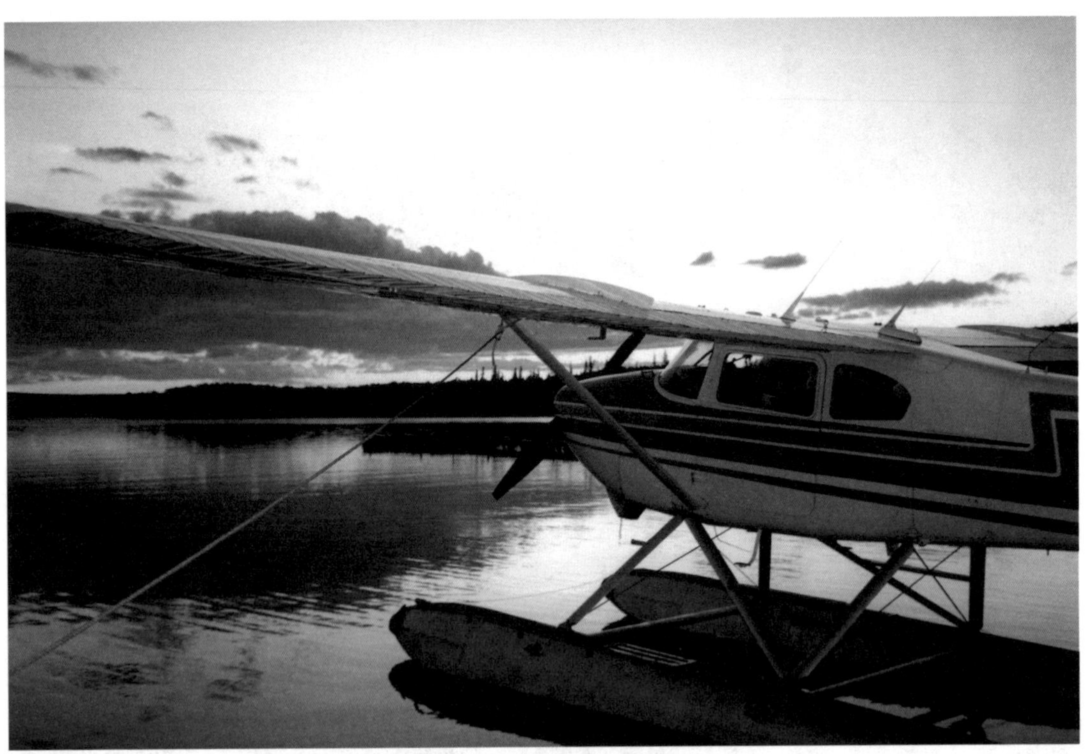

Near the end of a perfect day of seaplane flying in the Canadian bush.

Chapter 2
Resources and Information

For the seaplane pilot who wishes to review or learn more, and for the aspiring seaplane pilot, there are now a number of good sources for seaplane lore and knowledge. For the beginning sea-pilot, the FAA's Practical Test Standards are the bible by which you will be tested for the seaplane rating. A description of the PTS is in this chapter, and the entire single-engine sea PTS is printed in the appendix.

Books

When I started flying seaplanes, there wasn't much available to read on the subject, and what was available was written before WWII. Fortunately, that has changed. Here is a short list. Refer to the bibliography for more available resources.

See Bibliography, Page 369.

Other Books by this Author

Seaplane topics:

Seaplane Operations: Basic and Advanced Techniques for Floatplanes, Amphibians and Flying Boats from around the World;
Aviation Supplies & Academics, Inc. (ASA)

Water Flying Concepts: A text on wilderness water flying;
Aviation Supplies & Academics, Inc.

Other aviation related topics:

Aircraft Systems for Pilots; Jeppesen Company

Global Navigation for Pilots;
Aviation Supplies & Academics, Inc.

Other ASA seaplane publications

Notes of a Seaplane Instructor: An Instructional Guide to Seaplane Flying by Burke Mees

Figure 2-1. Other seaplane topics by Dale DeRemer

Once the seaplane rating is completed, you will find plenty of reading material to get ready for the next water flying season! The Seaplane Pilots Association (SPA) website has a significant list of books dealing with various aspects of seaplanes and their operation.

Seaplane Pilots Association

The Seaplane Pilots Association (SPA), over 7,000 members strong, provides its membership with Federal, State and local representation on matters of access to waterways and other issues. Publications include *Water Flying Magazine* and the *Seaplane Landing Directory*, which is the most complete directory of U.S. waterways available to seaplanes. You can find other seaplane information on SPA's website at **www.seaplanes.org**. The SPA national staff and field directors are a great source for seaplane knowledge.

Regional Associations

There are many regional associations where information is available. A list of these organizations can be found on the SPA website.

Water Flying Magazine

Water Flying Magazine is the only periodical in the U.S. devoted entirely to seaplanes. It is published by SPA, and the subscription is included in their annual membership dues. It is a must for pilots interested in seaplanes.

SPA Field Directors

SPA's field directors are experienced seaplane pilots familiar with their operational areas. They are a wonderful, willing resource for all sorts of information about seaplanes and their use in each area. A directory of field directors is on the SPA website.

Aviation Canada

Aviation Canada magazine is published quarterly and is rich in seaplane lore and information. Their website is **www.aviationcanada.ca**.

Figure 2-2. ASA's Practical Test Standards

Practical Test Standards

Most government publications are terribly dry reading. The PTS is no exception. However, we pilots know that when we go for a checkride, it is "judgement day," and it is nice to know the criteria on which we are going to be judged. The following discussion about the PTS is designed to help you understand the "rules of engagement" for you, your flight instructor, and the examiner.

Practical Test Standards books are published by the Federal Aviation Administration (FAA) to establish the standards for pilot certification. FAA inspectors and designated pilot examiners conduct practical tests in compliance with these standards. Flight instructors are expected to use this book when preparing applicants for practical tests, and you should find these standards helpful during training and preparation.

PTS Book Description

The PTS contains the **Areas of Operation** and **Tasks** that you need to demonstrate knowledge and skill.

Areas of Operation are phases of the practical test arranged in a logical sequence. They begin with Preflight Preparation, and end with Postflight Procedures (as do the chapters in this book). The examiner, however, may conduct the practical test in any sequence that results in a complete and efficient test.

Tasks are knowledge areas, flight procedures and/or maneuvers appropriate to an **Areas of Operation**. Descriptions of **Tasks**

These regulations, Advisory Circulars and more are on ASA's Flight Library CD, which can be ordered from ASA.

Figure 2-3. The Practical Test Standards list these references in the FAA regulations and other procedures publications.

14 CFR Part 43	Maintenance, Preventive Maintenance, Rebuilding, and Alteration
14 CFR Part 61	Certification: Pilots and Flight Instructors
14 CFR Part 91	General Operating and Flight Rules
14 CFR Part 97	Standard Instrument Approach Procedures
NTSB Part 830	Notification and Reporting of Aircraft Accidents and Incidents
AC 00-2	Advisory Circular Checklist
AC 00-6	Aviation Weather
AC 00-45	Aviation Weather Services
AC 61-23	Pilot's Handbook of Aeronautical Knowledge
AC 61-65	Certification: Pilots and Flight Instructors
AC 61-67	Stall Spin Awareness Training
AC 61-84	Role of Preflight Preparation
AC 67-2	Medical Handbook for Pilots
AC 90-48	Pilots' Role in Collision Avoidance
AC 91-69	Seaplane Safety for FAR Part 91 Operations
AC 120-51	Crew Resource Management Training
AIM	Aeronautical Information Manual
FAA-H-8083-1	Aircraft Weight and Balance Handbook
FAA-H-8083-3	Airplane Flying Handbook
FAA-H-8083-15	Instrument Flying Handbook

are not included in the PTS, but you will find them in this book. You will also find in this book the PTS references for particular tasks, which are listed in each section of the PTS. References upon which the practical test book is based are listed in the table in Figure 2-3.

Note: "FAR" is aviation jargon, short for Federal Air Regulations, which refers to CFR (Code of Federal Regulations), Title 14, or 14 CFR or CFR Title 14. See why someone shortened it to the commonly accepted nickname "FAR"?

These other references are available from the FAA, your local FSDO, or the manufacturer of your airplane:

- A/FD—Airport/Facility Directory
- NOTAMs—Notices to Airmen
- POH—Pilot Operating Handbooks
- FAA-Approved Flight Manuals

Do you need all these references at hand while studying for your seaplane rating? No, probably not. All the seaplane related issues are covered in this book. But having the information available on a CD you can pop into your computer is certainly useful. As a licensed landplane pilot, you are already expected to know a lot of the above information but, if you are like me, you need to review from time to time. Remember, the PTS says the examiner may ask you anything that you should already know as a licensed landplane pilot!

The **Objective** lists the important elements that must be satisfactorily performed to demonstrate competency in a **Task**. The **Objective** includes:

1. Specifically what the applicant should be able to do,
2. The conditions under which the TASK is to be performed, and
3 The minimum acceptable standards of performance.

In the PTS, information considered directive in nature is described in terms such as "shall" and "must," and means the actions are mandatory. Terms such as "will," "should," or "may," provide guidance and describe actions that are desirable, permissive, or not mandatory. They allow for flexibility.

Use of Rating Tasks Tables

If an applicant already holds a recreational, private, commercial or ATP pilot certificate and is seeking an additional class (seaplane) rating, sometimes referred to as an "add-on" rating, use the appropriate table at the beginning of the appropriate PTS to determine which required **Tasks** will be evaluated. However, at the discretion of the examiner, the applicant's competence in any **Task** may be evaluated.

See "Rating Task Table" example on Page 354.

An applicant's competence in ***any*** PTS task may be evaluated at the discretion of the examiner.

If the applicant holds two or more category or class ratings at the private level, and the table indicates differing required **Tasks**, the "least restrictive" entry applies. For example, if "All" and "None" are indicated for one **Area of Operation**, the "None" entry applies. If "B" and "B, C" are indicated, the "B" entry applies.

A close inspection of the rating tasks table may raise questions as to the FAA's intent. Generally, in developing these task tables, the FAA policy is to not retest a task that has been tested on a rating already held by the applicant. Also, some tasks are no longer even mentioned in the PTS, such as emergency descents.

This can be a bit of a trap for the applicant because (1) emergency descents are carefully described in the *Airplane Flying Handbook*, and (2) the applicant's skill in performing the emergency descent can be tested if the examiner calls for a simulated in-flight fire emergency with smoke in the cabin. Consequently, this book deals with such issues. To be the very best seaplane pilot you can be, you need to know these things, even if they are not specifically mentioned in the PTS.

OK, lets get on with the fun of learning about seaplanes. There is a lot to learn!

Burke Mees

There are several things the prospective seaplane student can do to ascertain the qualifications of a prospective instructor.

Chapter 3
Choosing a Flight Instructor or Flight School

One must keep in mind that not all flight instructors are created equal. To flight instruct in seaplanes, all that is required by the FAA for a landplane flight instructor to teach in seaplanes is the seaplane rating, which may require as little as 4.5 hours in a seaplane. While this scenario is not likely, it is possible.

It is apparent that an instructor, properly licensed by the FAA, who acquired the seaplane rating in a Super Cub and has not flown a turbo 206 or instructed in amphibians, is probably not qualified to instruct in a T206 amphibian. But the FAA seaplane instructor rating does not differentiate.

While it is not easy to predetermine the quality of flight instruction, there are several things the prospective seaplane pilot/student can do to ascertain the qualifications of a prospective instructor.

Ask the Prospective Instructor Some Questions

How long have you been instructing in seaplanes? What is your total time in seaplanes? Why do you like to instruct in seaplanes? Why do you feel you are qualified to instruct me? Of your last ten students, how many failed their checkrides on the first try? If the instructor is not providing the aircraft for instruction, I suggest you ask if he or she is competent to instruct in the aircraft and how many hours he or she has logged in this model.

There are no right or wrong answers to the above questions, but asking them will provide some feeling for the quality and ability of the instructor, as well as send a message that you expect nothing but the best instructional effort.

Check Other Resources

Aviation is a small community. Ask other flight instructors about the person you are considering. Within most FAA FSDOs, there is at least one inspector who is responsible for overseeing seaplane training. That inspector is not able to tell you directly about a given instructor because, after all, if the person is a flight instructor and has a seaplane rating, then the FAA requirements to teach in a seaplane have been met. But, if you really want to know, seek that inspector out. Go have a cup of coffee with him or her. Some carefully worded questions will provide a pretty good idea whether the flight instructor you are considering has a good or bad reputation. Keep in mind that seaplane flight instructors, like any other profession, have specialties. Some may do a lot of primary instruction. Others specialize in teaching in hull aircraft, or teaching advanced courses. You can find out who is good at what type of instruction.

The field director for the Seaplane Pilots Association in your area may be a good resource as well. You will find that person's name on the SPA website at **www.seaplanes.org**. In the annual issue of *Water Flying Magazine* and on the SPA website is a listing of senior or experienced flight instructors and their areas of expertise. A flight instructor need not be on this list to be good, but if your instructor's name is there, some of your questions about experience will be answered. If your instructor's name is not there, the list may give you a name or two in the local area to call for more information about your instructor. Also consider this: a "senior" seaplane flight instructor may not necessarily be the best choice for primary flight instruction unless he or she regularly accepts beginning students. A senior instructor may be a fine resource for ongoing or advanced training, and may be a good person to get to know when just starting, but he or she might not be the best choice as a primary instructor. It is always good to fly with different instructors, once the rating is acquired, to get different techniques and ideas.

A good flight instructor will ask you questions about your experience in different types of aircraft. He or she needs to find out what you know so they can help you build upon your knowledge level. Your instructor also needs to know what your goals are and how you think seaplane training will fit with them. Try to have answers to these questions ready.

Evaluate Your Flight Instructor After Every Lesson

Was there a lesson plan, or was each maneuver discussed prior to flight? Before engine start, did you have a pretty good idea what would be expected of you during the flight? If, after a flight or two, you are not comfortable with the professionalism of your flight instructor, seek another.

Your Responsibility as Part of the Crew

As a pilot-student you have a big responsibility as a member of the airplane's crew. The crew (you and the flight instructor) will take the airplane aloft to accomplish certain tasks. Those tasks are related to your learning. The feelings you experience during the lessons need to be communicated to your instructor, whether they be elation, frustration, or concern about any aspect of the task. Did the lesson end with a good feeling about your instructor? Did you enjoy the experience? If there were any negative aspects, discuss them with your instructor. If you are having any negative feelings about your own performance (everybody does), discuss them with your instructor. This may be hard to do, but keep in mind that the primary responsibility for you having a positive experience during your seaplane learning rests with you! Not all flight instructors will ask about your experience, but they should be there for you, with wisdom, facts and reassurance. Communicate! It is your responsibility as a crewmember, according to crew resource management (CRM) standards.

Seaplane Flight Schools

These training facilities are listed in the SPA Training Directory, which is updated each year and published in the *Water Flying Annual*, and on the SPA website. Since the add-on seaplane rating is usually a two or three day effort, consider combining a short stay at or near one of these training facilities with a vacation or business trip. The seaplane rating does not have to be done near home!

Enough talk. Let's preflight that floatplane, and fly it!

Section II
Preflight Procedures

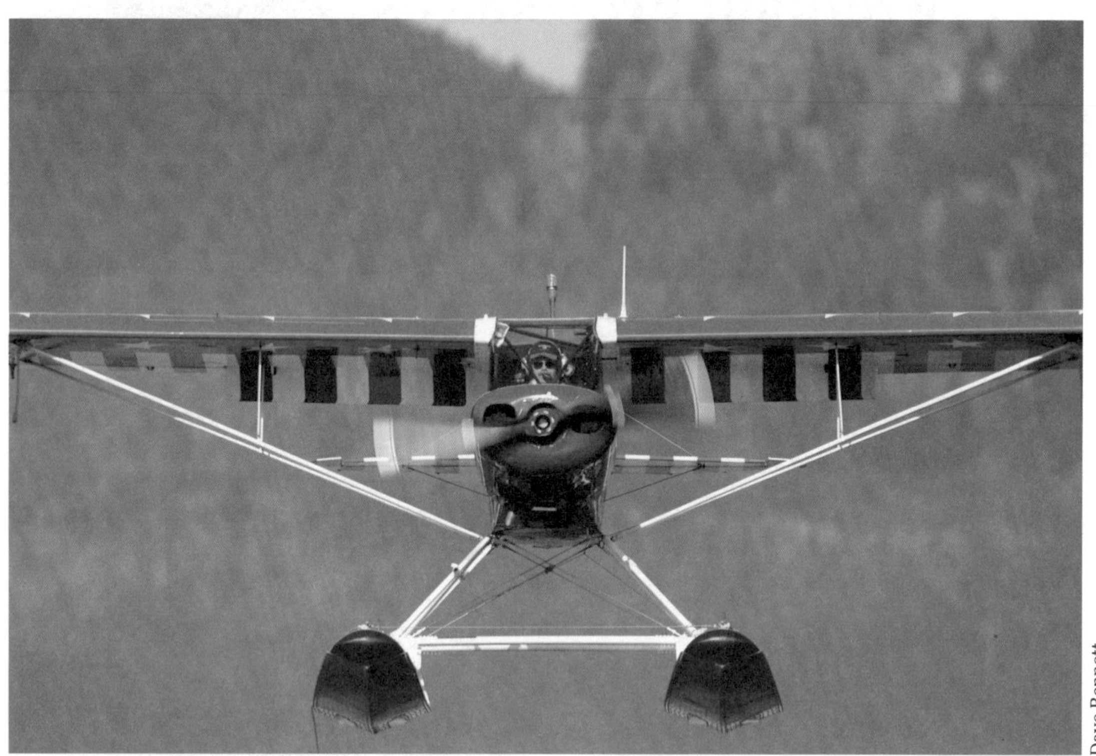

Dave Bennett

Super Cub on short final. Does this look like fun or what?

Chapter 4
Preflight Inspection

For the pilot preparing for the seaplane oral and checkride, I suggest you start by reading the FAA Practical Test Standards requirements (*see* sidebar) so you will know what is expected of you. The following pages will prepare you to meet these standards. For those of you who are already seaplane pilots, a review of this section will help refresh your knowledge for preflighting your seaplane, and I hope you will learn something new or something you have forgotten.

The preflight inspection may take place with the seaplane on the ramp or tarmac, up on a lift or rail system, heeled up on the beach or tied to the dock. If the seaplane is afloat, the preflight begins as soon as the seaplane is in sight. The first check is a glance to see if the wings are level. If they are not, there is probably more water in one float than the other, or fuel has transferred so there is an unequal quantity in each wing, or both.

Sumping

Preflight of the airframe is pretty much the same as for the landplane, except that it is more difficult to reach some parts of the aircraft. Special attention should be given to sumping the fuel system. Since the seaplane is operating in the water environment, it is much more likely that water will be found in the fuel. Over the years, I have found that many pilots are not aware that it is very important to **sump the fuel tanks first**, then the sumps, in sequence, working toward the engine. If there is water in a fuel tank and the pilot first sumps the gascolator up near the engine, water will be pulled into the fuel lines where it is both hard to detect (until the engine quits on takeoff) and hard to remove from the system. So, when sumping, **always start at the tanks and work toward the engine**. Sumping must be done, as a minimum, before the first flight of the day and after every fueling.

Important: Sump the fuel tank first, then the sumps, working toward the engine.

Sumping must be done before the first flight of the day and after every fueling.

A word to the wise about sumping: You have sumped and are holding a full cup of liquid in your hand. There is no meniscus (dividing line between fuel and water), so is it all fuel or all water?

How do you tell? Color? **Not**! If you use only the blue tinted U.S. 100LL, your sump cup will be stained blue, and hard to discern in the meager light of early dawn. If you run some 100LL and some autogas, no telling what the color will be. If you are fueling out of the U.S., don't bet on the color. Smell? **Not**! Water that has been in your fuel tanks will smell like fuel. Smell will only detect petroleum contaminants that are not gasoline, like jet fuel. The perfect test additive is just under the seaplane pilot's feet. Put a drop of water on your finger and drop it in the cup. If you can see the drop at the bottom of the cup, the rest is probably gasoline.

Fuel Quantity

No preflight inspection is complete without a visual inspection of fuel quantity in the tanks. Unless you are going to always fill the tanks before each flight, the only way to tell the amount of fuel in the tanks is with a calibrated dipstick. Since seaplanes are much more likely than landplanes to be loaded to gross weight, a seaplane without its own calibrated dipstick is like a blind man trying to find out what an elephant is like by touching it—he will think it's like a tree!

Figure 4-1. Fuel sumping, properly done, is a must!

Figure 4-2. Sumping a deHavilland Beaver can be quite a task, but necessary!

Propeller

The propeller should receive a special check as seaplane propellers undergo considerable abuse by water erosion. The experienced seaplane pilot knows how to care for the propeller with a burnishing bar, thus extending the life of the blade. If it is your own plane, find an experienced flight instructor or a good seaplane mechanic and have them show you how to do this. Water damage, at first, looks like what damage caused by tiny sand particles hitting the exact leading edge of the blade might look like. Tiny craters make the leading edge feel rough. If not treated, water will open these little craters up even more. I have seen propellers at the prop shop that had actually developed two leading edges from severe water erosion. They looked like the blade delaminated! Two new $4,000 blades had to be installed. There were two causes for this serious damage that happened over a considerable period of time. First, *the pilot failed* to exercise good operating practices to minimize damage to the propeller, and second, *the pilot failed* to properly care for the propeller during preflight.

Just a word about seaplane mechanics: not all good aircraft mechanics are good seaplane mechanics. Good seaplane mechanics are good mechanics with considerable experience working on seaplanes. They know about burnishing propellers to help them resist water erosion. They know about setting the seaplane engine idle to 450 RPM instead of 600–650 RPM (the lower RPM allows the seaplane to approach a dock slower and to power sail in less wind, a real advantage sometimes). So, if your seaplane is maintained by a mechanic with little seaplane experience, you will have to help him learn about your airplane and its differences.

Airframe

New wrinkles? Could signify damage from high stress loads.

An important check of the airframe is to look at the fuselage skin near the float attach points. Any new wrinkles within 18 inches of those attach points signify that the fuselage suffered high stress loads during a landing, has been bent and therefore, weakened. The floatplane is no longer airworthy and needs to be inspected by a mechanic before further flight. This type of damage is more likely to be found in seaplanes because hard landings or operations in very rough water transmit loads from floats directly to the fuselage. This is because there are no springs or oleo shock absorbing systems in water landing gear (floats or hull).

Tail Section

The tail section deserves special attention during the preflight. Stabilizers, rudder and elevator all receive quite a pounding from high velocity water during takeoff and landing.

Be familiar with the type of trim system on the aircraft you are flying and how to correctly check for any damage to the system that attaches it to the fuselage. For example, the Cessna 180, 185, Super Cub and some others have a moveable stabilizer trim system. It is a wonderful trim system, allowing a wider CG range than the trim tab system. However, that stabilizer is rigidly attached to the fuselage only at the hinge points, and the front of the stabilizer is attached to one or two screw jacks by which the pilot accomplishes pitch trim.

There is a very specific procedure for checking the integrity of those attach points. The hinge attach points are checked by holding the stabilizer at the forward, outboard corner (just inboard of the fiberglass tips on the Cessna) and moving that point up and down, fore and aft. If it moves much or moves differently than it did the last time you did it, a defect has developed in the attach hardware. To check the screw jacks, grab the leading edge of the stabilizer as close to the fuselage as you can and forcefully lift it up and down. Again, there should be very little, if any, movement. Movement indicates worn or corroded screw jack threads or worn pins/bushings. If a worn or corroded screw jack strips out, the airfoil is left to its own devices and will always, like any airfoil, move to reduce angle of attack (up, in the case of the stabilizer, which will cause an unexpected nose pitch down). So, pay special attention to your tail feathers. Without them, it's game over!

Floats

Two kinds of water in the floats: overnight and operational.

Preflight inspection of the floats includes a good visual inspection for new dents, holes and scratches, pumping of all the float chambers, inspection of the flying wires and float attach hardware for security. If the floats are "tight," they will not take on significant amounts of water while sitting in the water. It is common for some water to be taken in during takeoff and landings and if waves are washing over the top of the floats. The seaplane pilot knows there are two kinds of water that may be removed from the float.

Overnight Water

Overnight water is water taken in from below the waterline, signifying a leak. It is found by pumping the floats at the end of day, mooring the seaplane in calm water overnight, and pumping them again in the morning. Unless wind has blown waves onto the floats during the night, any water pumped in the morning came in from below the waterline, so there is a leak. If it is a significant leak needing prompt attention, there will be a lot of water to pump out. Ten strokes on the handpump for one chamber is roughly my personal decision point as to whether I will pump and fly or fix, then fly. (Remember, those ten strokes include both overnight and operational water.)

Operational Water

Operational water is water taken in from above the waterline from rain, wave action and spray during operations. Where does the water get in? Many places. Through inspection covers that are not absolutely tight, small cracks in the deck, pumpout plugs that are not sealing well, around spreader bar attach fittings. There is considerable flexing of the float during takeoff and landing which may provide a temporary pathway for water, pressurized from high speed, to find a way inside. A solution for preventing operational water, especially on old floats, is more difficult to find. Most pilots live with it, remembering to pump the floats at the end of day if there is a chance it will freeze overnight, especially if the float is out of the water overnight. When troubleshooting the problem of water showing up when pumping the floats, think in terms of these two types of water, and make a decision to fix overnight water problems when they arise.

When pumping floats, keep in mind that the hose from the pumpout funnel (riveted to the deck) that goes to the bottom of the bilge may have become detached from the funnel or may have developed a crack. In either case, any water in that compartment will not be removed, and your pump will move only air, signaling no water present! The savvy float pumper listens for the sound of water falling back to the bilge in the hose as the pump is removed or the sound of sucking air when the chamber is emptied. If you have very dry floats and rarely find any water at all, the level wing check will help you confirm that the floats really are dry. Remember, a gallon of water weighs well over eight pounds. Just imagine what a couple gallons in a rear float compartment can do to put you out of CG limits aft!

Water Rudders

Water rudders should be inspected for damage, bending, proper alignment with the float centerline when the air rudder is centered. (Alignment when the rudders are up affects in-flight trim, and alignment when rudders are down affects the seaplane's ability to turn against the wind while on the water.) You should also check whether the rudders move all the way up when retracted and all the way down when put down. Check for downspring flexing, as a broken or missing downspring renders a water rudder nearly useless. The water rudder hinges are inspected for wear and all three cables (left-right, balance, and retraction) are checked for freedom and fraying. Moving the air rudder by hand full left and right while observing movement of the water rudders is another good check.

Paddles

Paddles may be installed in brackets on the floats. Check their security and be sure you know how to get the paddle out quickly and efficiently. This means the paddle or paddles need to be accessible from both floats. They are handy for fending off, moving the airplane short distances if there is no wind, and maneuvering the seaplane in tight places if there is no wind. Read the rules about paddle use in Chapter 16 (Page 218).

Checklist

Always use the checklist! It can be used to guide you through the preflight or after task completion to be sure you didn't miss anything.

Review

Preflight is the same as landplane except parts of the aircraft may be hard to reach, and special emphasis is placed on sumping and doing it right. When sumping, always start at the tanks and work toward the engine. Sumping must be done, as a minimum, before the first flight of the day and after every fueling.

Visual inspection of fuel, and determining quantity when tanks are not full, is important. Also propeller inspection and burnishing, airframe check for hard landing damage, and a more thorough inspection of the tail surfaces is needed due to the abuse from high velocity water during takeoffs and landings. Checking floats for new dents, holes and scratches, pumping all float chambers, knowing about overnight and operational water, inspecting flying wires and float attach hardware for security are important aspects of the seaplane pilot's preflight. Water rudders should be inspected for damage, bending, proper alignment, full up and down travel, downspring operation, hinge security and bearing wear. All three cables need your attention as you look for security and abrasion. Check paddles for security, and remember the rules about paddles.

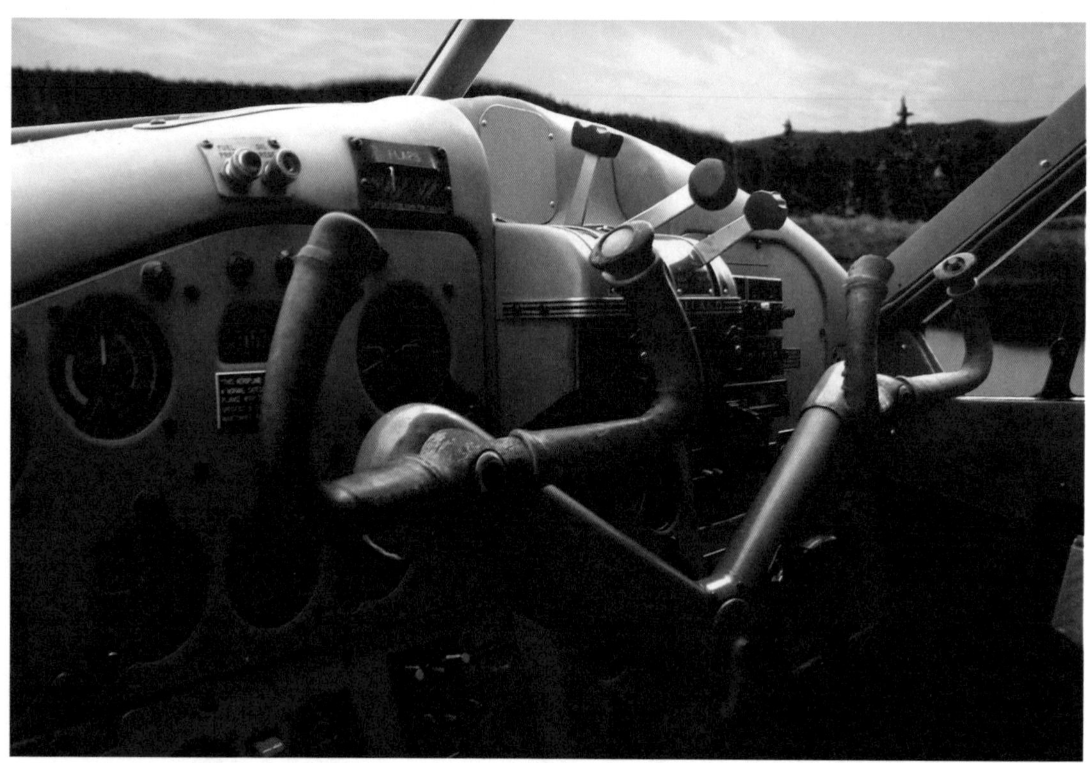
ASA

The Beaver seaplane pilot's "office."

Chapter 5
Cockpit Management and Passenger Safety

If you are studying for the seaplane oral and checkride, have a look at the PTS section II ◆ B before continuing. If you are already float-rated, this chapter provides information to improve the safety of your seaplane operations.

PTS ◆

Section II ◆ B
Cockpit Management

Human Resources

Cockpit management means the effective use of **all** available resources: human resources, hardware, and information. Human resources include crewmembers, passengers and persons near the aircraft. It means keeping a neat and orderly cockpit and cabin, with items needed for flight and for operation on the water (charts, anchors, lines etc.) safely stowed but close at hand. In the seaplane, one or all passengers may be considered crewmembers if the pilot has briefed them as to their duties beforehand. Since a preflight briefing of passengers is required, it is up to the pilot to effectively utilize the passenger-crewmember. For example, if a passenger sees other aircraft in the air or aircraft and/or vessels on the water *and* has been properly briefed on how to notify the pilot, he or she becomes a crewmember with respect to that task.

Loose Items in the Cockpit/Cabin

Loose items in the aircraft are probably a greater hazard in seaplanes than in other types of aircraft. Everything in the airplane should be secured for these reasons:

- In case of a rapid deceleration (crash or impact with the water), objects behind the pilot and passengers become high-energy missiles. A small Mag-lite holding 2 AA batteries, residing on the hat rack in a Cessna 180 or 185, in a 9 G deceleration will impact the back of the pilot's head *with more energy than a 9 mm bullet.* So, pay attention to what is loose behind you in any airplane.
- In case of an upset where the cabin fills with water, chances of survival improve if the occupants don't have to deal with debris during their escape from the submerged aircraft.

Loose items such as these can become dangerous missiles in a rapid deceleration!

- Loose items have been known to jam flight control movement, especially rudders, flaps and water rudder controls.

Organization

If the pilot is organized, this is evidence that he or she is capable of thinking ahead. If the chart is in the luggage compartment, or the checklist/pencil continually ends up on the floor, or the anchor doesn't already have a line (rode) attached and is stored where it can't be quickly reached, this is evidence that the pilot is not well organized or prepared.

Use of Checklists

The checklist should be accessible; that is, it doesn't easily end up temporarily misplaced, on the floor, or under the seat.

The proper checklist and its proper use are vital parts of any aircraft operation. The best checklist is one that lists tasks in the right order and is accessible. The checklist in my airplane is permanently attached to the instrument panel so I don't need a hand to use it. Proper order of tasks is important because if the order is not correct, the pilot is disinclined to use it. If this happens, consult with your flight instructor and create a new checklist. If a checklist came from the aircraft manufacturer, it was approved by someone; however if it has tasks listed in the wrong order or missing (as is often the case with landplanes converted to seaplanes), nothing says you can't change the order or add to it if better checklist is the result. Many senior pilots use checklists of their own making. The important thing is that there is a proper checklist and the pilot uses it.

Figure 5-1 shows a generic seaplane checklist. If you are going to use it, it probably needs to be modified to fit the airplane you fly, and it may need to be condensed. Consult your flight instructor or other experienced pilots about modifications you believe should be made. Then use it—every time!

There are many reasons why pilots don't use their checklists, including:

1. The checklist isn't correct or in the right order, or it is too detailed.
2. It is hard to manage in the cockpit. It falls on the floor, ends up under the seat, or it requires one of two hands to use.
3. A macho attitude: "I don't need that checklist; I know the airplane inside and out," etc.
4. Bad habits.

Continued on Page 50

A Generic Seaplane Checklist

Before Entering Aircraft:

- ❑ Check flight control freedom
- ❑ Determine weight and balance
- ❑ Check trim tab setting and freedom of movement
- ❑ Visually check fuel quantity
- ❑ Check oil quantity
- ❑ Drain fuel sumps in proper order
- ❑ Pump floats—check cables
- ❑ Visual inspection of aircraft and floats
- ❑ Remove tie downs
- ❑ Passenger briefing (outside)

Inside Aircraft:

- ❑ Position and secure seats
- ❑ Clear seat belts
- ❑ Finish passenger briefing (inside)
- ❑ Check trim indicator (takeoff)
- ❑ Check fuel selector
- ❑ Check cowl flaps open
- ❑ Master switch on (check gauges)
- ❑ Check radios off (after ATIS)

Start Up:

- ❑ Clear area ahead, to the sides and behind
- ❑ Mixture control "RICH"
- ❑ Carburetor heat "COLD"
- ❑ Propeller full in (high rpm)
- ❑ Prime if needed (none when hot)
- ❑ Throttle cracked (minimum)
- ❑ Clear!
- ❑ Engage starter
- ❑ Mags to both
- ❑ Look outside!
- ❑ Water rudders down
- ❑ Check oil pressure
- ❑ Idle engine 700 rpm
- ❑ Look outside!

Pre-takeoff Check:

- ❑ Check operations of flight controls
- ❑ Check doors and seat belts
- ❑ Set flight instruments
- ❑ Set radios—communicate as needed
- ❑ Check fuel
- ❑ Check engine instruments
- ❑ Check magnetos
- ❑ Check prop control—set HIGH
- ❑ Set mixture control for altitude
- ❑ Check carb heat—set COLD
- ❑ Set flaps, check trim
- ❑ Plan departure path for safety
- ❑ Recheck the things that can kill you (see discussion in Chapter 9)
- ❑ Clear area
- ❑ Check water rudders up (most cases)

Takeoff:

- ❑ Stick back
- ❑ Increase rpm to full power
- ❑ Check directional control
- ❑ Retract water rudders (if still down for crosswind takeoff)
- ❑ Transition to step taxi
- ❑ Seek least drag attitude
- ❑ Lift one float clear of water (optional)
- ❑ Allow turn (center ball)
- ❑ Accelerate in shallow climb
- ❑ Reduce flaps—accelerate to V_Y and flaps up by 50' AWL
- ❑ Reduce power at safe altitude
- ❑ Set climb or cruise power
- ❑ Adjust cowl flaps

Landing (except glassy water):

- ❑ PAX brief and seatbelt check
- ❑ Close cowl flaps—adjust mixture RICH
- ❑ Reduce power—apply carb heat as needed
- ❑ Reduce speed to white arc
- ❑ Apply 10-degree flaps (or appropriate)
- ❑ Approach at best glide speed
    - ❑ Check seat belts—unlock doors (Cessna)
    - ❑ Check landing gear—water rudders
- ❑ On short final (before ground effect)
    - ❑ Reduce power—increase flaps
    - ❑ Prop full rpm—mixture RICH
    - ❑ Carb heat COLD (except franklin)
- ❑ After entering ground effect
    - ❑ Bank to stop drift
    - ❑ Flair to landing attitude
- ❑ On the water
    - ❑ Maintain touchdown attitude until off step
    - ❑ Retract flaps
    - ❑ Adjust power to taxi
    - ❑ Open cowl flaps

Slow Taxi and Shutdown:

- ❑ Stow seat belts and headphones
- ❑ Throttle closed
- ❑ Carb heat as required
- ❑ Prop low RPM
- ❑ Switch mags off temporarily
- ❑ Kill engine with mixture or mags, as appropriate
- ❑ Turn off all switches

Figure 5-1. Generic seaplane checklist (modified from an original from Wiley's Seaplanes).

Items (1) and (2) are easy to fix. Correct the checklist. Make a better one. Paste it on the instrument panel, or put it on your clipboard if you use one. Items (3) and (4) are more difficult. They require self discipline and a conviction that, if you use the checklist, you will be a better pilot (which is undeniably true). Use the checklist!

Passenger Briefing

PTS: "Briefs passengers on the use of safety belts, shoulder harnesses, and emergency procedures."

The Practical Test Standards say, "Briefs passengers on the use of safety belts, shoulder harnesses, and emergency procedures." The PTS does not define what emergency procedures should be briefed to passengers, so consult with your flight instructor as he or she should know what will be expected of you by the designated examiner.

The following discussion covers the main components of a complete passenger briefing.

Preflight Passenger Safety Briefing

Presently, regulations are soft regarding passenger preflight briefings. If operating under Part 91 (giving sightseeing seaplane rides, flight instructing, etc.), §91.107(a) requires the pilot to give a proper briefing about seat belt and shoulder harness use. That's all! The seaplane flight test practical test standards require the ASES applicant to give a proper briefing about seat belts, harnesses *and emergency procedures*, but, at present, §91.107 does not require the pilot to brief passengers about emergency procedures. But, there are other incentives for pilots to provide a proper briefing about emergency egress from an upset seaplane. These include:

1. A court system and laws that hold the pilot responsible for the safety of all persons in and around the aircraft, not to mention our personal feelings as pilots, should someone lose their life in our airplane.
2. The knowledge that the survival rate in egress situations for passengers who have not been properly briefed is not good. We know, from study of accident statistics that:
   - 50% to 60% of seaplane accidents happen during takeoff.
     —Drowning was the cause of 67% of passenger fatalities in a recent Canadian study.

In these cases the drownings occurred "without other incapacitation"; that is, the passengers were conscious and otherwise unharmed yet they still drowned in attempt at egress.

- The floatplane's ultimate stability is achieved after upset (upside down).
  - —To take advantage of the fact that upset floatplanes will usually float forever, those inside must know how to get out.
  - —That one accident where passengers inside are found unharmed from the crash, sitting in their seats with seat belts fastened, but drowned, is one accident too many. (Unfortunately, there have been a few of these.)

The good news is that upset floatplanes usually float forever—take advantage of that and *inform your passengers in a briefing* on the best method of egress in an emergency!

I have discovered an even better reason to give a thorough briefing: It seems that whenever I "level" with a passenger regarding safety issues, the passenger, now trained from my briefing, accepts responsibility for their own egress and mentally becomes a part of the trained crew. They seem eager to learn more and to take on more responsibility, so I give them more to occupy their thoughts (as shown in the next section, "Passenger Involvement."). After the flight, they often say "that was fun, I learned so much!"

When you level with passengers about those "tough-to-discuss" safety issues, you'll find they willingly accept responsibility and become part of the crew!

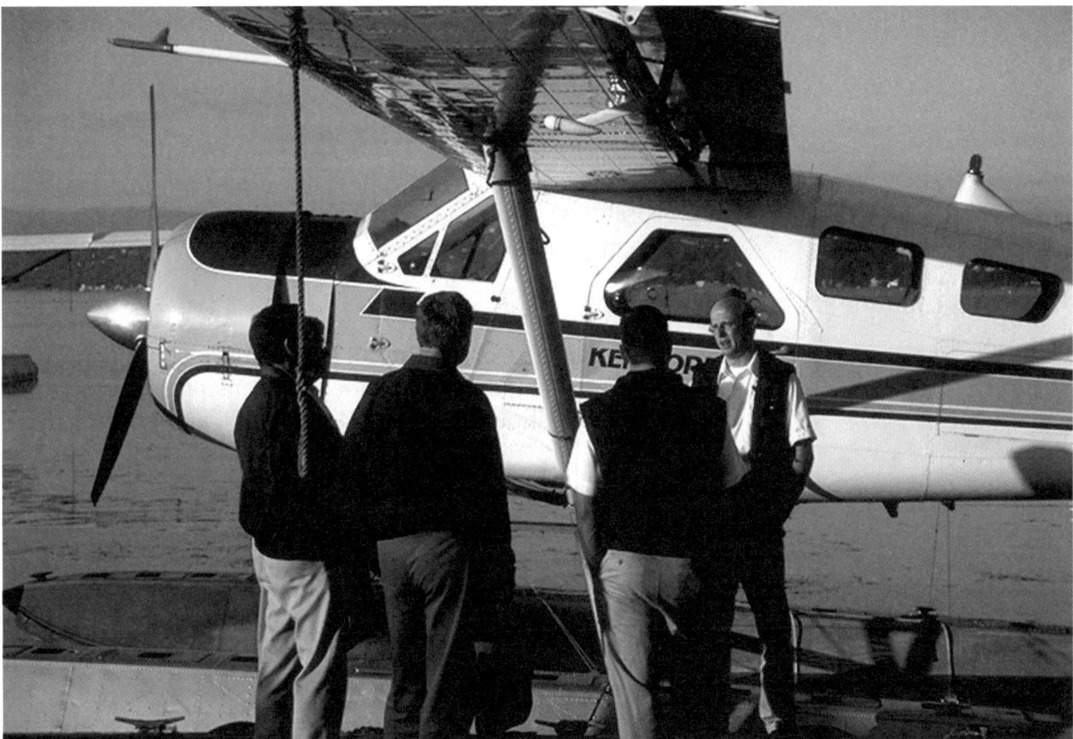
SPA

Figure 5-2. Completing the passenger briefing at Kenmore Air Harbor, Seattle

Get them involved: Brief passengers on how to visually inspect the wheels on their side of the airplane before landing an amphibian.

Passenger Involvement

It is not difficult and there are many ways to get passengers involved during the flight. If we are in an amphibian, the preflight briefing includes how to visually check that the wheels are up for water landing. After the passenger practices wheel up inspection on their side of the aircraft the first time, they are usually way ahead of me, doing their inspection before I ask for it.

All passengers, including youngsters, are good at spotting traffic on the water and other aircraft, and pointing them out to me during flight. I involve them in some Crew Resource Management (CRM) by asking them to point out other aircraft but not point at anything *other than* aircraft. Passengers enjoy practicing the "sterile cockpit rule." I have heard passengers say "sterile cockpit" to another passenger who is talking about trivia during final approach. It is amazing how they enjoy becoming responsible members of the crew rather than just "geese" (old airline term for the bodies in the back that are just along for the ride).

Can the passenger hear about all the bad news scenarios and still want to go flying with you? My experience indicates the answer is yes, if the passenger is involved as a crewmember with responsibilities and is properly briefed. The passenger needs to know everything necessary to be able to get out of an inverted airplane, even with an incapacitated pilot. The passenger needs to hear that the pilot cares. If it is apparent that the pilot cares, and if the passenger is made to feel like a part of the crew (with responsibilities), most of the fear is dispelled while the passenger concentrates on the tasks at hand.

Emergency Equipment

The location and use of the aircraft's emergency equipment, such as fire extinguisher, emergency locator transmitter, survival kit and equipment, should be pointed out to the passenger.

Personal Floatation Devicess

The preflight needs to include a briefing about personal floatation devices (PFDs), and my passengers are given the choice of wearing one. If they decline, I ask them how good of a swimmer they are. If there is any doubt, I help make the decision to wear the PFD, and I wear mine. Wearing a PFD is not a regulation, but rather a personal decision with common sense very much on the side of wearing one.

Note: Only inflatable PFDs should be used in an aircraft since the standard boat-type PFD is dangerous. It is too bulky to permit egress from small spaces and its floatation is constant, which studies have shown, could prevent egress, pinning the wearer against the highest point inside the cabin. Inflatable PFDs should never be inflated inside the aircraft for that same reason.

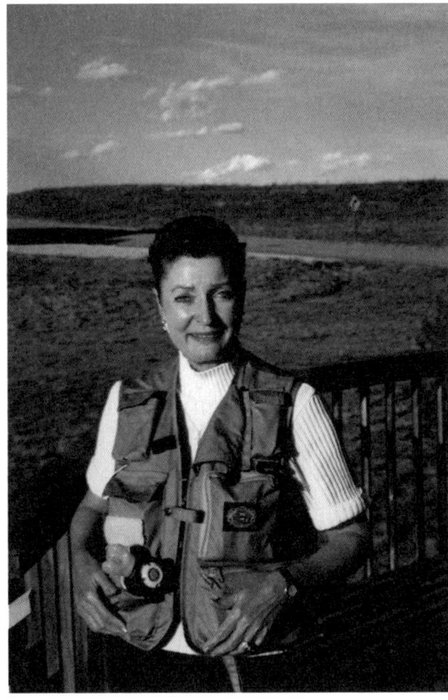

Figure 5-3. This co-pilot is wearing her PFD, which is a single-bladder, non-approved inflatable type that has many pockets for survival gear. Note the "spare-air" breathing apparatus in her lower right front pocket, a nice addition in an underwater egress situation.

Seat Belts

The next item in the briefing to discuss with the passenger is seat belts. Practice unlatching the buckle with eyes closed, then the seat belt again latched and rolled over 180°, as buckles sometimes do under the stress of high G loading. The passenger learns what the buckle feels like in that position and how to roll it back over to unlatch it. Discuss why it's a good idea to tuck in the loose end of the seat belt (the loose end, floating in water, may interfere with seat belt release), as well as why unlatching the seat belt is the last thing done before exiting a water-filled cabin. When the belt is unlatched, the body tends to roll over and float up or be deflected by currents of water flowing in, so disorientation is re-introduced. With belt removed and body floating, it is very difficult to push against anything to open a door or window.

All who've experienced upset and egress from the flooded cabin report disorientation, including the author! **Re-orientation is the key to starting off the process right.**

Underwater Egress

Next we discuss underwater egress from the cabin.

First, re-orient. Those who have experienced an upset and egress from a flooded cabin all report disorientation. I have experienced it in training, so I am a true believer. The passenger is briefed to do something like "This is my right knee, I am sitting on the right side, so plan A is to exit to the right, plan B is to exit left."

Second, get rid of headset and other paraphernalia. Be sure the headset cord is stowed out of the way so it doesn't impede egress. ***Do not*** release seat belt yet!

Third, clear a pathway out. The passenger is briefed as to the best way to clear a path out of the model aircraft used. It is much easier to push against a door or window if the seat belt is still holding you in place.

Fourth, get a good grip on some structure of the aircraft near the exit. Maintain that grip to prevent another bout of disorientation. As the body is released from the seat belt it will tend to float up and roll or be pushed out of position by water still entering the cabin.

Fifth, release the seat belt and exit the cabin with hand over head so the hand will encounter the step, struts and float deck obstacles, not the head. Don't kick your feet (USCG studies have shown a much higher incidence of getting tangled up with wires, cords or other structure, if you do that). Another reason to avoid kicking your feet is to prevent kicking (and possibly further disorienting, or disabling) other passengers on your way out. Once above water outside, hold on to the chine of the float and shout to establish contact with anyone who is in the water on the other side of the aircraft. If you feel the need to inflate your PFD, do so now, keeping in mind that doing so will prevent you from being able to dive back down to the cabin to help another person or to retrieve items from the cabin. Then, move along the chine (preferably into the wind as spilled fuel, oil, fire, etc. will be downwind) to the inside of the float, and use the spreader bar to get out of the water onto the float to avoid **hypothermia**. The passenger needs to know: the good news about an upset is that the airplane will continue to float!

Effects of Hypothermia (from FAA AC-91-69A)

Water Temperature in °F	Exhaustion or Unconsciousness*	Expected Time of Survival
Up to 32.5°	Under 15 minutes	15 to 45 minutes
32.5° to 40°	15 to 30 minutes	30 to 90 minutes
40° to 50°	30 to 60 minutes	1 to 3 hours
50° to 60°	1 to 2 hours	1 to 6 hours
60° to 70°	2 to 7 hours	2 to 40 hours
70° to 80°	2 to 12 hours	3 hours to indefinitely
Over 80°	Deferred indefinitely	Indefinitely

*Times given are for young adult in good condition and health with no alcohol or drugs in system.

Figure 5-4. Time of useful consciousness vs. water temperature.

Hypothermia

Hypothermia causes incapacitation and loss of consciousness due to lowered temperature of the body. Time of useful consciousness (TUC) is dramatically decreased in cold water as is seen in Figure 5-4, taken from AC 91-69A. It should be noted that while the TUC of an adult in good condition, dressed for outside activities, may be as much as 30 to 60 minutes in water temperature of 50°F (10°C), the USCG says that, at that temperature, we can only hold our breath for about 15 seconds. These are sobering thoughts considering that most of us fly from water that is often colder that that.

A Good Briefing

Only the basics of a good briefing have been covered here. The FAA's Advisory Circular 91-69 has a preflight briefing checklist that is a good place to start, or use the one in Figure 5-6 (Page 39). Throw out what you don't like, add to the list, test it with your flight instructor, and a great passenger brief checklist is born!

See Appendix 2, Page 367–368 for this suggested checklist.

A good briefing should be one that is especially developed by the pilot for the aircraft and the conditions under which it is flown. It will be successful at improving safety and building passenger confidence. It must get the passenger involved. A well-done briefing will return a big helping of good feeling to the pilot, and that's reason enough to do a complete passenger briefing every time.

Figure 5-5. Briefed and ready to go fishing.

AC 91-69 also suggests "the pilot should instruct passengers not to assist unless specifically requested to do so by the pilot." Seaplanes can be dangerous, especially at the front (propeller) and rear (horizontal stabilizer). If a passenger gets hurt it will be the responsibility of the pilot, under the law. For this reason, dockings and beachings that must be accomplished without an experienced dock hand on the dock should be done by the pilot if at all possible, with the passengers remaining safely within the cabin until the aircraft is secured. Ask your flight instructor to teach you how to do that under varying conditions.

Flying friendly with passengers also means shallow banks, prebriefing any unusual maneuver (getting close to obstacles, short lake takeoffs, sudden maneuvers, etc.), selecting flight times of day that minimize turbulence, keeping the flight short, continuously checking on passenger comfort and state of mind. In short, letting the passenger know you care and making him or her feel special is an important form of "fly friendly" as well as a strong safety statement.

Sample Passenger Preflight Checklist

External Preflight:

- ❑ Show passengers key items before start: lift strut, chine, propeller, where to stand on the float, location and use of emergency equipment, etc.

Pax Brief:

- ❑ PFD: use, wear, inflation (not in aircraft!)

Exits:

- ❑ latches up/forward, or down forward, or?
- ❑ baggage door: inside latch check, baggage door not locked

Seatbelts:

- ❑ Rolled 180°, loose end, last thing released

Exit Process:

- ❑ Orient, pathway, hand hold, seat belt, hand over head

Outside:

- ❑ Chine, communicate, wind direction
- ❑ Spreader bar, hypothermia
- ❑ Flotation, ELT, survival

PAX:

- ❑ Check condition of (mental and physical)

Figure 5-6. A sample passenger preflight checklist

It's Not Over Until It's Over!

After the landplane accident dust settles, there is usually someone there to help, and the aircraft stays put. Not so for the seaplane pilot. The floating aircraft is still subject to wind and current, the fixed ELT is useless on the upset aircraft (I carry a spare in my dry sack), and if the accident occurs in the wilderness, a good knowledge of survival skills will be most helpful.

Review

Before you go for your oral and checkride, you should:

1. Understand and be able to discuss the elements of cockpit management. Key points are use of human resources, neat and orderly cockpit and cabin, and orderly stowage of items used in flight and while the aircraft is moving.
2. Secure loose items in aircraft. Know why. Items behind you become dangerous missiles; loose items become debris that inhibits egress in a flooded cabin; loose items can jam flight controls (it happens more often than you might think).
3. Use a checklist for passenger briefings. Make one up, use it and know why each step is necessary.
4. Organize material you will use during the oral and the flight. A well-organized applicant is a sign of a pilot who can think ahead.
5. Have good checklists and use them!

Burke Mees

Skillfully departing a crowded dock like this is part of the engine starting process.

Chapter 6
Engine Starting

If you are studying for the seaplane oral and checkride, have a look at this PTS section to see what will be expected of you. If you are a certified seaplane pilot, look at this chapter to review your procedures and get some new ideas.

Before Starting

A number of tasks must be completed before engine start, so refer to the checklist to be sure all of them have been completed. Assuming the preflight inspection of the aircraft is complete, here are some tasks that should be done before engine start:

1. Passenger briefing (discussed in previous chapter)
2. Passenger security
3. Plan for departure from dock or beach
4. Brief the dock handler
5. Traffic check

Note about item #3: Also, plan for sailing if the engine quits after start. (*See* Chapter 8, "Sailing.")

Passenger Security

Passengers should be in their seats, with seat belts fastened prior to engine start. This is required by the Federal Air Regulations and is an appropriate operating procedure. The only exception to this is if a passenger has one or more specific tasks to perform during engine start, such as holding the aircraft alongside the dock. If the passenger has tasks to perform and has been properly briefed by the pilot as to the safe execution of the task, then he or she becomes a member of the crew and will be expected to fasten the seat belt when underway (taxi) and in safe water. Seaplane pilot and crew who may have tasks to perform during and just after engine start are exempt from the secured seat belt rule if the tasks would be impeded by a secured seat belt. The pilot's seat belt is rarely fastened at engine startup in a seaplane because a number of events could require the pilot to move quickly to another location in or on the aircraft. For example, if the engine starts then quits, the aircraft is in motion but subject to winds and currents. The pilot may need to move quickly to fend off or use the paddle. The pilot's seat belt is fastened as soon as the aircraft is under way in safe water and the pilot's hands are free to secure the seat belt. As soon as that task is done, the pilot should recheck that all passenger's belts are fastened.

Plan for Departure from Dock or Beach

The experienced seaplane pilot pauses as long as is necessary—often on the dock or beach—before casting off the lines or pushing off the beach, to determine the exact plan of action and the desired path to open, safe water. Wind, current direction and velocity, obstructions in the water, and traffic are considered, as well as what the aircraft will do as soon as it is freed from its tether. If what the aircraft will do when it is cast loose is in doubt, let the airplane tell you. Cast it free for a moment and see what it does.

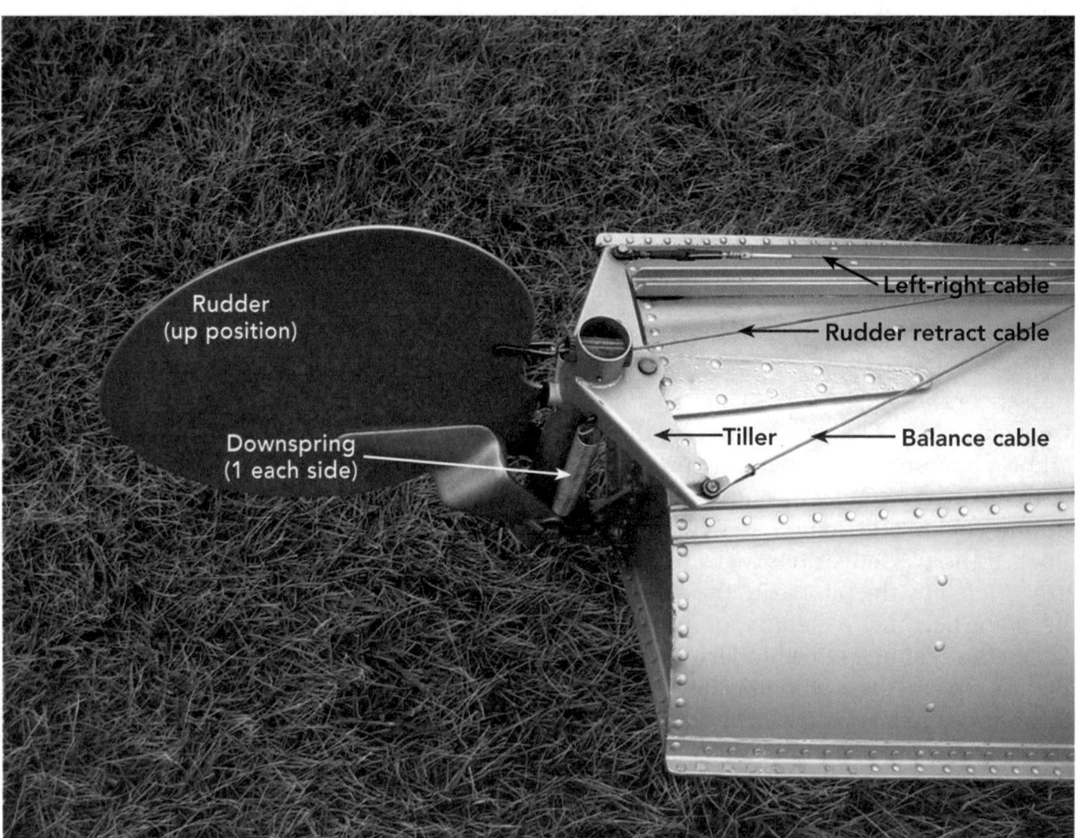

Figure 6-1. Close-up of water rudder showing up position, cables, and downspring.

At this time, take a moment and consider where you will end up if the engine starts, pulling the seaplane away from the dock or beach, then the engine quits (as it sometimes will). Considering the wind at the moment, where will you end up and what will you need to do if you can't successfully restart? It is possible to predict where the seaplane will sail to. Have a plan already formulated! This is just one example of the *thinking ahead* the good seaplane pilot must do.

Of course, if the wind is coming from the right at engine start, the airplane will attempt to weathercock into the wind (turn right). When not underway (moving through the water) it will weathercock more slowly if the **water rudders** are down, but it will weathercock with the rudders down until the aircraft is moving forward. The water rudders have authority (ability to turn or direct the aircraft) only when water is moving across their surfaces. Water rudders have no authority when forward velocity is zero. Authority increases as the aircraft moves faster through the water until about 8–15 MPH when water pressure exceeds downspring pressure and the water rudder rides up, losing authority. *See* Figure 6-1.

While we are on the subject of water rudders, let's mention a simple, yet constant rule about when water rudders should be up or down: When operating, **water rudders are always up, except when accomplishing one of these three maneuvers:**

Water rudders are always up except for displacement taxi, plowing turns and starting a crosswind takeoff.

1. Displacement taxi
2. Beginning crosswind takeoff
3. Plowing turn

Some may teach that water rudders are down during power sailing, when moving forward (a form of displacement taxi). That's OK, but I have never found it necessary to use the rudders in any phase of power sailing. Having to put the rudders up and down while power sailing adds unnecessarily to the pilot's workload during a busy time, so let's keep it simple and remember there are only three maneuvers where water rudders should be down.

What about water rudder position when moored at the dock? Well, depends on who you ask. Some say rudders should be down so the wind doesn't wear out the hinges, moving them back and forth all the time. Others say rudders should be up so the airplane's movements in the water at the dock don't wear out the hinges. You can decide for yourself which side of that argument you agree with.

Beach Departure

A common, stable mooring position for a floatplane is heeled up on a sand or pebble beach or wood ramp (Figure 6-2). This is a desirable mooring for overnight because the airplane cannot sink under any condition (*see* Figure 6-3) and is reachable during high wind or wave conditions to give attention, add mooring lines, etc. With the airplane sitting with the wing at a decreased angle of attack and, heeled up, it can survive near gale conditions and three foot high breakers if some of the float compartments are filled with water. Woe be the pilot who has to pump those floats out the next morning when the sun is shining and the birds are singing…unless he has an electric pump and strong battery. But, at least he has survived the storm with his floatplane intact. *See* Figure 6-4.

The beach departure is made more gracefully if the pilot will "float the aircraft" (push the aircraft off the beach, then bring it back so it is just touching the beach enough to hold it from mov-

Figure 6-2. Turboprop C-206 heeled up on a beautiful sand beach. Note grablines on each wing and ventral fin under the tail needed to maintain yaw stability.

Figure 6-3. Mild results of heeling up tail to the weather. No damage but lots of pumping required before further flight. Because of foliage near the shore, the pilot chose to moor bow-to the beach, but the wind blew waves onshore.

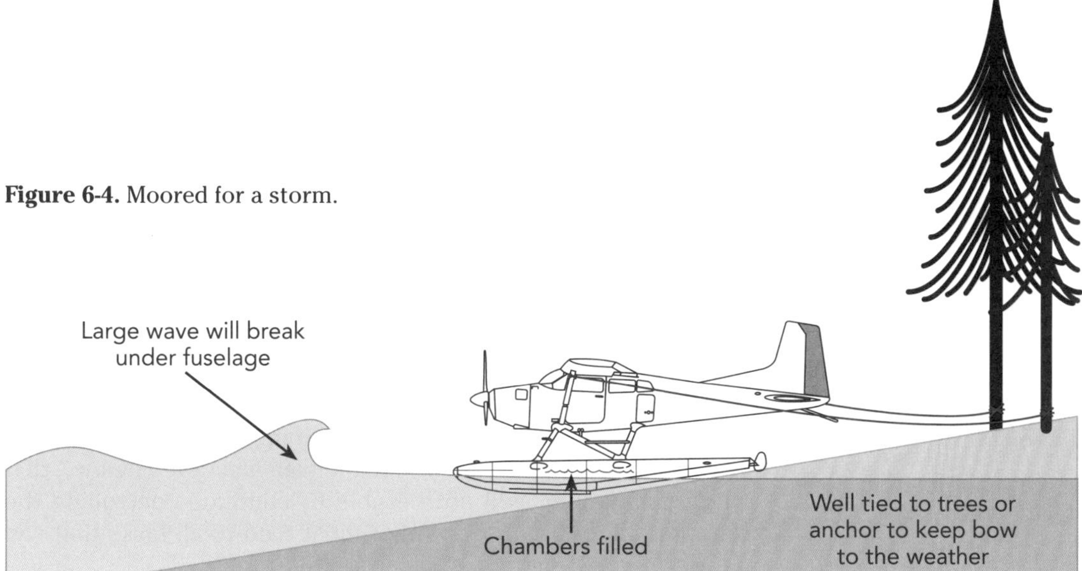

Figure 6-4. Moored for a storm.

ing) then load some cargo or a passenger, then float the aircraft again, load some more, float it again, repeating until all fuel, cargo and passengers are loaded. This will prevent the solid and immovable condition of the airplane on the beach. The final adjustment of the aircraft on the beach is done by the pilot just before going aboard, so that the aircraft will not be moved by wave or wind while the pilot is moving aboard and starting the engine. Just before going aboard, check for conflicting water traffic. Your added weight on the float will probably hold you until the engine starts. Don't take time to adjust your seat, or seat belt or do anything else. In fact, assume the one foot out on the step, or half in, half out position described in Chapter 16. Clear the area for traffic, start the engine and guide the seaplane into safe water. Don't forget to put the water rudders down as soon as the water is deep enough. Then do the rest of your chores and use the checklist. Until you get away from the beach, you need the ability to get out quickly. Once in awhile, one float will stick causing the airplane to turn around and face the beach when the engine starts. Be alert for this. If a turn starts, a burst of power and full opposite rudder may save the moment! If that doesn't work, the turn will continue. Shut down and start over. Better luck next time.

When departing the dock and especially the beach, the pilot is responsible for the safety of people and animals on the beach and around the airplane. Always warn onlookers away from the back of the airplane so they don't get sand blown in their eyes. Then take a good look behind the airplane just before the start. A good rule is: *Always depart the dock or beach looking back at your stabilizer as you start to move forward.* This is especially true when departing the dock.

Always depart the dock or beach looking back at your stabilizer.

When departing the dock or beach, the pilot does not have the luxury of time to get settled in his seat—unlike his landplane/pilot cousin. When the sea pilot moves from dock or beach to the cockpit, there is only one objective: to safely and quickly start the engine and move the aircraft out into safe, deep water. Then, and only then can the other tasks such as seat belts, checklist attention, etc., be accomplished. The reason for this is obvious. The aircraft is free to move in any direction at the whim of wind or wave. Or, if there is a dock handler, it is expected the pilot will not tarry after boarding, as this inconveniences the dock handler who has other things to do. Plus, it increases the chances, in some situations (like a tail-out maneuver, discussed below), that the dock handler will not be able to continue controlling the airplane's location. So, the pilot must tend to all tasks that can be performed prior to engine start before the aircraft is cast loose from the dock or beach. Most of these tasks are found in the prestart section of the checklist. In other words, do all you can do before cuttin' 'er loose from the dock or beach!

Brief the Dock Handler

The dock handler is the person who will control the airplane at the dock between the time when the aircraft is untied and underway with engine running steadily. The dock handler may then remain on the dock or, if leaving with the aircraft, step aboard and enter the cabin. Upon arrival at a dock, the dock handler is the person who brings the aircraft alongside and into contact with the dock. *See* Figure 6-5.

Again, this may be a person who is on the dock at time of arrival, or someone who steps off the aircraft onto the dock at the critical moment for the purpose of controlling final contact with the dock. The pilot should be capable of being the primary

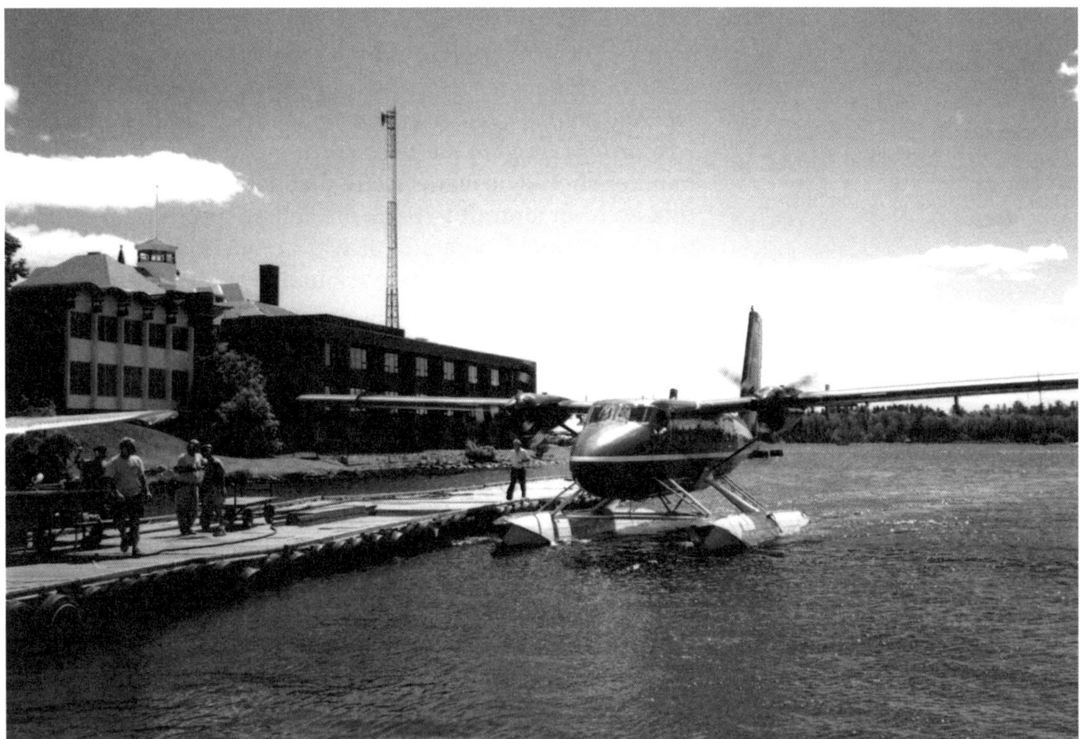

Figure 6-5. Dock handlers prepare to dock a De Havilland Twin Otter at Kenora, Ontario.

dock handler, regardless of which side of the aircraft approaches the dock. There are several reasons for this:

- The pilot is probably the most qualified person on the aircraft to accomplish this task.
- Only the pilot knows exactly how the aircraft will come to the dock.
- No other qualified person may be aboard.
- The pilot is ultimately responsible for the safety of all aboard and those around the arriving or departing aircraft. "It's not my fault" just won't cut it if there is an injury associated with operation of the aircraft.

That said, if a passenger is properly briefed by the pilot to accomplish a certain task, such as that of dock handler, that person effectively becomes a crewmember with certain limited responsibilities. Therefore, a proper and complete briefing by the pilot is needed.

Some points to cover in briefing a dock handler:

1. *If the dock handler is with the airplane, there is only a brief window of time when the dock handler can safely step aboard (departing) or go to the dock (arriving).* Generally, the dock handler should be made aware that if it isn't completely safe to step from aircraft to dock or dock to aircraft, no attempt to do so should be made. It will be easier for the pilot to come back to recover the dock handler if he is on the dock rather than in the water!
2. *When stepping to the dock to handle the aircraft, the dock handler **must** go to the dock with **both** feet.* One foot on the dock and one on the aircraft will always result in separation of the aircraft from the dock with the dock handler forming a human bridge. Inevitably, gravity takes over leaving a very wet dock handler with everyone laughing at him except the pilot, who is busy with an aircraft that is not attached to the dock. "Sounds like you've been there!" you say? Of course…more than once! It has been said that "pain is the beginning of wisdom." Sometimes that can be modified to "wetness is the beginning of wisdom," around seaplanes.
3. *Upon arrival, the aircraft's forward momentum should not be stopped by pushing rearward on the wing or lift strut.* Such action will not stop the aircraft but rather turn it toward the

dock, causing the front of the float to whack the dock. This is probably the most common mistake made by inexperienced dock handlers and is why most pilots decline efforts to help with the docking by strangers on the dock. If the dock is seaplane friendly (lined with rubber tires or other proper soft fenders), the aircraft is pulled toward and parallel to the dock so forward momentum is dissipated by rubbing against the fenders. *See* Figure 6-6. If the dock is not friendly, the aircraft must be held off the dock until speed is reduced by water friction.

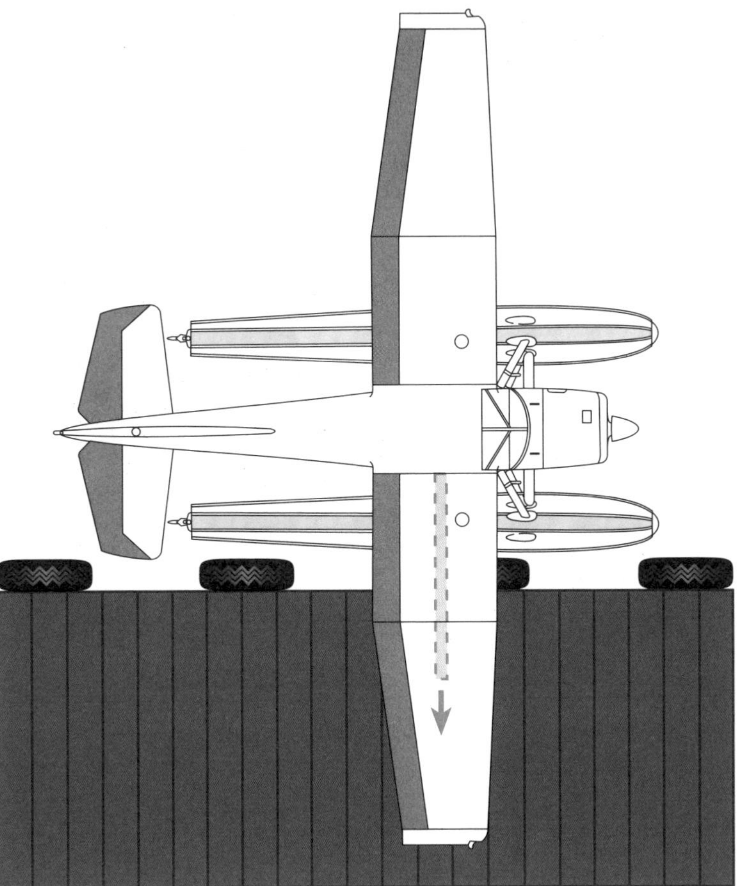

Figure 6-6. The seaplane is pulled toward the dock by the dock handler, taking care to keep the float parallel to the dock. Float to dock contact slows the floatplane, not the dock handler, who merely applies pressure on the lift strut *towards* the wing tip, while allowing the floatplane to move forward.

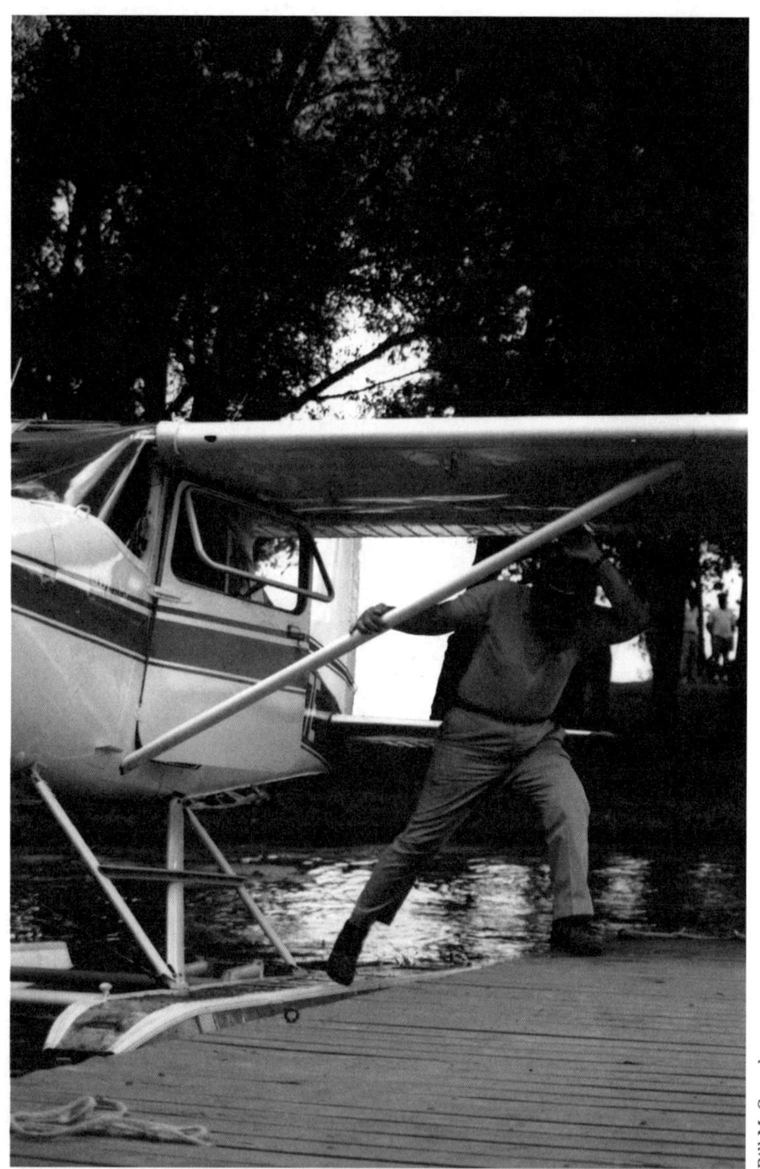

Bill McCarrel

Figure 6-7. The dock handler (in this case, the pilot) goes to the dock with both feet and controls the floatplane by using the lift strut "handle."

4. *The dock handler should be briefed to understand that the seaplane has many handles.* The lift strut beneath the wing, the wing itself, the floats, the tail, a bow line that may be taken ashore when the handler goes ashore, are all handles (*see* Figure 6-7). Some aircraft, particularly the larger ones, have grab lines attached to the wing tiedown ring or near the wingtip (look back at Figure 6-2).
5. *For departure, a dock handler may hold the seaplane parallel to the dock, slightly bow-out or, at a crowded dock, may "tail out" the aircraft*, as seen in Steps 1 through 5 of the photo series (Figure 6-8) on the next page. The pilot must understand that once the aircraft is in the "tail out" position, it is not totally under control of the dock handler and may be blown laterally into contact with the downwind aircraft. So time is of the essence in getting the engine started.

   In the absence of an experienced dock handler, the pilot may operate from a packed dock by tailing the aircraft out himself, then quickly going aboard via the back of the float to start the engine. This maneuver requires some experience and is not a maneuver for a windy day. Always clear the area of oncoming traffic, as well as people near the prop, before yelling "CLEAR"!
6. ***The last word:*** *if a dock handler is going to be a "frequent flyer," take a moment and teach him a proper cleat hitch, a bowline, and a double half hitch.* It will keep others from thinking you, the skipper, are a land-lubber (nautical term for one who doesn't run a tidy ship or doesn't know much and therefore can't be trusted). Also, you will do your frequent-flyer friends a favor if you teach them (a) wet wood docks and ramps are always slippery. If they can't walk on water, they can't walk on wet wood, especially that which is in the water (because of the slime growing on it); and (b) when walking on wood docks, walk on the nail heads. With time, wood rots. A foot through a dock board is usually good for a compound (bloody) fracture of the leg or ankle. The nail heads are where there is support. In addition, walking on seaplane docks is hazardous. There may be tiedown rings sticking up from the dock surface, fuel hoses, tools, baggage and cargo on the dock, and wings and tails extending over the dock at head level. Explain to them about the "Cessna diamond brand in the forehead," and then try to avoid it yourself. Watch your step...below and above!

Caution:
Wet wooden docks are slippery!

On wood docks,
walk on the nail heads!

Seaplane docks are hazardous!

Figure 6-8. Pilot tailing out from a crowded dock:
Step 1. The pilot pushes the floatplane away from the dock to allow clearance for the floats to swing.
Step 2. The pilot rotates the wing forward causing the tail to swing close to the dock.
Step 3. The pilot grabs the tail and walks it to left or right to point the floatplane away from the dock.
Step 4. The floatplane is pulled back until the water rudder just clears the dock.
Step 5. The pilot goes aboard, clears the area for traffic and quickly starts the engine.

Hand Propping

Most of today's aircraft have electric starters but there are some, especially the smaller ones, that do not, so they must be hand-propped. (These are said to have "Armstrong starters.") But the real reason the seaplane pilot needs to know how to safely hand-prop is that seaplanes often land on water in remote areas where there are no support systems. Many different things could cause the starter to malfunction, and it is a long swim home!

Not all engines can be hand-propped. Generally, three bladed propellers are not hand-propped because, since the blades are closer together, each blade comes by much quicker. The engine must be equipped with impulse magnetos to be easily hand-propped, and if fuel injected, a hand primer must be fitted. So, generally, only engines that have carburetors and two-bladed props are hand-propped.

Here is a checklist to go with the photos on the following page (Figure 6-9) to illustrate hand propping:

1. Before start checklist complete
2. Passengers and cargo safe and secure
3. Aircraft secured in starting position
4. Magneto switches off and mixture full lean/cutoff
5. Engine primed
6. Propeller pulled through two or three blades (not backwards) then set to proper start position (usually 2 o'clock)
7. Magneto switches on, mixture rich, throttle set to idle
8. Standing comfortably on the right float (clockwise rotating engines) with left hand on aircraft structure and right hand (fingers) about 8" from the propeller tip, quickly squat then follow through with arm thrust.

It is quite a thrill the first time the engine starts successfully!

If you have seen someone prop a landplane from in front of the propeller, keep in mind that some prefer to prop the landplane from behind the propeller, just like the seaplane pilot does, because it is safer. (*See* Figure 6-10.)

Of the checklist items above, #3 is the most complex, so let's talk about it. Since there are no brakes on the seaplane, it will begin moving as soon as the engine starts. Securing the seaplane for a prop start may mean many things. It can mean anything

Figure 6-9. Hand propping (*see* the checklist on the previous page):
(6) Proper start position set, fingers in position
(8) The squat and follow-through

from "tied up" to "just pointed in the right direction." In the case of the latter, the problem is getting the floatplane to stay pointed in the right direction until the engine is running and the pilot is in the cockpit, guiding it. Proper procedure is to secure the floatplane by tying it up until the engine is running smoothly. With landplanes, it is almost always possible to find a qualified person (pilot or aircraft mechanic) to sit at the controls while the airplane engine is prop started. In fact, many aircraft insurance policies require it. In the case of the floatplane, the pilot may be out somewhere in the wilderness by himself, so he should learn proper procedure to prop start the airplane by himself. It goes without saying that, if possible, a qualified person should be at the controls during a prop start.

Dave Bennett

Figure 6-10. Some floatplanes have no electrical system to save weight. This pilot always hand-props his Super Cub.

A normally crowded dock at Ketchikan, AK.

If the Airplane is at the Dock

See discussion of knots in Chapter 16, Pages 226–232.

Possibly the aircraft will lie quietly alongside the dock, pointed seaward. If you are lucky, the seaward pointing will cause the starboard (right) side to lie alongside the dock with the wind coming from the left side of the airplane and holding it gently against the dock. Or perhaps there is someone who can hold the airplane there until the engine starts. If not, your best bet is to use the slippery knot (Chapter 16) to secure the airplane to the dock so the engine can warm up a little at a slow idle. Once you are aboard and all is well, you can release the brakes by pulling the rip cord on the slippery knot. Unless you are alone, you are now flying the airplane from the *right* seat. If you are not comfortable with this, arrange beforehand to change seats with the passenger. I prefer the method of taxiing out to safe water, "parking" the seaplane (*see* Page 79), followed by both persons stepping out on the float to change positions. Or one person steps into the back of the floatplane to change positions. There is no reason why the seaplane can't be flown by the pilot occupying the right seat; seaplane pilots often do that if they must carry an external load on the right side. This way they can keep a close eye on the load.

See Chapter 8 of *Water Flying Concepts* for a complete discussion about external loads.

If the Airplane is Heeled Up on the Beach

The floatplane heeled up on the beach can be easier to secure for hand-propping. The trick is to position the bird on the beach solidly enough so that when you walk forward on the float to accomplish the propping, the airplane won't float free—but not so secure that a lot of power (and possible propeller water damage from high RPM) is required to get off the beach. Experience is needed to judge wind, waves, current and other forces that may be present, and to get the floatplane just right on the beach for the propping exercise. Remember to make sure there is no one behind the airplane and no traffic on the water in front before swinging that prop.

Refer to your checklist to be sure you haven't overlooked any item of this phase of the flight. Then, let's go taxiing, a somewhat more complex activity in a seaplane.

Review

Before engine start, you have completed the preflight checklist, briefed the passengers, seen to their security inside the aircraft, and developed a plan for departure from dock or beach. You have also completed a plan for sailing if the engine fails after first start, positioned the aircraft correctly for start, seen to the safety of persons near the aircraft, and done a traffic check. Too much to remember! Use your checklist before engine start and again after the engine is running and under your control in safe water. Go over each of the tasks mentioned above and be sure you know how to do them. Be sure you can describe to the examiner how you would prop start the engine if the need arises.

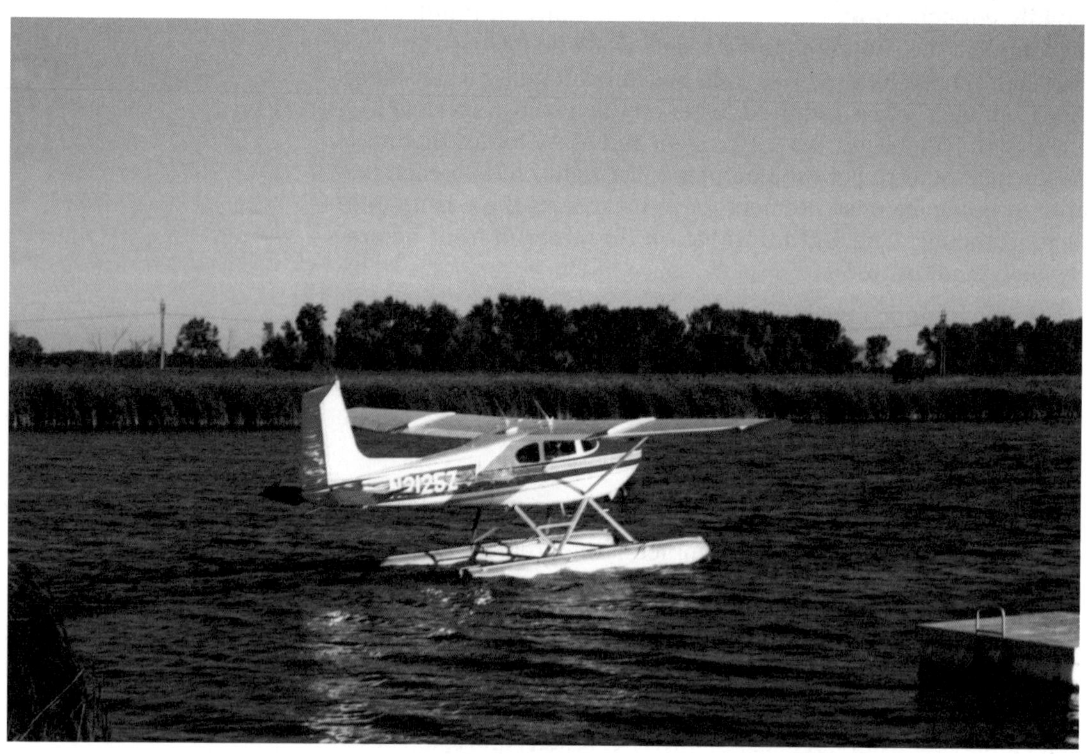

Figure 7-1. Taxiing out

Chapter 7
Taxiing

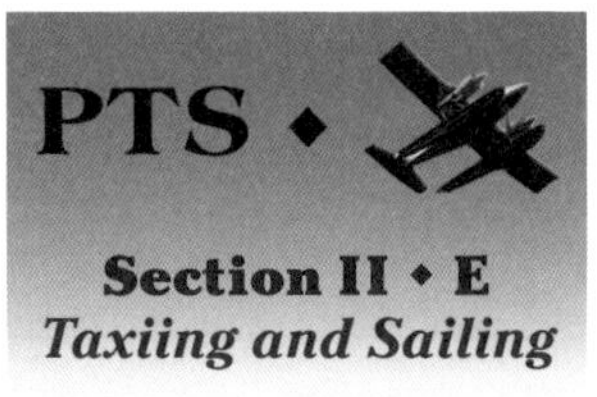

For the beginning seaplane pilot, there is a great deal to learn about taxiing on water. It will come easily, though, so when taxiing, don't forget to occasionally pause to appreciate being out on the water in a beautiful place.

Let's start this discussion by breaking taxiing down into three categories: displacement or idle taxi, hump or plow taxi, and step taxi. At this point, if you are studying for the seaplane oral and checkride, I suggest you pause here and read what will be expected of you in PTS Section II • E, which also contains the sailing task discussed in the next chapter. Figure 7-2 shows the seaplane's attitude in each of the three taxi modes.

See Figure 7-2 on Page 60.

Displacement Taxi or Idle Taxi

Displacement taxi or idle taxi begins immediately after starting the engine. The airplane moves forward at a speed akin to a fast walk, about 3–6 MPH. Rule number one for taxiing is: When the seaplane is on the water, the pilot must be sure that engine RPM is at idle unless there is a very specific reason to use more power. This means not more than 1,000 RPM, preferably 700 RPM. The purpose of this rule is to prevent damage to the very expensive propeller.

Note: This taxiing mode is illustrated on Pages 60–61.

When the seaplane is on the water, the pilot must be sure that engine RPM is at idle unless there is a very specific reason to use more power.

After engine start, if the seaplane is left alone to make its own trail, it will do one of two things. If there is no wind, the single engine seaplane will turn left. It will turn left at the fastest rate, scribing the smallest circle, at low RPM with the water rudders up. *See* Figure 7-3. As power is added, turn rate decreases and the path of the circle widens. If there is a significant wind, the seaplane will weathercock into the wind.

To better control the seaplane, the pilot lowers the water rudders. (If it is a departure from a dock, water rudders were probably already down.) With rudders down, the seaplane will turn left if there is no wind and no input to the rudders from the pilot, but rate of turn will be less than if rudders are up.

Figure 7-2. The three taxi modes

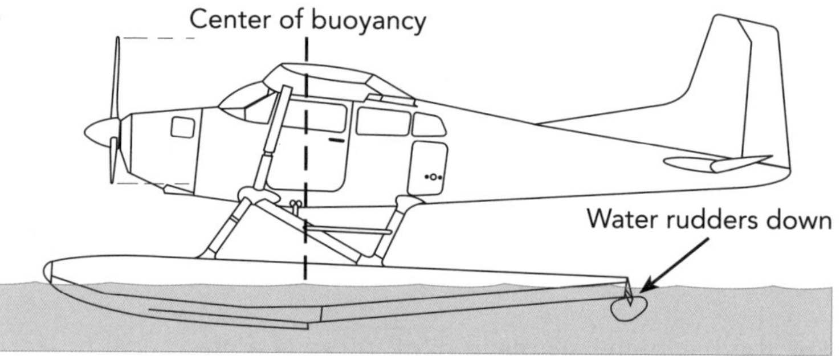

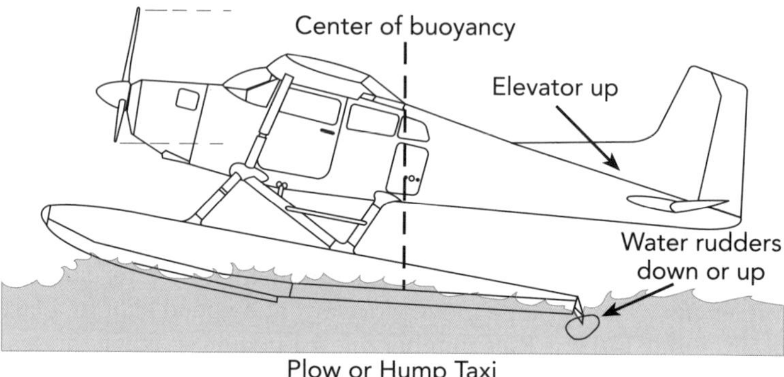

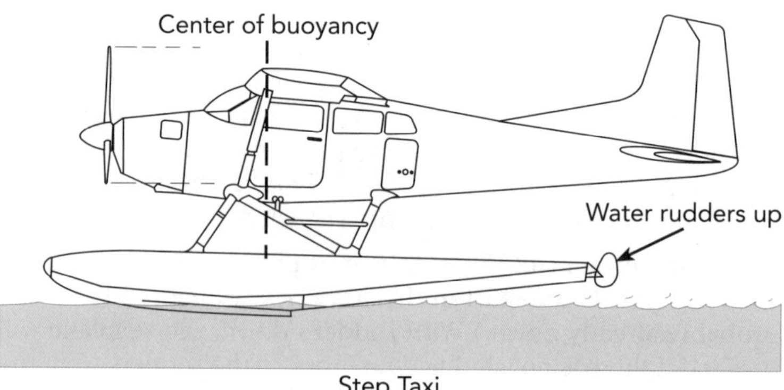

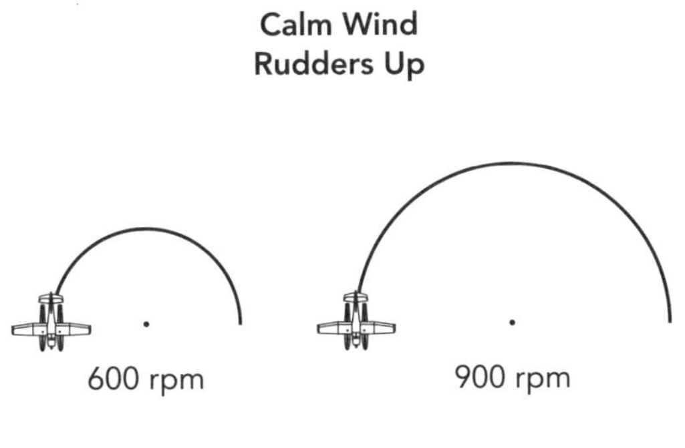

Rudders down but with no pilot input, adding power will increase radius and decrease rate of turn.

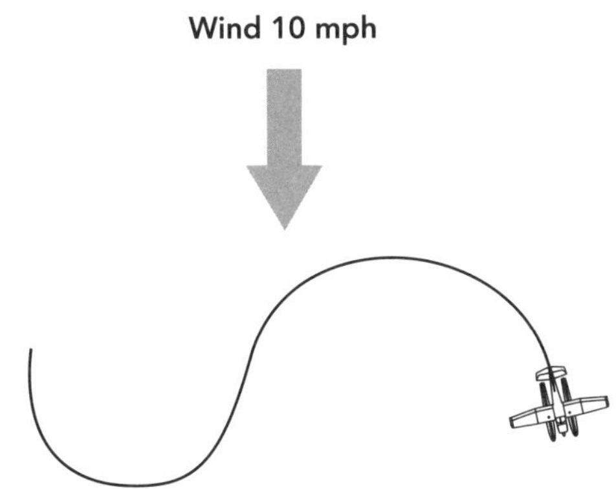

Rudders down: turn into the wind will be fast rate, small radius. Turn to downwind will be slow rate, very large radius—be sure you have enough room to turn!

Figure 7-3. Idle taxi turning radius

Turns

Turns are made using water rudders *and* ailerons. While displacement taxi turning, the seaplane pilot always uses ailerons. When the wind is strong, ailerons are a must. When the wind is light, it is good to stay in the habit and remember, even if wind is calm, the ailerons are "seeing" some wind by virtue of the seaplane's forward movement. How the ailerons are positioned depends on where the wind is coming from. The rule is: If the wind is coming from the front hemisphere of the seaplane, ailerons are positioned full opposite the rudder direction. If the wind is from behind, the wheel (aileron) is a steering wheel. So with wind from behind, the wheel (or stick) is positioned in the same direction as the rudder. The ailerons are of significant help in turning a seaplane, if positioned correctly. This can easily be demonstrated by facing into the wind with water rudders up, put one foot across both rudder pedals so they and the air rudder are neutral. Turn the aileron fully one direction. Note the nose swing toward the down aileron. Then reverse the aileron position and note the nose swing in the opposite direction. Because they are so far from the CG, ailerons are very effective at yawing the aircraft. Keep in mind that the down aileron is always the "draggiest" aileron, regardless of where the wind is coming from. Knowing this, the pilot can predict the result of putting an aileron down, as in Figure 7-4 on the next page.

If the wind is coming from the front hemisphere of the seaplane, ailerons are positioned full opposite the rudder direction. If the wind is from behind, the wheel (aileron) is a steering wheel.

The down aileron is always the "draggiest" aileron.

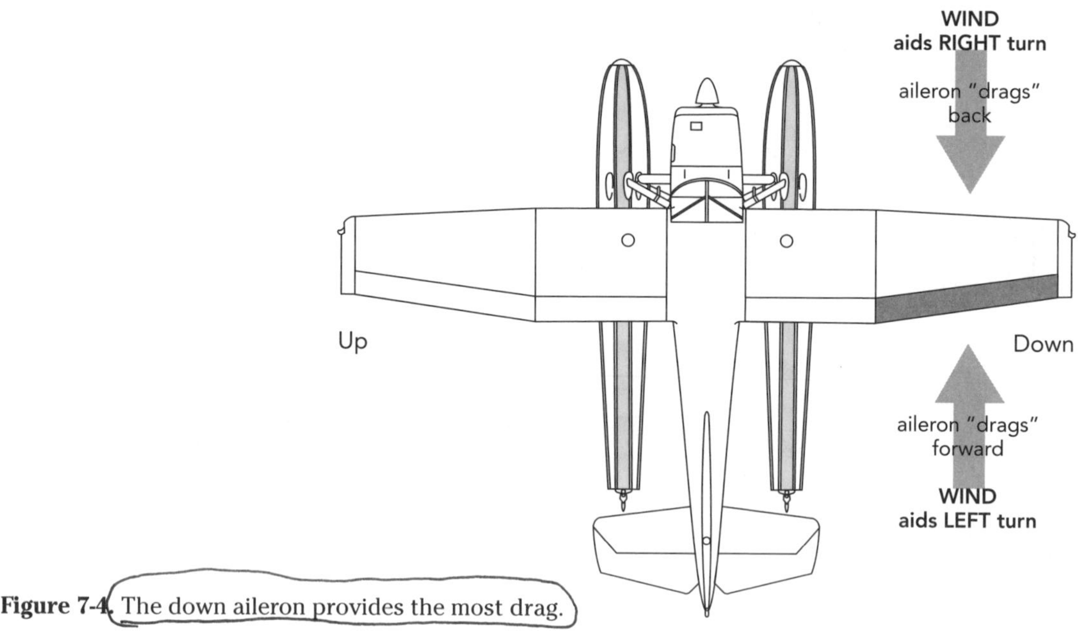

Figure 7-4. The down aileron provides the most drag.

For example, headed into the wind with a desire to turn left, the pilot fully depresses the left rudder pedal. Since the wind is from the front half of the seaplane, aileron is fully positioned to the right, putting the left aileron down, which drags back, aiding the left turn. Once the airplane has turned 90° left, the wind is soon going to be coming from the rear half of the seaplane, so the aileron is repositioned fully left (turning left, the steering wheel is turned left), putting the right aileron down, which drags forward, aiding the left turn. Once the turn is completed to downwind, the ailerons are centered, and the pilot must pay close attention to rudders and ailerons to keep the floatplane pointed downwind. The floatplane is only yaw stable when pointed into the wind.

When taxiing crosswind, use the aileron to decrease the need for rudder. Your leg will appreciate it on a long crosswind taxi.

Turns from into the wind to downwind in a stiff breeze require some skill and technique, because as the seaplane turns crosswind, the weathercocking forces increase, reaching their peak when the seaplane is directly crosswind. In how much wind can the seaplane still turn to downwind? Factors affecting this are aircraft model (amount of side surface area fore and aft of the pivot point), size of water rudders, pilot technique, and how the rudders are rigged. Some seaplanes will turn better to the right than they will to the left due to rudder rigging. So if your seaplane can't turn left in a wind, it may be a good idea to try turning to the right.

Turning in Wind

Pilot technique for turning in wind is not difficult. Let the seaplane itself determine how much wind is present and what technique will work to make that 180° turn. Start by attempting a normal turn (full rudder, full opposite aileron). If the turn is not completed, try turning in the opposite direction. Interestingly enough, this attempt in the other direction may stand a better chance of being successful for two reasons.

1. Rudder rigging may be such that better turning force is available in one direction.
2. The turn in the opposite direction is actually an inertia turn.

Inertia Turn

It is reasonable to expect a turn made to the left would stand the best chance of success due to the left turning forces. If the first (normal) turn described above was to the left and didn't work, and a second turn was attempted to the right (an inertia turn) but it didn't work, then the next step would be to try an inertia turn to the left.

The inertia turn is just like a normal turn except the pilot starts the turn in the opposite direction of the desired turn direction. An inertia turn to the left is started by turning right. When the seaplane has turned as far to the right as it will go, reverse rudder and aileron. When the nose passes through heading directly into the wind, it already has a turning inertia (hence the term), which should help oppose the weathercocking forces and allow the turn to be completed.

The inertia turn is the seaplane equivalent of rocking a car fore and aft to get a wheel out of a hole. If the inertia turn doesn't work, then try an RPM increase.

Increase RPM

Since water rudder authority depends on velocity of water flowing past the rudders, the rudders will be more capable of helping the seaplane through the turn if they are moving through the water a little faster. The downside of this is that higher RPM increases propeller erosion. The turn from into the wind will certainly put water through the propeller as waves splash back from the inside of the downwind float and are blown by the wind through the propeller. Therefore, an RPM increase should be small.

If the first attempt to turn was unsuccessful using 700 RPM, try 800, then 900. Trying to turn out of the wind with more than 1,000 RPM is a bad idea. The wind is strong enough that other strategies should be used.

With a little experience taxiing a particular airplane in varying wind and sea states, you will know what combination of RPM increase and turning technique will probably work.

Hump or Plow Taxi

This is the second phase of taxi the seaplane must go through during its acceleration to takeoff speed. The plow taxi is accomplished by holding the stick back (elevator up) and adding takeoff power. The seaplane will accelerate as the nose rises, hesitates and rises some more. If the stick is held back, the nose rise stops and the airplane continues to plow taxi. Speed is 10–15 kts. If back pressure on the stick is relaxed, the nose will start down again as the seaplane accelerates into step taxi.

Plowing Turn

The plowing turn is accomplished with water rudders remaining down (so they will be down when power is reduced to idle on the downwind heading) by positioning the elevator all the way up and holding it there until the maneuver is completed. Increase power to takeoff power or nearly so. As the nose rises, the center of buoyancy moves aft so the weather-cocking tendency changes to a tendency to weathercock downwind, thus aiding a turn to downwind. So, as soon as the turn is started, there will be a tendency to turn downwind, and the turn is easily completed. Aileron positioning is the same as for the idle taxi turn, which is the same as used in the landplane when taxi-turning in a strong wind. The plowing turn is typically done to the left due to the strong left-turning tendencies.

The plowing turn is a good training maneuver, but it is also a bit of an enigma. Besides seriously limiting forward visibility, in a strong wind the plowing turn can be dangerous. In light to moderate breezes the plowing turn teaches many techniques in seaplane handling, but it is really not needed, as most floatplanes will turn in these wind speeds using the displacement taxi techniques. In stronger winds, the plowing turn maneuver causes a high wing angle of attack. The airplane is moving forward into the wind, the right wing is moving forward faster than the left wing, and the wind is impacting the right side of the aircraft. All of these factors add together to help bury the left float and cause an upset.

So when the wind is strong and the white-maned ponies (large whitecaps) are racing across the surface of the water, and I need to taxi downwind, I would never opt for a plowing turn. So, what's to be done? There are two good options:

1. Don't land where you need to turn around on the water in the first place. The experienced seaplane pilot, if possible, will land and fall off the step close to the final destination and preferably, just downwind of it, so the taxi path doesn't have a downwind taxi component.
2. If the above strategy is not possible, sail back! It is far safer than attempting a turn to downwind and taxiing downwind in stronger breezes. Sailing is a topic coming up in the next chapter, one which is fun and rewarding for the seaplane pilot.

See Chapter 8, *Sailing*

No Rudders

Sometimes, the seaplane pilot must taxi without rudders. The rudders may be rendered inoperative by a broken cable or by the need to taxi in very weedy water. It is actually possible to taxi to almost any destination without rudders, using combinations of the techniques discussed above. If there is a strong breeze (12–15 kts or more), taxiing without rudders is a breeze. Just use the power sailing techniques discussed in the next chapter.

The Throttle as a Rudder

If the wind is less than that, just remember that the pilot can turn the throttle into a rudder by using the elevator. If that last sentence has you scowling, read on!

Turn the throttle into a rudder by using the elevator!

Let's start this short discussion with your seaplane displacement taxiing with the wind coming from 30° to the right of the nose. The seaplane wants to turn right into the wind, doesn't it? But if you pull the stick back and add lots of power, the nose comes up, the center of buoyancy moves aft, so there is more right side-surface area exposed to the wind forward of the center of buoyancy (the pivot point while taxiing). Now, the seaplane will turn left. *See* Figure 7-5 on the next page. Throttled back, the seaplane turns right. Add power and the seaplane turns left. Therefore, there must be some intermediate throttle setting where turning forces are neutral. Can we not argue that the seaplane pilot can use the throttle as a rudder?

Yes, we can. But we must also remember that propeller RPM above 1,000 can cause damage to our prop, and prolonged operations at or above 1,000 RPM at slow speed will overheat the

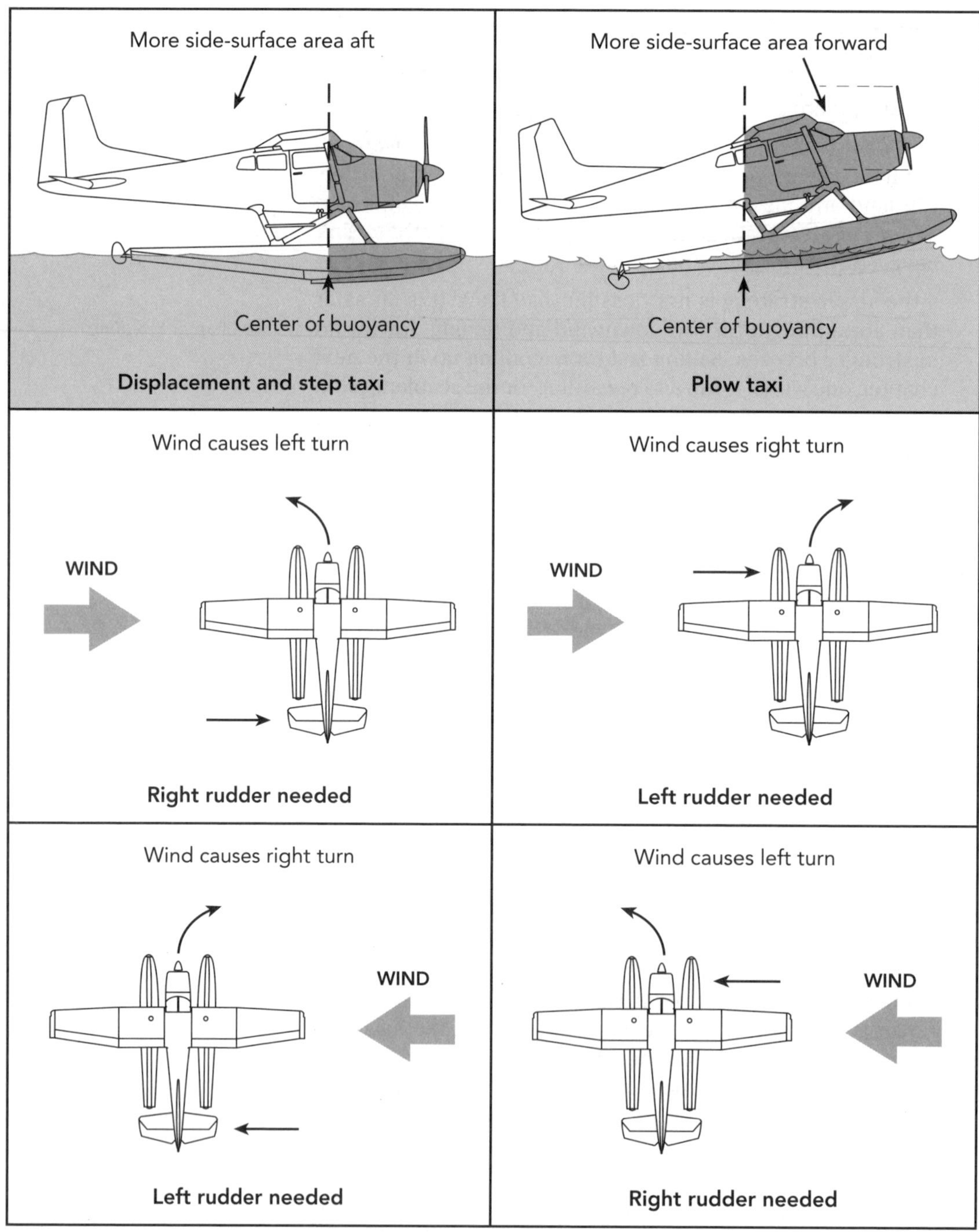

Figure 7-5. Turning effect of crosswind in level or nose high taxi modes.

engine. So, the above is not used for long distance taxiing. It is a very useful technique for ramping with a crosswind, though. Some combination of idle taxi and plow taxi will allow arriving at a taxi destination without rudders, if necessary.

Step Taxi

Once full plow taxi speed is reached, if backpressure on the elevator is relaxed, the seaplane will accelerate onto the step. If the pilot completely relaxes all pressure on the stick, as the seaplane accelerates, the nose will continue to lower. On the step, the faster you go the more the nose will come down until too much of the float is wetted forward causing drag. Before this happens, the pilot should start increasing back pressure to maintain takeoff attitude (which is just about the same attitude the seaplane had when displacement taxiing). If this attitude is held and power is full, the seaplane will accelerate to lift off speed. If power is reduced to just what is needed to remain on the step but not accelerate, step taxi is achieved.

While step taxiing, remember the characteristic of the floatplane on the step that as speed on the step increases, nose drops lower; and as speed decreases, the nose will rise (assuming no change in elevator input from the pilot). This is the best clue you will have as to whether you are accelerating or decelerating on the step. Power can be managed to maintain speed by managing the throttle to maintain nose attitude. On most seaplanes, the airspeed indicator is not useful for speed control on the water because (a) safe step taxiing is done at low to moderate step taxi speeds, in a range where the airspeed indicator is not useful or not accurate; (b) because wind velocity and direction will have a significant impact on the reading (error) of the airspeed indicator; and (c) the pilot should be looking outside, not at the instruments in the cockpit.

Remember the ailerons! If there is wind, ailerons must be fully applied to keep the upwind wing down. If the downwind wing lifts, you are going too fast or there is too much wind for the step taxi to be a stable, safe maneuver. If a wing lifts, the most dangerous thing you can do is neutralize ailerons and keep the same throttle setting. The airplane is trying to fly, so either throttle back or add power and fly away.

Step taxi speeds range from 15–18 kts up to liftoff speed. At these speeds, it is quite easy to punch a hole in a float bottom (they are typically only .03" thick) by hitting any object in the water. Unless you are lucky enough to hit an object squarely on the keel or sister keelson, even something as light as a floating soda pop can or bottle may make a hole in a float bottom. For this reason, step taxiing is for takeoff and landing only, especially in the wilderness where maintenance is a costly, major headache. Fly to the place where you want to be, land, and displacement taxi to shore. A good pilot flies an uneventful flight and arrives with grace and good technique, not showmanship. Practice step taxi in water you are certain is free of flotsam, primarily to develop and maintain your skill and comfort level with taxiing on the step and step turns.

Step Turn

The purpose of the step turn is to reverse course in the smallest possible space while on the step. It is used to decrease the distance needed for takeoff. The step turn is made only to the left due to the strong left turning tendencies found during a slow step taxi, which are so strong that the right rudder is needed to keep the turn from becoming too severe.

This maneuver is started when on the step (preferably at a slow step speed) with the application of left rudder and simultaneous full application of left aileron. Use absolutely all aileron input! Once the turn has started, a little more power will be needed to maintain speed. You should be scanning outside but looking primarily about 45° to the left of straight ahead, because that's where you are going. Keep in mind that if a rudder cable breaks, or the engine fails, the seaplane's path will instantly become a straight line, tangent to the original circular path. So don't plan your step taxi too close to shore or docks. While turning, continuously monitor what changes are taking place with pitch (nose) attitude. If the nose is gradually rising, more power is needed or you will continue to slow and fall off the step. Most floatplanes signal that they are falling off the step by beginning to porpoise. When that happens, you have let the speed decrease too much and now have only two options. You may abandon the step taxi by throttling back to idle, or to continue, apply full throttle until the seaplane is firmly back on the step. Full left aileron is a must throughout the maneuver.

Most seaplane pilots I fly with don't like step turns, or are not comfortable with them. This is mostly because the centripetal (tipping) forces are great, and these pilots are intuitively not feeling safe because no one has taught them how to know the safe limit of side forces. They haven't learned how tight a turn

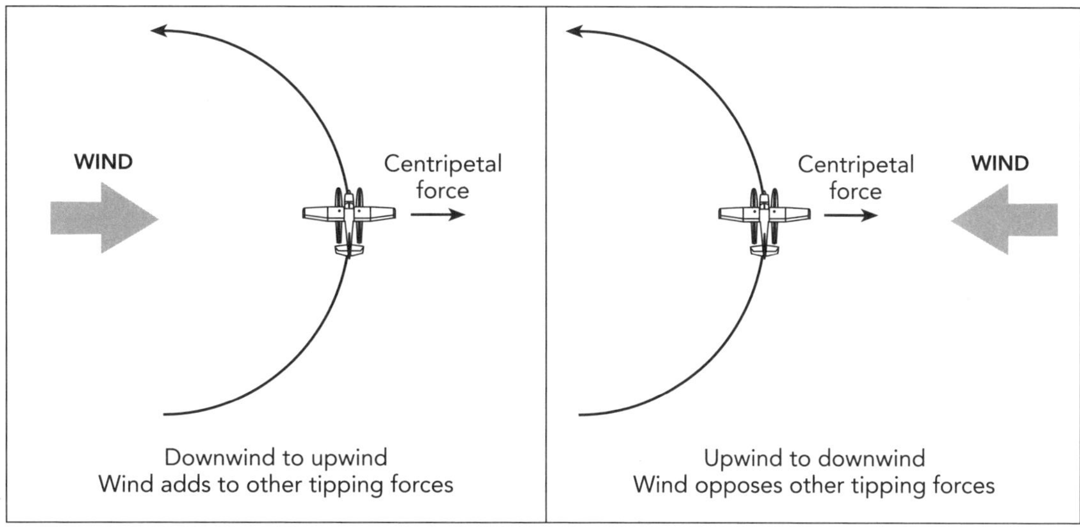

Figure 7-6. Step turns in wind

can be made without fear of tipping to the right, catching a wingtip and going for a swim. Their solution to this is a logical one: they don't do step turns! They make sure they don't have to take off from a small space by using a step turn. This is certainly a safe solution to the problem but it takes away a capability of the seaplane.

Any discussion of tipping forces and their management must include crosswind as a factor. For this discussion, let's assume no wind. The goal of the step turn is to make a small radius turn, on the step, and make it safely. There is an instrument in most seaplanes that can be used to keep from exceeding a turn rate that is safe. The turn coordinator can be used for this purpose by not allowing the wing of the little airplane to go past the top of the "L." The secret to making a small radius turn is speed control. The slower the turn, the smaller the radius with the same tipping force, so practice is needed to be able to maintain a turning speed just above the speed at which the seaplane wants to fall off the step. Keep in mind that the centripetal force increases with the square of the speed. Therefore, a little increase in speed causes a larger increase in tipping force.

Now let's add wind to this discussion. In the takeoff chapter, step turn takeoffs are limited to wind speeds not exceeding 10 MPH. Probably, this should be even less for small two-seater floatplanes and certainly less for ultralight floatplanes. The rea-

See the "Confined Area Takeoff" discussion on Page 120, for more on step turn takeoffs.

son for this is that during a turn from downwind to upwind, the crosswind component of the wind adds to the tipping forces of the turn. *See* Figure 7-6 on the previous page. So, turns from upwind to downwind on the step can be made with higher ambient wind speeds because the crosswind opposes the tipping force of the turn. Unfortunately, seaplane pilots find little use for this kind of turn.

Don't turn left on the step where the wind will be from the left.

What we floatplane pilots must guard against is any situation where we are making a turn on the step, and during any portion of the turn, the wind is adding to the other tipping forces. So, don't turn left on the step where the wind will be from the left or right with a wind from the right except in very light winds. More than one seaplane rating applicant has busted a checkride when a salty old examiner said, "OK, after this crosswind landing (wind from the left at 12 kts) stay on the step and give me a 90° turn." After the landing, the pilot, not thinking, did the natural thing, turning left to fall off the step into the wind and busted the checkride. The same scenario can develop during takeoff.

For a complete discussion of step turn instability, dynamic rollover, and teaching/learning step turns, consult Chapter 9 of *Water Flying Concepts*.

Review

Where is the point about which the aircraft pivots, and what is it called when the seaplane is in the air? on the water? The CG doesn't move much while flying except in response to fuel burn, but the center of buoyancy moves aft significantly during nose high operations on the water.

The three taxi categories are displacement taxi, plow taxi, and step taxi.

When displacement taxiing:

- When the seaplane is on the water, the pilot must be sure that engine RPM is at idle unless there is a very specific reason to use more power.
- Preferably not more than 700 RPM. The purpose of this rule is to prevent damage to the very expensive propeller.
- No wind, the single engine seaplane will turn left. It will turn left at the fastest rate, scribing the smallest circle, at low RPM with the water rudders up.

- With rudders down, the seaplane will turn left if there is no wind and no input to the rudders from the pilot, but rate of turn will be less than if rudders are up.
- When turning, always use ailerons.
- The down aileron is always the *draggiest* aileron, regardless of where the wind is coming from. How does this knowledge apply to turning the floatplane?

Cite the rule for proper aileron use.

For turning in wind, how do you let the seaplane itself determine how much wind is present and what technique will work to make that 180° turn?

Since water rudder authority depends on velocity of water flowing past the rudders, the rudders will be more capable of helping the seaplane through the turn if the seaplane is moving through the water a little faster. Trying to turn out of the wind with more than 1,000 RPM is a bad idea—other strategies should be applied.

Plow Taxi

To plow taxi, hold the stick back (elevator up) and add takeoff power. The seaplane will accelerate as the nose rises, hesitates and rises some more. If the stick is held back, the nose rise stops and the airplane continues to plow taxi. Speed is 10–15 kts.

- Describe how the plowing turn is accomplished and how water rudders should be positioned.
- Describe how and why the weather cocking tendency changes as the nose comes up.
- Describe aileron positioning during this maneuver.
- The plowing turn is typically done to the left due to the strong left-turning tendencies.
- In a strong wind the plowing turn can be dangerous, so use sailing or land where turning downwind is not needed.

Sometimes the seaplane pilot must taxi without rudders. It's possible to taxi to almost any destination with no rudders, using combinations of the techniques discussed above.

The seaplane pilot can turn the throttle into a rudder by using the elevator!

Step Taxi

Once full plow taxi speed is reached, the seaplane will accelerate onto the step if backpressure on the elevator is relaxed. On the step:

- The faster you go, the more the nose will come down until too much of the float is wetted forward, causing drag.
- Before this happens, start increasing back pressure to maintain takeoff attitude.
- Hold this attitude and keep power full, and the seaplane will accelerate to liftoff speed.
- If you reduce power to the amount needed to remain on the step but not accelerate, step taxi is achieved.

On the step, as speed increases, the nose drops lower and as speed decreases, the nose rises. On most seaplanes, the airspeed indicator is not useful for speed control on the water.

Cite three reasons why this is true about the AI (*see* Page 67).

Remember the ailerons! If there is wind, ailerons must be fully applied to keep the upwind wing down. If a wing lifts during step taxi, you are doing something wrong. Describe how to fix it. Step taxi speeds range from 15–18 kts up to liftoff speed.

At these speeds, it is quite easy to punch a hole in a float bottom by hitting any object in the water. For this reason, step taxiing is for takeoff and landing only. Practice step taxi in water you know is free of flotsam.

The purpose of the step turn is to reverse course in the smallest possible space while on the step:

- Step turn is made only to the left due to the strong left turning tendencies found during a slow step taxi—so strong that the right rudder is needed to avoid a too-severe turn.
- Start this maneuver on the step with the application of left rudder and simultaneous full application of left aileron.
- Use absolutely all aileron input! Once the turn has started, a little more power will be needed to maintain speed.

With respect to step turns, describe:

1. Where, outside, you should be looking during the turn.
2. What happens if the engine quits or a rudder cable breaks.
3. Why subtle changes in pitch attitude are important indicators.
4. Aileron positioning and its importance to safety.
5. Use of the turn coordinator.
6. Why turns into a wind from the left are a big no-no.

Taxiing in at the end of the day.

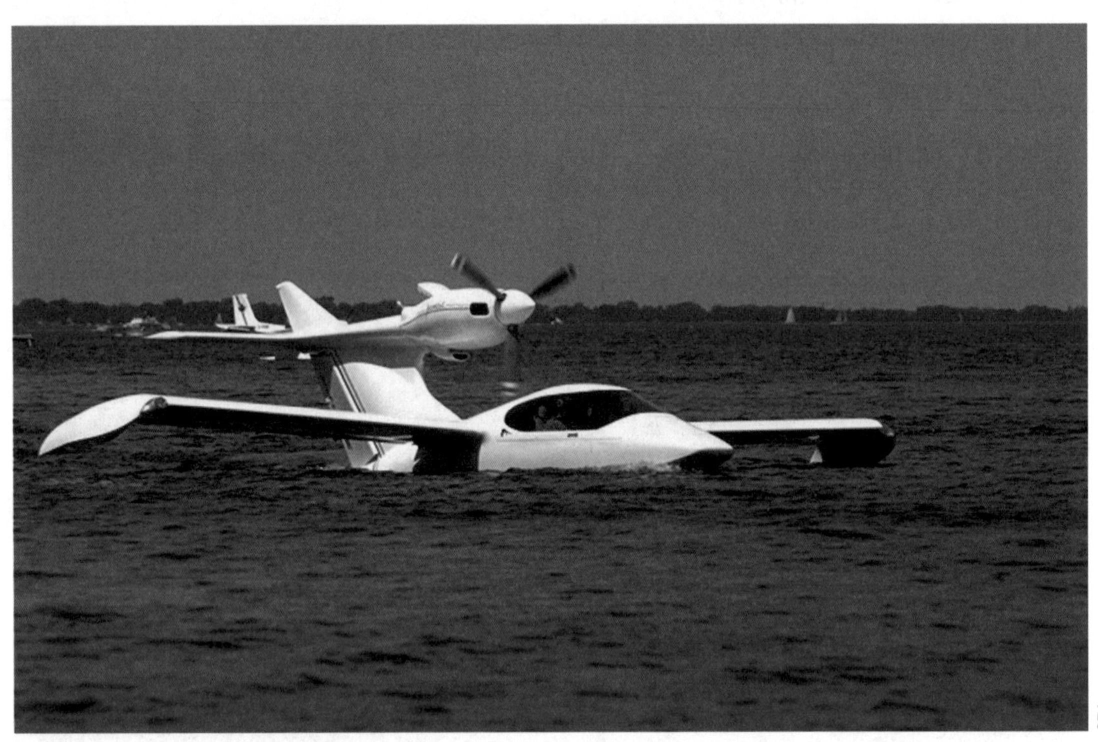

SPA

A Seawind, "parked" in a light breeze.

Chapter 8
Sailing

If you are studying for the oral and checkride, please read the PTS section shown at right, then return to the discussion below.

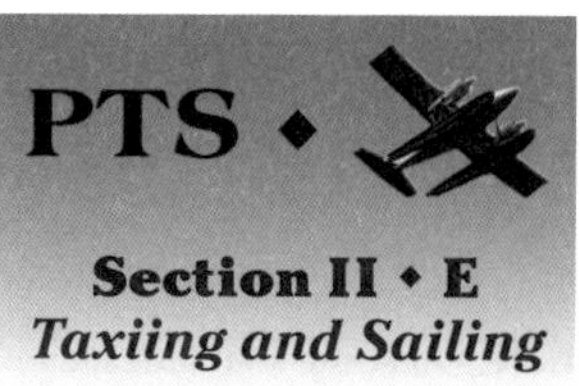

Water handling of the seaplane is what sets the expert seaplane pilot apart. Mastery of sailing provides the pilot with the confidence needed to precisely and safely put his craft anywhere on the water, under any circumstances. Under high wind conditions, the seaplane pilot can power sail with precision to anywhere on the lake, while keeping the nose pointed into the wind where the seaplane is safe from upset.

Let's start by breaking sailing into two categories: **power-off sailing and power sailing**.

Power-Off Sailing

Power-off sailing is further broken down into two subcategories called **accuracy** or **precision** sailing and **long distance** sailing. But first, some basics.

Power-off sailing:
- engine off
- water rudders up
- flaps usually up

Power-off sailing is done with engine off, water rudders up and flaps usually up. Water rudders are up because, moving backwards, they turn the seaplane in a direction opposite of the air rudder, so water and air rudders are fighting each other. Flaps are up for three reasons:

1. With flaps extended it is impossible to see where you are going (and the flaps become an impediment to walking aft on the float at the appropriate moment).
2. Extended flaps disturb the airflow over the fuselage, decreasing the authority of the air rudder and resulting in less directional control.
3. Unless the wind is light, with flaps down, it is possible to get moving rearward too fast, which may bury the back of the float and cause the seaplane to go over backwards. Flaps are used only in very light winds, so don't get in a hurry!

Power-off sailing: Point tail in the direction you want to go

When power-off sailing, point the tail in the direction you want to go. So, here you are, needing to sail back and to the left. You point the tail to the left, which means you point the nose to the right using full right rudder and full left aileron. Check rudders up and flaps up, unless wind is very light. Note the nose swing partially to the right. Don't expect to go exactly in the direction the tail is pointed. Your path will be one that is somewhere between where the tail is pointed and directly downwind. *See* Figure 8-1.

Some instructors prefer another way of teaching this. They teach if you want to sail back and to the left, use left aileron (put the aileron in the direction you want to go) and opposite rudder. Whichever way works best for you, the result is the same.

What makes this work is **keel effect**. Much like a sailboat uses its keel to "grab" the water to make the boat go where pointed, the seaplane's keel works in the same way, although not efficiently because it doesn't extend into the water very far.

Note: On some seaplanes, use of one door may turn the floatplane (if the door's center of wind pressure is not over, or nearly over the center of buoyancy). Give it a try—if it works, use it.

Doors, when opened, cause drag—therefore if more drag is needed in light winds or when power sailing, the doors may be opened.

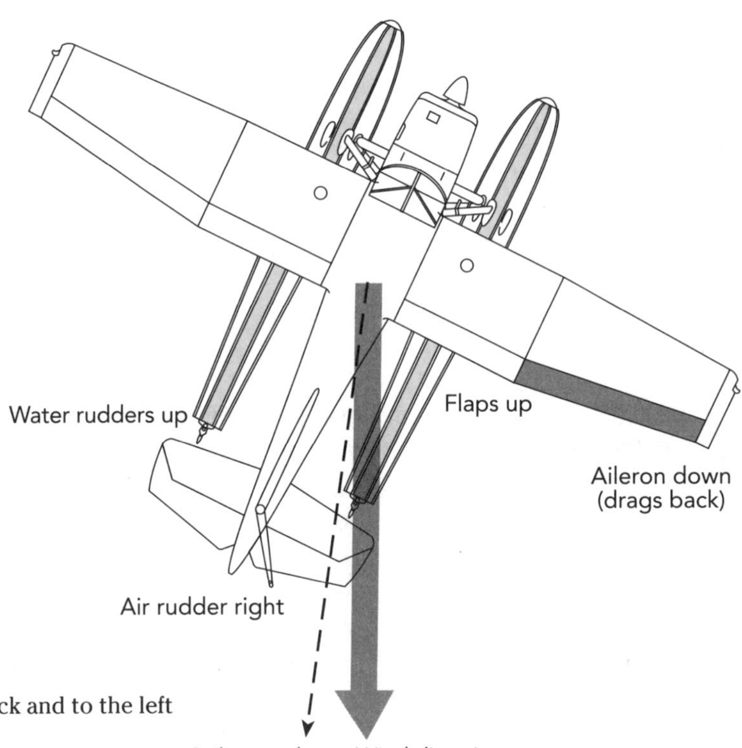

Figure 8-1. Power-off sailing back and to the left

Accuracy (precision) sailing is done to position the seaplane at an exact spot on the beach. Perhaps there is a tree, where you want to tie the tail. The primary rule here is the shorter the distance you sail back, the more accurate the sailing. If you only have to sail back three feet, you won't miss your goal very far! So, do whatever you can to position the aircraft as near as possible to the destination using power (displacement taxi).

The shorter you sail back, the more accurate your sailing will be.

Sailing back to the beach or into a slip (a real challenge) in winds less than 13–15 MPH may be done with accuracy sailing. You will find a full description of this on Page 216.

Long distance sailing is a skill needed if you have landed on the water without power after a power failure in the air. Depending on where you touch down and the size of the lake, you may have quite a ways to sail back. And downwind of you there may be a rocky shore with a small sand beach off to one side, which you must get to or your aircraft will be damaged on the rocks.

Let's pretend that you are involved in the above scenario. The wind is about 8–10 MPH. Sitting in the pilot's seat looking back while sailing a quarter to a half a mile is a neck-wrenching experience. If you have an able-bodied person with you, there is a better way. Quickly instruct that person how to use the rudder and aileron controls. Check that water rudders are up, then hop out and position yourself as if you were checking the fuel, facing aft looking over the top of the wing (*see* Figure 8-2).

Figure 8-2. This pilot has taken the position for long distance sailing and is directing the person in the co-pilot's seat to correctly position the controls.

There, you are master of all you survey! You can see the air rudder and ailerons and have a perfect view of where you are going. Since you are facing aft, control inputs are reversed back to being correct (for you). If you want to sail to your right (of directly downwind), instruct the person in the cabin "right rudder, left aileron," check visually for correct control input, and watch for the tail swing to your right. Now, focus on your goal—that sandy beach to the right (*see* Figure 8-3). And remember that once the wind gets near the beach, it will be influenced by the shore (especially if there are trees on the shore), and change direction to more parallel the shore. So you probably need to position yourself to the right so you won't be blown into the rocks on the left side of the sandy beach. See if you can spot two objects, one behind the other, at the far right end of the beach, such as a specific tree behind where the right side of the beach ends in rocks. Use those two points as **range markers**, (*see* the discussion of range markers on Page 315) and try to sail a path directly there. While up there, looking back over the wing, enjoy the fresh air and experience of knowing what it is like to be a sailor! This is a fun maneuver to practice. After all, you are going somewhere in a seaplane, and it isn't costing you anything for fuel. When you are getting close to shore, hop down, grab the paddle, and go aft to fend off and heel up.

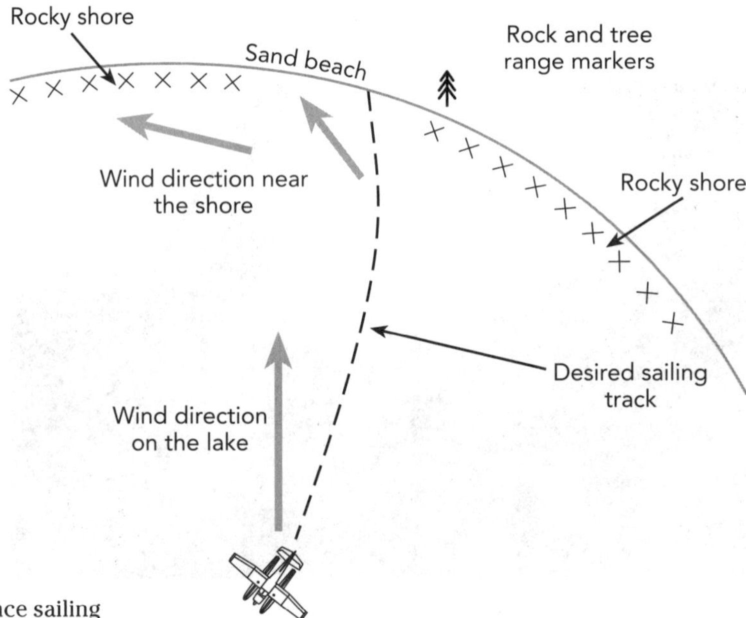

Figure 8-3. Long distance sailing

Power Sailing or Tacking

If the wind is strong (13–18 MPH or more, depending on the aircraft), the technique of power sailing allows the seaplane pilot to move in any direction, under absolute control, while headed nearly into the wind where the seaplane is most stable and safe from upset. Power sailing is done with engine near or at slow idle, water rudders up, and flaps as needed. Some may teach that water rudders are down during power sailing, when moving forward (a form of displacement taxi). But I have never found it necessary to use the rudders in any phase of power sailing. Having to put the rudders up and down while power sailing adds unnecessarily to the pilot's workload during a busy time, so let's keep it simple.

Power sailing:

- engine near or at idle
- water rudders up
- flaps as needed

Once the technique is perfected, very precise positioning such as sailing back into a slip can be accomplished with relative ease. Let's start with a discussion of the simplest form of power sailing called **parking**.

Parking the Seaplane

This is done anywhere on the water by throttling back to idle (the seaplane should idle at 450–500 RPM), extending the flaps, and waiting for the forward speed to decrease to zero. If there is sufficient wind to power sail, the seaplane will slow down, stop, then move slowly backward. Now adjust the flaps and RPM so the seaplane remains fixed in position on the water. You have parked the seaplane! The great value in this, besides determining if there is enough wind to power sail, is that once you have parked the seaplane, you can divert your attention to other tasks: getting lines or anchors ready; casting an anchor at a specific spot in a wind; putting a line on a stern cleat in preparation for going ashore; programming a GPS; completing a passenger briefing; checking the chart; or finishing a pretakeoff checklist. Even if the wind is too light to power sail, parking is a maneuver that allows the seaplane to continue straight ahead slowly without requiring attention, as long as there is a little wind. If there is little or no wind, the seaplane will gently scribe left circles, and free the pilot to attend to other tasks (if in a large enough area without traffic).

Now that we have learned how to power sail in place, let's do it with precision! Use a buoy or float. Taxi toward the buoy from directly downwind. Put your water rudders up and stop with your left wingtip directly over the buoy. Once stabilized there, using power, rudders, and flaps to remain in place, use some left rudder to bring the buoy up to a foot from the float, under the wing.

Stop there by again facing directly into the wind. Now move the buoy back out to under the wingtip with a little right rudder. With practice you will learn how to anticipate corrections and watch the water in front of you for signs of stronger or weaker wind and gusts that may be coming at you.

Point the nose toward the direction you want to go.

When power sailing, you move the seaplane back when drag from the wind exceeds thrust from the propeller. Forward happens when thrust slightly exceeds drag. When power sailing, point the nose toward the direction you want to go. While using right rudder, the seaplane moves to the right because of wind acting on the left side of the fuselage and because of the component of propeller thrust acting to the right. (*See* Figure 8-4.)

Manage these forces and you can move in any direction. Practice will improve your skill. Try to taxi (power sail) in a circle around the buoy, keeping a constant distance and the nose of the airplane more-or-less into the wind. (*See* Figure 8-5.)

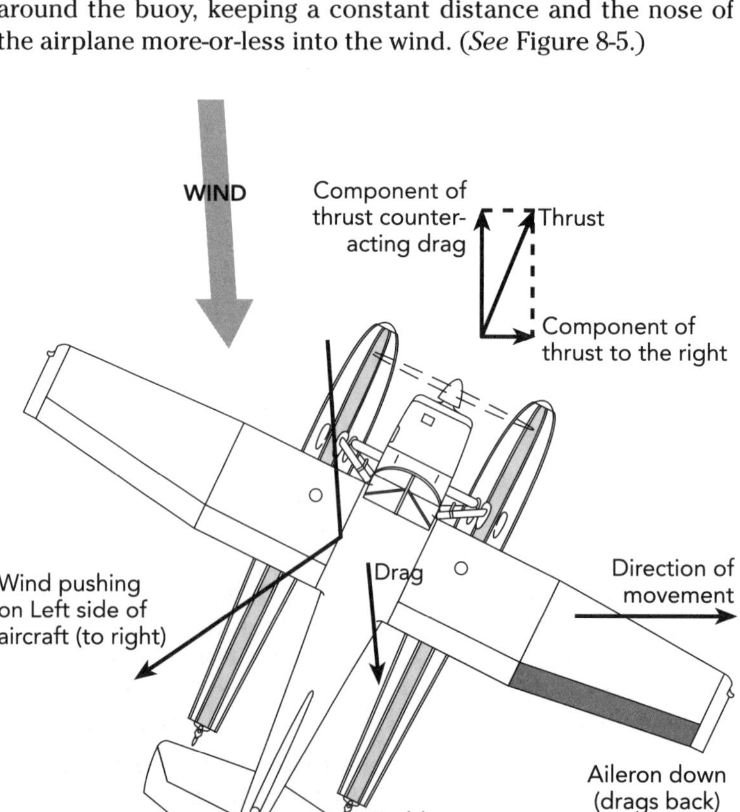

Figure 8-4. Power sailing to the right

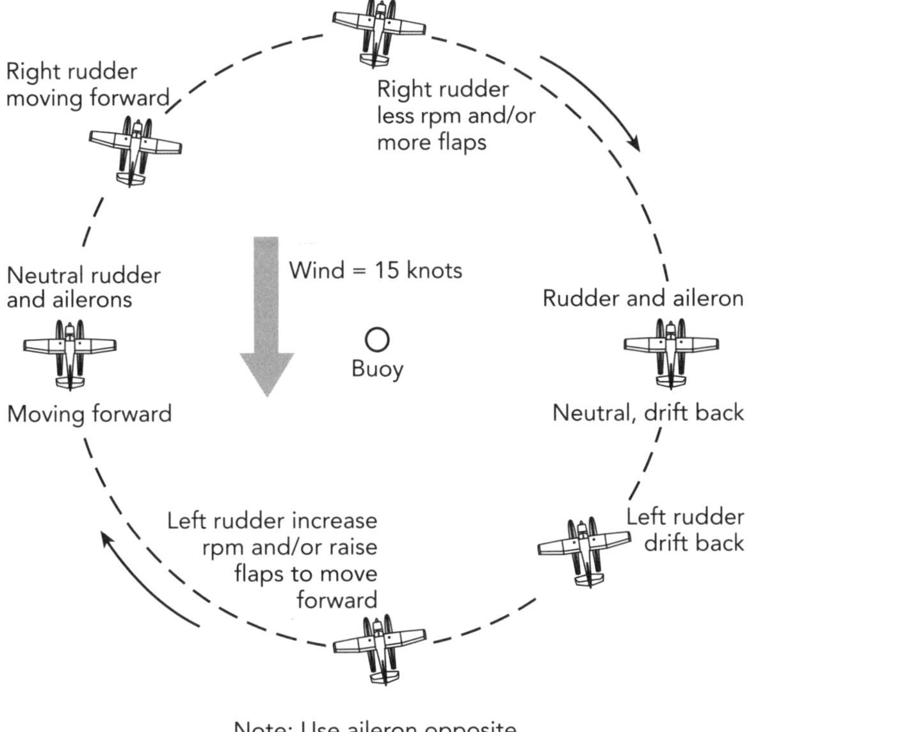

Figure 8-5. Power sailing exercise

Review

The two categories of sailing are **power-off sailing** and **power sailing**.

Power-off sailing is further broken down into two sub-categories called **long distance** and **accuracy** or **precision** sailing.

Power-off sailing is done with engine off, water rudders up and flaps up. Water rudders are up because, moving backwards, they turn the seaplane in a direction opposite that of the air rudder. When power-off sailing, point the tail in the direction you want to go. What makes this work is **keel effect. Accuracy sailing** positions the seaplane exactly where you want it. The shorter the distance you sail back, the more accurate will be the sailing.

Long distance sailing is a skill you need to land on water without power and with considerable distance to sail back to the shore.

Use two points on shore where you want to go as **range markers** and try to sail a path directly there.

If the wind is strong the technique of **power sailing** allows the seaplane pilot to move in any direction, under absolute control, while headed nearly into the wind.

Power sailing is done with engine at or near idle, water rudders up, and flaps as needed.

Parking the seaplane is done anywhere on the water by throttling back to idle, extending the flaps, and waiting for the forward speed to decrease to zero. Once you have parked the seaplane, you can attend to other tasks such as getting lines or anchors ready, casting an anchor at a specific spot in a wind, or putting a line on a stern cleat in preparation for going ashore.

When power sailing, you move the seaplane back when drag from the wind exceeds thrust from the propeller. Forward happens when thrust slightly exceeds drag. When power sailing, point the nose toward the direction you want to go. The seaplane moves to the right because of wind acting on the left side of the fuselage and because of the component of propeller thrust acting to the right. Manage these forces and you can move in any desired direction. "Practice makes perfect!"

SPA

Displacement taxiing while completing the pretakeoff check.

Chapter 9
The Pretakeoff Check

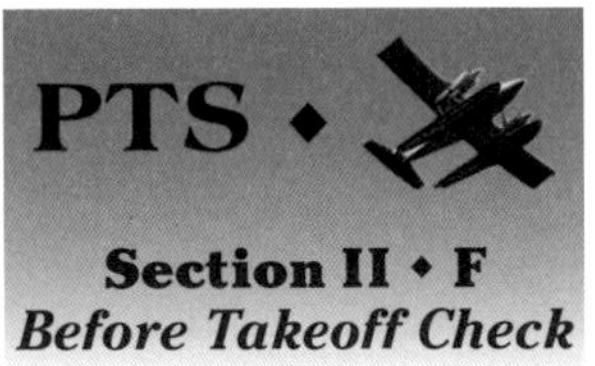

If you are studying for the oral and checkride, please read PTS Section II • F, then return to the discussion below. If you hold the landplane rating at the private level or better, the PTS task table says this task is not tested, but you will be performing it under the watchful eye of the examiner, so you want to review this chapter. If you are a seaplane pilot interested in reviewing, read on!

Checklist Differences

The main difference between a landplane and seaplane pretakeoff check is that the seaplane is always in motion while the pilot is accomplishing the check. This means that the seaplane pilot needs to accomplish the check while his eyes are outside (looking out) at least 90% of the time. So, techniques need to be developed to aid the pilot in this difference. They are discussed below as we cover each item in the generic pretakeoff list from Chapter 5. Remember, the order of the generic list, or the order of the checklist in your airplane may not be quite correct for your operation, and the items in the generic list may differ somewhat from the checklist in your airplane. Get with your flight instructor regarding those differences, and establish a checklist that works best for you.

See Figure 5-1, Page 31.

Establish a checklist that works best for you.

Checklist Timing

When is the seaplane pretakeoff checklist accomplished? Usually while taxiing downwind and/or toward the spot where the takeoff run will begin. All the pilot's chores must be finished before the seaplane reaches that spot. As a landplane pilot, you have developed the habit of taxiing to the takeoff runup area, then doing the pretakeoff check. You must now change that habit. Get used to the idea that you should feel uncomfortable while taxiing to the takeoff spot unless you have completed the pretakeoff checklist. When you get to that spot, you are going to turn and take off so you must be ready, with all tasks completed, when you get there. There are tasks that can be checked while

The checklist: when and how.

the engine is warming up, so do those first. Those items should appear on your checklist before runup. If they aren't, change the checklist. It is good cockpit management!

The Pretakeoff Check in Detail

Check Operations of Flight Controls

In God we trust, ALL ELSE WE CHECK, every time!

Have you ever checked the flight controls for "free and correct" and found them not OK? It doesn't happen very often. I have had it happen twice in more than 20,000 hours of flying. In both instances, a wire bundle behind the instrument panel had sagged just enough to snag the control column. Both times, had I not checked, the flight probably would have gone badly. So, *in God we trust, ALL ELSE WE CHECK, every time!*

The correct procedure is to visit, with the controls, the extremes of the four corners (forward-left, back-left, back-right, forward right). While moving the controls, feel for smoothness, snags, rough spots in the travel, etc., that would indicate a frayed cable (which would make the aircraft unairworthy), or a bearing in a pulley that is failing or something fouling the control surface itself. When the control is at the left and right limit, check to make sure your thumb is pointing to the up aileron, a good habit to be in for the day when the controls of the airplane have been worked on, and cables reversed.

The seaplane pilot's control check.

Also, as a seaplane pilot, when the wheel or stick is at the left and right limits, make a mental note of just where that control is. Teach yourself, before each flight, where FULL aileron input is located, because you will be using it!

Note that all of this can (and should) be done without looking inside the cockpit! Eyes outside for safety!

Check Doors and Seat Belts

A door popping open on takeoff or climbout is no big deal... for the pilot. But what about the passenger? A passenger trying to crawl into your lap during takeoff could make things go rather badly! So, a door, window and seat belt pretakeoff check is a good idea.

Again, there is no need to look inside while this check is done. Feel for the doors and windows and query the rear seat passengers about their belts. If you have briefed them properly, they can accomplish this check for you.

On single-engine Cessnas and some other aircraft, some pilots prefer to leave the doors latched but not locked to facilitate rescue if things go badly. To me, this is an acceptable practice, but it would be a good idea to brief your right seat passenger about the possibility of a door popping open. They would be comforted to know that the airplane will still fly and the door won't (can't) be opened more than an inch or two. Just tell your passenger to expect a louder noise and leave the open door for you (the pilot) to close when you are ready to do so.

Set Flight Instruments

Limit your "eyes inside" time during this task. The altimeter can be set before engine start so it will only require a quick check. The gyrocompass will need to be set, but don't bother looking at the magnetic compass until you have established and held a constant heading for about 15 seconds (eyes outside to do this), or the magnetic compass card will be swinging when you look at it. If you use the GPS track indication for magnetic heading information, the same thing applies as there will be a few seconds lag between actual heading and indicated track. If the examiner sees the gyrocompass being set while the seaplane is changing heading, he will wonder what, if anything, you know about navigation. This will start a navigation question and answer session you really don't need, because examiners are supposed to distract you at various times during the checkride. You may choose to defer such conversations to a less busy time, so don't let yourself be distracted. But, you will still be held accountable!

Examiners are required to create distractions to test your concentration—don't get distracted!

After takeoff, the seaplane's gyrocompass will need to be checked during climbout and as soon as wings are level on course. Expect to see greater errors in gyrocompasses after takeoff and after climb in a seaplane. So do not make the mistake of thinking that the gyrocompass you set while on the water will direct you on the correct course when airborne. The reason for this is complex but it is a fact of life.

A mistake: Thinking the gyrocompass you set while on the water will direct you on the correct course when airborne.

If you feel the need to set the attitude indicator, remember that the seaplane pitch attitude is slightly nose up during displacement taxi. Best to set it in level, cruise flight unless you know the exact setting for on the water.

Set Radios—Communicate As Needed

When setting radios, remember... eyes outside unless absolutely necessary! The GPS is a new enigma for pilots, especially seaplane pilots. Studies have shown that seaplane pilot's eyes-out-

GPS: an enigma for seaplane pilots.

side time decreases dramatically if there is a GPS (or LORAN) in the cockpit. It is called "television syndrome" because, just like a TV set, when it is turned on, the eyes of everyone in the room gravitate to that screen. When the GPS or LORAN is turned on, it goes through a period of initialization, then signals that it is ready to be programmed. Don't be a slave to that nav radio. Program it when you are ready, not when the radio is ready, because your most important task is to guide the moving seaplane safely. Wait to program the nav radio until you are in safe water, have parked the seaplane safely out on the water with engine running, or are safely in the air. Some pilots have their GPS installed so that it can be turned on before any other equipment, in order to initialize and program it before leaving the dock.

Check Engine Instruments

PTS: "Ensure that engine temperature and pressure are suitable for runup and takeoff."

One of the eight preflight tasks in the PTS says: Ensure that engine temperature and pressure are suitable for runup and takeoff. Pressures are checked on the engine instruments, but temperature, especially oil temperature is not the best indicator of when the engine is ready for runup or takeoff on many airplanes. Check with your flight instructor as to the correct procedure to use and why, if not using the oil temperature gauge.

Again, limit your eyes-inside time; select a time to look at instruments when all is stable and safe outside the airplane.

Check Fuel

Fuel gauge check actually checks the *fuel gauges* themselves.

This checklist item is really two tasks. One is to check fuel quantity on the gauges. (You have already conducted a much more accurate fuel quantity check with the dipstick or confirming full tanks during the preflight, so this check is really a reality check regarding accuracy of the fuel gauges.)

The second task is to confirm that fuel will get to the engine, so check the mixture control position and fuel selector valve for correct position. (Flight instructors and examiners love to play with the fuel selector valve position, so be sure you visit this task or it will be ride over!)

Check Magnetos

In a seaplane, there are only two acceptable directions to taxi during the runup. The first choice is directly downwind (going with the waves, there is less splash to go through the propeller), or directly into the wind as second choice. If you wish to save erosion of the propeller, there is no other acceptable heading.

To decrease propeller erosion, runup RPM is kept to a minimum. Minimum is defined as the lowest RPM at which the engine will run smoothly, and on engines equipped with constant speed propellers, the governor will control propeller pitch. For example, 1,200 RPM works fine for my Cessna 180 while 1,700 RPM is called for during the runup on land.

Again, EYES OUTSIDE! Your hand should know where the magneto switch is and your ear is very capable of telling if there is any difference in RPM or roughness between left and right magneto switch positions. You should really only need to look inside to confirm you guessed right when setting runup RPM.

Check mags while looking outside!

Check Prop Control—Set HIGH

I like to exercise the propeller three times on the first flight of the day to move some warm oil into the propeller hub. On later flights, once is enough to determine proper function of the control. This is strictly an eyes-outside operation. Learn to discern between the controls on the throttle quadrant without visual aid. You should be able to accurately place your hand on the throttle, propeller control, mixture, cowl flap, carburetor heat, flap, and pitch trim controls with your eyes closed. If you can't, go get acquainted with your airplane while it's tied up. You want it to be a friend, not a stranger!

Set Mixture Control For Altitude

Check with your flight instructor about this. Seaplanes are usually low altitude airplanes and don't require leaning before takeoff. If you are flying above 3,000 feet with a normally aspirated engine, perhaps leaning will help takeoff performance.

Check Carb Heat—Set COLD

This is one of the preflight check items that can kill ya! Seaplane takeoffs with carb heat set hot are veerrry long. Often too long. It won't be a takeoff, it will be an abort!

This is an especially critical item to check because so many seaplane operations occur in northern climes, where use of carb heat just prior to takeoff can help (for some models of aircraft) to help remove any carburetor ice accretion from taxi. In any case, remember to remove that carb heat before takeoff!

Set Flaps, Check Trim

Set flaps while looking outside!

On airplanes with manual flaps, learn to set them without looking inside. If they are electric, find the flap switch and set the flaps, counting to yourself. Then confirm the setting on the flap indicator. Trim should be set correctly during the preflight so all that is needed is a quick glance to confirm that you did check it and the flight instructor or examiner hasn't messed with it.

Most seaplanes will get on the step a little faster with flaps up, but the performance difference is so small that I almost always set takeoff flaps before beginning the takeoff run, thus reducing pilot workload while on the step. It is good to occasionally practice setting the flaps when on the step with eyes outside constantly! If your seaplane acts like it doesn't want to get on the step, put the flaps up until you are on the step. There is reason to practice putting flaps both up and down with eyes outside while under full power.

Plan Departure Path for Safety
Review Climb Airspeeds and Emergency Procedures

We have previously discussed the need for departure path planning to reduce risk. Before takeoff power is applied, be sure you have planned out your climb departure path. You don't have to climb straight ahead to 500 feet like you do at your friendly airport. Seaplanes aren't restricted by the rigidity of the airport environment, so do what is safest but enjoy the freedom!

Before you apply takeoff power, also review proper climb and power-off glide airspeeds and emergency procedures. Brief the examiner, or crew and passengers. If you are riding right seat with someone else flying, wouldn't you appreciate knowing the pilot's plans for takeoff and what he is going to do? Sure, it is just good crew resource management (CRM).

Recheck the Things that can Kill You

A very high-time Canadian bush floatplane pilot taught me this, and it really applies to seaplanes due to their higher rate of takeoff accidents.

So, what are the things that can kill you? Anything that, if set incorrectly, will contribute to decreased takeoff performance or controllability. Prop, mixture, flaps and trim are surely to be found on this list. You may have some lively discussions with your flight instructor about some others.

Clear Area

You can see almost 180° of sky and water on any given heading. Most seaplane takeoffs require a turn from taxi heading to takeoff heading, so clear the area while making that turn. Prime consideration needs to be given to traffic on the water. Boats under way are constantly changing the traffic picture. If there is any doubt about surface traffic, wait for the area to clear. If it looks like it will be a wait of more than a few seconds, park the seaplane so you don't use up valuable takeoff run distance. Or circle, so you can recheck the sky behind you.

Check Water Rudders Up (Most Cases)

The typical scenario is to taxi to the takeoff spot, then if a left turn (preferred) is required to align with the takeoff path, the pilot kicks left rudder then quickly puts the water rudders up and smoothly brings the power in as the heading becomes 10–30 degrees to the right of the takeoff path.

Be careful if a particular takeoff is done differently than the above described scenario, causing you to forget to put the rudders up. An old seaplane tradition is if a pilot is observed coming out of the water with rudders down, he owes the observer a case of beer!

Does leaving the rudders down cause problems on takeoff? If the water rudders are perfectly rigged, not really. The problem with rigging water rudders is that they can be rigged correctly in the up position so they don't adversely affect rudder trim in flight, or they can be rigged correctly when down so they work well while taxiing and when starting a takeoff with rudders down. Rarely can they be rigged correctly for both. If they are not properly rigged, the pilot may notice some strange directional problems. But, if the rudders are down for takeoff, they may also be down on landing. Best case scenario is that all that high speed water running is just hard on the rudder hinges and attach points. There are two "worst cases": landing with poorly rigged water rudders down may cause serious directional control problems; landing with water rudders down during a checkride may be grounds for a pink slip. A seaplane is considered a "retractable." That is why it can qualify as a "complex" and why landing with your rudders down is akin to landing with your wheels up, on a checkride.

In my years of instructing seaplane pilots, the two items most often forgotten on takeoff are water rudders and flaps. Flaps, by far, were the most often forgotten. And flaps, you'll remember, are on the old bush pilot's "can kill ya" list. This is a very good reason for practicing "no flap" takeoffs occasionally, so you will be able to know what your airplane is telling you during the takeoff run. It will be saying or shouting "flaps are up!" but you need to know its language!

Runup complete. Remaining checklist items are flaps, window, things that can kill you, clear area and stick back.

Review

Because the seaplane is always moving, pretakeoff and runup are done differently, with eyes outside most of the time. Control check is done to all four corners, and the full aileron position on both sides is noted because full aileron is used often in seaplane operations. Doors and seat belts are checked with eyes outside.

Techniques for setting the gyrocompass are different in a seaplane, and gyrocompass precession, while on the water, is of greater magnitude than experienced in a landplane. Setting nav radios requires special techniques in the seaplane. Be sure you are confident that you can interpret engine instrument indications.

A fuel gauge check is really to check the fuel gauges themselves, since you know quantity from the preflight. The pilot's fuel check verifies mixture and fuel selector valve settings to be sure adequate fuel is getting to the engine.

In a seaplane, there are only two acceptable directions to taxi during the runup. What are they, which is preferred, and why? Runup RPM is often set lower to save the propeller. All of the runup is done with eyes outside. Explain how.

Flap management and the need for changing flap settings should be done with eyes outside. Flaps are the most forgotten item on the "things that can kill ya checklist," along with carb heat, pitch trim and prop. They should be checked again just before power up.

Before you apply takeoff power, review not only your departure path but also proper climb and power-off glide airspeeds and emergency procedures. Brief the examiner, or crew and passengers. It is just good CRM. Clearing the area is done a little differently in the seaplane with major emphasis on surface traffic. Don't forget the water rudders.

Use the checklist!

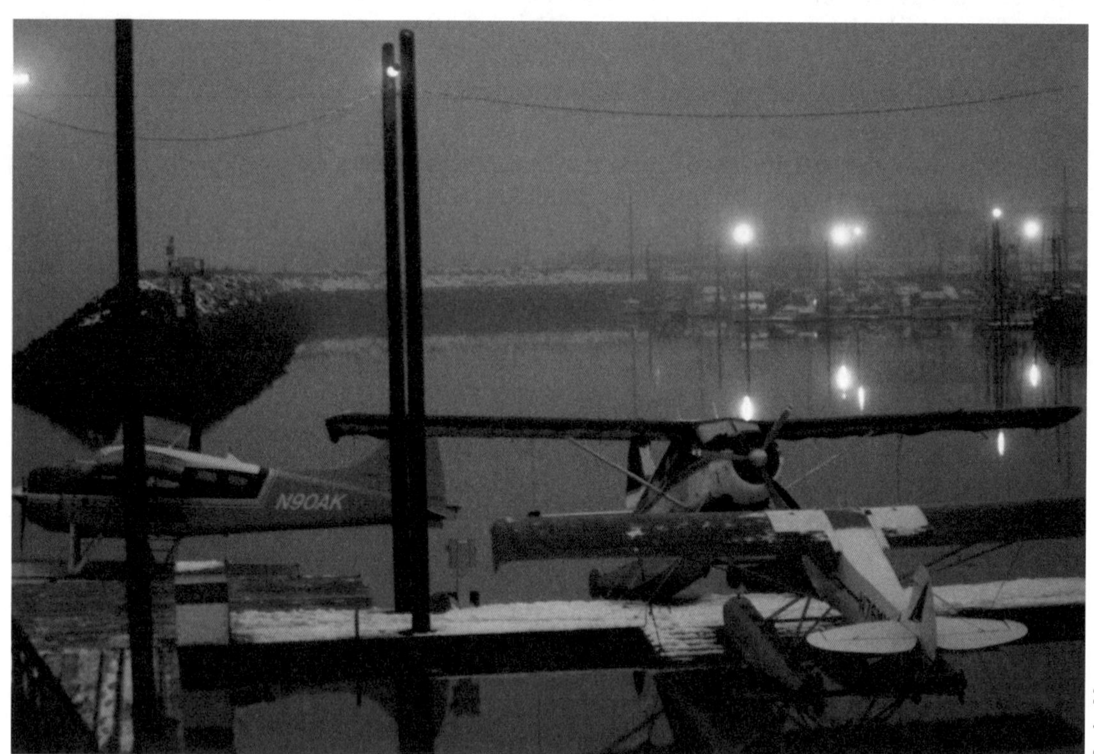

Burke Mees

Early morning in winter at the boat harbor in downtown Juneau, AK.

Chapter 10
Seaplane Base and Airport Operations

Communications Procedures

As a landplane pilot, it is expected that you are familiar with radio communication procedures and light signals, but perhaps it's been a while. It is best to review this material since you would like your oral exam to be a pleasant experience. It will be easy and fun...if you know the answers! I suggest you review radio communications, including radio failure procedures, ATC light signals, seaplane base/airport and landing area/runway markings and lighting. That, and lots more that would be good to review can be found in the *Pilot's Handbook of Aeronautical Knowledge* (FAA Advisory Circular 61-23C). It provides basic knowledge essential to pilots. It introduces pilots to the broad spectrum of knowledge needed as they progress in their training. Except for the Code of Federal Regulations pertinent to civil aviation, most of the knowledge areas applicable to pilot certification are presented. This handbook is useful to beginning pilots, as well as those pursuing more advanced pilot certificates. This publication, along with the *Aeronautical Information Manual*, the regulations, *Airplane Flying Handbook* and most all other FAA publications, can be found on ASA's Flight Library CD or on the Internet.

Please note that, in the latest version of the PTS, if you hold the private landplane rating, tasks A (radio communications and light signals) and B (traffic patterns) are not required to be tested. However, in most cases you will be doing both on the checkride, under the watchful eye of the examiner, and seaplane traffic patterns are a little different. So discussions of these items are included in this chapter.

Radio Use

An important skill I find sometimes missing among U.S. pilots is giving a proper position report with the radio. It may be done as a "blind transmission" (a general message for all that can hear with no expectations of a reply). I find it rarely contains all the

A proper position report is professional and may save a midair.

information I need as a pilot regarding the reporting aircraft. (Canadian pilots generally give better position reports than those I hear in the U.S.) If there is another aircraft in the uncontrolled airspace where you are flying, what would you like to know about that aircraft? Here is a list of what will help you avoid a midair collision:

1. Tail number (so you can talk to him if you need to).
2. Aircraft type and color (so you know how fast he is moving and, if you see him, a more positive way to identify him)
3. Location, and reference to some well known point. (Preferably, one that will be known to strangers—something that is at least on a sectional chart; announcing an instrument intersection or "inbound on the ILS runway 28R" or "over the paper mill" does nothing to tell most other pilots where you are.)
4. Altitude and level, descending or climbing (so you know whether to look up, down or level).
5. Intentions (so you know what he will do next).

That position report might sound something like this: "Traffic advisory, Golden Lake area, this is November 2125 Zulu, a red and white Cessna 180, silver floats, 5 east of Golden Lake at 3700, descending, landing Golden Lake."

Don't be a loon...give good position reports...the life you save might be your own! Remember, only the pelican and his cousins fly slower than you in your seaplane, and you can't see what is approaching you from behind. Let everybody know where you are by radio, and do it completely!

Seaplane Base

Lighting

The seaplane base beacon is described in AIM ¶2-1-8. Basically, seaplane base lighting is not standard. There are very few lighted seaplane bases. Those that have lighting are well described in the appropriate landing directory. Beacons indicating seaplane bases are standardized and are white and yellow. Or the pilot may see white and green with flashing yellow if airport and seaplane base are colocated. Just because there are a handful of lighted seaplane bases doesn't mean it's a good idea to fly a seaplane at night. Mother nature puts logs, fenceposts and other debris in landing area waters at night as well as in the daytime, and there is the odd chance someone in a boat or canoe without a light will be out for a nighttime cruise. All of these things in your landing path may not be visible at night. In Canada, it is illegal to take off or land a seaplane more than 30 minutes after sunset and until 30 minutes before sunrise.

Traffic Patterns and Procedures

Most seaplane base operations are without serious restrictions. Imagine what airport operations might have been like back in the 1920s. Pilots back then did what they needed to do to operate safely. Freedom from restrictions is one of the joys of seaplane flying. In many cases, one need not even turn on or have a radio, although it is certainly a good safety practice to announce your location and intentions, etc.

Because the seaplane pilot needs to inspect the landing area, preferably while flying upwind (ground speed is slower so more time to look) at not more than 500 feet above the surface, traffic patterns are nonstandard. So, the pattern flown is whatever the pilot deems is the safest path. Chaos? Not really. The pilot has a need to fly upwind over and just to the right of the landing area to inspect it closely. This may be repeated if the pilot feels the need for a better look, or it may be repeated at a lower altitude for a different perspective. Of course, this will be followed by a left or right turn to the downwind. There may be more or less of a squared base leg or just a circular path, with brief roll to level to check for traffic that might be farther out on final. The seaplane pilot always flies with his eyes outside, scanning for traffic, and the radio is used to give frequent updates of his whereabouts. Generally, expect seaplane pilots to fly a much tighter pattern than most landplane pilots. This is in order to keep near the water in case of engine failure and also to keep the touchdown point in sight—a real problem if you stray from the landing site at low altitude (500 feet). You may not be able to see your destination a quarter mile away. Also, over unfamiliar or hilly terrain, it is easy to lose orientation to the landing site.

The pilot needs to fly upwind along the landing area.

This is not to say that some seaplane bases don't have traffic pattern operating limitations and requirements. Expect them in congested areas to help the seaplanes avoid noise sensitive areas and assist the orderly flow of traffic. Always check for these limitations and operating rules, but don't be surprised if none are found in the directory. If the seaplane base is in a congested area or is near or adjacent to a busy airport, and the directory gives little or no information, a call to solicit local knowledge is a good idea.

◆ ***LINO LAKES— Brown's Base South SPB*** (MY74) **Location:** Reshanau Lake, 2 mi E of city. **Coordinates:** N045-09.5; W092-06.0. **Telephone:** 612/426-7595. **Hours:** 24. **Elevation:** 885. **Pattern altitude:** 1480 MSL all aircraft. **Landing lanes:** 02-20 6,000 × 1,000; 04-22 5,250 × 1,000; 18-36 5,300 × 1,000, tower 495' S. **Mooring facilities:** beaching, anchor buoys. **Frequencies:** CTAF 122.9, FSS 123.5, ATIS 125.699. **Sectional:** Twin Cities. **Local attractions:** Surfside SPB 1 mi W on Rice Lake. **Transportation:** Emergency only. **Camping:** 1 mi N at George Watch Lake. **Fuel:** 100, emergency only. **Notes:** Avoid overflying bldgs on E & W shores.

LINO LAKES— Surfside SPB (8Y4) **Location:** Rice Lake, 2 mi S of city. **Coordinates:** N045-09.0; W093-07.0. **Telephone:** 612/780-4179. **Hours:** Daylight. **Elevation:** 880. **Pattern altitude:** 1480 MSL all aircraft. **Landing lanes:** E-W 5,000 × 1,000, fresh water; N-S 5,500 × 1,000, fresh water; NE-SW 6,500 × 1,000, fresh water. **Mooring facilities:** hangar, tie-down, pull-out, ramp, docking, beaching. **Obstructions:** 500' tower 2 mi S of bldgs. **Fees:** tie down, hangar. **Frequencies:** CTAF 122.9, FSS Princeton/122.2, 120. **Sectional:** Twin Cities. **Local attractions:** Seaplane Pilots Annual Picnic. **Transportation:** Courtesy car, Rental Car. **Restaurants:** Shirley Kays 780-4181, Mardee's 1/2 mi. **Lodging:** Mounds View Inn 6 mi 786-9151. **Camping:** Available on site. **Fuel:** Seaplane Services 612/792-4703 100LL. **Services:** Flight instruction, Repairs. **Noise abatement:** Noise sensitive area SW of landing area; make apch & dep ovr water when possible. **Notes:** intensive flight training, rc models.

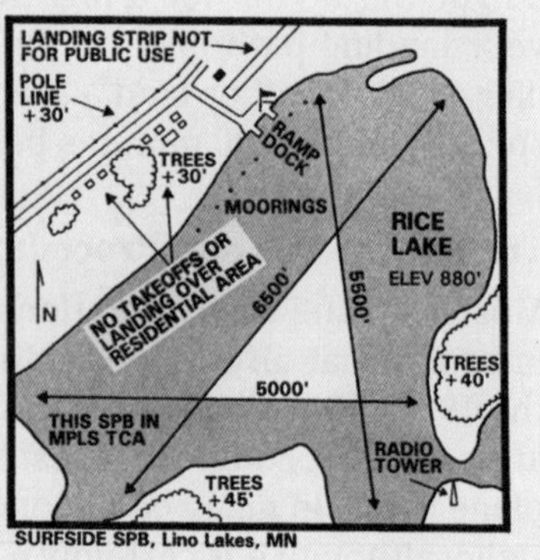

Figure 10-1. Example of seaplane base operating limitations from the *Water Landing Directory*. Operating limitations in text and on chart are highlighted. In addition, there is limiting airspace above, west and east of the SPB. Be sure to consult airspace restrictions on your aeronautical chart as well.

When planning a trip to a congested seaplane base, it is helpful to review any available sectional and terminal charts in conjunction with local street maps and marine charts, because there may be numerous geographical "callouts" used by local pilots that would otherwise be unrecognizable. One example includes the numerous points, bridges, bays, and other landmarks used by seaplane pilots transitioning the busy corridor of Seattle's Lake Washington. In any case, avoid the landplane traffic patterns if at all possible. Figure 10-1 is an example of operating limitations found in the *Water Landing Directory*.

Airspace

Since seaplanes usually fly at low altitudes and VFR, Figure 10-2 provides a good look at the U.S. and Canadian airspace categories from the seaplane pilot's perspective. It is unlikely you will be tested on this during the oral or flight test, but not impossible. Surely, you will need to know it if flying in the airspace.

Review

The Radio

Here is what should be in a good position report, which may be given "in the blind":

1. Tail number
2. Aircraft type and color
3. Location and of reference some well known point
4. Altitude and level, descending or climbing
5. Intentions

ALPHABET AIRSPACE FOR SEAPLANE PILOTS

CLASS ALPHA* is the old positive control **IFR airspace from 18 to 60 thousand feet MSL** in both U.S. and Canada. Above FL 600 is uncontrolled in the U.S., and Class D in Canada. The floor is FL 230 in northern Canada and FL 280 in the Arctic. We don't care—it's not on the VFR charts and we are not going there anyway.

CLASS BRAVO in the U.S. is the old TCA "flipped wedding cake." It goes from the ground to 10,000' MSL (some exceptions, i.e., MSP to 8,000). A clearance and Mode C are required (Mode C is required 30 NM from primary airport—from the surface to heaven). VFR is one mile and clear of clouds with radar separation. In Canada, it is like our old continental control area. It goes from 12,500 or MEA (whichever is higher) up to Class A. Clearance is required for VFR and IFR. In the U.S., the continental control area from 14,500 to 18,000 is general controlled airspace (Class E).

CLASS CHARLIE is the old ARSA, with a 5 NM mile ring from ground to 4,000', 10 NM mile ring 1,200' AGL to 4,000' plus Mode C required to 60,000'. Radio contact required before entry. Three miles and the old cloud separation requirement (500' below, 1,000' above, 2,000' horizontal). In Canada, Class C is all controlled airport traffic areas—clearance required to enter, but not Mode C. Can overfly above 3,000 AGL.

CLASS DELTA is the old airport traffic area and control zone—contact with operating control tower required before entry. The top has been lowered to 2,500' AGL, more or less. Actual top printed on sectional chart. Communications required, but no Mode C. The size has been reduced to 5 statute miles (give or take a little). Three miles and the old cloud separation requirement (500' below, 1,000' above, 2,000' horizontal). No comm is required in the Class E control zone extensions. In Canada, Class D is outside controlled airport airspace, along airways from 700' AGL or 2,200' AGL up to 12,500' MSL. It is limited horizontally to the range of the navaid, beyond which is Class E.

CLASS ECHO is all general controlled airspace, such as low-altitude airways. It goes to the ground at airports with no tower but with a control zone (which is now called a "Class ECHO surface area"). Otherwise it starts at 700' AGL (magenta) in the old "transition zones," or 1,200' AGL (blue) elsewhere. Below 10,000' it is 3 miles and the old cloud separation requirement. In Canada, Class E is uncontrolled airspace and it goes from the ground to the bottom of Class A, but no VFR-on-top unless you and your aircraft meet some rather stringent requirements.

CLASS FOXTROT in Canada is all special areas such as Alert, Danger and Restricted. This airspace can be controlled or not. In the U.S., prohibited, restricted, warning and MOAs aren't considered to be a class of airspace so there is no class F. (Good grief!)

CLASS GOLF is uncontrolled airspace in the U.S. It includes space under the airways and, in the few areas remaining, goes as high as 14,500'. Then there is Class ECHO airspace from 14,500 to the bottom of Class A. One mile and clear of clouds (daytime), and within 1,200' above the surface. From 1,200' to 10,000' (daytime) it is one mile and the old cloud separation. Canada has no class G, as uncontrolled airspace there is Class E.

*Airspace classes are written "Class A, B," etc. but are spoken "Class Alpha, Bravo," etc.; it is written here the way it is supposed to be spoken, to help you remember.

Figure 10-2. U.S. and Canadian Airspace Classification for the seaplane pilot. Revised from an original by Dave Wiley. *(Continued on next page.)*

Other notes:

1. We can no longer fly in uncontrolled airspace above 1,200 AGL with one mile visibility at night. During the day above 1,200 AGL, one mile is OK but standard cloud clearance applies. (14 CFR §91.155)
2. In the U.S., only recreational pilots are restricted to maintaining visual contact with the ground under them. In Canada, VFR-on-top and night VFR are heavily restricted. Otherwise, uncontrolled airspace is more uncontrolled.
3. The purpose of alphabet airspace was to bring the U.S. more into line with ICAO (worldwide) regulations (such as used in Canada). The nomenclature changed from "old" to "new" as a result.

A Way to Remember Them:

Class	U.S.	Canada
A = Altitude	IFR ONLY	Same, higher base north
B = Busy	TCA	cont. control above 12,500'
C = Contact	ARSA	Mode C/contact required
D = Destination	ATA/CZ	dialog (must talk)
E = Elsewhere	other controlled airspace	uncontrolled
F = Fire	none	military airspace
G = Go For It	uncontrolled	none

Figure 10-2. *(Continued from previous page)*

Seaplane Base Lighting

- Non-standard. Check appropriate landing directory.
- Beacons are standardized white and yellow; or white and green with flashing yellow (if seaplane base and airport are colocated).

Traffic Patterns

- Non-standard, but predictable (since seaplane pilots must inspect the landing area).
- Nevertheless, seaplane bases have traffic pattern operating limitations, requirements; you should expect them in congested areas.
- In a congested area or near a busy airport when directories give little or no information, call to find out what the local seaplane base operating limitations may be; either way, avoid landplane traffic patterns if at all possible.

Airspace

- Review Figure 10-2 for airspace categories with a seaplane-flying perspective.
- Examiner may or may not test on airspace, but you need to know it anyway.

Section III
Flight Operations

SPA

A Grumman Goose on the step.

Chapter 11
Takeoff and Climb

Pilots who are preparing for the seaplane rating: It is recommended you read the PTS Section IV (the parts shown at right) in the appendix first, before reading this chapter. Please note that task A is not directly followed by task B. This is because task B will be found in the "landings" section. Section E deals with seaplane takeoffs, so it follows A, for purposes of this chapter. For better understanding, takeoffs are discussed first, then landings, then go-arounds.

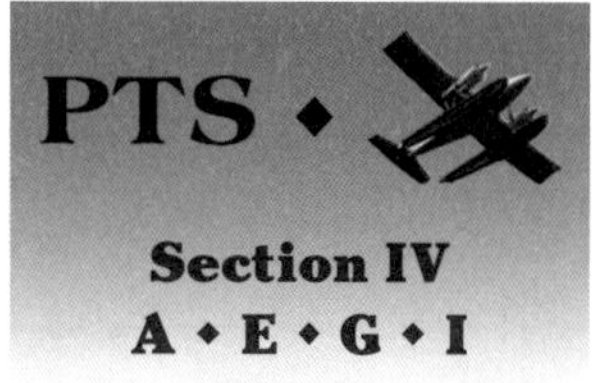

Takeoffs in the PTS

If you read the above mentioned PTS section first, your reaction will probably be "good grief, how can I remember all this?" Don't despair. In the discussions that follow here, each aspect of the takeoff will be covered in detail, followed by landings and go-arounds. In each chapter's summary you will find a table that should help you remember what you learned in the discussion section. It condenses and describes the basic differences from the normal takeoff or landing, danger areas, etc. So, look over the tasks in the PTS, study the discussion, and review the table until you are confident you've got it!

There are five primary types of seaplane takeoffs: normal, crosswind, rough water, glassy water and confined area. We will completely describe the normal takeoff first, then discuss the differences between the normal and other types of takeoff. There are two additional takeoff techniques that are not required to be demonstrated on the checkride, as they are considered advanced techniques. They are float-lift takeoff and flap-change takeoff. Put them on your list of things to learn after your single-engine sea certificate is in your pocket. But first, some basics.

Primary takeoff types:
- Normal
- Crosswind
- Rough water
- Glassy water
- Confined area

V Speeds for Climb

V_X is defined in 14 CFR Part 1 as the speed at which the aircraft will climb at the steepest angle, or will achieve the greatest altitude in the least forward distance. Virtually all aircraft will accomplish this best with gear and flaps up (clean). So, V_X is really a

Figure 11-1. A Super Cub takes off from land using homemade skates that brake quickly to a stop once the Cub's weight is lifted from them.

clean configuration airspeed and has no direct application to takeoff performance. V_X is ***not*** obstacle clearance speed ($V_{OBS\ CL}$), even in a seaplane (or landplane) that is not equipped with flaps, because of the acceleration factor. So why is it mentioned in the PTS takeoff section? Because there are a lot of older airplanes that do not publish a $V_{OBS\ CL}$ speed in their pilot's operating handbook (POH), or manual and V_X is usually the published speed closest to $V_{OBS\ CL}$. $V_{OBS\ CL}$ is a little lower than V_X for every aircraft I know except one. (For some models of the Cessna Turbo 206, Cessna says the two speeds are the same numerically.) If your airplane's POH lists a $V_{OBS\ CL}$, use it. If not, the FAA is saying you may use V_X for purposes of demonstrating your ability to climb over an obstacle at a specific, slow speed.

$V_{OBS\ CL}$ or obstacle clearance speed is the speed the manufacturer has determined the aircraft will climb the highest in the least forward distance, starting at zero forward speed to clear a 50-foot obstacle. $V_{OBS\ CL}$ assumes takeoff flap setting. See the difference between V_X and $V_{OBS\ CL}$? V_X will provide the most height/forward distance but assumes starting the measurement at some point in the climb where the aircraft is already at V_X speed and clean. $V_{OBS\ CL}$ provides the best height/forward distance if starting at zero speed and the forward distance is relatively short. Takeoff configuration is required for this. V_X provides the best angle of climb but $V_{OBS\ CL}$ will get you over an obstacle in a shorter total distance if the distance is measured from the spot where you powered up. (*See* Figure 11-2.)

V_X is not really a part of takeoff performance discussions, other than it is a speed usually close to $V_{OBS\ CL}$ speed. So, what is V_X used for by the pilot? Beats me! The only thing I can think of is if the pilot has already gotten himself in a bad spot, like a box canyon, needs to climb over a higher obstacle ahead, and the maneuver is started at or above V_X.

A BIG word of caution: when climbing over an obstacle (or demonstrating it) the aircraft is only a few knots above power-off stall speed and the nose is high. If there should be a power fail-

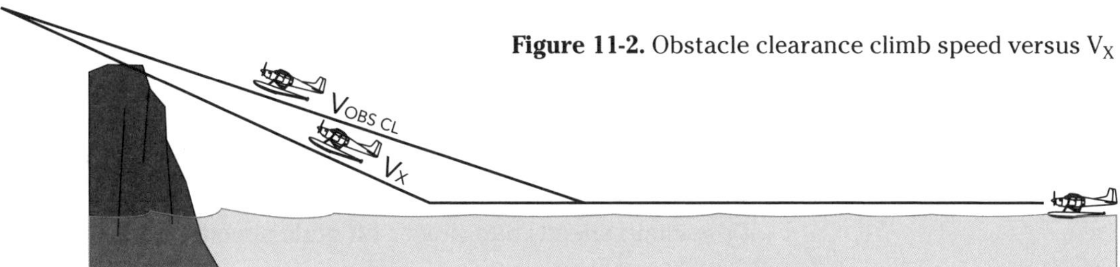

Figure 11-2. Obstacle clearance climb speed versus V_X

ure in this configuration at any height above about 10–15 feet, the descent rate will be very large when reaching the surface and there will be no excess airspeed for a flare. The aircraft will "fall through" any attempt to flare, going directly to stall, which will actually increase the descent rate and remove the last bit of control the pilot may have had. *In any power-off descent, airspeed is life itself!*

Caution: in power-off descent, remember—airspeed is life itself!

So, there is risk involved when practicing the confined area takeoff. If you are not a true believer, try it at a safe altitude (a good place to practice). At a safe altitude, set up takeoff configuration and reduce speed to $V_{OBS\,CL}$. Note the altitude on the altimeter and consider that ground level. Climb at $V_{OBS\,CL}$. Note the attitude of the nose above the horizon. At 50–150 feet above the starting altitude, simulate engine failure by throttling back to idle. Then note the sink rate as you pass through the beginning altitude. Even if you try to flare for a simulated landing at that altitude, there simply isn't enough airspeed to stop the high rate of sink. Did you hear the stall warning horn? Sure! It started when the engine quit and never stopped until you lowered the nose quite a lot, which increased the rate of sink even more.

There is no way to save the day in this scenario. The energy simply isn't there for the pilot to manage. How does one manage this risk? Avoid it as much as you can. Practice at altitude. Then practice from the surface at $V_{OBS\,CL}$ + 10. Then practice at $V_{OBS\,CL}$ only enough to be sure you can do it well. A word to flight instructors: You are at the greatest risk because you are involved in this scenario often.

$\mathbf{V_Y}$ is well known by pilots as the speed at which the aircraft achieves the best rate of climb. It is typically published in the POH and if not, is easily determined by the pilot by climbing at climb power at several speeds and measuring the rate of climb. (Use the altimeter and clock, not the vertical speed indicator, as it is not a reliably accurate instrument.*) Plot the results. V_Y is considered the goal speed after liftoff to ensure enough airspeed for the pilot to manage in case of engine failure. V_Y is used during the early part of the climb, until a safe altitude is reached.

* Why? See the discussion of this topic ahead in Chapter 20, Pages 286–287.

$\mathbf{V_{CC}}$, or cruise climb speed, is used after reaching a safe altitude. It is usually a speed that is 1/3- to 1/2-way between V_Y and indicated level cruise speed. It allows for better engine cooling, better visibility over the nose, and more passenger comfort.

If your aircraft's POH doesn't publish the above speeds, all of the climb speeds and power off glide speeds, except $V_{OBS\,CL}$, can be determined by you with a 5-minute flight test. How to do this is documented in Chapter 5 of *Water Flying Concepts*.

What is safe altitude? There is no true definition, in terms of distance above the surface. It is more of a feeling—an altitude where the pilot feels safe. The logical decision of when safe altitude has been reached is complex. This is because the decision is based on the character of the terrain below, the aircraft's stall speed, how lucky the pilot is feeling, and other obscure things, such as how much altitude the amphibian will loose after engine failure (until the gear is fully extended or retracted). Generally, safe altitude will be somewhere between 400 feet (Super Cub on straight floats over water) and 1,200 feet (heavy amphibian over swamp or forest). It may even be just 10 feet if there are 7 miles of safe water ahead on climb out!

Seaplane Takeoffs: An Overview

One well-known aviation saying is "Takeoffs stress the aircraft, landings stress the pilot." This is especially true for seaplanes. Seaplanes typically take four or five times more distance for takeoff than they do for landing. Their engines work harder than those on landplanes because the takeoff run is longer.

A recent, 15-year study of accident statistics showed that seaplane accidents typically occur more often in the takeoff and climb phase as compared to landplanes. The difference is dramatic: 60–65% of seaplane accidents occur in the takeoff/climb phase. With landplanes, it is 30–35%. This means we seaplane pilots need to be really careful during takeoff. Seaplanes have much more drag than landplanes on the surface and in the air. Seaplane pilots usually don't know the exact length of the takeoff path. Seaplanes are easily overloaded. These are a few reasons why pilots must be careful and develop high level judgment skills.

60–65% of seaplane accidents occur in the takeoff/climb phase

Seaplane takeoff planning must be taken seriously! Before increasing power for takeoff, be sure that (a) the checklist is complete; (b) thought has been given to the safest climb path after liftoff (don't climb straight ahead down the center of the lake then out over the trees at a low altitude. If you can, drift to the right and circle the lake while climbing to a safe altitude; and (c) remind yourself that this takeoff attempt is really going to be an abort maneuver if you sense that anything at all is amiss. Do whatever you can to decrease the risk factor (assuming noise abatement or other factors are not contributing). Practice the abort-stop short maneuver (*see* the discussion of the aborted takeoff later in this chapter).

Save the propeller!

Save the propeller! Water is capable of causing dramatic erosion to a propeller that is turning at speeds greater than 1,000 RPM. In fact, my rule is no more than 700 RPM unless absolutely necessary. Taxiing crosswind at higher RPMS will cause propeller erosion because waves bounce off the inside of the downwind float and up through the propeller. So keep this in mind while operating on the water.

Seaplane Takeoff Performance

As a landplane pilot, it is assumed that you can access the takeoff performance tables in the POH, extract the correct takeoff performance data, apply it to a landplane. The information for the seaplane is the same, except that the takeoff distances are considerably greater. This is because the seaplane is probably heavier, but it is mostly because of the great hydrodynamic (water) drag experienced by the seaplane. Figure 11-3 shows the drag vs. speed curve for a typical seaplane.

This graph clearly makes the point that there are two periods of high drag during the seaplane takeoff where net accelerating force (NAF) is minimized or becomes zero, causing no further increase in speed. The first of these two events occurs during the hump or plow phase just before step speed is reached. The second occurs at a higher speed on the step. Note that at 6,000 foot density altitude, takeoff would not be possible because thrust available is insufficient to overcome drag, so the seaplane would not reach step speed. It is not unusual for this to occur, for nor-

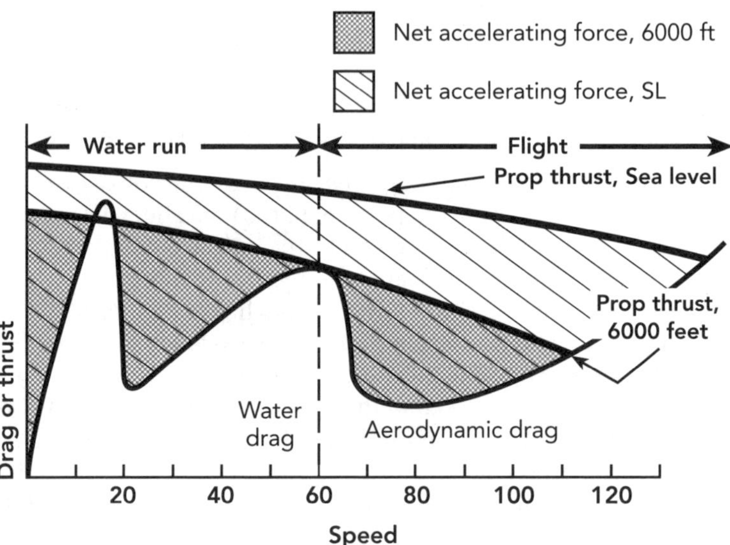

Figure 11-3. Graph of total drag vs. speed for a typical seaplane

mally aspirated engine seaplanes, at 4,000–6,000 feet density altitude. The seaplane may easily land at these altitudes, but it can't take off.

To learn more about seaplane takeoff performance, read Chapter 3 of *Water Flying Concepts.*

Takeoff Area Assessment

The best time to assess the takeoff area is *before* you land on it. From aloft, you are the master of all you survey. You can measure the length of the takeoff area, evaluate depth and obstructions, determine the safest taxi path from shore to the takeoff area and determine the best climb path for safe departure. This is all part of the landing area assessment discussed in Chapter 12. Hopefully, while looking over the takeoff area, you noted the compass heading for takeoff, because things often look a lot different when you are down on the water. When you use the takeoff area, some time has passed since you looked at it from above, and Mother Nature is always busy, changing things. Therefore, back taxiing along that takeoff path before departure is a good idea. While back taxiing, the pretakeoff checklist must be accomplished. But don't get so busy that you forget to scrutinize every foot of that water for deadheads and debris. The seaplane pilot's eyes *must* be outside when moving on the water! Back taxiing also provides an estimate of how long the water run will be. *See* the discussion of back taxiing in the next chapter.

Back taxiing along that takeoff path before departure is a really good idea.

Chapter 12, Pages 134–135

The Normal Takeoff

Section IV ◆ A
Normal and Crosswind
Takeoff and Climb

Probably the most often used takeoff type, the normal takeoff, is accomplished by positioning the seaplane into the wind if the wind is strong, or 10–30 degrees to the right if it is light (to allow for strong left-turning forces that tend to turn the seaplane to the left. Water rudders are retracted, elevator is positioned full up and held, and power is smoothly increased to takeoff power. The nose rises as the seaplane accelerates to 8–12 knots. As long as the elevator is held full up, the aircraft will remain in the plowing or plow-taxi phase. Typically, the nose will rise, hesitate and rise some more. At the top of the second nose-rise, elevator back pressure is relaxed (completely, if the aircraft is correctly trimmed), and the seaplane will accelerate onto the step. The faster the seaplane moves across the water, the more the nose will pitch down. When the nose attitude reaches that of proper takeoff attitude (about the same as the attitude during displacement or slow taxi), the pilot will add elevator back pressure to maintain that

SPA

An amphibious Husky just coming up onto the step.

attitude. The proper takeoff attitude (the attitude with minimum drag, or "sweet spot") is maintained until the aircraft lifts off, both floats coming out of the water at the same time.

During the water run portion of the takeoff, the pilot's eyes are looking outside, to maintain the proper attitude and to scan for water traffic and obstacles in the water. The only need to look inside comes early in the takeoff, just after full power is achieved, to do a power check. There is no need to look at the airspeed indicator since the aircraft will lift from the water when it has achieved the correct speed.

The Climb Phase

The *very important* climb phase…

If after liftoff, the seaplane maintains the same attitude, it will accelerate promptly to V_Y while maintaining a proper climb angle away from the surface. The goal is to reach 50 feet above water level (AWL) and V_Y speed with flaps up at the same time. The saying "V_Y and clean before 50" is known among seaplane pilots as appropriate takeoff climb planning, because it gets the aircraft to a speed that allows the pilot some energy to manage the aircraft before it is high enough to develop high vertical velocities should the engine fail. Fifty feet can usually be measured by

"V_Y and clean before 50" is good climb planning in a seaplane.

using the trees in the area. Direction of the takeoff path is important, too. Try to avoid flying over houses at low altitudes so you can be a good neighbor. Stay over water if you can, in case of a power failure while at low altitudes. If not over water, choose the safest climb path, considering terrain and obstacles. Seaplanes have no rigid traffic pattern when flying from water, except when departing congested seaplane bases. Do what is safest when choosing direction of flight during climb.

The Crosswind Takeoff

The crosswind takeoff can be started in two ways:

Two ways to begin a crosswind takeoff

1. Directly into the wind with a turn to the crosswind takeoff direction when the plowing phase is achieved; or, if there is room, just as the seaplane gets on the step. As the aircraft is turned to the crosswind heading, FULL aileron into the wind is applied. Starting into the wind saves the propeller, allows the floatplane to get up on the hump quicker, and makes directional control easier.
2. In the direction of the takeoff run. This choice will probably put some water through the propeller and increase the difficulty of directional control. If this method is used, ailerons are held FULLY into the wind from the start, and water rudders remain down until full power has been applied, then retracted. This will help with directional control. More about that in a moment.

Importance of Ailerons

Full aileron into the wind means just that: 100% aileron control deflection. It has been my experience that most landplane pilots, especially those who fly large aircraft, are disinclined to apply full ailerons. Learn where full aileron position is, both left and right, when you do a pretakeoff control check, and remember it. Use it, especially during crosswind takeoffs and landings, and step turns. Why is it so important? So that there is little chance of an upset. For a complete discussion of the forces involved, I refer you to Chapter 9, "Seaplane Stability on the Water," in *Water Flying Concepts*.

Full aileron is applied until the downwind float lifts slightly from the water. Aileron input is then reduced to keep the downwind float just barely out of the water until liftoff, which will occur quickly after the downwind float comes out of the water.

Drifting downwind after liftoff is a no-no.

After liftoff, the upwind wing will be low. Don't be in a hurry to level the wings. As soon as the aircraft is out of the water, it will tend to begin a downwind drift unless you stop it. Drifting downwind after liftoff is a no-no because, in the event of a power failure, landing while drifting downwind will probably cause an upset. So, have a plan to stop the downwind drift just after liftoff. I can think of three ways to do this:

1. Leave the upwind wing down and turn into the wind. This is the safest option, if there is room and water below, because if the engine quits now, you won't be drifting and can land into the wind.
2. Crab into the wind, if you must maintain the takeoff heading. At least the drift is stopped and the ball is centered.
3. Leave the upwind wing down and apply a little opposite rudder, slipping ahead while climbing. This will result in reduced climb performance because the ball isn't centered but will stop the drift.

You might observe some pilots lifting the upwind wing, claiming they get off the water faster. They may, but the dangers they are exposing themselves to are not worth the risk, and doing so will surely disqualify you on a checkride.

Directional Control When Takeoff is Started Heading Crosswind

Let's go back to the beginning of the crosswind takeoff and look at the turning forces that affect your ability to control the direction of travel on the water. Especially in a seaplane, left turning forces are great during the early (slow) part of a takeoff.

If the wind is from the left, it will add to those left turning forces in all phases of the takeoff, except the nose-high or plowing phase, possibly even making them uncontrollable unless the water rudders are down. In some airplanes, with a brisk breeze, even the water rudders won't keep the airplane from turning left. When the nose rises to the plow or hump phase, there is more side area exposed to the wind. So if the wind is from the left, left turning tendencies are decreased (you may wish to review the discussion of this in the "No Rudders" section on Page 65). Also, remember that when the nose starts to lower to go on the step, precession (one of the strongest of the left-turning tendencies) comes into play, requiring even more right rudder. So be prepared.

If the crosswind is from the right, it helps cancel the left turning tendencies in the very early phase of the takeoff, before the nose is up, so some left rudder may be needed. But as the nose comes up, two other forces come into play:

- While the nose is coming up, precession provides a right turning force. The faster the nose comes up, the stronger that force will be.
- While the nose is quite high, more side surface area forward of the center of buoyancy is exposed to that right crosswind, which adds to the left turning tendencies. If the pilot's foot is still pushing the left pedal, as was needed a moment before in takeoff, the airplane will turn rapidly left as the nose stops rising (because the right-turning precession force stopped when the nose stopped rising). Lowering the nose brings precession forces back into play, but this time as strong left turning forces that apply only while the nose is rotating downward.

When the examiner gives you a crosswind takeoff to do, you can bet it will be with a right crosswind because this is the most difficult for the inexperienced pilot. He or she must maintain directional control, especially during and just after the critical plow phase of the takeoff run.

The examiner may ask you during the oral whether you can expect better takeoff performance during a crosswind takeoff with the wind from the left or the right. "Right" is the correct answer because you don't have to create as much drag with the rudder to maintain heading. You just need to be quick and well timed with rudder applications as the need for rudders changes from left to right and back to left (strong crosswind). Another good question: "Is the need for rudder greater during the time the nose is high with a left or right crosswind?" The answer is that a right crosswind adds to the left turning tendencies requiring strong right rudder until the nose is back down and the floatplane is accelerating on the step.

A third good question is "When is the need for right rudder the greatest during a crosswind takeoff?" Your answer will be during a right crosswind takeoff, when the nose is highest and just starting down—just after the pilot moves the stick forward. Because then, precession and the wind on the large side-surface forward are aiding the other left turning forces.

Faced with a crosswind takeoff with the wind from the left, what can be done to maintain directional control?

1. Leave the water rudders down until full throttle, then smoothly reach down and put the water rudders up. Practice this maneuver until you can do it without looking down. You need to be looking outside all the time to maintain directional control during changing forces on your aircraft. Full throttle provides maximum airflow over your air rudder, which should allow you to maintain directional control after you put the rudders up.
2. Cheat a little: Start the takeoff run headed 10–30 degrees to the right of the desired direction. Explain to the examiner why you are doing this and watch him or her relax a little. And don't forget the full ailerons!

If it's a right crosswind, do both of the above, plus be ready for the change to right rudder as the nose comes up, and even more right rudder when you release back pressure to go onto the step.

Crosswind takeoff danger areas include loss of directional control due to very strong left turning tendencies during the plow phase and engine failure after takeoff if the aircraft is drifting downwind.

Section IV • I
Rough Water Takeoff
and Climb

The Rough Water Takeoff

You probably noticed similarities between the water and land crosswind takeoff. Similarities exist between the rough water and rough land takeoffs, too. Look for them.

Rough water takeoffs are easy for the pilot and hard on the airplane, especially the floats. After a few real rough water takeoffs, expect some seepage leaks in the floats due to stretched rivets below the water line. They are not hard to repair but do require maintenance. So, takeoffs and landings on really rough water are to be avoided, if possible.

Types of Rough Water

The seaplane pilot deals with rough water differently depending on its character.

Wind-Generated Waves

Rough water can be made by wind causing a chop. Wave amplitude (height) may be considerable, but wave frequency is high.

(The wave crests are close enough together that the floats will be touching more than one crest most of the time.) This is the most commonly encountered type and is discussed in detail below.

Waves from Boat Wakes and Reflected Waves

This type of rough water is difficult to deal with because waves may be traveling in many directions at once. The wave crests may amplify each other or cancel each other out and this effect is constantly changing. Waves reflected from vertical shorelines will cross the waves coming from the original source. In short, it's a mess! Some bodies of water become unusable for seaplanes as the day proceeds, due to boat traffic. Crossing a boat wake during takeoff will be hard on the floatplane. It is best to wait until the wake has dissipated.

Swells

Swells are made some distance away and travel long distances on large bodies of water. There may be swells from two, three or four different directions at once. The distance between crests is greater than the length of your floats, indicating the need to land parallel to the swell. This is difficult because the swell may be hard to see from the air, especially when close to the surface; and the swell is probably moving in a direction other than downwind, requiring a crosswind landing that becomes problematical because the swell is moving, causing a tendency to drift when touching down. This is indeed a complex maneuver.

Landing in Wind-Generated Waves

Always make the rough water takeoff directly into the wind or pay a significant penalty in propeller erosion. The rough water takeoff differs from the normal takeoff in these ways:

1. Application of power is done quickly just as the nose reaches the lowest point in its pitch oscillation. This is done so that, when the nose rises to the top of the oscillation, full power is already applied, allowing the elevator to keep the nose up from that point on in the takeoff run.
2. As the seaplane comes onto the step, the step acceleration run is made with the nose lower than if the water were smooth. Resist your normal tendency to keep the float tips high because doing so will make for a rough takeoff run. Lower the nose and feel the ride smooth out, because the floats are now cutting through each wave rather than having the float

bottoms pounded by the waves. Continue that attitude until liftoff speed is reached, then lift the aircraft out of the water. Remain in ground effect until speed builds a little, then go for "V_Y and clean before 50 feet."

3. Advanced techniques, such as the flap-change, are often used by experienced pilots to get the floats out of the water at a lower speed. This reduces the beating the floats receive, but don't worry about that until after the checkride. Then go see your experienced flight instructor...there is always more to learn! Avoid float-lift takeoffs because the beating the floats take is concentrated in one float briefly rather than equally distributed.

See the discussion of advanced takeoff techniques later in this chapter (starting on Page 122).

Remember:

- Rough water takeoffs in heavy chop are done directly into the wind. Avoid takeoffs across boat wakes.
- Both floats come out of the water at the same time, to avoid subjecting one float to all the abuse.
- Learn to watch the gusts as they come toward you across the water. It will help you anticipate turbulence or increased lift, and determine whether it is momentary or not.

Section IV ◆ G
Glassy Water Takeoff
and Climb

The Glassy Water Takeoff

Ah, the pleasure of taxiing out on a sunny morning while the water is still glassy smooth. The passengers won't even know when the seaplane leaves the water! Nor will they have a clue of the dangers involved.

There is ***absolutely*** no way for the pilot to judge height above glassy water, to know when to flare when landing.

The glassy water takeoff is a normal takeoff with some extra planning. Expect the takeoff run to be noticeably longer because there are no wavelets to aerate the water passing under the floats. The air-water mixture presents less drag. Use of the float-lift technique is often incorporated by the pilot to further decrease drag during the high speed component of the water run.

Special planning is needed, not only for the longer takeoff water run, but especially to counteract the dangers associated with the glassy water takeoff. After liftoff, since there is absolutely no way for the pilot to judge height above the water, two separate dangers occur. They are listed below along with ways to avoid them.

1. **Inadvertent drift down** to the water after liftoff and during early climb. This puts the aircraft back into the water at higher speed and with lower nose attitude, which is the scenario for a water loop. A **water loop** occurs when the water contacts the float at a point on the float that is forward of the aircraft's CG. When this happens, the aircraft behaves like a taildragger during a ground loop. The result is usually dramatic with the aircraft ending upside down, and pilots and passengers swimming (PPS). The water loop is usually thought of as causing landing accidents, when landing too fast or when using a flat approach into a sheltered area on a large body of water, or ocean, where swells are present. Swells sometimes combine making a "super-swell" or **rogue wave** which is higher than the rest. If one of those spanks the bottom of a float when at higher than landing speed, a dramatic accident occurs. Low, fast approaches are poor technique!

   The inadvertent drift down after a glassy water takeoff can easily be avoided. Before takeoff the pilot must remember that it is a glassy takeoff, and the exact pitch attitude at the moment of liftoff must be noted and held until depth perception returns (at about tree top height). This is one scenario where "V_Y and clean before 50" is sacrificed in the face of a greater potential danger—the inadvertent drift-down. Once depth perception returns to the pilot, the climb becomes a normal climbout, with one exception, and that's during engine failure.

2. **Engine failure during climbout** over glassy water is really the seaplane pilot's equivalent of "up a creek without a paddle." Without power to make a gentle let-down, a flare will be required, and there is no way, looking at the water, to know when to flare. A power off descent at or near touchdown attitude is going to result in a very high vertical speed, resulting in severe contact with the water.

   To improve chances of being able to pull off such a landing, the pilot can design the takeoff path so that clues are available. Here are two techniques I like and one I don't care for:

   - Design for a visual glide slope. On bodies of water more than a mile in length, it may be possible to design the takeoff path by positioning the seaplane's starting point so the takeoff run is toward a distant point-of-land with water beyond it, or toward an island or any visible object on the water. When airborne, the object and the far shore beyond

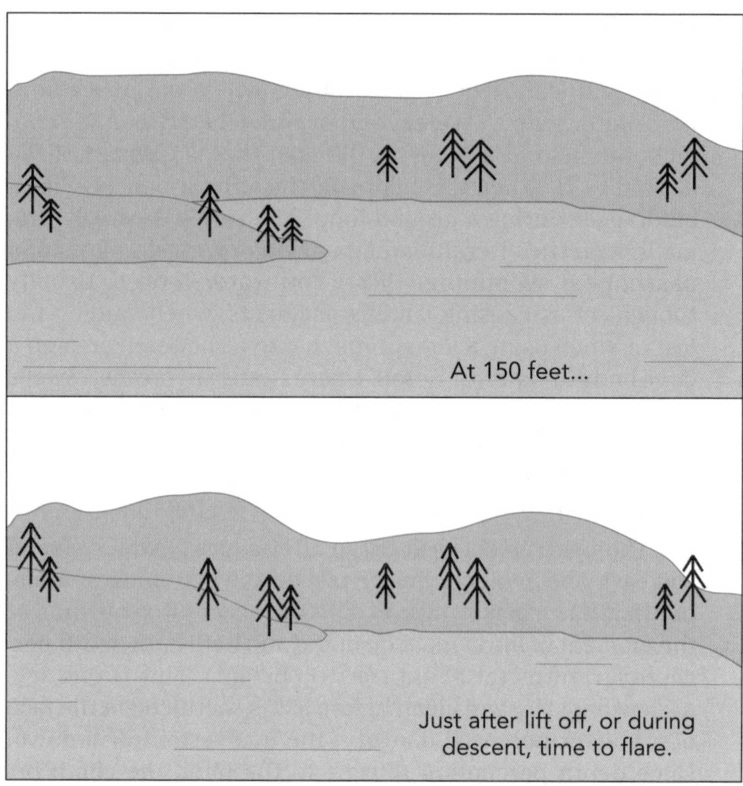
At 150 feet...
Just after lift off, or during descent, time to flare.

Figure 11-4. The point-of-land visual glideslope indicator

About 50′ AWL

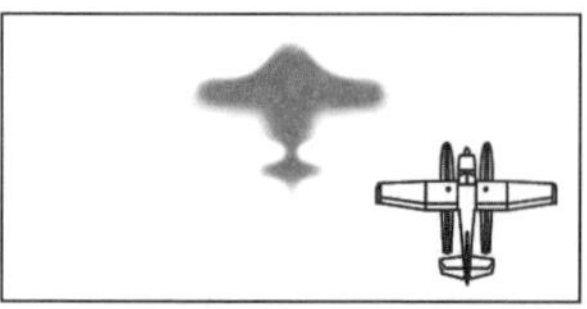

About 20′ off the water

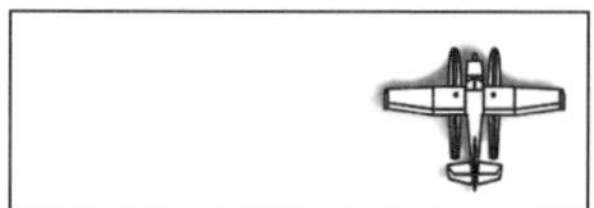

At the surface

Figure 11-5. Using the sun's shadow

act like range markers for glide slope information (instead of left-right information). *See* Figure 11-4. The pilot notes the relationship between the point and the far shore just after takeoff and, in case of power failure, completes the flare when that same picture is seen again.

- Design to use your shadow. If the body of water is round, with no protruding features to provide a visual glide slope, one trick that works well is to position the aircraft for takeoff so the sun is over your right shoulder. Then, as the seaplane lifts off, your shadow moves away from you, in your left-forward peripheral vision. If the engine fails, and you must return to the glassy water, do so at near touchdown speed and flare as your shadow gets near. Of course, this only works in the morning or afternoon, not when the sun is high in the sky, nor on cloudy days. *See* Figure 11-5.

- Takeoff and land along the shoreline if the water is glassy. This is the technique I don't care for. It never made much sense to me. Its principal advantage seems to be that, if things don't work out, you won't have so far to swim! Shorelines are rarely straight enough to provide a constant distance from shore. Rocks are just under the water and difficult to see when looking at the sky reflection off the glassy water. The pilot shouldn't be looking at the shoreline when maintaining the aircraft's pitch attitude is so critical.

If I am familiar with the surrounding terrain and know I can climb out over a level, flat, vegetated field, I will do so, as I would rather land in a field than on glassy water, if I have experienced an engine failure.

Glassy water takeoffs are a pleasure, but remember the danger areas and prepare for them to minimize your lifetime risk level.

Burke Mees

A glassy water morning on Lake Hood, Anchorage AK.

Section IV ◆ E
Short-Field Takeoff
(Confined Area)
and Maximum
Performance Climb

The Confined Area Takeoff

There are two types of confined area takeoffs. Whichever one is used will depend on the shape of the takeoff surface area and wind velocity.

If the wind is stronger than 8 knots (10 MPH), or less for very small seaplanes, or if the confined area is elongated, a takeoff straight ahead is appropriate, utilizing every available foot of the takeoff area and practicing excellent takeoff technique.

If the small body of water is more rounded, at least at the departure end, *and* the wind is less than 8 knots, an acceptable technique is to begin the takeoff run while headed down wind, and reverse direction using a 180° slow step turn to complete the takeoff into the wind. Caution must be exercised when using this technique since wind and centrifugal force will be acting in the same direction and could result in an upset. This is the reason for the wind velocity restriction mentioned above. If the wind is light and the pilot is skilled in the slow step-taxi technique, a loaded seaplane can be flown from a surprisingly small body of water. A review of the discussion of step turns may be appropriate here (*see* Pages 68–70).

To use all available space during the straight takeoff run technique, complete the pretakeoff checklist except for water rudders, while taxiing downwind to where the takeoff will begin. When that location is reached, the pilot kicks left rudder. As soon as the nose begins to swing left, water rudders are retracted and the left turn rate increases, so the seaplane makes a very small radius 180° turn. When the aircraft is pointed about 30° right of the desired takeoff heading, power is applied briskly. Left turning tendencies will swing the aircraft left onto the takeoff heading as the nose rises. The pilot does a quick glance at the gauges for a power check, then, for the rest of the takeoff run, concentrates on looking outside while doing everything correctly, and being careful not to lift the aircraft out of the water too soon. After liftoff, $V_{OBS\ CL}$ speed is attained and maintained until the obstacle is cleared. Only after the obstacle is cleared are the flaps raised while accelerating to V_Y speed.

The float lift technique may be appropriate if the aircraft is heavily loaded or the water is glassy. If there is an obstacle, the flap change technique is ***not*** appropriate in most aircraft (*See Water Flying Concepts*, Chapter 4). There are other techniques used by experienced pilots for getting out of short, obstacled ponds, but they are not discussed here. After you are rated, find a highly experienced flight instructor to help you learn those techniques.

The two most dangerous aspects of the confined area takeoff are:

1. The potential for power loss while climbing at $V_{OBS\ CL}$. See the above discussion of $V_{OBS\ CL}$ speed. An experienced examiner once said that sitting through this task on a checkride is fearsome. I certainly agree.
2. The difficulty of determining if the takeoff area is large enough to allow liftoff and climb over the obstacle. It may be possible to determine the distance needed from the POH. The difficulty is determining the actual distance available. Most seaplane takeoff areas are not measured and published. Factors like water condition (glassy water, most often found on small bodies of water, greatly increases the required takeoff distance and is not dealt with in the POH), and seaplane condition (old engine, eroded propeller), and pilot technique are factors that cannot be calculated in black and white.

   For the seaplane rating oral, the candidate will be expected to determine required takeoff distances from the POH, modify those numbers for changes in atmospheric conditions, and make decisions based on good judgement. So, if you are not sure you can make a takeoff in the available distance, you will be expected to waive the takeoff and seek alternative options, (such as finding a longer takeoff path, relying on an experienced pilot to help, or just not trying it).

The licensed seaplane pilot must make these decisions on many flights, and the wrong decision has led to numerous seaplane takeoff accidents and fatalities. The only positive way to know if the airplane is capable of making it out of a short, obstacled body of water (before the accident or sweaty clearing of the obstacle) is with the use of the Delta Ratio. The Delta Ratio technique tells the pilot if the aircraft is capable of clearing the obstacle *before* the aircraft leaves the water. This is an advanced technique, well documented in several places, such as Chapter 3 of *Water Flying Concepts*.

The Aborted Takeoff

Every takeoff should be considered by the pilot to be a practice takeoff abort procedure. If everything is just right and nothing of concern is detected by the pilot, the abort is continued to liftoff. So, before powering up for takeoff, remind yourself that this is going to be an abort unless everything is perfect.

Practice the abort procedure periodically. It is easy to do but must be done in the correct sequence and instinctively. Hence the need for practice. See how short you can stop your seaplane, decelerating from liftoff speed. The procedure, in the correct sequence, is

1. Throttle back
2. Flaps up
3. Stick back
4. Maintain heading
5. While falling off the step, rudders down
6. Turn left or right 90° (to stop forward progress)

Flaps up is done slightly before or concurrently with stick back to keep from flying, due to increased angle of attack. To stop in a shorter distance, instead of #4 (maintain heading), walk the rudders. Left, right, left, right smoothly to add drag. Don't do this on the checkride, though, unless you have gotten the examiner's approval to do so. You should be able to stop a Cessna 180-185 size floatplane and turn 90° in 600 feet; smaller aircraft in less distance than that.

Some Advanced Takeoff Techniques

Float lift takeoff is a modification of the normal takeoff. It is used in calm wind (glassy) conditions, when departing directly into the wind and with mild crosswinds (the downwind float is always the one lifted). The pilot lifts the right float (calm and headwind) by using full aileron input at a speed several MPH (typically 5–8) below normal liftoff speed. Full aileron deflection is held until the right float begins to lift out of the water. Aileron deflection is then decreased just enough to hold the right float barely above the water. The decrease in water drag allows the seaplane to accelerate rapidly, and liftoff occurs very soon after the right float lifts. For example, in the Cessna 180 at gross weight and a density altitude of 2,000 feet, liftoff occurs at about a count of "three" after the right float comes up. Once the float comes up, the aircraft is banking so lift is attempting to turn the airplane. If the pilot resists this turning force with opposite rudder in order to hold a straight course, a side load is imposed on the float which increases drag considerably. For best performance and least drag, allow the turn (keep the ball centered). There are further modifications of this technique that an experienced flight instructor can show you after you get your rating.

How is this different than crosswind takeoff technique?

1. With a crosswind, full aileron application is used from the beginning. With the float lift technique, full aileron is applied at the correct moment. To use ailerons sooner adds drag.
2. Crosswind technique always lifts the downwind float. Float lift technique always lifts the right float. The reason for this is because the propeller (American made engines with propellers rotating clockwise as seen from the pilot's seat) rotating clockwise torques the fuselage counterclockwise causing the right float to be "lighter," therefore more easily lifted out of the water. If you watch enough seaplanes doing float lift takeoffs, you will probably see a pilot lift the left wing instead of the right. What can I say? They are victims of poor

SPA

Float lift takeoff at Greenville, ME

instruction. The difference in performance is neither dramatic nor a safety issue. It is just an indicator of poor technique or lack of understanding.

The float lift technique is used to get the aircraft out of the water sooner. It is most useful for takeoffs from glassy water, or under high density altitude conditions, or if the aircraft is heavily loaded. Studies indicate that takeoff performance over a 50-foot obstacle is only improved under the above described conditions. Obstacled takeoff comparisons at 15% under gross weight were won by the normal takeoff, not the float lift technique, in studies using a Cessna 180. *See* Chapter 4, *Water Flying Concepts* for details.

Flap change takeoff is an advanced technique not normally taught and not demonstrated by the applicant for the sea rating. It is a technique that should be learned with the help of an experienced flight instructor. It is only possible to use this technique in aircraft equipped with "johnson-bar" or manual flap handles. In the Cessna 180 or 185, for example, normal takeoff flap setting is 20°. Flap settings of 0, 10, 20, 30 and 40 degrees are possible. When using this technique, the pilot starts the takeoff with 10 or 20 degrees of flaps. It is generally considered that most seaplanes will accelerate onto the step best without flaps so that the propwash will be directed more rearward. Flaps interfere with the propwash, directing some of it downward, so if the aircraft is having trouble getting on the step, try it with no flaps, then set the flaps after step taxi is achieved. However, in the case of the flap change takeoff, a flap setting of zero is not used because it requires the pilot to bend forward to reach the flap handle, which usually causes application of down elevator at a critical time. So, 10 or 20 degrees is used because the flap handle is easily reached in that position.

At an indicated airspeed of 8–12 MPH below normal liftoff speed (to be determined by experimentation with the airplane and modified depending on load and density altitude), the pilot, ***while looking outside***, removes hand from the throttle, depresses the flap position lock button, and pulls the flap handle smoothly to its limit (40° in this case). The flap position lock button is kept depressed, until the flap handle is back to 20° or less. When the flap handle is pulled to its limit the aircraft should lift out of the water. If it doesn't, the pilot may raise the nose just slightly. If that doesn't get the floatplane airborne, the maneuver was attempted at too low an airspeed.

If the airplane does become airborne, it should be kept in ground effect until flaps are returned (gently and slowly) to normal takeoff flap setting and a speed above V_S is attained. At that point, a normal climb departure is accomplished.

This technique should never be used if there is an obstacle (except for the few floatplanes that won't get off the water without this technique). It is best used for rough water takeoffs where there is plenty of water ahead or for getting out of short ponds that have no obstacle. It is not appropriate for glassy water because of the need to remain in ground effect until flaps are back up to climb flap setting (which cannot be done in glassy conditions because the pilot cannot determine where the water surface is).

Another modification of this technique is the **constant attitude takeoff** in which the attitude of the seaplane does not change once step taxi is achieved, and until cruise altitude is reached. Airspeed changes, but not attitude, which passengers like. The flap handle is used much like the collective control in a helicopter. Another advanced technique for your highly experienced flight instructor to show you!

High Altitude Takeoff

If you are planning a trip to a place where the altitude of the lake surface is higher than you are used to, you can easily simulate the performance your aircraft will exhibit at that higher altitude.

First, since aircraft performance is dependent on *density altitude*, estimate the density altitude of the high altitude landing site. As a licensed pilot, you already know how to do this, but let's review. Let's say you expect to take off from a lake where the surface is 4,000 feet MSL and you expect the temperature to be 80°F when you take off. Density altitude is pressure altitude corrected for nonstandard temperature. Since variations between elevation and pressure altitude are minor, we can ignore those and assume that elevation = pressure altitude. Standard temperature at various altitudes is shown in Figure 11-6 but you can do it in your head by remembering that standard temperature at sea level is 59°F, and it decreases 3.5° for each 1,000-foot increase in altitude.

Standard temperature at 4,000' pressure altitude is 59° – (3.5° × 4) = 59 – 14 = 45°F. On an 80° day, temperature is 35° warmer (degraded performance) than standard. Then use the old rule that for every 15° warmer than standard, density altitude is 1,000 feet higher than pressure altitude. So, 35/15 = 2.33. Density altitude is 2,330 feet higher than the 4,000 feet pressure altitude. Density altitude will be about 6,300 feet.

To simulate power available at that altitude, decrease the takeoff manifold absolute pressure (MAP) by .75" per 1,000 feet of density altitude change from the low level lake to the high altitude lake. For example, if your MAP gauge reads 27.5" during the takeoff run from your home lake at elevation 300 feet, the difference in altitude between the two lakes is 6,000 feet. So 6 × .75 = 4.5, and then 27.5 – 4.5 = 23" MAP.

If you want to know approximately what that high altitude takeoff will feel like, or even if your airplane will be able to get on the step and take off, load the airplane to gross weight, and try some takeoffs using 23" MAP. Patience and perhaps some new techniques will be needed to get your seaplane on the step and flying. An experienced flight instructor on board will help you learn a lot more, and faster!

During the seaplane checkride, your examiner may have you do a simulated high density altitude takeoff, because more skill is needed to get the struggling seaplane airborne.

As a general rule, seaplanes with normally aspirated (not turbocharged) engines will experience considerable difficulty getting airborne at elevations above 4,000 feet, so plan carefully before flying into landing sites at these high altitudes. If you do, practice first and be sure there is a lot of water surface available for the long takeoff. As with all takeoffs, performance will improve if you leave early when it is cooler and depart in a nice breeze. For more about planning takeoffs and determining the length for the takeoff, see Chapter 3 in *Water Flying Concepts*.

Pressure Altitude, feet	Temperature, degrees F
Sea Level	59
1,000	55.4
2,000	51.9
3,000	48.3
4,000	44.7
5,000	41.2
6,000	37.6
7,000	34
8,000	30.5
9,000	26.9
10,000	23.3

Note: Add .35 degrees per 100 feet, to interpolate between 1,000-foot levels.

Figure 11-6. ICAO standard atmosphere temperatures

Review

Seaplanes typically take four or five times more distance for takeoff than they do for landing. Their engines work harder than those on landplanes because the takeoff run is longer.

Seaplane accidents typically occur more often in the takeoff and climb phase as compared to landplanes. The difference is dramatic: 60–65% of seaplane accidents occur in the takeoff/climb phase; with landplanes the percentage is 30–35. This means we pilots need to be really careful during takeoff.

Takeoff planning for seaplanes must be taken seriously! Before increasing power for takeoff, be sure that (a) the checklist is complete; (b) some thought has been given to the safest climb path after liftoff. (If you can, drift to the right after liftoff and circle the lake while climbing to a safe altitude.) And (c) remind yourself that this takeoff attempt is really going to be an abort maneuver if you sense that anything is amiss. Practice the abort-stop short maneuver. Water can cause dramatic erosion to a propeller that is turning at speeds greater than 1,000 RPM. In fact, my rule is no more than 700 RPM unless absolutely necessary!

Seaplanes differ from landplanes in that they require a takeoff area assessment before departure. When you use the takeoff area, some time has passed since you looked at it from above and things change. So, it is a good idea to back taxi along that takeoff path before departure.

During the water run portion of the takeoff, the pilot's eyes are looking outside to maintain the proper attitude and to scan for water traffic and obstacles in the water. The only need to look inside comes early in the takeoff, just after full power is achieved, to accomplish a power check. There is no need to look at the airspeed indicator since the aircraft will lift from the water when it has achieved the correct speed.

After liftoff, if the same attitude is maintained that existed at liftoff, most seaplanes will accelerate promptly to V_Y while maintaining a proper climb angle. The goal is to reach 50 feet AWL and V_Y speed with flaps up at the same time. Remember the saying: "V_Y and clean before 50." It means the aircraft achieved a speed that allows the pilot to manage the aircraft before it is high enough to develop high vertical velocities if the engine fails.

Try to avoid flying over houses at low altitudes. Stay over water if you can, in case of a power failure while at low altitudes.

Or choose the safest climb path. Do what is safest when choosing direction of flight during climb.

The following table (Figure 11-7) is a summary of takeoff types, their differences, when they are used, and when they are not used. Refer to the table when reviewing the discussion section above.

Practice high density altitude takeoffs before operating out of high lakes. Remember, you might not be able to get airborne in a heavily loaded seaplane with a normally aspirated engine at lake altitudes over 4,000 feet on a warm day.

Takeoff type	Difference from normal	Used for	Do not use for	Danger elements
Normal	See "normal takeoff" description (p.109).	General use.		
Crosswind	Start into the wind or crosswind. Start with full aileron, lift downwind float; after liftoff turn into the wind, crab into the wind, or slip into the wind. Be sure you understand rudder requirement changes.	All crosswind conditions.	[Crosswinds ONLY]	Engine failure if drifting downwind in climb.
Rough water	Apply power when nose down, nose lower when on step, rotate at liftoff speed or use flap change, accelerate in ground effect.	Rough water.	Any takeoff not directly into the wind.	Taxiing any direction except directly into strong wind. No flap change if obstacled.
Glassy water	Need to plan takeoff path in order to neutralize the two dangers. Note attitude at liftoff and maintain to 50'. Use normal or float lift technique only.	Any glassy or near glassy conditions.		Inadvertent driftdown, power loss after takeoff.
Confined area	Liftoff after straight run following 180° displacement taxi turn or after a 180° step taxi turn, climb to obstacle at $V_{OBS\ CL}$	Areas offering only short takeoff.	If obstacled, do not use flap change technique.	Pilot's inability to judge whether the seaplane is capable of takeoff in the available space.
Abort	Before powering up for takeoff, remind yourself that this is going to be an abort unless everything is just perfect. The correct sequence is: 1. Throttle back 2. Flaps up 3. Stick back 4. Maintain heading or walk rudders 5. While falling off the step, rudders down 6. Turn left 90°	Every takeoff.		
Float lift technique	Right float lifted by full aileron input at 5-8 mph below normal liftoff speed.	Calm wind (glassy) conditions or when departing directly into the wind with a full load or high density altitude.	Not for rough water, crosswinds or obstacled takeoffs at less than gross weight.	Damage to float in rough water.
Flap change technique	See description for flap change technique in the text above (p.124). Advanced technique not needed for the sea rating. Learn it later. Gets aircraft out of water the fastest.	Rough water, short takeoff without obstacle.	Absolutely not for obstacled or glassy water takeoffs.	

Figure 11-7. Summary of takeoff types

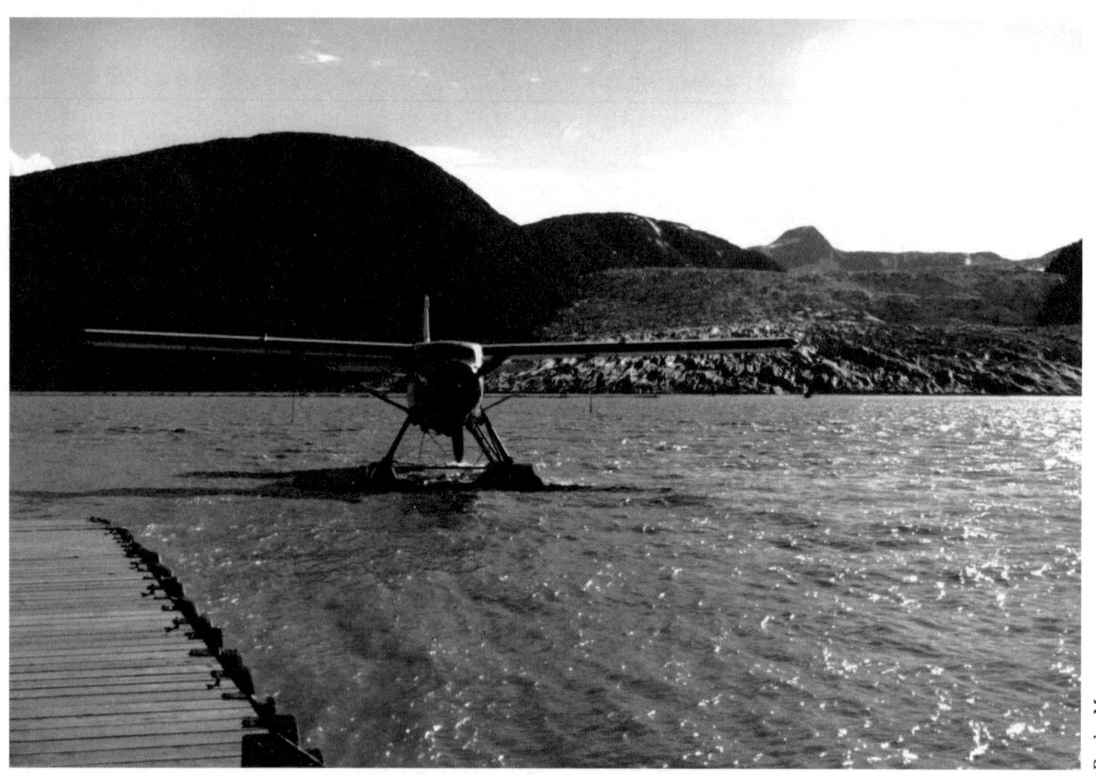

Burke Mees

Docking in a fast current with "Hole-in-the-Wall" glacier in the background (Taku River near Juneau, AK).

Chapter 12
Landing Area Assessment

A Vital Part of Every Landing

For the pilot preparing for the seaplane oral and checkride, I suggest you read the FAA PTS requirements so you will know what will be required of you. The following pages will prepare you to meet these standards. For those of you who are already seaplane pilots, a review of the discussion below will refresh your knowledge of assessing landing and takeoff areas.

As I write this, I am watching a landplane do a right downwind for the dirt airstrip about 1,000 feet from where I live in Mexico during the winter months. This airstrip is nearly 400 miles south of the nearest civilized (paved, maintained) airport. Every day, that dirt airstrip has people, dogs, chickens, burros, four-wheelers and an occasional vehicle on it. It's a nice strip. It is even maintained with a drag of some sort once in awhile.

I am wondering when that pilot last landed on that strip. Yesterday? Last week? Last year? Never? ***Why*** is he flying a right downwind? You can't inspect a runway from a right downwind (if you are sitting left side)!

Landing area assessment is a vital part of risk reduction.

Landing area assessment is a vital part of risk reduction when operating off and away from civilized airports. For the seaplane pilot, it is a vital part of ***every*** landing. Even if it is your home base and you have landed there a thousand times. Mother Nature constantly changes the water surface. Wind direction and speed, floating debris, other traffic (boaters rarely look up, unless experienced and knowledgeable about operating in an area where seaplanes come and go), shifting sandbars, alligators sunning, a new flock of migrating white pelicans (very slow and very dumb!), an old, male polar bear lounging on the beach where you want to heel up, and cannibals on the shoreline with spears at the ready, starting a fire under a big pot are examples of a few hazards that must be identified before selecting a landing place on the water. There is no end to the types of potential hazards.

Boaters rarely look up.

A New and Different Technique

Trying to look at everything on the ground while whizzing rapidly by, flying the airplane and formulating a landing plan is, at first, a bewildering task. Wouldn't it be nice if you could hang the airplane on a skyhook right over the landing area, so you could take your time to look at everything, make and critique a landing plan for taxiing in, docking or beaching, and selecting a takeoff water strip and climbout path?

The Procedure

The process starts 5 miles back...

Well, yes, it would be nice, but skyhooks are very scarce so let's get organized and do this multi-faceted task in a way that makes it easiest for us. Let's start this process of landing area assessment about 5 miles back from our destination landing area.

Make a position report and do it right!

Step 1. Make a position report. Do it right! See the discussion about radio use on Pages 95–96. Canadian regulations require a position report 5 *minutes* out from any landing site.

Plan to arrive at 500 feet over the water's edge at V_Y.

Step 2. In preparation for the landing area assessment, you want to arrive over the near shoreline of the water you intend to land on at 500' AWL and slowed to landing area assessment speed, which is about V_Y in most airplanes. So do the math and start your descent at the appropriate time. Why 500 feet? It is the highest altitude at which a pilot with normal vision can see detail the size of a baseball.

Get the big picture.

Step 3. Make whatever predeterminations you can. If you pass over any water while inbound, wind direction and speed can be determined and the ambiguity of direction resolved (*see* the discussion of wind direction determination below). Listen for other traffic. Look at the big picture. Absorb the general local weather picture (are there any convective clouds in the area that may impact the conditions in the landing area, etc?).

Make a second position report, slowing to V_Y.

Step 4. A half mile or more back from the shoreline, start slowing to V_Y, and make another radio call. Arrive over the shoreline in landing area assessment configuration.

Landing Area Assessment Configuration

Landing area assessment airspeed of the seaplane is V_Y, approximately. It is a slow but comfortable speed to allow more time to look. A notch or two of flaps lowers the nose for better visibility. Trim the seaplane carefully—most new seaplane pilots tend to drift down gradually during the assessment process. Learn and remember the power setting that will hold you level in this configuration, and use it.

Configuration:

- V_Y
- Flaps
- Trim
- Power setting

Landing area assessment configuration of the seaplane *pilot* is even more important. It is a mindset with three management tasks while above the landing site.

Fly the Airplane!

Once the landing area configuration is achieved (80 indicated, a notch of flaps and about 18" of manifold pressure and trimmed in the Cessna 180-185), the pilot may look outside to do the assessment, as long as the wings are approximately level. When the seaplane is banked for turning, the pilot's full attention shifts from looking at the surface to flying the airplane and looking for traffic.

Plan the Assessment and Prepare to Execute the Plan

Landing area site assessment is a complex task. Much like preflight inspection, it is made up of many subtasks. It is best accomplished in a standard, routine manner...every time! Here is how I do it. There are five steps.

First look over the place you want to go ashore.

First: Check out the place you plan to go ashore. Identify and fly toward the point where you plan to go ashore. While en route and at 500 feet AWL, assess the general sea state (water surface condition), which tells you wave height, wind speed and direction. When you have located where to go ashore, fly by and look, then immediately enter a maneuver that will allow the next fly-by into the wind (lowest ground speed, more time to look). I repeat this maneuver as many times as necessary until satisfied that I know exactly where I am going ashore. I identify a distinctive landmark to help me find the place when I am on the water (everything looks different on the water). I assess what hazards are there, estimate the wind direction and velocity in the microenvironment at the shore, plan what type of approach (to the shore) I will use and what the going-ashore plan is for the pilot and passengers (right down to what length line I will need to tie up and what knot I will use). In the beginning, you will lack the experience for detailed planning, but learning is the goal. Soon, you will be doing the assessment, making mistakes, and learning. (Look for the assessment hints that follow the third phase of the assessment process.)

Assess while flying into the wind.

Assess the landing and taxi area.

Second: Define and assess the landing area and taxi path to shore. Select the exact location where you will touch down, and where you will fall off the step. This is done by selecting the fall-off-the-step location first, which is as close as possible to where you will go ashore, considering safety. Directly downwind of that spot, about one thousand feet, is the touchdown point. I try to define that point by using some landmark.

Precisely define the touchdown point.

In other words, the place to land is ***not*** just wherever the airplane comes to rest, because it is impossible to completely survey a large water area for debris, sandbars, rocks, etc. Pick out a place to land, survey it well, land there, and fall off the step where you had planned. Once you master this, you will be taking home prizes from spot landing contests!

Now that you know where you will fall off the step, examine the taxi path to shore for obstructions, shallow spots and other hazards. Find some landmarks ashore so you will know, when down on the water, that you are taxiing in the area you inspected. It is important you view this area with the sun at your back. Power poles, mostly submerged wood, logs, and rocks under a clear water surface are best seen with the sun behind you.

Select the safest approach path.

Third: With the landing site chosen, define the safest approach path. Select the safest approach path for landing at the location you have chosen. You have already read that seaplanes don't have prescribed traffic patterns. The correct traffic pattern is chosen based on what path is safest. Imagine what the examiner would think about your sanity and ability to use good judgment if he told you to "land there," and you set up a rectangular traffic pattern that brought the seaplane in low over trees and big rocks, when a circular final approach could have been made over water or shoreline all the way! *See* Figure 12-1.

Select the safest takeoff and departure path.

Fourth: While still aloft, choose the takeoff path. Select where you will begin the takeoff run. Note the compass heading to define direction or choose a prominent feature on the far shore. When in wilderness areas, it is a well-proven practice to always take off precisely along your previous landing path because it is proven water. This may require you to **back taxi** along the takeoff path. This is ***always*** a good practice! It should be done at displacement taxi speed while watching carefully for debris in the water. Back taxiing will also help you know where your liftoff point will be, once you know your airplane. For example, a C-180 at gross weight, 2,000 foot density altitude, with a very light headwind and normal takeoff technique, will lift off just before a point that is 5 minutes back if the back taxi is done at 700 RPM. Once you know the numbers for your airplane, you will know how much back taxi is required to inspect the entire water run area, as well as have a pretty good sense of where you will lift off

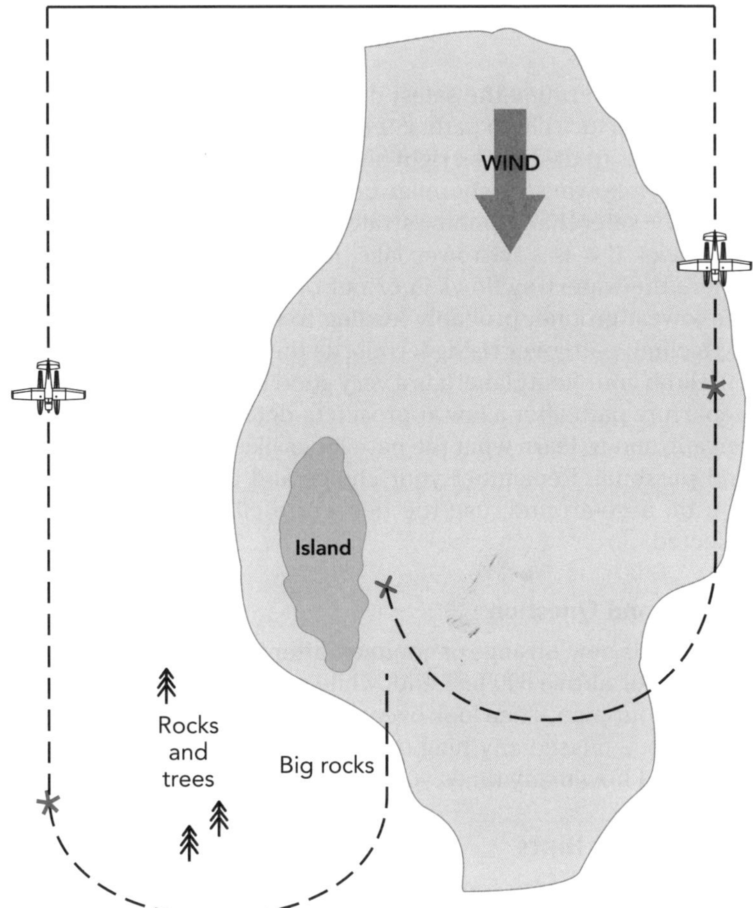

Figure 12-1. Which is the safest approach path to land at X? The asterisk marks beginning of descent from 500 feet AWL.

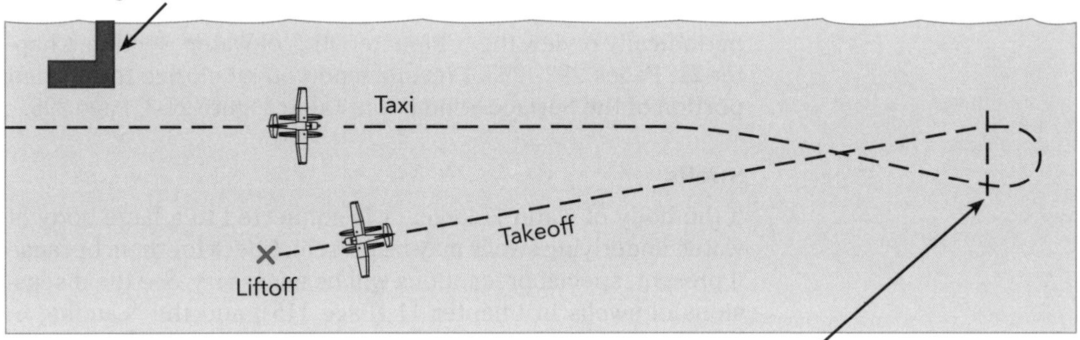

Figure 12-2. Water run estimate from back-taxiing.

(assuming no change in seaplane capability and pilot technique). *See* Figure 12-2.

Fifth: Determine the safest departure climb path. Select the safest departure climb path. If it is a round lake, perhaps the safest tactic is to drift to the right after liftoff and make a left climbing turn, following the shoreline until a safe altitude is reached. It would be safer than climbing straight, passing low over trees and big rocks. If it is a narrower lake, it would be helpful to know where the waterway flows in or out of the lake because that is the lowest ground, probably leading to the next lake. Don't fall for a climb path over rising terrain, as the terrain very likely will outclimb your floatplane! It is a very good idea to fly your chosen departure path after a low approach to determine it is not rising terrain, and to learn what the path looks like when you are close and personal. Remember your choice and use it after liftoff. If you do a go-around, use the departure climb path you have selected.

Review and Question

Crituque your plan.

If the site is new, strange or complex, after formulating your plan, climb to or above 500 feet and, while scanning for other traffic, review your plan. Then look over the entire area and ask yourself if you have missed anything or is there a safer way. You will be surprised how many times you will find changes are in order.

Assessment Hints

Assessing the Water Surface for Wind Speed, Direction and Waves

Learn to read the water.

One of the finest tools that seaplane pilots have, and that is lacking in the landplane pilot's world, is that the water surface makes the wind, and what it is doing, visible. In order to equip yourself with the knowledge you need to enable you to read the water, periodically review the "Characteristics of Water" section, Chapter 21, Pages 292–293. I recommend you memorize the bolded portion of the Surface Wind Force Table, Figure 21-3, Page 295.

Swells

If the body of water is large, or is connected to a large body of water, underlying swells may be present. Check for them because if present, special precautions will be necessary. *See* the discussions of swells in Chapter 11 (Page 115), and the "Landing in Swells" section in the next chapter (Page 154).

180° Directional Ambiguity

When you identify the direction of the wind streaks (have a look at the waves and streaks discussion, and their idiosyncrasies on Pages 293–294 in Chapter 21). With that knowledge, check to see that the wave faces are about 90° to the wind streaks. Then, check for ambiguity. You think you know where the wind is coming from, along the streaks. But, the last thing you want to have happen, ***ever***, is to be 180° wrong about the wind direction and attempt a rough water landing, downwind, in a 25 knot wind. So, always check for ambiguity! My favorite way for doing this is to look for the shoreline where the waves are coming ashore. The white waves breaking at the shore are visible from a considerable distance. Land the airplane going away from that shore.

Don't ***ever*** let the 180° ambiguity get you!

Gusts, Catspaws and Microbursts

The surface of the water also tells the pilot about gusts, which are seen as dark patches on the water. The darkness is caused by the increased wave height, locally, due to the higher velocity of wind on the water. The darkness is caused by the greater wave face area, which gives the appearance of looking down into the water. The view from this angle appears darker than the sky reflection when looking at the surface some distance away.

The seaplane pilot can "see" gusts.

While the gust may be higher velocity air moving in the same direction as the general air mass, it may also be the result of a downburst or microburst. A downburst is a faster moving column of air whose direction may have more or less of a vertical component coming from above. If this is the case, when it reaches the surface, it is deflected in many directions, depending on the angle it encounters the water, and forms a pattern called a **catspaw** because that's what it looks like. *See* Figure 12-3 on the next page. The direction the dark patch of water is moving, compared to the seaplane's movement and by the wavelet pattern of the dark patch clues the pilot about whether that higher velocity air is coming at him or moving as a crosswind. The information gained from reading the water is extremely useful. It tells the seaplane pilot whether to expect a momentary airspeed increase, lift increase (or the opposite) or roll when operating close to the water.

Terrain and Wind Current Considerations

The seaplane pilot must keep in mind two things about terrain. One is that it really affects wind direction and speed for a quarter to a half mile, or more, offshore. The new seaplane pilot soon

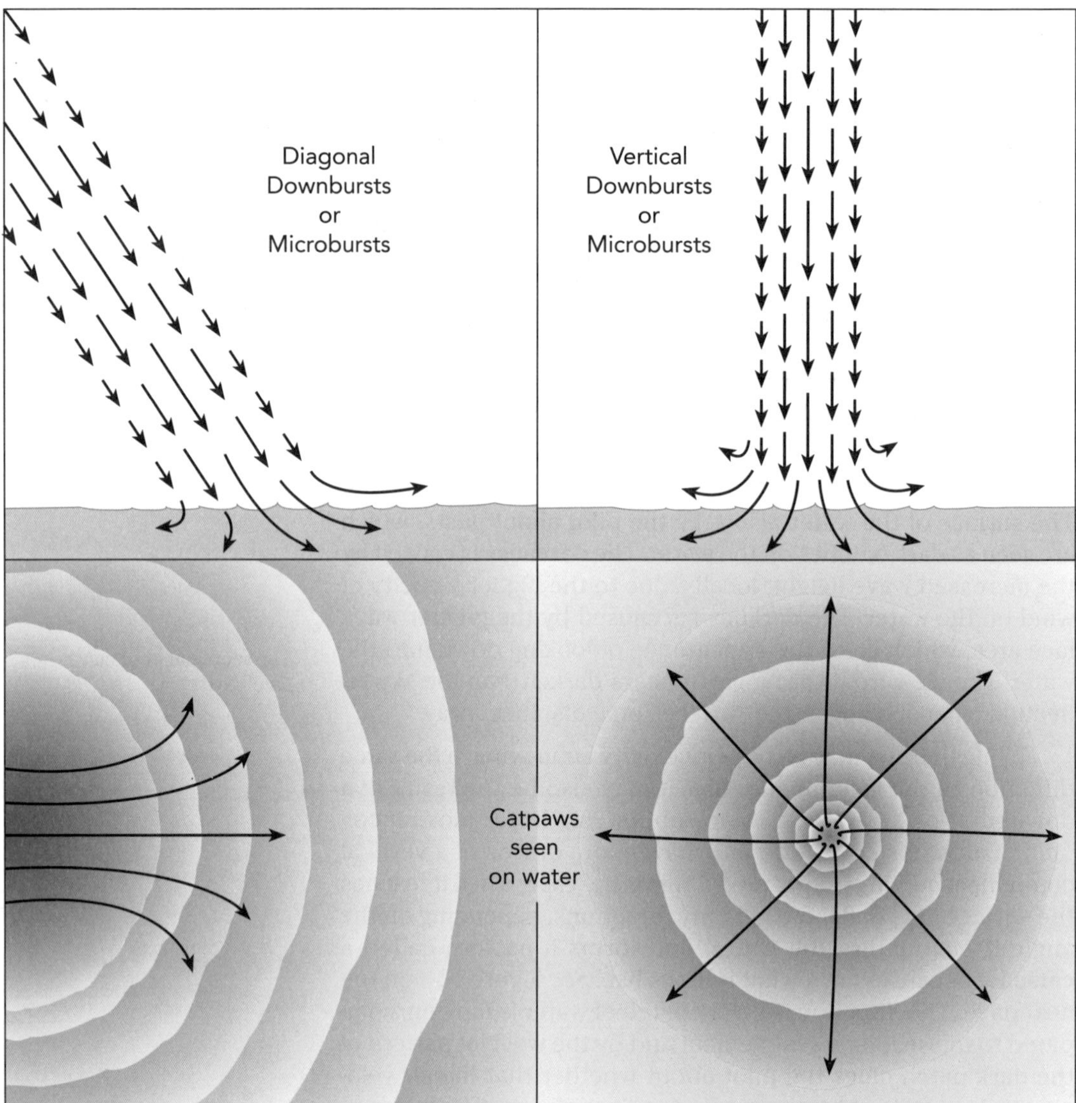

Figure 12-3. Catspaws and microbursts

learns, by watching wind streaks on the water, that the wind tends to follow the shoreline, especially if it is covered with trees or rises rapidly. When landing on waterways with higher terrain along the sides, try to visualize how the wind is channeling down canyons. When it reaches the water, it flows out in all directions, creating wind shear. Sudden airspeed losses will be experienced when flying near the surface, past these canyon mouths or stream inlets. Not a good place to be with low airspeeds just after liftoff or before touchdown! *See* Figure 12-4.

The other fact about terrain concerns whether to utilize the smooth water, just downwind of high terrain, for takeoff and deal with the turbulence and rolling tendencies (*see* Figure 12-5), or to accept a rough water takeoff into the wind, toward the high terrain, with a turn to fly over lower terrain during climbout. If the calm water is utilized, get ***lots*** of airspeed before leaving

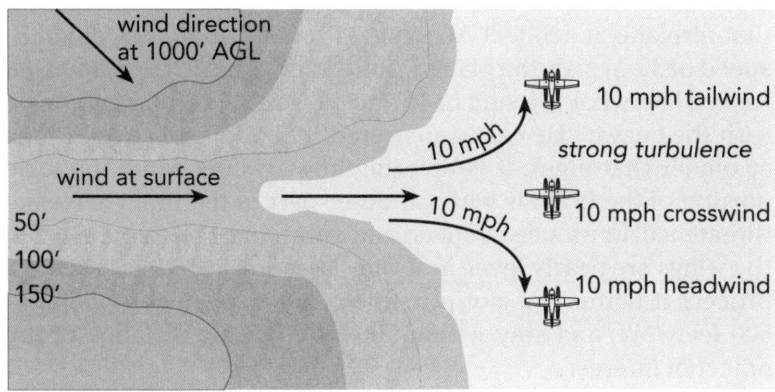

Figure 12-4. Wind shear: The airplane experiences up to a 10-MPH airspeed increase and more lift, then a 10-MPH airspeed decrease with a crosswind. Another 10-MPH airspeed loss occurs, followed by that sinking feeling. A "catspaw" may be seen on the water surface.

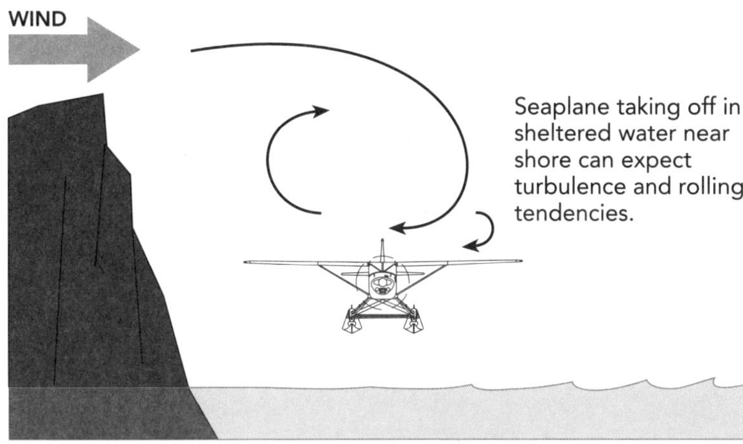

Figure 12-5. Roll turbulence

ground effect and brief your passengers about the turbulence you expect. That way, they will be prepared and feel confident that you know what you are doing. They should then be less likely to climb in your lap and dig their fingernails into your tender body parts when the turbulence starts!

The seaplane pilot needs to consider terrain during all phases of the landing area assessment from the standpoint of flightpath design. In other words, don't hit it! Take advantage of low terrain when designing the flight path into and out of water areas. Rising terrain at the departure end of the lake needs special attention. It often climbs faster than your seaplane!

Best Assessment: Wings Level, into Wind, Maximum 500 Feet AWL

I had a wilderness course client one time who was very proud of his Helio Courier on floats. He wanted to do assessment with that airplane at 500 feet AWL, in a 45° bank at an indicated airspeed of 35. Yes, the airplane would do it. While in the maneuver, I asked him what the sum of 12 and 14 was. He couldn't come up with the answer. He easily answered that and similar questions at dinner that night. It is amazing how dysfunctional the logic portion of the brain is when another part of the brain is feeling threatened! Use a safe airspeed and only look at the ground when the wings are nearly level. You will see more, and your brain will process it better. It is not possible to do turns about a point at 500 feet AWL and stay within 500-foot viewing distance of the object of interest.

How dysfunctional the logic portion of the brain is, when another part of the brain feels threatened!

Take Your Time

I once rode with an 8,000-hour seaplane bush pilot who spent 25 minutes overhead, assessing a landing site before he landed. Yes, it was complex... a shallow, fast river with lots of large rocks in it. The sand beaching site was some distance from where he could land, accessible only with a complex taxi path. Take your time. Don't commit to a landing until you are confident that both the landing and takeoff can be accomplished safely.

Don't hurry when assessing.

Review

Landing area assessment is a vital part of risk reduction of ***every*** seaplane landing. Mother Nature constantly changes the water surface. List 20 hazards to watch for before each landing. There is no end to the different types of potential hazards, so listing that many should be easy!

About how many miles back from the destination landing area should the landing area assessment process start? The 5 steps are listed below; see if you can describe how to do each and check your answers in the text above:

Step 1. Make a position report.

Step 2. Plan ahead to arrive over the near shoreline of the water you intend to land on at 500 feet AWL, slowed to landing area assessment speed.

Step 3. Make whatever predeterminations you can.

Step 4. A half mile or more back from the shoreline, start slowing to V_Y, make another radio call, and arrive over the shoreline in landing area assessment configuration.

Step 5. Landing area assessment configuration, what is it and what are the reasons for using it? What is landing area assessment configuration power setting for your airplane?

What are the landing area assessment configuration elements of the seaplane *pilot*? What are the five steps of the landing area assessment, once over the landing site? When does "review and question" fit into this process?

Describe the elements of each assessment hint listed below, and how to utilize them:

- **Assess water surface for wind speed, direction, and waves.** Back taxiing along the takeoff path is *always* a good practice! What are the two main reasons why?
- **180° directional ambiguity.** The last thing you want to happen, ***ever***, is to be 180° wrong about the wind direction and attempt a rough water landing, downwind, in a 25-knot wind. Describe how to avoid this.
- **Gusts, catspaws and microbursts.** The information gained from "reading the water" is extremely useful. How does the seaplane pilot relate this to wind shear?
- **Terrain and wind current considerations.** Terrain really affects wind direction and speed for a quarter to a half mile, or

more, offshore. How does wind interact with the shoreline? How do trees or rapidly rising terrain near the shoreline affect this interaction? When landing on waterways with higher terrain along the sides, try to visualize how the wind is channeling down canyons. When it reaches the water after flowing out of canyons or streamways, what does that wind do and what does it create?

Another dilemma is whether to utilize the smooth water just downwind of high terrain for takeoff and deal with the turbulence and rolling tendencies, or to accept a rough water takeoff into the wind, toward the high terrain with a turn to fly over lower terrain during climbout. Faced with this decision, what are your options as the pilot? Consider the terrain during all phases of the landing area assessment from the standpoint of flightpath design. Explain the considerations to address while accomplishing the assessment.

- **Best assessment is done wings level, into the wind at not more than 500 feet AWL**, using landing area assessment configuration.
- **Take your time.** Don't commit to a landing until you feel confident!

Dave Bennett

A very patriotic Super Cub turning final for the water.

Chapter 13
Approaches, Landings, and Go-Arounds

If you are studying for the oral and checkride, read the PTS sections indicated in the sidebar. If you are already a seaplane pilot and are reading for review, the following pages will provide an opportunity to review and perhaps learn something new.

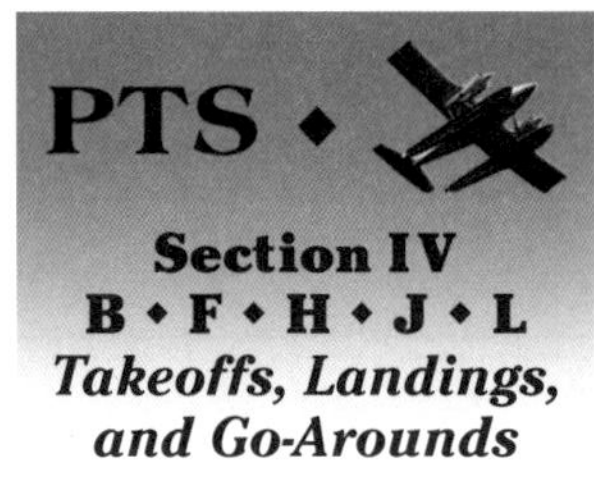

PTS •
Section IV
B • F • H • J • L
Takeoffs, Landings, and Go-Arounds

The Normal Approach
(All Landings Except Glassy)

The seaplane pilot's normal approach differs somewhat from that in a landplane. A left-hand, rectangular pattern may be used, but the "safest approach path" rule applies. If it is safer to use a path that differs from the old, familiar rectangular pattern, then it is appropriate to do so.

Fly with eyes outside!

The seaplane pilot correctly flies his craft with eyes looking outside more than 95 percent of the time. Scanning for other traffic continuously and making frequent radio position reports are proper safety procedures, especially when operating near landing areas.

The Downwind Leg

After completing the landing area assessment, if a rectangular pattern is used, the downwind leg is flown, keeping the pattern in close and slowing to about 1.4 V_{SO} if not already at that speed. Turn base closer in than you think you should, probably not more than a quarter mile past the point on the downwind that is abeam the touchdown point. Develop the seaplane pilot's habit of flying a tight pattern. Once you get used to it, you will find the close pattern will make approaches seem easier.

Why does the seaplane pilot fly a close pattern?

1. The traffic pattern is at 500 feet to permit scanning the landing area again on downwind. So descent starts 300 to 700 feet lower than the landplane's pattern.
2. The seaplane has more drag than the landplanes you fly so the glide angle with partial or no power will be steeper, permitting a close pattern.

3. When flying in wilderness areas, approaches are often flown to landing areas embedded well below terrain and tree tops. It is easy to lose sight of the touchdown point unless a close pattern is flown. Descent from traffic pattern altitude should not begin unless the touchdown spot on the water is in sight.

Don't start down until touchdown point is in sight.

A properly flown "close" pattern does not require steeply banked turns. It does require good airspeed control and proper planning as to when the turn from base to final must be started.

Base Leg

Base leg is relatively short, with partial flaps applied while wings are level (if a split-flap condition arises, better to have it happen when wings are level). The turn to final is made early enough to permit a medium bank of not more than 30°. Twenty degrees is better for passenger comfort. Practice making good "close in" patterns since this is not a maneuver typically used by landplane pilots, who often like to do a grand tour of the county in what they call a traffic pattern, a habit probably started by operating in busy traffic patterns.

Final

Final is flown normally, except it will be short because you are flying a close pattern. So set landing flaps after leveling wings on final so the seaplane will be stabilized in landing configuration, allowing you to fine tune the power setting. ***Always*** be looking outside when you change flap setting so you can stay up with the corresponding pitch change (there shouldn't be a pitch change; manage it with elevator and, if manual flaps, make the flap change slowly enough to accomplish the flap change with no apparent pitch change). Find the flap lever without looking at it so you can continue looking outside.

Always be looking outside when changing flap setting.

All airplanes have specific power settings for use with certain configurations. Learn from the airplane what they are and use them. It will make your life so much easier! *See* Figure 13-1.

Use a specific power setting to accomplish a specific task.

I still remember one time, many years ago, when I was the most nervous in an airliner I had ever been. I was a passenger in a B-727 that was making an instrument approach into SFO. There were *seventeen* power changes after the wheels came down at the outer marker! I hope that was a new copilot making his first approach, and I hope that that copilot got a good lecture about power management from the captain after engine shutdown.

I like to demonstrate this point by setting the manifold pressure at 12" (Cessna 180 floatplane) and putting the prop control to high pitch at a point abeam the touchdown spot on a 500 feet AWL downwind, and then not touching the throttle until on the water. The airplane flies the most perfect seaplane approach all by itself if properly trimmed! Try it! See if you can find the *one* power setting for approach. Then use it, because it is so easy on you, the pilot. You will need to make a few, minor adjustments on some approaches, usually to compensate for wind, load or density altitude changes. It is truly amazing how many seaplanes and landplanes that, if you are coming down the perfect looking 3° final approach path and you glance at the manifold pressure gauge, it will be reading 12 inches! (Normally aspirated engine, constant speed prop set to flat pitch.)

Keep your speed up in the pattern!

Airspeed on final? Use what the POH or your flight instructor recommends. Keep it simple. Use one airspeed in the pattern, about 1.4 V_{SO} (rounded to the next higher airspeed indicator marking because it is easier to remember and see) until your wings are level on final, because the turn, close to the ground, will be safer. Floatplanes like to slow down, and mush, developing high rates of sink. I like to keep my speed up until on short final so all the factors of speed, descent rate, glide angle and power setting don't change.

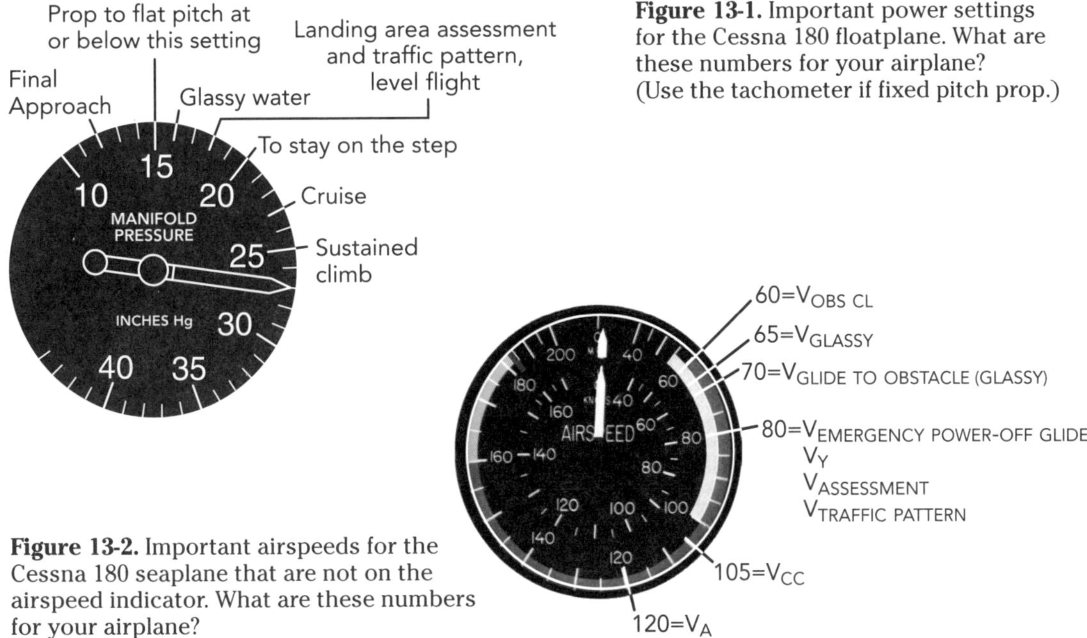

Figure 13-1. Important power settings for the Cessna 180 floatplane. What are these numbers for your airplane? (Use the tachometer if fixed pitch prop.)

Figure 13-2. Important airspeeds for the Cessna 180 seaplane that are not on the airspeed indicator. What are these numbers for your airplane?

Figure 13-3. A cub demonstrates a good normal landing attitude on sod or water.

The Final Check

Recheck the "things that can kill ya"!

That same 8,000-hour bush float pilot taught me that, on final before the flare, "check the things that will kill ya!" It is a confirmation that you checked the really important things. What should be on that checklist? Mixture, prop, flaps? Wheels would top this list if in an amphibian. Discuss with your flight instructor and other pilots what is needed on this check. Whatever it is, memorize it and make it second nature, because you shouldn't be looking inside on short final.

The Roundout, or Flare

The roundout, or flare, should start a little higher than in a landplane, and the pilot must assure that a safe touchdown attitude is achieved (usually the same attitude as when displacement taxiing on the water) before getting close to the water. After that, continue a slow pitching up until the water is contacted smoothly. Then, ***don't*** do what the tricycle gear pilot does habitually...don't relax pressure on the elevator! Continue to fly the touchdown attitude or, if you wish to decelerate faster, raise the flaps and use full up elevator.

The reason for not getting close to the water in a nose down attitude is that if the water touches the float at a point on the float that is forward of the center of gravity, directional stability goes out the window, and a water loop (similar dynamics to a ground loop but with much more damaging results) is the likely result. Long, low, flat, fast approaches near the water are potentially very dangerous. You may wish to review the water loop discussion in Chapter 11 on Page 117.

One fine flight instructor I know likes to teach flares-to-a-landing to novices in this way: he asks the pilot to accomplish the flare using five distinct flares. The first at 50' AWL, the second at 25', the third at 15', then the last two as needed. He tells his student "After the third flare, I relax a little."

Hint: As you may know, a smooth landing in an aircraft that is slowing requires that the nose is rising at the moment of surface contact.

Normal Landing

The normal landing is accomplished with both floats touching the water at the same time. The water touches the float at the step first or at the step and back near the transom (heel) at the same time, or the heel may touch first. A full stall landing is not appropriate because there is no shock absorbing mechanism built into a floatplane. Always land with airspeed just above full stall. The floatplane will never skip or bounce if the heel of the float touches first, for the same reason a tail dragger won't bounce if

Wipaire

A DeHavilland DHC-6 Twin Otter on Wipline 13000 amphibious floats demonstrates a good normal landing attitude.

Figure 13-4. A Republic SeaBee demonstrates a nice "heels first" touchdown.

the tailwheel touches first. (*See* Figure 13-4.) Surface contact at the heel of the float or tailwheel causes the nose to pitch down slightly, decreasing the angle of attack of the wing, which decreases lift.

After splash down, keep flying the airplane!

Again let me stress, that after touchdown, do not allow the stick to move forward! Continue to maintain the landing attitude by "flying" the airplane. This will be the most comfortable attitude for passengers, or if you wish to stop more quickly, put the flaps up (first) then elevator full up.

Once off the step, put the water rudders down and complete your checklist.

Crosswind Landing

The same basic principles and factors involved in a normal approach and landing apply to a crosswind approach and landing; therefore, only the additional procedures required for correcting for wind drift are discussed here.

On final, crab into the wind with the wings level so that the airplane's ground track remains aligned with the centerline of the landing area, just as you would do in a landplane. Just before the roundout is started, smoothly change to the wing-low slip method to maintain track for the remainder of the landing.

In the landplane, you learned to put the upwind wing down enough to stop the drift across the runway, then maintain that angle of bank until touchdown. If you do that in a seaplane, you will still be drifting downwind... a lot! This is because the surface of the water runway you are seeing (wavelets) is moving downwind!

No worry! There is an easy fix. Just establish the angle of bank needed to stop the sideways movement of the wavelets, then double it. Landing on one float is just like landing on one main wheel. Keep the same aileron control input you had at touchdown, and the downwind float will come down soon, but smoothly. Then smoothly input FULL aileron into the wind as soon as both floats are in the water and keep it there.

If the downwind float comes down quickly and hard, your teacher (the airplane) is telling you that you were indeed drifting downwind at the moment of touchdown. Drifting downwind at the moment of touchdown is dangerous because when the floats touch, they "trip" on the water, which starts an upset moment that is augmented by the wind. If the drift is significant, an upset is possible. *See* Figure 13-5. If you have to be drifting, doing so into the wind is better because the sidewind will counter the upset moment. If you feel like too much bank angle is needed (concern over catching a wingtip in the water), go around and don't land there. Landing in strong crosswinds should be avoided. There is rarely a need to do so. If the wind is strong, the seaplane's landing distance is very short, often allowing a landing across a narrow body of water, into the wind.

Don't forget:

- **go smoothly to full aileron as soon as both floats are down**
- **water rudders (expect the seaplane to weathercock into the wind)**
- **finish your checklist!**

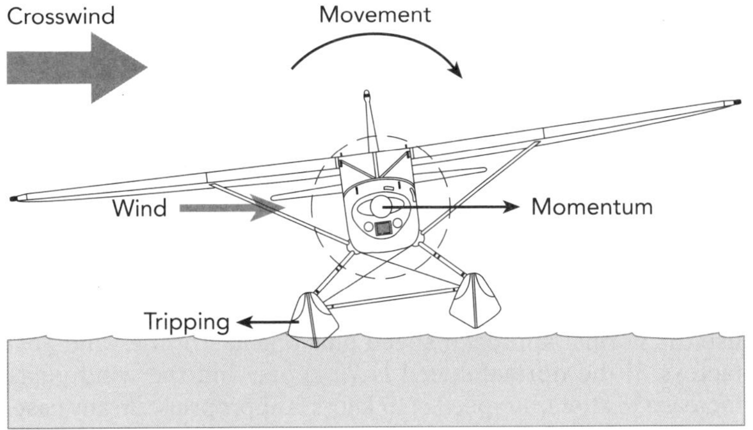

Figure 13-5. Three strong forces (momentum, tripping and wind) create an upset moment if drifting downwind in a crosswind landing.

Rough Water Landing

Rough water means the wind is probably blowing. If the wind is blowing, it is probably gusty. If the water is very rough, probably the gusts are strong. Here are a few things to consider when flying near the surface in strong gusts:

Protect the airplane. When the wing encounters an up-gust, the angle of attack increases, lift increases, and load on the wing increases. Most general aviation aircraft are stressed for a positive load factor of 3.8 Gs. That means the wing can handle 3.8 times the load that's on it in level flight. That wing can make your body weigh 3.8 times your body weight, slam you hard to the bottom of your seat cushion travel and really get your attention. Actually, the seaplane can handle even a little more and keep flying. ***But***, extend the flaps and the allowable load factor decreases to 2.0, almost half the structural strength you had before you lowered the flaps. Think *tender*. Lower flaps and you make the airplane *tender*.

Flaps make the airplane ***tender***.

Maintain aileron authority. Gusts provide strong roll tendencies as well. When the aircraft is rolled, the primary roll control is the aileron. Roll is corrected with the aileron, but only if aileron authority (ability to roll the airplane) is adequate. Only airspeed determines how much aileron authority is available. So, in gusty conditions, keep your speed up until you are in ground effect where the surface decreases the gust's ability to roll the aircraft.

So when it's gusty, keep your flaps and speed up until you are in ground effect (20 feet above the water). If the gusts are still requiring near full aileron input, go around and don't land there. If it has smoothed out, apply flaps and land. If you are landing in sheltered (smoother) water in a strong wind, consider not using flaps. Your speed over the ground is already low. Practice an occasional no-flaps landing, just to stay sharp. Remember to expect more of a pitch down moment upon touchdown due to the higher drag from faster moving water, when doing a no flaps landings in light wind. Land on the heels first (nose up more) to slow your speed.

When it's really gusty, ***keep flaps and speed up***.

Operating in Strong Gusts

The FAA *Airplane Flying Handbook* says, "One procedure is to use the normal approach speed plus one-half of the wind gust factors. If the normal speed is 70 knots, and the wind gusts increase 15 knots, airspeed of 77 knots is appropriate. In any case, the airspeed and the amount of flaps should be as the airplane manufacturer recommends."

Very few seaplane pilots have the pleasure of a tower telling them "wind 340 degrees at 14 gusting to 29." So, how do we know the gust factor? If it is really gusty (remember, you can see the gusts on the water and/or if it is turbulent at assessment altitude) a low pass (at 50 feet) while noting turbulence and variations on the airspeed indicator will give a good idea of the gust factor. Add 50% of the difference between high and low airspeed readings observed (while over the water on the low pass, with power and pitch attitude constant) to your usual approach speed on final. When you get to be an old "silver side" with thousands of sea hours in your logbook, you will be able to look at the water from 500 feet and know what you are in for and what to do about it. Remember when doing that fly-by at 50 feet: flaps up and not faster than V_A speed to protect the airplane.

V_A Speed Defined

If you are at or below V_A speed, the aircraft will not be damaged by full control movements in calm air and won't be damaged by excessive turbulence if no severe control movements are used during the turbulence. In effect, the wing will stall before being overstressed if at or below V_A. Remember, V_A speed decreases when the aircraft's weight decreases.

V_A speed is important and it decreases when the seaplane's weight decreases

Caution

Really rough water (wave heights approaching 10% of the float length) is extremely hard on the floats. You can expect increased seepage into the floats due to stretched rivets after continued operations in really rough water. Can safe landings be done in this roughness of water? If properly done, yes.

Plan Ahead

In strong winds, after you fall off the step, it will be difficult if not impossible to turn around and/or taxi crosswind. Taxiing crosswind, if possible at all, will be hard on the propeller. Sailing will be required. Keep that in mind when planning (during landing area assessment) for the spot where you will fall off the step, in relation to your shore-side destination.

The Rough Water Landing in Chop

A rough water landing is very similar to a rough field landing in a wheel airplane. On floats in a wind-driven chop, a rough water landing must always be done into the wind with both floats contacting the water at the same time (to spread the loading evenly between the floats). Use full flaps and whatever power is needed to let yourself gently down into the smoothest water patch you can find, at just above stall speed. The smoothest water is the lightest colored water patches.

Once on the water, lower the nose to a flat attitude. The ride will smooth out considerably because the floats are now cutting through the wave tops instead of each wave whacking the bottom of the float. Continue to fly that flat attitude. As the seaplane slows, more and more forward elevator will be needed to maintain the flat attitude. When the nose finally rises uncontrollably as the floats settle to displacement attitude, the elevator control will be all the way forward. Once displacement speed is reached, full aft elevator is needed to protect the propeller.

Remember: Pitch level just after touchdown, run out with a flat attitude ending up with the stick all the way forward, stick all the way back as soon as in displacement taxi mode; water rudders and checklist.

The pilot who brings the stick back just after touchdown in very rough water causes tremendous shock loads to the airframe and floats and is using poor technique.

Landing in Swells

Recall the discussion of what causes rough water in Chapter 11, in "The Rough Water Takeoff." The above discussion applies to landing in wind-generated chop. Landing in swells, especially underlying swells that are hard to see, is problematic. Swells, if all coming from the same direction, will have a pattern of two or three larger swells followed by three to five smaller ones. It is possible that there may be faster moving swells superimposed which occasionally create "rogue" swells that are much higher than their counterparts. This makes long, low approaches very dangerous. If the float bottom is smacked by one of these swells while still above touchdown speed, a water loop is the likely result. Be sure you are in touchdown attitude before approaching the water when landing in swells (which will be present on any large body of water or in inlets to large bodies of water).

See Pages 114–116 in Chapter 11; you may also wish to look ahead at the Chapter 21 section, "Waves" starting on Page 293.

If the swells are significant, landing parallel to the swell may be required. This will likely be a crosswind landing with the added problem that the swell (and the water at the surface) are moving perpendicular to the direction of landing, and the surface of the water is rising or falling. It is indeed a complex landing!

Confined Area Landing

The confined area approach and landing is very much like a short field approach and landing in a landplane except different deceleration techniques are used once on the surface. There is little need to put extra effort into decelerating the seaplane. Here are some hints:

- Apply full flaps after wings are level on final.
- Don't descend from 500 feet until the water touchdown spot is in sight and a 3° glidepath picture is seen.
- You may touchdown heels first but remember, speed is dissipated faster on the water than in the air. Use recommended "over the fence" speed, and use a little power during the roundout if you feel you need it because you *will* land short, and safety is most important.
- After touchdown, its power back, flaps up, then stick back, rudders down and, as soon as in displacement mode, turn 90°, and complete the checklist. Optionally, you may, after stick is back, walk the rudders slowly left, right, left, etc., to increase drag (but don't do that on your checkride without examiner's prior approval nor with a flight instructor aboard unless he or she has been briefed). The water run will be very short. The important part of this maneuver is the spot landing (a good approach with airspeeds "right on" is required) with proper flare and touchdown.

Glassy Water Approach and Landing

"Fly down close to the water with flaps and at 1.2 V_{SO} and 12" of manifold pressure. Pitch up to landing attitude. Count to three. Bring power to 16". Hold landing attitude until on the water."

Sound simple? Yes, but ***don't*** try it until you have logged several thousand glassy water landings and are doing at least twenty a month! The old, high-time bush pilot who described a glassy water landing with the words above knows all the tricks of how to judge "close to the water" without looking at the water. He knows the landing attitude of his floatplane precisely and how to control it. He knows exactly what power settings will provide what performance.

The Illusion

When the water is glassy, or the light is poor, or it is raining and the combination of water on the windshield and raindrop patterns on the water create an illusion of height above the surface, or the sun is in your eyes, or anything else that adversely affects your ability to clearly see the water surface, use a glassy water approach and landing! If you are not sure, use a glassy water approach and landing…it's safer and you need the practice.

If any of these conditions exist, the seaplane pilot will not be able to accurately judge height above the water. The only safe landing technique is the glassy water one.

The Glassy Water Landing Technique

The seaplane pilot positions the seaplane at a low but safe altitude above the water with the correct flap setting and correct pitch attitude, which gives correct airspeed and correct power setting, which in turn gives correct vertical speed. He or she then maintains this stable condition (absolutely no change in pitch attitude) until touchdown.

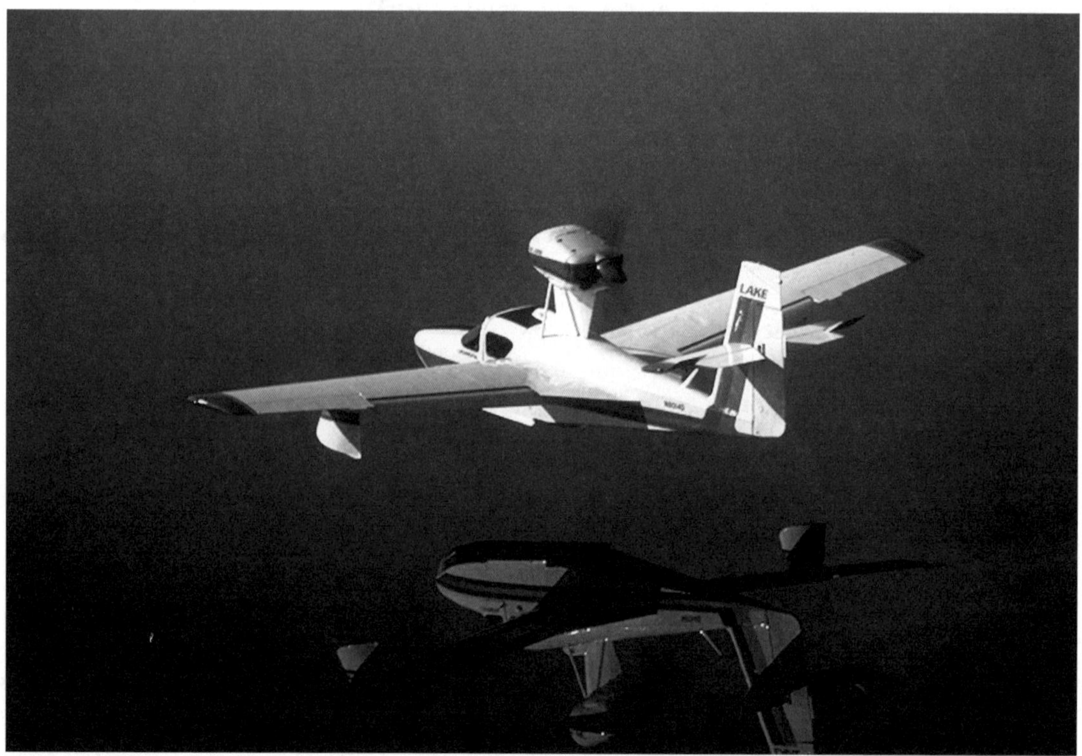

SPA

Figure 13-6. A Lake Amphibian just before a glassy water touchdown.

Here is how it is done.

Determining the Glassy Water Power Setting

While still at cruising altitude, if it looks like you might need to do a glassy water landing, take a moment while still inbound at a safe altitude and slow the airplane to the recommended glassy water landing speed (usually 1.1 to 1.2 V_{SO}). Set the recommended flaps, put the prop to flat pitch, and determine what power setting will provide a descent rate of 150 feet per minute at the correct airspeed. Don't use the VSI as it is not to be trusted (reference the VSI discussion in Chapter 20, Pages 286–287). Use the altimeter and clock.

Then remember that, any time you use that power setting (prop at flat pitch), airspeed, and flap setting with that load and density altitude, the airplane *will* provide *that* vertical speed.

Glassy Water Landing Area Assessment

The landing area assessment is the same as described in Chapter 12, except as follows: Choose the **glassy water landing path**. It needs to be:

- A **long stretch of water** because the gradual let down into the water uses up a considerable distance.
- preferably with the approach **over or near land** to provide the height information necessary for the initial positioning of the aircraft.
- with approach planned that takes advantage of any **low terrain** near the water, so the aircraft can be positioned initially at a lower altitude.
- with **Sun** position considered. It would be foolish to plan the landing path into the sun since, without wind, any landing direction may be used. If the sun is out and it is before mid morning or after mid afternoon or anytime at high latitudes (sun not more than 45° above the horizon), consider planning the landing path to put the sun over your right shoulder (*see* the shadow discussion on Page 118 of Chapter 11). Using the shadow is of primary importance should you need to land out in the middle of a large body of water.

A **landing path along the shore** is of questionable value for the same reasons as that of a takeoff along the shoreline. *See* the discussion about this in Chapter 11, Page 119.

Plan a longer than usual final to provide more time to correctly position the seaplane, acquire the correct altitude over the shoreline, and stabilize the airspeed.

The Stabilized Glassy Approach Configuration

Flaps

At the specified airspeed, more flaps will lower the nose and make the float entry to the water flatter. Most floatplanes, when a lot of flaps are used, will approach the water at a dangerously flat attitude that may result in a water loop. NEVER use more flaps than the manufacturer's recommendation for the glassy water flap setting.

Pitch Attitude

Once the correct flap setting and airspeed are achieved, note the pitch attitude (by looking outside, toward the horizon) and maintain that attitude precisely. Set the correct power setting, maintaining the noted pitch attitude. If the nose rises slightly,

Bill McCarrel

Figure 13-7. The sun shines on a Cub on a glassy, no horizon morning.

airspeed will decrease, drag will increase, and descent rate will increase. Maintaining the correct pitch attitude is critical.

If there is no discernable horizon, pitch reference must come from the aircraft instruments. It is far more difficult to maintain an accurate pitch attitude when looking at the attitude indicator than when looking at a distant object or line outside the window. While the attitude indicator gives general attitude information, the most accurate pitch instrument in this situation is the airspeed indicator. For all glassy approaches, set abort airspeed limits. For example, I add power and go around if airspeed on approach falls below 55 or goes above 65 (60 being the target airspeed). If pitch adjustments are needed, make very small changes.

Trim

Once wings are level on final, the final flap setting has been made, and airspeed is correct, trim to neutral control pressure. Since elevator (pitch) always controls airspeed, proper trim will help you control airspeed for the rest of the approach. If doing an obstacled glassy approach, the last power adjustment (at 50' AWL) occurs after trimming and will provide a slight need for forward pressure, but you will hardly notice it. As the aircraft soon comes into ground effect, the nose will pitch slightly down, thus neutralizing that brief need for light forward stick pressure. See the discussion of ground effect below.

Power

Power always controls vertical speed (stabilized airspeed). If flap setting is correct and airspeed is on target, the correct power setting will provide the correct vertical speed. Therefore, there is no need to look at the VSI. (Its indications are 7 or 8 seconds behind what the airplane is doing, and it will probably lie to you even if you are willing to wait.) If you must steal a glance inside, look at the airspeed indicator, but only for an instant because you cannot fly the correct pitch attitude if you are not looking outside!

Ground Effect

For reasons well explained in most books on aerodynamics, ground effect decreases elevator effectiveness. Since the elevator is helping the entire horizontal tail surface to lift downward (holding the nose up), a decrease in downward lift (caused by ground effect) will cause a very mild nose-pitch-down moment.

The seaplane will tell you when it descends into ground effect.

On a very calm, glassy water day, if you "freeze" the elevator control, you will see the nose pitch down as the seaplane comes into ground effect. If you don't freeze the control but do pay attention to the fact that you are automatically pulling back slightly on the stick to maintain the correct attitude, you will know that the airplane has entered ground effect, so you will have a clue as to how high you are. Don't use that clue as reason to change anything! Just know that the approach is going as planned and your floats are now about 15–20 feet above water.

The Glassy Approach Over Obstacles

There are many ways to teach and conduct a glassy water approach over an obstacle. Some of those ways are good, some are terrible! The worst I have seen utilizes the VSI during the approach. Don't let anybody teach you this, as it is a recipe for disaster (see discussions of the VSI elsewhere in the book). Here is how I like to do it.

Never use VSI during a glassy approach.

After the assessment where I have chosen a stretch of water that is long enough with an approach path that utilizes the lowest terrain near the water, I make a slightly longer than normal final to allow more time to get stabilized and to correct the glidepath. Since I want a fairly steep approach angle over the obstacle to keep from using up too much water distance after the obstacle, and once wings are level on final, *and* I can see the touchdown point on the water, I set recommended glassy flap setting and my "standard approach" power setting (12" manifold pressure in most seaplanes and landplanes with normally aspirated engines). I then trim for 1.3 V_{SO} (about 70 in most seaplanes). I keep the wings level and adjust power so the seaplane arrives over the obstacle with the float bottoms just barely above the obstacle at 70 IAS. If you are higher than that, you will waste valuable water runway, gliding down. Note: use the manufacturer's recommended airspeeds and flap settings.

Once the obstacle is cleared, I look out, usually 30–45° to the left, and wait until I am level with the top of a tree that is closest to the beach, or I use some other terrain feature to judge when I am 50' AWL. At that point, I pitch up to landing attitude and wait for the airspeed to bleed down to 1.2 V_{SO} (65 IAS). I briskly bring the power up to the predetermined value (16" ±0.5" for a Cessna 180 that isn't plagued with having a "U" engine). By the time power is applied, speed will further decay to about 60 IAS, the target airspeed. Then, looking outside, I maintain that exact attitude until water contact, stealing a quick, occasional glance at the airspeed to be sure it is within limits (55 to 65). Once I think I'm on the water, I use my peripheral vision to look for spray coming out from the floats to confirm I am on water before pulling the power back to idle. Then remember, rudders, flaps and checklist!

A good glassy landing is so smooth you need to check for spray to be sure you are on the water before throttling back.

The Glassy Approach: No Obstacles

After the assessment during which I have chosen a stretch of water that is long enough and has an approach path that utilizes the lowest terrain near the water, I make a slightly longer than normal final to allow more time to get stabilized at glassy water touchdown speed, with correct flap setting. Before losing sight of the beach, I must be at correct attitude, airspeed and preselected power setting, and low over the beach. Then, looking outside, I just maintain that exact attitude until water contact, stealing a quick, occasional glance at the airspeed to be sure it is within limits. Once I think I'm on the water, I use my peripheral vision to look for spray coming out from the floats to confirm I'm on the water before pulling the power back to idle. Then remember, rudders, flaps and checklist!

Go-Around

If you are not an expert at go-arounds, perhaps you should be, because it is a safety maneuver. Every approach to a landing should be thought of as an approach to a go-around which, if everything is perfect, will be converted into a landing maneuver. A go-around is a good maneuver. It reeks of safety. It is done by good, safety-minded pilots.

If this airplane is new to you, or if you haven't done a go-around on floats for awhile, it is recommended that you practice at a safe altitude to get used to the control forces that will be required to counteract the strong nose-up trim forces and avoid an elevator trim stall (*see* discussion of this on the next page).

Smoothly apply maximum allowable power, level the airplane's wings, and transition to a climb pitch attitude that will slow or stop the descent. After the descent has been stopped, landing flaps should be partially retracted and set as recommended by the manufacturer. In the absence of such a procedure, the flaps should be positioned to a climb or takeoff setting until V_Y speed is achieved. Then remember, all airplanes climb better with flaps up. Caution must be used in retracting the flaps. Depending on the airplane's altitude and airspeed, it may be wise to retract the flaps in small increments to allow time for the airplane to accelerate properly.

Particularly when operating into confined areas, or onto water surfaces that have high terrain close to shore (embedded water surfaces), a good general rule is that the go-around must be initiated before going below tree-top or top-of-terrain height. Generally, the aircraft is committed to landing once below tree-top height.

For the go-around and climb out, use the departure path that was planned during the landing area assessment.

Elevator Trim Stall Avoidance

The elevator trim stall can occur when full power is applied for a go-around and control of the airplane is not maintained. Such a situation may occur during a go-around procedure from a normal landing approach, or a simulated forced-landing approach, or immediately after a takeoff. The objective of practicing go-arounds at a safe altitude is to demonstrate how important it is to make smooth power applications, to overcome strong trim forces, and to maintain control of the airplane in order to hold safe flight attitudes. Use proper and timely trim techniques to both avoid stall and to become proficient at go-around recovery with no or minimal altitude loss.

At a safe altitude and after ensuring the area is clear of other air traffic, the pilot should slowly retard the throttle, extend full flaps, close the throttle, prop to high RPM and maintain altitude until glide speed is established. Then trim to maintain glide speed just as you would during a landing approach (nose up trim).

During this simulated final approach glide, when a target altitude is reached, the throttle is advanced smoothly to maximum allowable power as would be done in a go-around procedure. The combined forces of thrust, torque, and back-elevator trim will tend to make the nose rise sharply and turn to the left. When the throttle is fully advanced, climb pitch attitude is established and climb flaps are set which results in a positive climb rate and very slow acceleration. Remember the altitude loss (if any), attitude, and required control pressure so you will know what to expect next time. Most aircraft will require a decrease in flap setting before they will climb well. Trim for climb airspeed.

This maneuver should be practiced at a safe altitude until it is apparent that no stall danger exists and altitude loss is negligible once the go-around is initiated.

Landing type	Difference from normal	Used for	Do not use for	Danger elements
Normal	See normal landing description.	General use.		
Crosswind	Establish the angle of bank needed to "stop" the sideways movement of wavelets, then double it. Landing on one float is just like landing on one main wheel. Keep the same aileron control input you had at touchdown and the downwind float will come down soon, but smoothly. Then smoothly input FULL aileron into the wind as soon as both floats are in the water and keep it there. In displacement taxi mode, water rudders and checklist. If you feel like too much bank angle is needed (concerned about catching a wingtip in the water), go around and don't land there. Landing in strong crosswinds should be avoided.	Crosswind conditions	[Crosswinds ONLY]	Drifting downwind at touchdown.
Rough water	Carefully plan for the taxi to shore. Landing is always done into the wind with both floats contacting the water at the same time. Use full flaps and whatever power is needed to let yourself gently down into the smoothest water patch you can find, at just above stall speed. The smoothest water is the lightest colored water patches. Pitch level just after touchdown, run out with a flat attitude ending up with the stick all the way forward, stick all the way back as soon as in displacement taxi mode, water rudders and checklist.	Rough water.	Any landing not directly into the wind.	Turbulence; attempting a taxi turn to downwind.
Confined area	Very much like a short field approach and landing in a landplane except different deceleration techniques are used, once on the surface. The important part of this maneuver is the spot landing (a good approach is required) and proper flare and touchdown. • Apply full flaps after wings are level on final. • Don't start down from 500 feet until the water touchdown spot is in sight and a 3° glidepath picture is seen. • It is fine to touchdown heels first. Use recommended "over the fence" speed and probably a little power during the roundout. • After touchdown, it's power back, flaps up then stick back, rudders down, and as soon as in displacement mode, turn 90°, complete checklist.	Short landing area.	Confined area glassy landings are for highly experienced seaplane pilots only.	Takeoff from that confined area.
Glassy water	When the water is glassy, or even nearly glassy, or the light is poor, or it is raining and the combination of water on the windshield and raindrop patterns on the water create an illusion of height above the surface, or the sun is in your eyes, or anything else that adversely affects your ability to clearly see the water surface, use a glassy water approach and landing! If any of these conditions exist, you will not be able to accurately judge height above the water. The only safe landing technique is to use the glassy water technique. You position the seaplane at a low-but-safe altitude above the water with the correct flap setting, correct pitch attitude which gives correct airspeed and correct power setting which gives correct vertical speed, then maintain this stable condition (absolutely no change in pitch attitude) until touchdown. Refer to the discussion of the subject in the main text for details (Page 155).	Any glassy or near glassy conditions, poor visibility or night landings. Get good glassy water landing recurrent instruction annually and practice periodically.		Failure to recognize the need to use glassy procedure; engine failure over glassy water; confined area glassy landing attempts.
Go-around	Every approach to a landing should be thought of as an approach to a go-around which, if everything is perfect, will be converted into a landing maneuver. A go-around is a good maneuver. It reeks of safety. It is made by good, safety-minded pilots. Smoothly apply maximum allowable power, level the airplane's wings and transition to a climb pitch attitude that will slow or stop the descent. After the descent has been stopped, landing flaps should be partially retracted and set as recommended by the manufacturer. When operating into water surfaces that are embedded, with high terrain close to shore and especially into confined areas, a good general rule is that the go-around must be initiated before going below tree-top or top-of-terrain height. Generally, the aircraft is committed to landing once below tree-top height. Use the departure path that was planned during the landing area assessment.			

Figure 13-8. Summary of landing types

Review

The seaplane pilot's normal approach differs somewhat from that in a landplane. The "safest approach path" rule applies.

Remember, eyes outside at least 95 percent of the time. Make frequent radio position reports. It is proper safety procedure. Downwind leg is flown, keeping the pattern in close and slowing to about 1.4 V_{SO}. Turn base closer in because:

1. The traffic pattern is at 500', not 800' or 1,200' as you are accustomed to in a landplane.
2. The seaplane has more drag than the landplanes you fly, so the glide angle with partial or no power will be steeper.
3. It is easy to lose sight of the touchdown point unless a close pattern is flown.
4. Descent from traffic pattern altitude should not begin unless the touchdown spot is in sight.

A properly flown close pattern does not require steeply banked turns. It does require good airspeed control and proper planning as to when to turn from base to final. All airplanes have specific power settings for use with certain configurations. Learn from the airplane what they are and use them.

Keep it simple. Use one airspeed in the pattern, about 1.4 V_{SO} (rounded to the next higher airspeed indicator marking—it is easier to remember and see), until your wings are level on final.

Floatplanes like to slow down and mush, developing high rates of sink.

Base leg is relatively short, with partial flaps applied while wings are level. The turn to **final** is made early enough to permit a medium bank of not more than 30°; 20° is better for passenger comfort.

Final is flown normally except it will be short because you are flying a close pattern.

Set landing flaps after leveling wings on final. ***Always*** be looking outside when you change flap setting.

The **roundout**, or **flare**, should start a little higher than in a landplane and the pilot must assure that a safe touchdown attitude is achieved (usually the same attitude as when displacement taxiing on the water) before getting close to the water.

Upon touchdown, don't relax pressure on the elevator! Continue to fly the touchdown attitude or, if you wish to decelerate faster, raise the flaps and use full up elevator.

A few things to consider when flying near the surface in strong **gusts**:

Protect the airplane. If you are at or below V_A speed, the aircraft will not be damaged by full control movements in calm air or excessive turbulence if no severe control movements are used during the turbulence. Lower flaps and you make the airplane *tender*.

Roll turbulence. Only airspeed determines how much aileron authority is available to counteract roll turbulence. When it's gusty, keep your flaps and speed up until you are in ground effect. Use normal approach speed plus one-half of the wind gust factor. Be sure you know how to determine the gust factor.

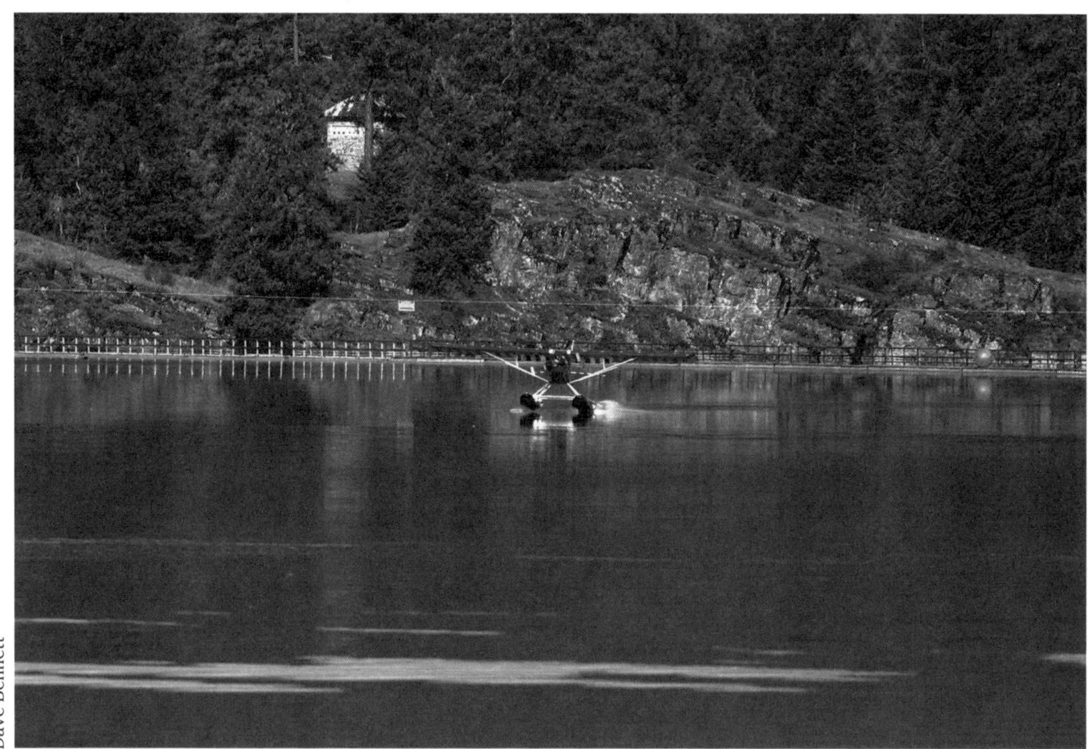

Dave Bennett

Just after touchdown on a nearly glassy resevoir in Montana. Glassy water technique definitely needed here!

SPA

When floats are installed, they typically lower the aircraft's stall speed somewhat.

Chapter 14
Slow Flight, Steep Turns, and Stalls

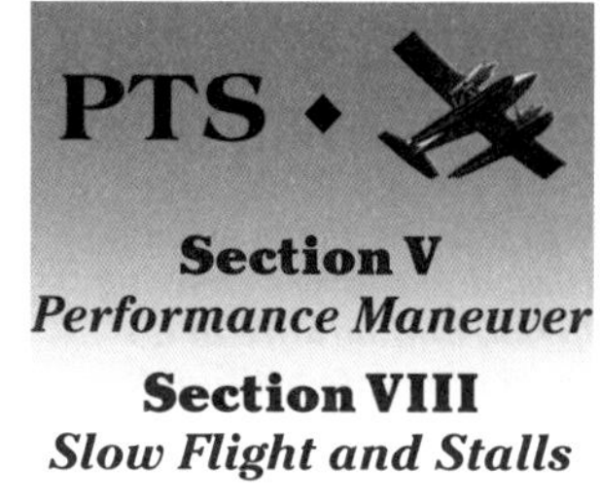

PTS •
Section V
Performance Maneuver
Section VIII
Slow Flight and Stalls

When I was a young pilot, I just couldn't understand why I should regularly practice maneuvers like slow flight, steep turns, and stalls. When I became a flight instructor, I found that many pilots did not like to practice or demonstrate their skills of stall recovery. Then I looked at the accident statistics, and it became very clear to me why the FAA and NTSB stress stall awareness. Far too many fatalities are the result of stall/spin scenarios. For seaplanes, the statistics show an even higher incidence of fatal accidents are stall/spin related. As a licensed seaplane pilot, you may think "couldn't happen to me." I hope you are right. A review of this chapter should help that come true.

If you were preparing for the seaplane checkride before August 2002, you could expect your examiner to stress this area because the FAA, in its accident prevention program, was asking examiners to do so. With the advent of the Practical Test Standards that became effective August 2002, the requirement for demonstrating these maneuvers on the checkride ended. The reason given was because you demonstrated this skill as a landplane pilot. In my opinion, it is still ***very*** important that you acquire these skills in a seaplane with your flight instructor, then practice them periodically! Be sure your flight instructor covers this information well and lets you practice until you feel confident performing these maneuvers. The life you save may be your own! Seaplanes, particularly heavily loaded seaplanes, recover from stall more slowly than their landplane counterparts with much greater altitude loss. Reading this chapter may help you understand why.

Heavily loaded seaplanes recover from stall more slowly than their landplane counterparts, with much greater altitude loss. Stall recovery should be practiced!

Slow Flight

The objective of maneuvering during slow flight is to develop the pilot's sense of feel and ability to use the controls correctly, and to improve proficiency in performing maneuvers that require slow airspeeds. Maneuvering during slow flight should be performed using both instrument indications and outside visual reference. Hint: it is a lot easier to do in a seaplane if you are looking outside 90+% of the time!

The floatplane will seem heavy and lumbering compared to the landplane. Somewhat like transitioning from a sedan to a truck. More power will be needed, and it is likely that your feet will discover what the rudder pedals are for, since there are now three air rudders (the two water rudders, if they are up, provide another 20–40% air rudder surface area); the rudder system is encumbered with many more cables and pulleys that increase friction, which resists control movement. If you are transitioning from landplanes, it is normal to experience a little trouble keeping the ball centered at first. You will soon get past this problem.

Slow flight and stall recovery are much easier to do if you are looking outside.

A little practice doing slow flight will have you doing it well and gaining confidence in your ability to control the seaplane at low airspeeds. However, I suspect you will join me in agreeing that, when near the surface (landing area assessment, turns to base and final, etc.), there is a real need to keep your speed up!

When doing these maneuvers, don't forget clearing turns, and be sure to do them at a safe altitude!

Slow flight is defined as flight at any airspeed that is less than cruise airspeed. However, flight should be practiced at the slowest airspeed at which the airplane is capable of maintaining controlled flight without stalling, usually at 3 to 5 knots above stalling speed. The FAA defines the term "flight at minimum airspeed" as a speed at which any further increase in angle of attack or load factor, or reduction in power, will cause an immediate stall. This airspeed will depend upon various circumstances, such as the gross weight and CG location of the airplane and maneuvering load imposed by turns and pullups. Flight at minimum airspeed should include climbs, turns, and descents. It requires positive use of rudder and ailerons to counteract three things: asymmetrical loading of the propeller (to counteract yaw to the left), the action of the corkscrewing slipstream (to counteract yaw and roll to the left), and torque (mostly roll to the left and some yaw left from the down aileron) reaction. Rolling in and out of turns requires more rudder input than rolling at normal airspeeds because of decreased airflow over the control surface and greater displacement of the ailerons needed at minimum airspeed. Remember, the down aileron is *always* the "draggier" of the two ailerons. The down aileron provides yaw to the outside of the turn (adverse aileron yaw) causing the need for more rudder while rolling into the turn. As a new seaplane pilot you can expect some trouble keeping the ball centered while maneuvering, but your feet will soon learn what pressures on the rudder are needed to keep the ball centered.

The down aileron is always the draggiest aileron.

Hint: Have you ever wondered how your flight instructor knows, while looking out the window, that you don't have the ball centered? It's easy. Your body leans in the same direction as the ball. So, if the ball is off center to the right, you will lean to the right. Whichever cheek you are sitting on the most, is the rudder that needs more pressure. Now you are freed forever from having to watch the ball. Just "feel" it! Why does the ball have to be centered?

Your body leans in the same direction as the ball!

1. The airplane flies faster, climbs better and glides farther if the ball is centered.
2. When the airplane stalls, a spin is much less likely to develop if the ball is centered.
3. It is an indicator (to the examiner and anyone else that is watching you fly) that the seaplane is under your control and you are using good piloting technique.
4. Uncoordinated flight increases the likelihood of passenger's discomfort and airsickness.

Slow flight also demonstrates to the seaplane pilot one of the most important climb performance characteristics: A positive rate of climb may not be possible at slow speeds due to the lack of available power in excess of that required to maintain straight-and-level flight at the minimum airspeed. In most seaplanes, an attempt to climb at slow airspeeds (much below V_Y) results in poor climb performance and may result in a loss of altitude, even with maximum power applied—a perfect demonstration that the airplane climbs best at V_Y. Speeds below V_Y may result in negative rates of climb even at full power. Raising the nose to clear an obstacle can easily result in ***not*** clearing the obstacle. Airspeed management is the key!

A positive rate of climb may not be possible at slow speeds, even with full power.

The airplane climbs best at V_Y and most airplanes climb best with flaps up.

The above described characteristic is sometimes referred to as the *region of reverse command*, a potentially dangerous flight condition wherein pulling back on the stick causes the airplane to go down, not up. You will read about this flight condition again in the discussion on emergency power-off glides (Page 182), a situation that is *really* dangerous.

Flight at minimum airspeed will help you develop the skill to estimate *by feel* the margin of safety above the stalling speed. With floats installed, the seaplane may stall at a lower airspeed due to the lift provided by the floats, so first ask the airplane to show you what the values of V_{SO} and V_{SFE} really are by stalling the seaplane, flaps up and power off, with airspeed decreasing 1 to 3 MPH or knots per second. Then repeat, with flaps extended. Note the airspeeds, which should be at or just below the bottom of the green/white arcs on the airspeed indicator. Make sure the throttle is completely retarded and that you accomplish these maneuvers at a safe altitude.

How to calibrate your airspeed indicator.

Having completed a V_{SO}/V_{SFE} check, you have also accomplished another very necessary task of the seaplane pilot…an airspeed indicator calibration (low airspeed end). A number of things can adversely affect the accuracy of the airspeed indicator, such as partial blockage of the pitot or static ports or tubes, cracks in the plastic pitot or static port tubes, or accumulations of particles in the Bourdon tube of the instrument itself. Accuracy of the airspeed indicator is rarely, if ever, checked unless the pilot checks it! Accuracy in the low airspeed range is what we pilots are most interested in, isn't it? It is easy to check. If the airspeed indicator is lying to you, it is nice to learn that…at a safe altitude!

Steep Turns

Although the steep turn maneuver is not performed during everyday flying, it aids the pilot in analyzing the forces acting on the airplane and in developing a fine control touch, coordination, and division of attention for accurate and safe maneuvering. Its most relevant application is for performing an emergency descent (which is discussed in the next chapter).

Steep turns should never be attempted with flaps extended.

The steep turn maneuver consists of a turn in either direction, using a bank angle between 45 and 60°. This will cause an overbanking tendency (the airplane wants to bank even steeper) during which maximum turning performance is attained and relatively high load factors are imposed. A 60° banked turn imposes 2 Gs on the airplane and its contents (you). Because of the high load factors imposed, these turns should be performed at an airspeed that does not exceed the airplane's design maneuvering speed (V_A). Steep turns should never be attempted with flaps extended, because the maximum design load factor, with flaps extended, of most general aviation aircraft is 2.0. Up elevator force during a 60° bank would exceed this.

The principles of an ordinary steep turn apply, but as a practice maneuver, the steep turns should be continued until 360° or 720° of turn have been completed. You can judge your proficiency with steep turns to be good when you can continue the turn through 720°, roll into a steep turn in the other direction, then fly it for 720° while maintaining target angle of bank and altitude within ±100 feet (±50 feet for commercial). Take your time entering and exiting the steep turn. Just be sure to complete the entry or exit within 90° of turn.

Keep in mind that if a steep turn is made, the increase in angle of attack to maintain altitude may result in a stall, so don't combine slow flight with steep turns. A stall may also occur as a result of abrupt or rough control movements when flying at slow flight. Abruptly raising the flaps during slow flight will cause a sudden loss in lift and the airplane will lose altitude, stall or both. It is easy to calculate what the increased stall speed will be in a steep turn. It will be the level flight (load factor = 1.0) stall speed multiplied by the square root of the load factor. For example, if your seaplane's stall speed is 50, in a 60° bank the load factor is 2.0, so stall speed = $50 \times (2)^{1/2}$. The square root of 2 is 1.41, so $50 \times 1.41 = 70.5$. To fly safely in a 60° bank, airspeed must be kept above 70.5 and below V_A speed. Keep in mind that any increased back pressure, such as that needed to regain lost altitude, will further raise the stall speed we just calculated! I just remember that stall speed will increase by about 40% when going from level flight to a 60° bank.

In a 60° bank, stall speed increases by over 40 percent.

You will find the seaplane like a truck compared to the landplane you have been flying. Heavy control pressures and lots of power will probably be needed. If you are flying a Cessna with a seaplane kit installed, the V bars between you and the windshield make wonderful references for establishing bank angles. Learn to use the V bars to measure the correct angle with the horizon, and you will have a "heads up display" to replace the attitude indicator. It is so much easier to do this maneuver while looking out the window! The rollout from the turn should be timed so that the wings reach level flight when the airplane is exactly on the heading from which the maneuver was started. While the recovery is being made, back-elevator pressure is gradually released and power reduced, as necessary, to maintain the altitude and airspeed. Practice makes perfect! I hope you will agree with me that a steep turn is ***not*** a maneuver to be used for landing area assessment. Don't forget clearing turns and safe altitude, and ***never*** do 60°-banked steep turns with flaps extended (remember, with flaps extended, limit load factor is only 2.0).

You should become skilled in doing steep turns.

You should become skilled in doing steep turns, because that skill is the basis for doing emergency descents while performing two other tasks simultaneously. You will understand the above sentence better after reading the discussion about emergency descents in the next chapter.

Stalls

Stalls in the seaplane are a little different than those in the landplane. Like the landplane, stalls may differ in each airplane due to variations in rigging, bends, dents, etc. The seaplane will seem heavier, drag is greater, and recovery performance will be slower.

Since the seaplane often flies closer to the ground, recovery from stalls with minimum altitude loss is important, and this takes practice in a heavily loaded seaplane on a warm day. To recover most heavily loaded seaplanes with minimum altitude loss, it is necessary to fly the seaplane *through* the secondary stall rather than avoiding the secondary stall as you have been taught to do. This is an advanced technique that should be learned from and practiced with a highly experienced flight instructor, at a safe altitude, in an airplane you are familiar with. By doing so, you will come to understand that, in the first scenario described in the "stall-spin fatal accident" section below, only a small amount of elevator back pressure separates a stall-spin fatal accident from adequate control of the seaplane.

I highly recommend you also read the section about stalls in Chapter 5 of the **Airplane Flying Handbook** ***(FAA-H-8083-3) while studying this section.***

Power-Off Stall

Acquire sufficient altitude so that you can finish the maneuver at least 1,500 feet AGL, then reduce power to slow to about V_Y speed, and hold altitude while doing clearing turns. Then set flaps. Both flaps up and approach flap setting should be practiced. Apply carb heat as necessary, and reduce power to idle while holding altitude until stall. Your flight instructor may want you to establish a glide, simulating approach, and stall from the glide as well. A good exercise I like to use is for the pilot to demonstrate all stalls, including power-on, without gaining or losing more than 100 feet from the target altitude. This requires recovery from the stall in less than 100 feet of altitude loss (this may take some practice) as well as power management during power-on stall demonstrations to keep from climbing above target altitude +100 feet.

Power-off stalls will result in the greatest altitude loss.

One of the most important parts of stall recovery to prevent altitude loss is getting that nose up to climb attitude as soon as the airspeed indicator increases to above V_{SO}. Otherwise, you lose too much altitude. The climb attitude used should be such that the airspeed will continue to increase slowly to V_Y. Don't forget the carb heat! Get in the habit of pushing the carb heat control in as soon as power is applied. When carb heat is on, the engine's ability to produce power is significantly limited.

Power-On Stall

Power-on stalls seem easier because, if the ball is centered during the stall, all that is needed to recover is to lower the nose to climb attitude and ensure that the airspeed is increasing.

If the ball is not centered during the stall, a wing will drop quickly, beginning a spin entry. Recovery from this is the same as normal spin recovery. Altitude loss will be great, and if it happens within a few hundred feet of the ground, it's usually "game over."

Spin Awareness

The Stall-Spin Fatal Accident

An astonishingly high percentage of *fatal* seaplane accidents are stall-spin accidents. They occur primarily in two scenarios:

An astonishingly high percentage of fatal seaplane accidents are stall-spin accidents.

The first, and most common, is a heavily laden seaplane departing from a waterway that is obstacled and too short for the loading, pilot technique, and density altitude conditions. The seaplane becomes airborne but won't climb over the obstacle in time. In an attempt to climb, the pilot pulls back on the stick, induces a full power-on stall, a wing drops, followed by the nose, resulting in an out-of-control crash.

An alternate to this scenario is where the pilot realizes impact with the obstacle is eminent and throttles back with nose high, inducing stall, wing drop, etc.

For the above, prevention is the best solution. The pilot analyzes the situation and makes a decision to err in favor of safety by not attempting a "close" takeoff, or by using the Delta Ratio method to determine whether the takeoff is possible before leaving the water. That method is well documented in the book *Water Flying Concepts*.

If ever faced with the above scenario and already airborne, most experts agree that it is far better to maintain climb airspeed and power, even if the result is a controlled impact with the obstacle, rather than an out-of-control impact with a high rate of sink. The high rate of sink puts you into the harder, stronger parts of the tree before the aircraft has had a chance to slow down. Many seaplanes have landed without fatal injuries in the tops of trees because vertical speed was zero at the time of contact with the tree's foliage.

The second scenario I have witnessed many times while conducting biennial flight reviews. It occurs when the pilot is faced with an engine failure and the need to glide the maximum distance. It is very tempting, when needing to stretch the glide, to pull back on the stick to coax the airplane over that last obstacle. Just the opposite actually happens: the nose pitches up, the airspeed decreases, drag increases, sink rate increases, so instead of gliding farther, the glide path steepens, the stick is brought back further, and the pilot experiences stall and loss of control. *See* the "airspeed is life itself" discussion in Chapter 15, Page 182.

Seaplane stall accidents almost always result in fatalities. This is why stall recognition is so important. You must know the scenarios where stalls are likely to occur in order to be forewarned. You must know how to recognize the onset of stall in order to take preventative action. You must train yourself in stall recovery and know that, once a spin is induced, recovery is impossible if the seaplane is within a few hundred feet of the surface. When within a few hundred feet of the surface, *stall avoidance is mandatory* if you expect to see another sunrise!

When within a few hundred feet of the surface, stall avoidance is mandatory if you expect to see another sunrise!

John Lowery

One gruesome result of a stall-spin accident.

Review

Slow Flight

Objective: to develop the pilot's sense of feel and ability to use the controls correctly, and to improve proficiency in performing maneuvers that require slow airspeeds. Should be practiced and demonstrated at 3 to 5 knots above stalling speed, and include climbs, turns, and descents.

- The down aileron provides yaw to the outside of the turn (adverse aileron yaw) causing the need for more rudder while rolling into the turn.
- If the ball is off center to the right, you will be leaning to the right.
- A positive rate of climb may not be possible at slow speeds; very poor climb performance and possible loss of altitude is the result in most seaplanes, even with maximum power.
- Raising the nose to clear an obstacle can easily result in ***not*** clearing the obstacle.
- The seaplane with floats installed may stall at a lower airspeed due to the lift provided by the floats. Ask the airplane to show you what the values of V_{SO} and V_{SFE} really are by stalling the seaplane—which also accomplishes an airspeed indicator calibration (low airspeed end).

Steep Turns

Consists of a turn in either direction, using a bank angle between 45 and 60°, which will cause an overbanking tendency, maximum turning performance, and relatively high load factors.

- A 60° banked turn imposes 2 Gs on the airplane and its contents.
- In a steep turn, the increase in angle of attack to maintain altitude may result in a stall.
- A stall may also occur as a result of abrupt or rough control movements when flying at slow flight speed.
- Abruptly raising the flaps during slow flight will cause a sudden loss of lift and the airplane to lose altitude, stall or both.
- It is easy to calculate what the increased stall speed will be in a steep turn.

Stalls

Stalls in the seaplane differ from those in the landplane. The seaplane will seem heavier, drag is greater and recovery performance will be less. Describe the characteristics of a power-off stall and how to recover with minimum altitude loss. If the ball is not centered during the stall, a wing will drop quickly, beginning a spin entry. Recovery from this is the same as normal spin recovery, but expect a tremendous altitude loss.

Spin Awareness

Stall-spin accidents are a high percentage of *fatal* seaplane accidents:

- Often it is a waterway that is obstacled and too short for the loading, pilot technique, and density altitude conditions. The seaplane becomes airborne but won't climb over the obstacle in time, and the pilot induces a full power-on stall, a wing drops, followed by the nose, resulting in an out-of-control crash. Prevention is the best solution. The pilot analyzes the situation and makes a decision to halt a close takeoff, or use instead the Delta Ratio method; the pilot maintains climb airspeed and power, even if the result is a controlled impact with the obstacle, rather than out-of-control impact with a high rate of sink.
- Or, a pilot is faced with an engine failure and the need to glide the maximum distance. When needing to stretch the glide, the pilot is tempted to pull back on the stick to coax the airplane over that last obstacle. Instead the nose pitches up, the airspeed decreases, drag increases, sink rate increases. Instead of gliding farther, the glide path steepens, the stick is brought back further, causing a stall and loss of control.
- Airspeed is life itself!

A little humorous pilot advice from 1919: "If you are going to crash, try to hit the softest, cheapest thing you can as slowly as possible." Good advice! But please, not so slowly that you stall and lose control, because then you are no longer pilot-*in-command* and will be unable to follow the above advice.

Burke Mees

Busy docks in floatplane country.

Chapter 15
Emergency Operations

In the air, the seaplane differs little from the landplane. As a licensed pilot, you are expected to be familiar with emergency procedures. At this point I recommend you review them by reading the *Airplane Flying Handbook*, Chapter 12 "Emergency Operations." Then read this chapter about emergency strategies as they apply to seaplanes.

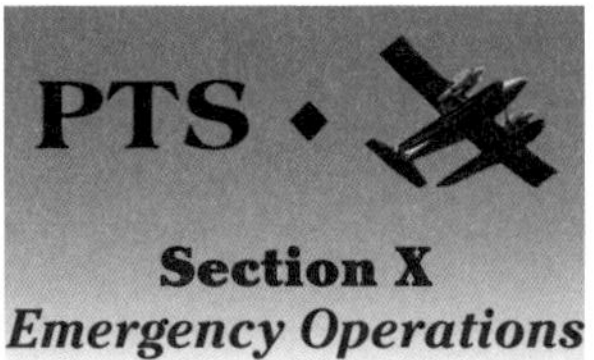

Emergency Descents

An emergency descent is a procedure for descending to traffic pattern altitude as quickly as possible without overstressing the airplane or its components. The principal reason for use in a seaplane is in the case of an in-flight fire. Let's take a moment here and talk about handling in-flight fires. The emergency descent technique is discussed in detail after that.

In-flight Fires

I have had four in-flight fires in my 45 years of flying, so I have been a great listener when the subject has come up. To me, the biggest danger of an in-flight fire is inhaling pyrotoxins. All smoke is toxic when inhaled, but the combustion products from some materials are extremely toxic. Smoke from burning insulation (including electrical wire insulation), carpet, upholstery and padding is extremely toxic. Even if you recover from breathing it, the event will probably shorten your life and cause respiratory problems in later years. In the event of an in-flight fire, the thing I want most is *out of the airplane, and quickly!* This is where the emergency descent is most useful.

Pyrotoxins are a major personal danger.

Second, but still very important, is the structural damage fire can cause, if it is allowed to continue. So, time is of the essence! Once smoke is detected, start that emergency descent! On the way down, analyze the problem, locate the fire, its fuel source and ignition source. Your nose will probably tell you whether the smoke is from an electrical fire or a fuel/oil fire, although some burning paints smell like burning electrical insulation, so it is possible to misdiagnose a fire (another reason why time is of the essence).

Electrical Fire

If electrical, remove the ignition source by shutting off ***all*** electrical systems and attempt to clear the smoke by opening a window. If the smoke clears, land as soon as possible and investigate. If one or more electrical systems are essential, bring only those back on line. If, after shutting off all systems, the smoke persists, land immediately.

Fuel/Oil Fire

If your nose detects what smells like burning oil, or smoke/flames can be seen coming from the engine compartment, or a smoke contrail can be seen after a 45° turn, shut off the fuel completely. The pilot's judgment becomes very important here as a decision must be made whether to stop the engine or continue to use it to reach a position over a safe landing place.

Include the exhaust stack on your daily preflight.

The best defense against fuel/oil fires is a thorough preflight inspection. Always include the exhaust stack as a preflight check item. Grab it and see if you can move it. If it moves, something inside is loose in the exhaust manifold system, which can allow exhaust fire to be loose in the engine compartment. Check the belly of the aircraft aft of the firewall for indications of oil or fuel stains (100LL will stain blue, autogas will stain yellow/brown). Check the inside of the engine compartment for oil and gas leaks.

Emergency Descent Techniques

Pilots who fly parachutists can teach us a few things about quick descents. They typically beat the parachutists to the ground, and they do it without overstressing the airframe or rapidly cooling the engine. Here are the basics:

Airspeed control is of utmost importance. Higher airspeed provides the most drag but V_A speed should not be exceeded if the air is rough. In smooth air, speeds up to V_{NO} are OK with a 45° bank but only with flaps up. If flaps are used, V_{FE} must not be exceeded. Typically, flaps are not used because rougher air is usually encountered at lower altitudes, which adds to the load factor in the steep banked descent. Remember, with flaps out, load factor decreases from 3.8 or more down to 2.0. The airplane is more "tender" with flaps out. The emergency descent is terminated with the emergency approach (discussion follows) and that is usually the time for flaps. Always follow the manufacturer's recommendations for the maneuver.

Properly done, the emergency descent is performed with constant airspeed and bank angle (45° to 60°) with power set above idle to prevent rapid engine cooling. Some pilots like to use carburetor heat as well, to decrease rapid engine cooling. If the airplane is equipped with constant-speed propeller, prop should be set to flat pitch (high RPM) for most drag. Practice the emergency descent until you can maintain a constant airspeed and steep bank angle while diverting part of your attention to troubleshooting the fire problem and analyzing where and how to make the emergency landing. Workload is very high during the emergency descent, so you need to be very familiar with flying the airplane in a steep turn, because it is the steep turn that allows the high rate of descent without exceeding speed limits.

Emergency descent:
- Airspeed control
- No flaps
- 45° to 60° bank
- Prop in (high RPM)
- Carb heat on, cowl flaps closed
- Maintain airspeed while assessing problem and selecting landing site

A Final Note Regarding Emergency Descents

With the advent of the revised PTS that was effective August 2002, demonstrating emergency descents is no longer required. However, there is no reason why your examiner can't give you an emergency in-flight fire simulation at altitude with persistent smoke in the cockpit. And, there is no reason why the "trouble god of aviation" can't give you a real in-flight fire someday. These are really good reasons to learn and practice the emergency descent, followed by an emergency approach and landing, followed by a sail-back to shore or anchoring. When simulating the above, cool the engine first and use carb heat for the long, minimum-power descent.

Emergency Approach

The emergency approach is the same technique used in case of an engine failure, but it is also used at the bottom of an emergency descent, usually starting about 1,000 feet AWL.

Many times I have asked seaplane pilots "If the engine quit now, where would you go?" The answers were many and varied. Almost all chose a place that was too far away. One pilot pointed to a safe harbor almost seven miles away, while we were flying 1,000 feet above the ocean! It is important that you know exactly how far your floatplane will glide with power off, and it is easy to become a real authority on this subject—let your airplane teach you!

The POH will tell you that the glide ratio is about 6 to 8:1. That is, 6 to 8 feet forward for each foot down. But that is under ideal conditions and with no wind. My rule of thumb is, I can comfortably glide down and make a landing site that is on a 45° slope, even with a 15 MPH headwind. That is conservative. Stretching beyond that requires the pilot to do everything exactly right!

Glide Performance

To glide the greatest distance, you need careful airspeed control. Here's how you do it:

1. Acquire (hold altitude until achieving) and maintain precisely the maximum distance glide speed. If this speed is not published for your airplane, it is easy to determine. The procedure is described in *Water Flying Concepts*. That discussion also tells you how to determine and use minimum sink glide speed, a useful speed that isn't published in any of the general aviation POHs that I can recall.
2. Flaps up. Virtually all airplanes glide and climb better with flaps up. Don't forget flaps before landing, however!
3. If equipped with a constant speed prop, pull the prop control all the way out (lowest RPM). The increase in glide distance will be apparent as it feels like someone gave you a push from behind when the prop changes pitch. Conversely, once you know you can make it to the chosen landing spot, push the prop control back in. In most airplanes, pushing the prop control back in is more effective for adding drag than pulling on full flaps. Once done, add flaps as desired. Early in the glide, closing cowl flaps may help a little by reducing drag, but it will be more help keeping the engine from cooling too much.

The prop in low pitch produces more drag than full flaps in most airplanes.

Again—airspeed is life itself!

4. While gliding down, remember that ***airspeed is life itself***. Do not, under any circumstances, let the airspeed get lower than best glide speed when lower than 1,000 feet AGL, until you are ready to flare. To do so insures a high rate of sink, inability to glide as far, and insufficient airspeed to flare and stop the descent rate. It creates an energy management problem for which there is no solution and no chance to return to correct glide speed without creating an even higher rate of sink. In effect, letting the airspeed get low on approach seals a contract for disaster you can't void. The one thing I still vividly remember from my one *real* floatplane forced landing on land was how fast the ground seemed to be coming at me,

causing a strong urge to pull back on the stick. But I did not succumb to that urge, maintaining best glide speed until it was time to flare. The landing worked out just fine.

The Airplane Teaches Glide Distance

It is difficult to translate the numbers in the POH book to tell how far you can glide when looking out the cockpit window, so it is best to let the airplane teach you what it will do.

With the four glide performance points above in mind, here is how the airplane teaches how far you can glide so you will know where to look for emergency landing sites.

Climb to 1,000 feet AWL. Cool the engine gradually by decreasing manifold pressure gradually (a couple inches MAP every minute) while maneuvering into position. Set up an approach into the wind that takes you from over land toward the water on which you will land (*see* Figure 15-1). Fly toward the water. When you think you can glide to the water and just barely clear the land obstacle, throttle back to idle (be sure the throttle is completely retarded), and see if you can make it. Note the angle below the nose by noting where on the aircraft structure the touchdown point is just as you retard the throttle. Practice the four points for good glide performance.

Hold the nose up until the airspeed decreases to best glide distance speed. Check flaps up, prop control back, close cowl flaps, and trim for best glide. While gliding, go through the process of troubleshooting why the power failed, just like you learned to do in landplanes, so you will retain that habit. Continually analyze the point at which the glide will reach the surface. When it appears you will reach the water, put the prop control back in (lowering the nose to keep speed up as drag increases) and use flaps as needed (keep airspeed up). Start the flare a little closer to the water than you usually do since you have no power. If all goes well during the approach, you can complete the power off landing. If that goes well, while you are patting yourself on the back for a job well done, remember that the (simulated) engine quit so you have no power. Now what? Can you sail to a friendly shore? If there is anything at all you don't like during the approach, add power and go around. Analyze whether you were short, long or just right on the approach, and go practice the maneuver again until you are confident you know the sight picture. You are now half done with this exercise.

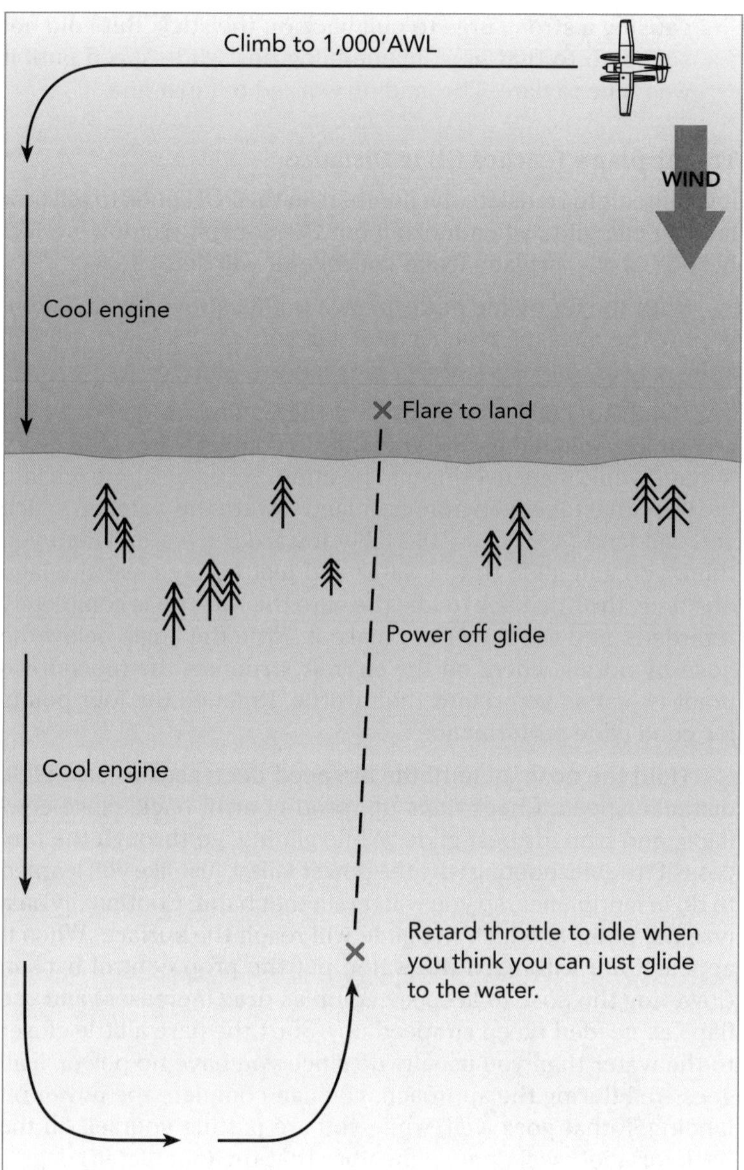

Figure 15-1. Learning glide distance from the seaplane, straight in.

Now, repeat the above, starting the approach flying downwind over the touchdown site on the water, then out over the land. Continue flying away from the water as far as you think you can, cut the power, accomplish a 180° turn and make the approach, noting where the shoreline was, back on the floats, as a reference. *See* Figure 15-2. There are two secrets to the successful outcome of this maneuver. First, you must start the 180° turn immediately. Don't wait until you have slowed to best glide distance speed. Second and most important, a 60° banked turn will give the best turn/glide performance. To become a true believer, try one at a 30° bank, then one at 45°. The difference is amazing! Now you know why you practiced those steep turns! Don't forget prop and flaps at the bottom!

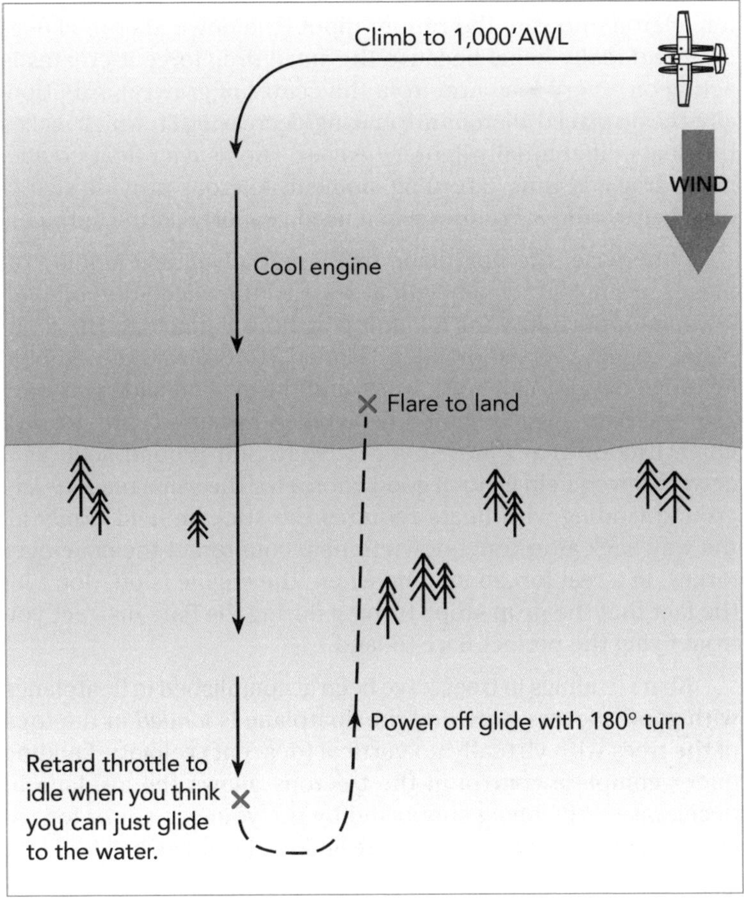

Figure 15-2. Learning glide distance from the airplane, with 180° turn.

Forced Landings in Floatplanes

I consider the "land as soon as possible" admonition to be a forced landing situation much like engine failure. If there is no water surface or airport nearby, and a great need exists to get the aircraft on the surface, an off-airport landing must be accomplished.

The floatplane has a distinct advantage over a wheeled airplane in that the floatplane can accomplish a safe landing on a greater variety of surfaces. Even in dry country, usually water surfaces are more numerous than airports. The floatplane can land safely everywhere a wheeled airplane can with the exception of crowned (almost all) roads. Without directional control on the ground, the floatplane will likely slide off the crowned road into the ditch. If you must land on a road, be ready with lots of rudder and aileron input. Just as when displacement taxiing, use full aileron opposite the rudder input (the down aileron causes drag and really helps because the small drag force it creates is acting on a very long arm from the center of gravity). Additionally, the displaced ailerons are making/decreasing lift which makes the floats differentially lighter/heavier. The heavier float creates more drag and thus, a turning moment. Ailerons provide significant help to the air rudder when used properly on the surface.

Otherwise, the floatplane has a real advantage landing on most terrain. Flat terrain with at least a little vegetation on it allows an opportunity for a landing with no damage to the floatplane. Expect a very short slide. I landed a C-180 in a wheat stubble field one day, into an 8 MPH wind, and the ground slide was only 255 feet! Bare ground should be avoided because it provides so much friction that a nose-over is likely. Soft ground such as a newly plowed field is not a good choice for the same reason. Any ground landing with floats requires the stick be held firmly all the way back after touchdown to help counteract the nose-over forces. In a real forced landing where the engine is off, don't let the fact that the prop stops turning during the flare distract you from flying the perfect flare-to-land.

Many landings in trees have been accomplished in floatplanes with good success provided the floatplane is *landed* in the tops of the trees with virtually no vertical (descent) velocity. Landing under complete control in the treetops allows the airplane to decelerate while being supported by the younger, softer foliage so the airplane slows down before finding the larger, harder parts of the trees below. The floats do a good job of absorbing the shock of deceleration and snagging the tree limbs so the aircraft doesn't fall through to the ground. Just be careful climbing down out of the tree! Consider using your mooring lines to rappel down to the ground.

Medical Emergencies

Since the seaplane is flown into remote areas, knowledge of the location and access of emergency health services is worth having. If you are going into a remote area, it is important to give some thought to how emergencies could be handled. If there is only one pilot (you), he or she probably shouldn't perform higher risk tasks such as chopping wood. It would not be good if the pilot is the one who needs to be transported to emergency medical service.

Plan ahead for the possibility of medical emergencies.

Include research into where and what emergency medical services are available as part of your preflight planning if flying into remote areas. Across the vast reaches of northern Canada, for example, the Indian reservations have nursing stations where first response medical services are available and airstrips from which serious cases can be flown to larger, better equipped medical facilities. As pilot, you must assess the problem and decide whether to utilize nearby but minimal facilities, or fly the person directly to a more distant community with larger, better facilities. Some northern hospitals have their own seaplane dock.

Systems and Equipment Malfunctions

Split flaps and hung flaps

With the exception of water rudders and floats, the system malfunctions are the same as in a landplane. Figure 15-3 lists some of the common system malfunctions that you may wish to review with your flight instructor before the oral and checkride. We have already discussed fires in this chapter. A split flap condition (where only one flap is down) is an interesting management problem when the down flap won't come up. First try to get both flaps up. If that doesn't work, remember that the ailerons are more effective at higher airspeeds, so try to cruise at a speed just below V_{FE} to make the ailerons more effective at controlling the asymmetric lift condition that is attempting to roll the aircraft. I have never had an in-flight split flap. I have had a hung flap. It was a slow trip back to the airport with 20° of flaps. The split flap condition is certainly possible, caused by a failure of any part in the flap control system. This is why I have a personal rule that I never change flap settings unless the wings are nearly level. Adding flaps while turning from base to final (close to the ground) seems foolish, because I can manage my flaps so I don't have to add them while turning. If that flap change did cause a split flap condition, it would be my luck that the low wing would be the one where the flap suddenly went up, causing an unexpected roll that would put me on the knife edge at a slow speed, close to the ground, where my ailerons are less effective. I just don't do it.

- ❑ partial power loss
- ❑ engine roughness or overheat
- ❑ carburetor or induction icing
- ❑ loss of oil pressure
- ❑ fuel starvation
- ❑ electrical system malfunction
- ❑ flight instruments malfunction
- ❑ landing gear or flap malfunction
- ❑ water rudder malfunction
- ❑ inoperative trim
- ❑ inadvertent door or window opening
- ❑ structural icing
- ❑ smoke/fire/engine compartment fire
- ❑ split or hung flap

Figure 15-3. Some system malfunctions: Make sure you can explain how to handle them.

Water Rudder Malfunction

The only item in Figure 15-3 that is seaplane specific is "water rudder malfunction." I have always considered a malfunctioning water rudder to be an inconvenience rather than an emergency. The time will come when you will have to land on a very weedy lake, requiring that you leave the water rudders up as you make your way to the dock or beach. So learn how to maneuver without using the water rudders.

There are many ways to steer without water rudders.

You already know how to power sail, so if the breeze is brisk, that procedure will get you anywhere you need to go. In a weedy lake you can't sail back as the weeds will hang up on the step, stopping you. If the breeze is strong you won't be able to go to a destination that is downwind of your location. That one scenario is really about the only situation where you cannot go anywhere without rudders. (Actually you can sail downwind in a weedy lake, but it involves getting out of the pilot's seat and using the paddle to continually disengage weeds from the step areas.) If the breeze is lighter (less than about 15 MPH) you can use the "throttle becomes the rudder" technique described in the section on ramping with a crosswind. There are ways to get around without rudders.

The light or no wind condition is perhaps the most difficult under which to steer a course but even there, with a little experimentation, plow taxi gives better air rudder authority. The ability to think, combined with knowledge of the forces involved, often produces solutions to problems like these. At idle in calm winds with the rudders up, the seaplane tends to turn left.

One salty pilot demonstrated that he could steer the floatplane straight or do wide right turns when idle taxiing by using a paddle while kneeling on the float (right float is best if you want to turn right). Another ingenious pilot demonstrated that he could steer the floatplane (calm wind, rudders up) from on top of the wing. If he stood on the wing just outboard of the right fuel filler cap, the floatplane would track straight. If he walked toward the right wingtip, the bird would turn right. Back in to the center of the wing, a left turn was produced. His weight acted to partially sink the right float and raise the left one, causing differential water drag and thus steering the floatplane without rudders! Don't get me wrong: I am not advocating this as a normal practice, and it shouldn't be tried unless there is another pilot on board to shut the engine off. If the wing-walking pilot were to slip and take a dive into the drink, it leaves the taxiing seaplane without competent crew. Rather, I offer the above as an example of a solution to a problem when the pilot uses his or her head. Other solutions include taxiing into the wind to the far shore to repair the water rudders. Don't forget what you learned in the taxiing chapter: when displacement (idle) taxiing, the seaplane will have a faster turn rate to the left with lowest RPM (no wind). So that is a hint: less tendency to turn left with higher RPM, but more tendency to damage the prop.

To repeat, inoperative water rudders are an inconvenience rather than an emergency.

Strategies for Inoperative Landing Gear and Other Malfunctions in Amphibians

If you are flying an amphibian, there are some things you must know and some more things to consider. In my 45 plus years of flying, the most prevalent system malfunctions have been in the landing gear systems of amphibious floatplanes. The gear extend/retract mechanism and the gear position indicating systems are outside the airframe and exposed to a hostile environment of water, spray and temperature extremes. So, expect occasional problems and stay current on how to handle them. Know how the gear system works. It is probably electro-hydraulic, using a power pack that sends hydraulic fluid to or from the hydraulic cylinders that actuate the gear retraction mechanism.

The questions in bold are some of the kind you might expect in the FAA oral exam...

Where is the power pack mounted in your airplane or floats? You have to know because checking the hydraulic fluid level in the reservoir is on the daily preflight inspection checklist—at least it should be. Are there two hydraulic cylinders or four? If only two, how is it that all four wheels are actuated? These are some questions you can expect in an oral. Some others are:

How do you check for hydraulic leaks in the floats? By watching for red-colored fluids when you pump the floats during the preflight.

If you get only three green lights after putting the gear lever in the down position, what do you do? Follow the procedure in the POH. It will probably read like this: First, check the unlit bulb to be sure it isn't burned out. Be sure you know how to do this by having done it, not just had it explained to you by someone else. If that is not the problem, expect one of two things: either the indicated gear is not fully down and locked, or the limit microswitch is malfunctioning. By now you have accomplished a visual check of the mechanical gear position indicators. Flying by the tower so the controller can take a look sometimes provides useful information. If the mechanical gear indicator says the gear is down, it probably is. The problem is likely a malfunctioning gear-light limit microswitch or circuitry, but you don't know for sure. Now the crew must make a decision. Read what the POH emergency procedures section tells you to do. It may suggest that you put the gear up and, if you get four up indicator lights, land on water and investigate. Doing so may be a considerable inconvenience if there is no water nearby with maintenance services. If there is a landable grassy area at your airport where there is good emergency and maintenance services, that may be a reasonable option. I have landed amphibians on grass with both one main and one nosewheel stuck in the up position, with no problems—not even paint scratched off the keel strip—and no directional problems. Our decision was easier, though. The gear wouldn't go back up so water landing was not an option.

If you fly an amphibian, it would be a good idea to meet with the airport manager and explore grassy areas of the airport for potential "emergency" landing areas. Then go walk any areas you both decide might work. Note in the sentence above that I put emergency in quotes. In my opinion, landing an amphibian on grass is not an emergency... it is just a nonstandard operation.

The airport manager, unless he is a salty seaplane pilot, will consider it an emergency, however. That's OK; he or she might be more cooperative if the idea is to prepare for an emergency.

Here is another question: **What is the critical altitude of your amphibian?** Critical altitude is the number of feet AGL needed to get the gear down, in case of engine failure. It is an important number for amphibian pilots because the amphibian can land on land either gear up or gear down. Faced with an engine failure, I would rather **land gear down** on:

- roads (better directional control)
- hard surfaced smooth fields (same reason)
- short fields (same reason, so I can choose to go between the fence posts rather than hitting them)
- rocky fields (I can steer between rocks, use the brakes, and if I do hit rocks, the landing gear is just one more thing between those rocks and my soft body)

For landing gear up:

- On furrowed fields (landing across the furrows)
- In wetlands, bogs, soft fields, soggy fields
- If you're not sure the surface is hard enough

But, if you are below critical altitude when the engine fails and the gear is up, you don't have the option of choosing gear down. So, when departing the airport, you need to be examining the terrain ahead. If you would prefer to land gear down on that terrain, you will leave the gear down until after reaching critical altitude. (Don't let that crafty examiner catch you putting the gear up during recovery from a simulated forced landing where you selected gear down for the existing terrain until you have climbed back up to the critical altitude!) So, you see, critical altitude is a decision making altitude. Generally, leaving the gear extended on amphibians has little effect on climb performance, so don't be in a big hurry to put the gear up. Do leave your hand on the gear switch, call critical altitude (verbalize it), then put the gear up so you don't make the disastrous mistake of leaving the gear down, thinking it is up and landing on water.

Don't let that crafty examiner catch you here!

Critical altitude is decision-making altitude.

Critical altitude is a function of how long it takes the gear to cycle down in your amphibian, and it is easily determined. At a safe altitude, slow to V_Y speed or best glide speed while cooling the engine. Throttle back completely to idle. Glide at max distance glide speed. At a noted indicated altitude, select gear down. Note the altitude when the gear is completely down. The difference is critical altitude. Try it again with takeoff flap setting and see if it makes any significant difference. Trying to get the gear down while gliding from critical altitude would be a good time to know your amphibian's minimum sink glide speed, wouldn't it?

Note that there are really two critical altitudes. The other one is the altitude you would lose if you had to put the gear down manually. Naturally, it is a lot higher. Since the odds of a gear extension system failure combining with an engine failure are very high, we don't normally worry about this second critical altitude. Having both failures would really be like having a bad hair day… sort of like the amphibian pilot who forgot and left the gear down, landed on the water, flipped over, managed to escape the water filled cabin, swam ashore, and then got eaten by a big bear…definitely a bad hair day!

While we are on the subject: if you have an **alternator failure** while enroute in an amphibian, keep in mind that you will have to do a manual gear extension (*how many strokes?*) when nearing the destination unless you are *very* conservative with electrical system use for the rest of the trip. Plan to put the gear down quite a ways out from the airport, probably right after first contact with the tower, because it is going to take awhile. Don't forget to be looking out the window for traffic while doing the manual extension. It is a good idea at this time to alert the tower to watch for you, because after you put the gear down you might not have enough battery to call at the specified reporting point.

Enroute alternator failures require specail management strategies.

Insurance rates on amphibians are considerably higher than for seaplanes with straight floats. This is because there have been so many gear-down landings in water that always result in upset with the cabin filling with water. A high incidence of drownings occur. Prevention is a must! Electronic gear warning systems help, but pilot discipline is important. Don't ever land on water without visually checking all four *visual* gear position indicators located out on the floats! If you are by yourself, this is a chore, probably requiring momentary seatbelt release to view the indicators on the opposite float. If you are carrying a right seat passenger, brief that passenger on how to check the visual indicators, when and why. They will soon be calling out "two up over here!" even before you ask. Follow and use the checklist. If you don't like the checklist, make your own and use it. Permanently install it on the instrument panel for easier use. *See* the more complete discussion of checklists in Chapter 5.

Emergency Equipment and Survival Gear

Emergency equipment must be located within reach to resolve the specific emergency. Survival gear is equipment used to survive after the emergency is past. Some items may be both. For example, a firearm may be used to acquire food during an extended survival situation, but it would be emergency equipment if you had engine failure while flying along the coast of Hudson's Bay, and you made a successful emergency landing only to find a couple of hungry, mature, male polar bears waiting for you at the shoreline. Examples of typical emergency equipment are listed in Figure 15-4 and survival gear is listed in Figure 15-5.

Be sure that you know where each item is in the airplane you fly and how to properly use it. Is each item in a logical place? Can you reach it? Can you reach the fire extinguisher and remove it from its bracket without opening the door? Is the fire extinguisher appropriate for use in an airplane? How, when and where is the fire extinguisher inspected? How is it used? *See* Figure 15-6 and also the local fire station can help with these answers.

Fire extinguishers should be checked annually. If the fire extinguisher has a gauge that checks in the safe range it can be returned to use. If no gauge, it must be weighed by a qualified service agency.

The anchor becomes emergency equipment during scenarios like one where you have landed on a river with downstream rapids, the engine quits, and you can't get it started; or you have

Examples of seaplane emergency equipment

- ❑ emergency checklist
- ❑ seatbelt cutter
- ❑ fire extinguisher
- ❑ personal floatation device (PFD)
- ❑ window penetration tool
- ❑ anchor
- ❑ emergency locator transmitter (ELT)

Figure 15-4. Examples of seaplane emergency equipment

Examples of seaplane survival gear
Note: this list is by no means complete.

- ❑ axe, knife, matches and other fire starting devices
- ❑ signaling equipment
- ❑ firearm
- ❑ water making, gathering, purifying and storage devices
- ❑ sleeping bag, tent and other shelter-making devices

Figure 15-5. Examples of seaplane survival gear (this list is not complete by any means).

Fire Extinguisher UL Ratings

Class	Use
A	Wood, paper, cloth, rubber and most plastics fires
B	Flammable liquids such as gasoline, kerosene, oil and grease
C	Electrical and electronics fires

Fire extinguishers should be checked annually. If the fire extinguisher has a gauge that checks in the "safe range" it can be returned to use. If no gauge, it must be weighed by a qualified service agency.

Figure 15-6. The ABCs of fire extinguisher UL ratings

Be sure that you know, and brief your passengers so they know, for each item:

1. location in the seaplane
2. method of operation or use
3. servicing requirements
4. method of safe storage
5. equipment and survival gear for various climates and topographical environments

pulled off an emergency landing and the wind is strong, and it is blowing you back onto a very unfriendly, rocky shore. The anchor should be carried, already attached to 100 feet of line, and located where it is immediately available to you when you get out of the cockpit onto the float. I suggest it be carried with the shank pointed forward, under/behind your seat. The attached line, of course, is coiled and secured to allow quick deployment. Practice anchoring so you're prepared. Review the discussion of anchoring techniques and practice in the next chapter.

For detailed checklists and techniques of survival, read the chapter on survival in *Water Flying Concepts*.

Review

Emergency Descents

This is a procedure used to descend to traffic pattern altitude as quickly as possible without overstressing the airplane or its components. The principal reason to use it in a seaplane is an inflight fire.

In-flight Fires

A big danger with in-flight fire is inhaling pyrotoxins. Not only is all smoke toxic when inhaled, but some materials' combustion products are extremely so. Another important danger is the structural damage fire can cause if allowed to continue. Time is of the essence and this is where the emergency descent is most useful—so, once smoke is detected, start that emergency descent! On the way down, analyze the problem, locate the fire, its fuel source and ignition source; usually you can tell by smell whether the smoke is from an electrical or a fuel/oil fire. Describe how to handle an electrical and an oil/fuel fire and check yourself with the discussions above.

Emergency Descent Techniques

Practice the emergency descent until you can maintain a constant airspeed and steep bank angle while at the same time troubleshooting the fire problem and analyzing where and how to make the emergency landing. Workload is high during the emergency descent, so you need to be very familiar with how to fly the airplane in a steep, descending turn.

Emergency Approach

The emergency approach is used in case of an engine failure but it is also used at the bottom of an emergency descent, usually starting about 1,000 feet AGL. It is important that you know exactly how far your floatplane will glide with power off. Describe how you can have your airplane teach this important knowledge to you, then check yourself with the discussions above.

Glide Performance

To glide the greatest distance, careful airspeed control is needed:

1. Acquire and maintain precisely the maximum distance glide speed.
2. Flaps up. (But don't forget flaps before landing!)
3. If equipped with a constant speed prop, pull the prop control all the way out (lowest rpm). But once you have the chosen landing spot in sight, push the prop control back in. Then add flaps as desired. Close the cowl flaps.
4. While gliding down, remember that ***airspeed is life itself***. Do not, under any circumstances, let the airspeed get lower than best glide speed when lower than 1,000 feet AGL until you are ready to flare. Why? Check your answer with the discussions above.

Forced Landings in Floatplanes

The "land as soon as possible" admonition is a forced landing situation just like an engine failure: an off-airport landing must be accomplished if there is a great need to get the aircraft on the surface, and there's no water surface or airport nearby,

Floatplanes have advantage over wheeled airplanes in that they can accomplish a safe landing on a greater variety of surfaces. List what you know about making a forced landing with floats and check to see if your answer is complete by referring to the discussions above. Landings in trees have been accomplished in floatplanes with good success when the floatplane was *landed* in the tops of the trees with virtually no vertical (descent) velocity.

Medical Emergencies

It's good to know the location and access of emergency health services since seaplanes are operated into remote areas. If you are going into a remote area, give some thought to how emergencies are to be handled. Research where and what emergency medical services are available as part of your preflight planning, and check yourself to see what you remember of the discussions above on this subject.

Systems and Equipment Malfunctions

These are the same as in a landplane, except for the water rudders and floats. Review Figure 15-3, as it lists some of the common system malfunctions you may wish to go over with your flight instructor before the oral and checkride.

The only seaplane specific item in Figure 15-3 is "water rudder malfunction." A malfunctioning water rudder is more an inconvenience than an emergency. You must learn how to maneuver without using the water rudders so you will be prepared to land on a very weedy lake, which requires you to leave the water rudders up as you make your way to the dock or beach. Review what you know about maneuvering without water rudders.

Strategies for Inoperative Landing Gear in Amphibians

Amphibian fliers should review this chapter and be able to answer the following questions (if you haven't read the chapter, but think you know the answers to the questions, read this part of the chapter to see if you agree with it!):

- Where is the power pack mounted in your airplane?
- Are there two hydraulic cylinders or four?
- If only two, how is it that all four wheels are actuated?
- How do you check for hydraulic leaks in the floats?
- If you only get three green lights after putting the gear lever in the down position, what do you do?
- What is the critical altitude of your amphibian and how is it used?
- Are there really two critical altitudes?
- If you have an alternator failure while en route in an amphibian, will you have to do a manual gear extension?
- How many strokes?
- What planning strategies are important if alternator failure occurs?

- Why have there been so many gear-down landings in water, which always results in upset with the cabin filling with water?
- Why is there always a high incidence of drownings?
- Prevention is a must! How are gear-down landings in water prevented? How are drownings prevented if upset occurs?

Follow and use this **checklist**. If you don't like the checklist, make your own, but use it. Permanently install it on the instrument panel so it's accessible.

Emergency Equipment and Survival Gear

- Emergency equipment: must be located within reach to resolve the specific emergency.
- Survival gear is for use while surviving after the emergency is past.

Some items may be both of the above. Be sure that you know where each item is, in the airplane you fly, and how to properly use it. Is each item in a logical place? Can you reach it? Can you reach the fire extinguisher and remove it from its bracket without opening the door? Is the fire extinguisher appropriate for use in an airplane? How, when and where is the fire extinguisher inspected? How is it used? The anchor can become emergency equipment—practice using it in emergency scenarios.

Know:

1. Each item's location in the seaplane.
2. Its method of operation.
3. Its servicing requirements.
4. Its method of safe storage.
5. The various types of equipment and survival gear.

Figure 16-1. A straight-in final approach to a dock on the Rainey River, MN.

Chapter 16
Postflight Procedures

If you are a seaplane pilot, this chapter will provide a good review of techniques from landing until you are moored. I will be very surprised if you don't learn something new from this chapter! If you are preparing to get your sea rating, have a look at the PTS to see what is required of you during the checkride, then read on and good luck!

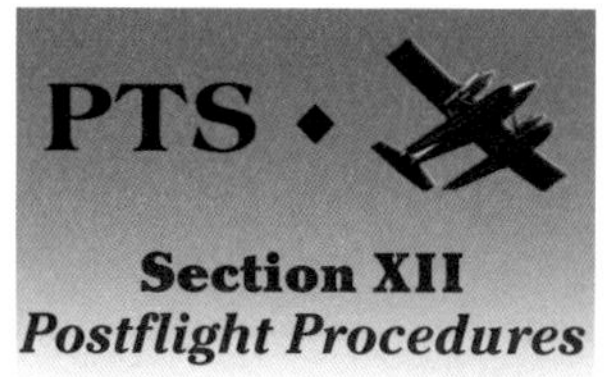

After Landing

If the water is smooth enough that the seaplane isn't telling you through vibration in the seat that you have landed on the water, first use your peripheral vision to check for spray coming out from the floats before pulling the power back to idle. Then, remember—rudders, flaps, and checklist! The examiner will now be watching to see that you use proper taxi procedure with ailerons properly positioned, and head up and swiveling for traffic-watch, and that you follow your taxi route to the dock or beach planned during the landing area assessment.

PTS Section XII
• A •

Mariner's Lingo

Much of this chapter deals with the skills that mariners must have, and many of the words used to describe the techniques and equipment are theirs. So that we may continue and function as mariners, here are a few terms you should know (the bolded ones, at least):

Generally, the word "rope" is not used in the marine environment, except in reference to wire cable or as part of a name to describe its use, such as "towrope." The correct term is **line**. Lines used for a specific purpose are referred to by specific names that indicate their purpose, such as **rode** (anchor line), painter (attached to the bow of a small boat or seaplane), halyard (flag line), sheet (used to control a sail), dockline, bow line, stern line, and **spring line** (used at the dock to keep the seaplane from moving fore and aft). **Standing line** or **working line** is the line, coming from a knot, that is under load (doing the work).

PTS Section XII
◆ B ◆

The anchor and the skill to use it may be the seaplane pilot's last option before disaster.

Anchoring

Anchoring a seaplane with an anchor on board is considered a temporary means of mooring. It is used for short stays and for emergencies when the seaplane's movement needs to be restricted on the water, such as to prevent drifting without power toward an unfriendly shore or a rapids downstream. Anchoring is an important skill because it is the seaplane pilot's last defense in any of the above scenarios. The anchoring process should be practiced periodically so that you can quickly and properly deploy an anchor without tangling lines, falling overboard or having the anchor not **set** (grab the bottom).

Because the anchor is sometimes needed as emergency equipment, it should be stored within easy reach of the pilot with line already attached using an anchor bend, and neatly coiled and secured (not buried under piles of baggage and still in its original box like some I've seen).

Ground Tackle

For **ground tackle** (anchors, rode and associated fittings) a 5 Kg (11 pound) Bruce or claw type anchor is my choice, fitted to 100 feet of 3/8-inch twisted nylon line, without chain. This is a reasonable compromise between not enough anchor and too much weight and is probably adequate for seaplanes up to 3,500 pounds. It can be expected to hold in reasonable breezes and currents to 8 knots on bottoms ranging from mud to small gravel. Hard mud is unlikely to take any anchor, and faced with it in the Guatemalan rain forest lakes, I found a gunny sack filled with rocks to work better. A rocky bottom will quickly abrade any anchor line except chain. The Bruce anchor was developed for holding drilling rigs in the storm-plagued North Sea, so it has fared well in comparison tests with other types. Its main disadvantage is that it does not fold, but its small dimensions allow it to fit beneath and behind the pilot's seat in most Cessnas. The Danforth type is most common, and a lot of seaplane pilots buy the aluminum version of this design because it is light and stows flat. Then they throw them away after a few attempts to use them. If you favor the flat Danforth type, buy the stronger galvanized steel version. Mushroom anchors are often found in inland boat stores. Forget them, as they are for small dinghies and calm winds.

Anchoring Technique

If you practice enough, you will develop your own style and learn what works and what doesn't. I suggest you start with, and then work the bugs out of the following:

First, I stow my anchor under and just behind the pilot's seat with the shank facing forward, (to restrain it in case of a rapid deceleration). Stored there, it is easy to access. Keeping in mind that the seaplane is going to come to rest about 100 feet downwind or downstream of where I place the anchor, I position the seaplane appropriately, estimating how far it will drift from the time the engine is killed until I get the anchor down. If the wind is 15 knots or more, I will "park" the seaplane with engine running until the anchor is placed. (*See* parking in the section about power sailing, Chapter 8.)

Anchoring, like landing, is a skill that needs practice.

To place the anchor, step out onto the float, slide your seat forward a little to ease removal of the anchor. Place the anchor on the float deck, turn around and sit down on the step with your feet spread apart on the float deck, the anchor between them. If the wind is blowing/prop turning, leave the door open to shield yourself from the wind, otherwise close it and lean your back against it (Cessnas). Slip your hand through all the loops of line on the coil so the coil of line hangs from your wrist (so both hands are free). Remove the wrapping securing the line bundle. Secure the **bitter end** (end of the anchor rode away from the anchor) to the vertical strut to your right with a simple knot that can be easily untied. I use a bowline or a slipknot on a bight, so I can pull the loose end and it unties. Lower (don't throw) the anchor over the outside of the float, paying out the rode quickly until all of it is in the water. If you have parked the seaplane, now is the time to kill the engine (or throttle back if the wind is strong).

As the seaplane drifts back, the rode will become taught and the seaplane will turn to the right about 30–40° if the anchor sets (because of where the rode is attached to the airframe). If the anchor does not set, you will observe the rode vibrating as the anchor drags across the bottom, or you can hold it like a fishing line and feel the anchor dragging much like a large fish nibbling on your bait. If you think the anchor has set, look ashore 90° to the direction of drift and find two landmarks that line up. Watch them for a moment to see if they stay lined up. If they do, the anchor has settled in. Now it's time to fashion a bridle and move the bitter end to the center of the bridle so the seaplane will lie faced into the wind/current, which is the position presenting the least drag on the anchor. I just tie my two permanent bow lines together, then untie the rode from the strut and secure it to the bow line/bridle and I am done. Some pilots prefer to carry an already-fashioned bridle with them. Bridles that attach to the prop or to the bow cleats work well.

The above paragraph contains a hidden clue about seaplane handling you might have missed. You can turn the seaplane around in lighter winds by moving (carrying) the bitter end of the rode aft to the stern of the float, or cause the seaplane to lie facing across the wind by moving amidships on the float. Where the seaplane is attached to the rode becomes the most windward part of your "boat."

Recovering the anchor is the same process, but in reverse. Just coil up the rode as best you can and put it in the cabin or float locker to dry and properly coil later. Your attention now shifts to getting underway.

Things to remember:

- You need two hands for handling the rode. Sitting on the step with feet wide apart on the float deck gives you security and stability and removes the need to use the old mariner's saying "one hand for the ship and one hand for yourself." (In landlubber's terms, hang on!)
- Uncoiling a 100 foot bundle of line quickly without tangles is an acquired skill. Each loop ***must*** come off the bundle to the outside of the bundle. You simply cannot accomplish this if the anchor is already tugging on the rode, so the uncoiling (at least partially) must precede lowering the anchor overboard. You can throw at least some of the individual loops in the water because: line will not tangle if loose in the water (98% of the time). Tangled line will sometimes untangle itself if in the water. And most anchors will not set if the bottom is heavily vegetated (weedy). Nor will it set if the rode is around one of the flukes of the anchor.

Scope (ratio of length of rode to depth of water) should be at least 6:1 if the anchor is fitted with chain and 10:1 (100 feet of rode in 10 feet of water) without chain. Hence the need for 100 feet of rode on your anchor. I have marked my rode at 10 feet so when I lower the anchor over the side, I know the water depth.

Swing is the area of the circle whose radius is the length of rode. If the wind or current changes, the anchored seaplane can go anywhere within this circle, so consideration must be given to this if the seaplane is left unsupervised.

There are advanced anchoring techniques about which you can read in *Seaplane Operations* or Chapman's "bible" on seamanship and boat operations titled "Piloting."

Docking and Mooring

PTS Section XII
◆ C ◆

Docking may be accomplished by coming alongside, with the seaplane's float parallel to the dock and just a few inches away, or bow-to, if obstructions on the dock make parallel docking impossible.

The docking maneuver is easier if two pervading rules of docking are followed. They are:

1. When docking, beaching or buoying, always do it into the wind. If you can't do it into the wind, expect trouble.
2. If at all possible, plan a straight-in final approach to the dock for the last 50 to 100 feet. This rule applies primarily to parallel docking.

When docking, beaching or buoying, always do it into the wind.

If at all possible, plan a straight-in final approach to the dock for the last 50 to 100 feet.

So often we see a floatplane approaching the dock on a course that is about 45° to the heading needed to parallel the dock. Both skill and luck are needed, in this case, to make that 45° turn to parallel the dock while the floatplane is slowing down, losing water rudder authority and being impacted differently by the wind (due to the change in heading) and current (which decreases or even becomes a back-eddy near shore). Good luck! Docking is made much easier if the pilot executes a straight-in approach, letting the seaplane tell him what the wind and current are doing near the dock. *See* Figure 16-2 on the next page.

If it is necessary to dock with the dock on the starboard (right) side, and you are flying a side-by-side floatplane, don't guess where the dock is. Move over to the right seat after briefing the passenger to either step out onto the float deck and stand just behind the aft doorpost (so you have a clear path to the dock) or, in larger aircraft like a Beaver, have the passenger step aft between the seats until you move over. Plan ahead if you can. If you know there will be a right side docking at the destination and your passenger is not able-bodied, fly that leg from the right seat.

Docking Technique

When approaching a strange dock, scrutinize it thoroughly from the air. When approaching it on the water, make a close pass-by keeping the dock on your left (if you are sitting on the left) and looking for anything you might have missed from the air. Note

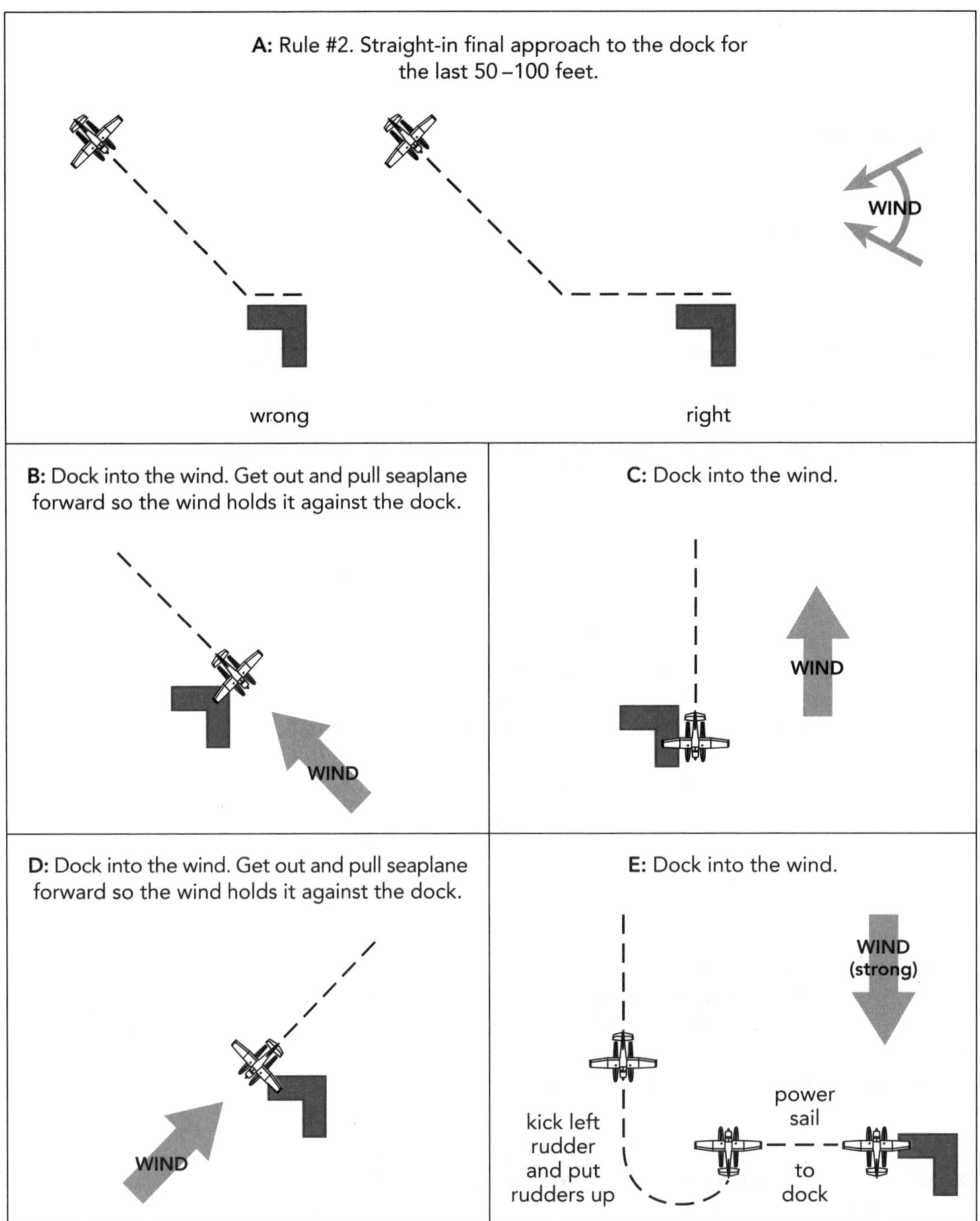

Figure 16-2. Straight-in final approach, and docking into the wind.

Figure 16-3. A unique experience: docked bow-to on a small iceberg in Glacier Bay, AK.

wind direction close to the dock, obstructions in the water, condition of the dock (nails sticking out, obstructions for the wing or stabilizer), current or back-eddys, swimmers or any other potential dangers.

While taxiing back out to begin your final approach to the dock, brief your passengers regarding their role in the docking (even if it is just "stay in your seat until you receive further directions") while you get yourself ready. Getting ready means getting unencumbered: headphones off and cord stowed so it doesn't hang down and catch your toe as you get out, dumping you on your nose in the water or on the dock; seatbelt and shoulder harness off and out of the way; seat all the way back with you sitting on the front edge; electrical systems off, door open and left foot out on the step while right foot works both pedals (if docking right side, the above left-right scenario is reversed).

Do you need a short line for the initial tie-up? Your back pocket is a good place for it because you don't want to be out on the dock, holding your airplane against the wind with no way to secure it to the dock. (Note: the above description is for Cessnas. You may need to modify it for your seaplane.)

The **half-in, half-out position** of seat slid back, sitting on the front edge, door open, left foot out on the step, right foot steering is one you should become comfortable with. You have total control of the seaplane while halfway out of it in case you need to get outside quickly. This position provides excellent visibility of the front of the float when looking between the door and door jam in Cessnas. It is also a comfortable position for dock or beach departure.

Don't forget the dockside safety skill and knowledge discussed in Chapter 6 (*see* Page 48).

Only experience will tell you when to kill the engine. Stay with the rudder pedals until the last possible moment, when you will step out, grab the lift strut, and step on the dock with ***both*** feet. One foot on the dock and one foot on the float creates a human bridge over an ever widening water gap, often followed by splashing sounds, soon followed by sounds of laughter, but not yours. If your floatplane is still moving forward, bring the floats parallel to the dock and let parallel contact with the dock be the brake.

Many seaplane pilots have lines permanently attached to the bow cleat or front vertical strut. I much prefer the line on the bow cleat. It is always ready to secure the bow or pass around

Figure 16-4. Bow-to in the bush on a remote Manitoba river. The brush would interfere with the tailfeathers if heeled up.

the front vertical strut to the dock for a single tie, or to take with me off the front of the float to dock or beach. The main disadvantage of this placement is that it lies on the deck, always ready to roll sideways under an improperly placed foot causing the foot to "roll" off the float. If the bowline falls off the float in flight, it is a simple matter to slip the seaplane so that the wind rolls the line back up on the float. Bowlines can be used to change the seaplane from right-side docking to left, or vice versa, by using the bow line of the outboard float combined with an outward push on the tail (used when there is a tailwind).

Bow-to docking is done where high walls, pilings or posts present danger to wing or tail. Timing of engine shutdown is critical and the **critical float** (the windward float, called the "serious float" in some parts of the south) must be tied up immediately, or the wind will swing the tail causing the wing to bump the obstruction. A permanent bowline is a big help to this maneuver, as is a grab-handle on the cowling. The Louisiana rigged floatplane is distinctive in that it is equipped with larger bumpers (often an aircraft tire cut in half laterally) over the bows of the floats, handles on the cowling and permanent bowlines. Almost all dockings in southern Louisiana are done bow-to, so the pilots there are very good at this maneuver.

Bow-to docking requires practice to be proficient.

More details on docking can be found in *Seaplane Operations*. See the section about lines and knots later in this chapter for details on securing your aircraft to the dock and facilitating departure from the dock.

Mooring at the Dock

There are docks and then there are docks. It does little good to tie your floatplane securely to the dock if the dock itself is not sound and securely anchored. Give some thought and investigation to the dock and how it is secured before deciding to leave your floatplane there overnight or for longer periods. Take a moment to look around. How much fetch is there in exposed directions? The more fetch, the larger the waves will be if the wind blows. If it appears to be a solid dock, try to moor on the side away from long fetches. If the dock is not well cushioned with bumpers or old tires, consider tying bow-to with the floatplane facing into the wind. If there are slips, tie in the center of the slip with lines bow and stern on both sides.

If tying alongside, use a springline (Figure 16-7) to keep the floatplane from surging fore and aft with wind and wave action. If you have grablines fitted near the wingtip, it is easy to rig a standoff line to keep the floatplane from continuously rubbing the dock (Figure 16-8). Lines from the dock can go to bow and stern cleats on the floats and/or to the bases of the N vertical struts.

If heavy weather is anticipated and the floatplane must remain at the dock, a tiedown from the wing tiedown ring to the dock may be installed but should be fitted with a rubber snubber to avoid undue stress when the dock and floatplane roll out of synch. If snubbers aren't available, tie the floats securely but with considerable slack to permit rolling but not flying. Floatplanes at the dock must be continuously watched in heavy weather because waves washing across the floats will eventually sink them. If they are in deep water and waves begin to wash over the floats, the aircraft must be moved ashore or to a location that is over shallow water and a sand bottom so that when the floats do sink, they won't sink far and can be pumped out on the next sunny day.

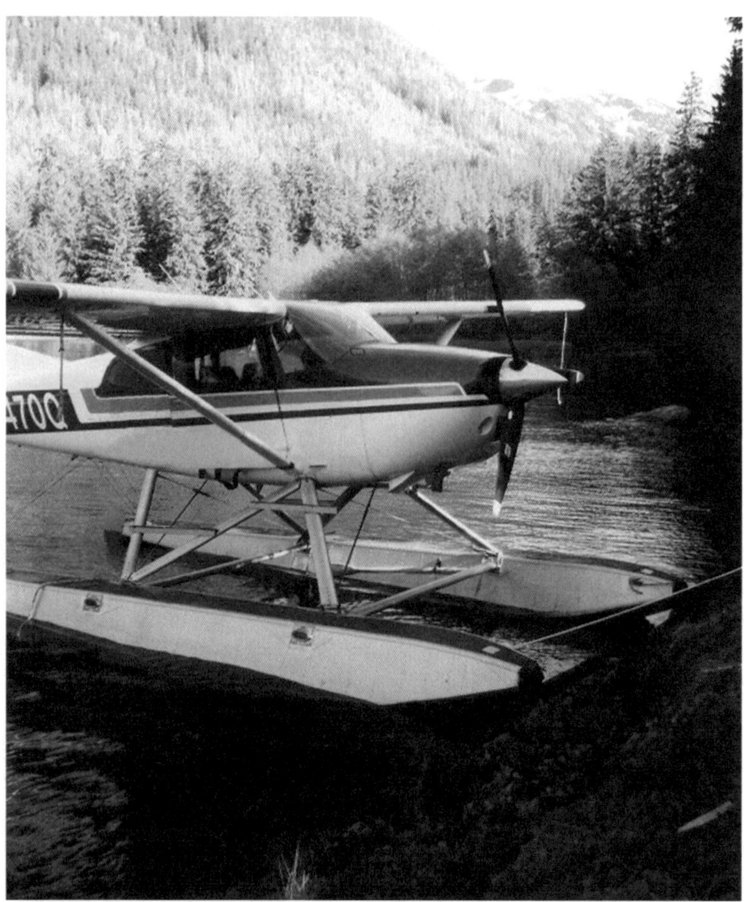

Figure 16-5. Bow-to docking on a sloping rock wall on a wilderness lake devoid of sandy beaches.

Figure 16-6. The author debugs the left wing at a convenient dock in the Ontario bush. Note the permanent bowline has been brought back around the forward vertical strut to the dock, and a tiedown line is used to secure the aft vertical strut to the dock, as a temporary tie-up.

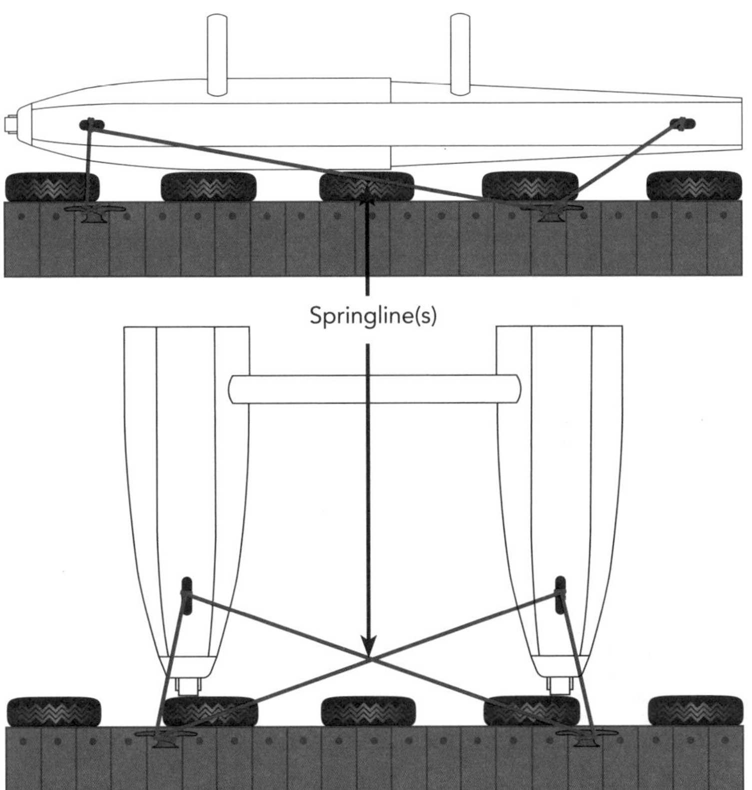

Figure 16-7. Springlines stop much of the surging at the dock.

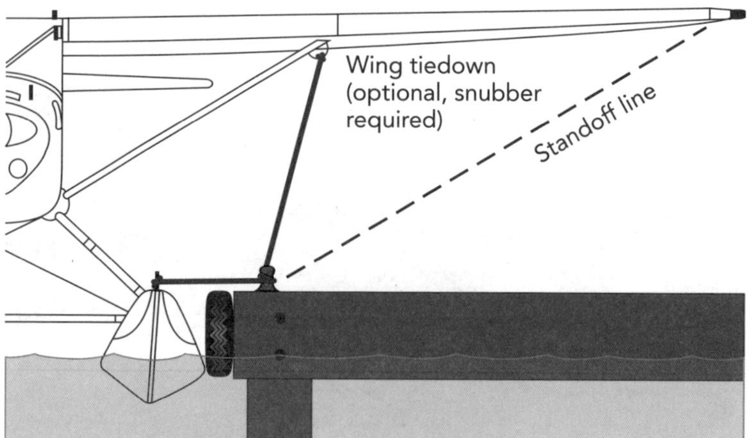

Figure 16-8. A standoff line minimizes float contact with the dock. A springline is required for it to work well.

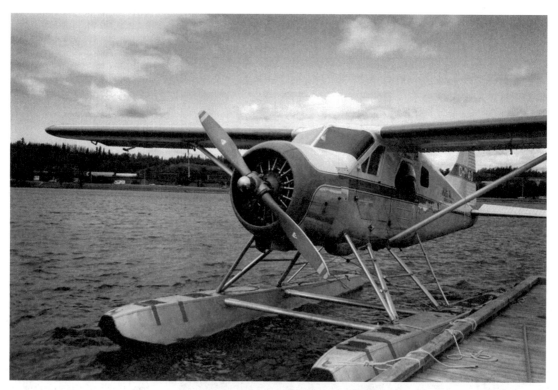

Figure 16-9. A Beaver well moored, tied at the bow, amidships at both vertical struts and at the stern.

Departing the Dock

With a dock handler to help you depart the dock, the process is simplified but two things are important:

1. Be certain both you and the dock handler know exactly what is to transpire.
2. Once the lines are free, if the dock handler has "tailed you out" (pointed your nose out by holding the tail) don't dawdle at getting the engine started for two reasons. If there is a breeze, the dock handler can only point your aircraft. He can't keep it from drifting. Second, the dock handler has other jobs to do, so don't leave him holding your airplane while you put your seatbelt on, adjust your headphones, etc. Start the engine promptly and take care of those other chores once taxiing in safe water. Be sure passengers are strapped in, etc. before casting off the lines.

If you are departing from a dock solo, with no help, the wind is blowing and there is an unfriendly shore downwind, here are some things you can do.

Use the braking effect of a lee dock. If the wind is pushing your floatplane up against the dock, the friction of dock contact tends to hold the floatplane—at least long enough for you to get in and get the engine started. Preferably, the seaplane should have been moored with the dock on the windward side. (If you are having a problem with windward and leeward, keep in mind that these directions are *from the mariner,* so imagine yourself sitting in the pilot's seat with the dock on *your* windward side.) This would be position A in Figure 16-10. When you are absolutely, positively ready to go, cast off the lines and move your floatplane to position C in Figure 16-10. While pushing forward on the lift strut, pull on the bow line to get around the corner (not easy to do in a strong wind). Note that position C is as far forward on the dock as you can position the airplane without it trying to turn left. It will weathercock downwind using the corner of the dock as the pivot point if there is more side surface area forward of the pivot point.

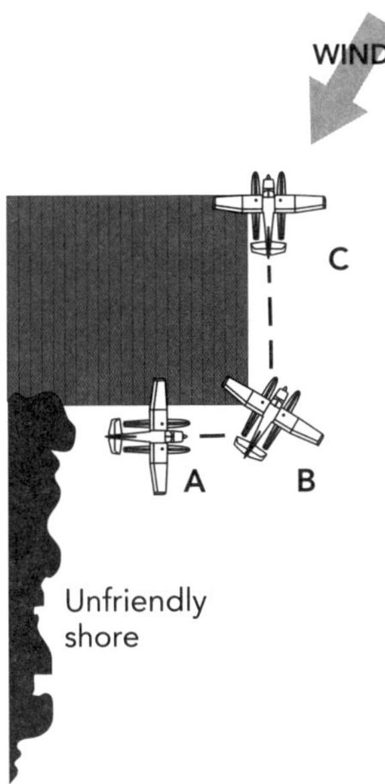

Figure 16-10. Using the braking effect of a lee dock

Now test to see what the floatplane does if left to its own devices (by letting go of it). If it stays in place, hop in and start the engine. You will not be able to turn right, away from shore until the stern of the left float clears the dock. In fact, as the floatplane moves forward, it will first try to turn left, so it is important that you carry enough power to move briskly forward until the float clears the dock. Then expect the tail to swing left over the dock. Make sure there are no obstructions on the dock. Once clear, the floatplane will turn right, away from the shore and into the wind. As with any dock departure, you should leave the dock while looking back at the tail so you will know if anything hits it, because that is an absolute no-go item. If the tail is struck, return to the dock—you don't want to fly with a damaged tail!

Use the slippery knot. Another option is to move the floatplane up from position A (Figure 16-10) to the corner so the floatplane heads into the wind (position B). Secure it there with a line you can release from the cockpit when the engine is running. One way to do this is to pass a line through or around some structure on the dock, bringing both ends back into the cockpit. When the engine starts, release one of the ends and hope the line doesn't snag on anything while half of the line runs out and around whatever you tied to. If it snags, you must release the other end of the line, sacrificing it or coming back for it later. Another disadvantage of this method is the pull on the line is likely to be excessive in order to hold the seaplane in place. You are having to bear the full force on the line, because you can't tie one end to the airplane in case it snags. If one end were tied and the other end snagged, your airplane would become like a tethered calf reaching the end of its rope. (Calves have ropes, seaplanes have lines, right?)

Slippery knot: *See* Pages 230–231, later in this chapter.

A somewhat more sophisticated method is to use the **slippery knot**, which solves both problems but adds a new one: you have to learn how to tie the slippery knot, then practice it occasionally so you don't forget. Tie one end of a 40 footer (3/8 inches × 40 feet) to the strut just outside the pilot's door. Tie it with a bowline (easy to untie after having a heavy strain on it) using a long loop so you can bring the knot up to your position as pilot to untie it later. Tie the other end, using a slippery knot, to some structure on the dock at a point that is forward of the lateral axis of the aircraft, and bring the release line back to the cockpit with you. Note that only about one foot of line has to pass back around the dock structure so the chance of a snag is virtually eliminated. Once the engine is running well, release the slippery knot and recover the line as you taxi away. From position B at the dock you can taxi directly into the wind away from the dock.

Buoying

PTS Section XII
◆ C ◆

Buoying is the process of taxiing up to and securing the floatplane to a buoy. The PTS has chosen to apply the broader term "mooring" to mean the same thing. We'll let them get away with it…they're nice guys.

Many seaplane pilots find this maneuver difficult. I believe this is primarily because they don't practice it or may never have been shown a few little things that make it easy.

Figure 16-11. The author's C-180 moored at a buoy (in the Northwest Territories) to keep the camp's dock clear for other seaplanes to come and go.

The buoy ***must*** be approached from *exactly* downwind. This is because, when you take your feet off the rudders to grab the buoy, if the floatplane is not headed directly into the wind, it will weathercock, either into the buoy (bump) or away from the buoy so you cannot reach it.

How do you tell if you are approaching from directly downwind? Easy! Let the airplane tell you. If you believe you are exactly downwind from the buoy, take your feet off the rudder pedals for a moment or put the water rudders up. If your floatplane continues toward the buoy, you've got it nailed! If your bird turns right, you need to be more to the left, etc. *See* Figure 16-12. Continue to adjust and test as you approach the buoy. When close, you may be able to compensate if the last test still shows a small tendency to turn.

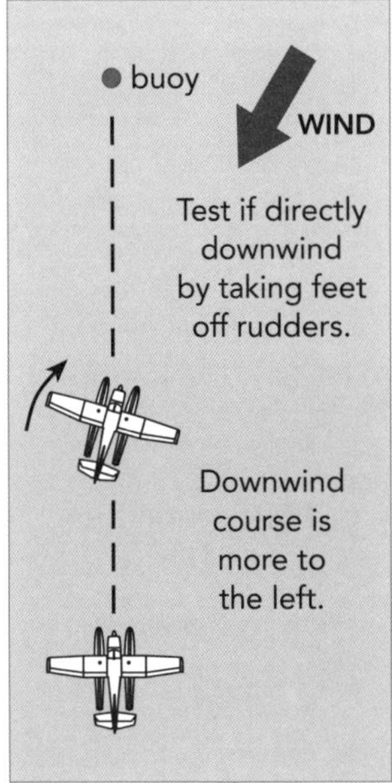

Figure 16-12. Determining if directly downwind of buoy

Bring the buoy alongside (outside) the left float (if you are going to get out on the left side). Experience will teach you when to kill the engine. If there is no wind, kill it at probably 25 to 50 feet before reaching the buoy, depending on the mass (inertia) of your airplane. The half in, half out technique will greatly decrease the time it takes you to get out and grab the buoy. Continue to steer until the last possible moment. This is the most common error my students make when docking and buoying—leaving the cockpit too soon. Don't bail out until the buoy is at least abeam the bow of the float and less than a foot away from the float.

When you do go to the float deck, wait for the buoy to come to you. Grab the buoy from amidships, where you stepped out of the cockpit. Don't go forward to reach it unless necessary, because amidships you have the step to hang onto while reaching out for the buoy. Forward, there is nothing to stabilize you.

A proper buoy (one intended for seaplane use) will have a bumper around it so it can't damage the floats and will have two lines already connected to the top, ready to be tied to the two forward cleats with a cleat hitch (*see* the knots section). If it doesn't have such lines, and there are no permanent bow lines on your bird, you must take one with you, in your back pocket or through your belt, when you leave the cockpit to grab the buoy. Thus, the need to first taxi by the buoy to assess it.

Buoy mooring lines can be attached to the bow cleats or to a bridle to the propeller. While some argue that the propeller attachment holds the nose down and decreases the wing's angle of attack in a strong wind, I prefer the redundancy of a separate line to each bow cleat, which also reduces "sailing" to and fro that any anchored craft does. Leaving the water rudders down helps decrease sailing at the buoy as well. If using a propeller bridle, I suggest a second "just-in-case" line attached to a bow cleat unless buoyed in very sheltered water.

In heavy weather, I much prefer to have my airplane heeled up on a protected beach where it won't sink and I can get to it. The beach option is not always available however.

PTS Section XII
◆ D ◆

Beaching

The floatplane can be beached either bow-to or heeled up (heels on the beach so the floatplane is facing the "weather" or open water).

If it is a sand or small, round pebble beach (friendly to the floats), heeling up on the beach is the preferred method (unless the water level is influenced by tides) to go ashore in unimproved areas for three reasons:

1. Heeled up, the aircraft faces any weather (wind and waves) that may come while on the beach. The tail is high, decreasing the angle of attack of the wing, so there is much less chance the seaplane will "fly" in a strong wind.
2. I would much prefer to leave the aircraft overnight heeled up than at the dock because it can't sink. I can secure it with lines to secure points on shore. If the waves get over two feet high and the float bottoms are pounding as the waves come and leave, I can fill one or more float compartments with water to solidly anchor the floats to the beach while the waves pass harmlessly over them and under the airplane's belly. The waves will actually move the floatplane further up on the beach. (Problems tomorrow will be pumping floats out and getting the bird off the beach, but they are solvable and we've weathered the storm.)
3. It is far easier to walk off the heel of the float onto the beach.

Refer to Figure 6-3 in Chapter 6, the results of mooring bow-to overnight. The wind came up in the night and filled the aft float compartments. Waves passing over the top of most any float models will gradually fill and eventually sink them. Wind from the back of the airplane also blows the rudder, elevator and aileron controls around, causing wear and possible damage. A bow-to mooring on a steep shore with deep water beneath the floats spells trouble if the wind comes up during the night. Sometimes a bow-to mooring can't be avoided, but the pilot must keep its risks in mind.

Figure 16-13. Heeled up for the night on a beautiful beach. The author prepares to secure the starboard wing tiedown. The tail tiedown is left for last because it inhibits left-right movement on the beach behind the tail.

Sailing back to the beach or into a slip (a real challenge) in winds less than 13–15 MPH may be done using accuracy sailing. If the wind is greater than 15 MPH, power sail back. It will take longer, but is the safest way. For reasons I will explain in a moment, I only use the accuracy sailing maneuver when the wind is blowing onto the beach at nearly 90° to the shoreline. Position the aircraft directly upwind of the point you wish to reach on the beach (*see* Figure 16-14). Shut down the engine, raise the rudders and hope for the best!

If you have positioned yourself close to the beach, there will be little left-right correction you can do (because of the short distance to the beach), but you can try. When 30–50 feet from contact with the beach, hop out on the float, grab the paddle and walk aft on the float. Once there, you can direct the tail direction with the paddle, but the primary reason for being there is to watch for rocks, obstructions, etc., and fend off from them with the paddle. Once the keel grounds, hop off and grab the tail stinger, raise the elevator by hand so you can see the water rudders and, keeping them straight with the air rudder, pull the seaplane onto the shore. This process is called "**heeling up**."

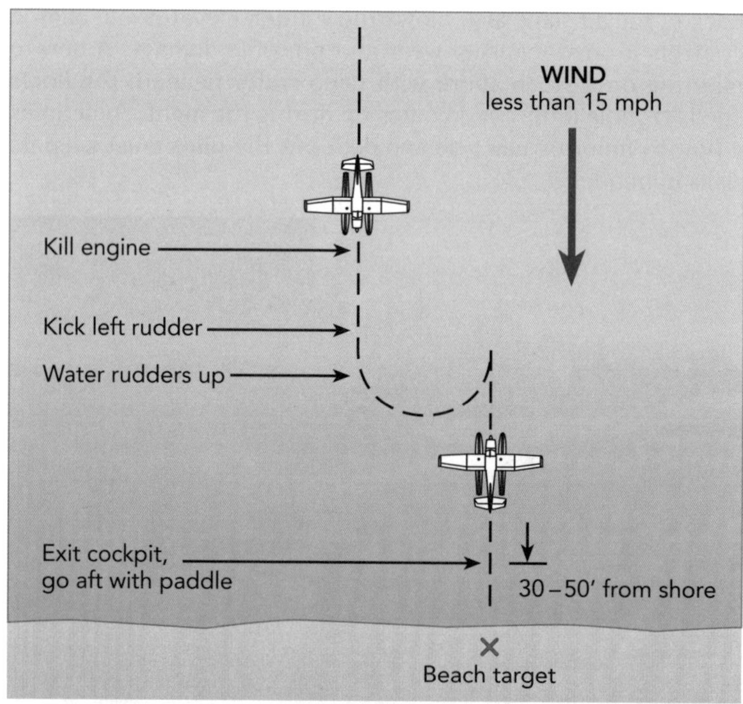

Figure 16-14. Sailing back to the beach

This all sounds very easy, but I've been made a fool many times doing this until I learned that the wind direction near shore is often quite different than that out on the lake. Experience has taught me that the wind streaks on the water close to shore are no longer indicating the true wind direction. Light winds along the shoreline tend to have a direction more parallel to the shoreline. For this reason, power off sailing back to the beach is not my favorite way of accurately placing myself on the beach. But when it goes as planned, it is easy and looks very professional.

Beaching Technique, Dry Feet Style

Anybody can taxi into shallow water, jump overboard and position the floatplane on the beach. Let's look at doing this while keeping our feet dry, and save jumping in the water (to save the airplane from damage) as a last resort.

Calm Winds Beaching

First, just as you did when docking, make a close pass to have a good look at the beach, obstructions, rocks in the water, hungry looking polar bears on the beach, etc. Choose a landmark on the beach at the exact point where you want to heel up. Assess the slope of the beach. Does the beach slope up enough so you will be able to reach the wingtip or wingtip grabline? If not, you will need a line attached to the stern cleat that you can take ashore with you.

The 45° approach to the beach.

After having a good look, taxi back out into safe water, park the seaplane and affix that line, if needed. Brief your passengers,

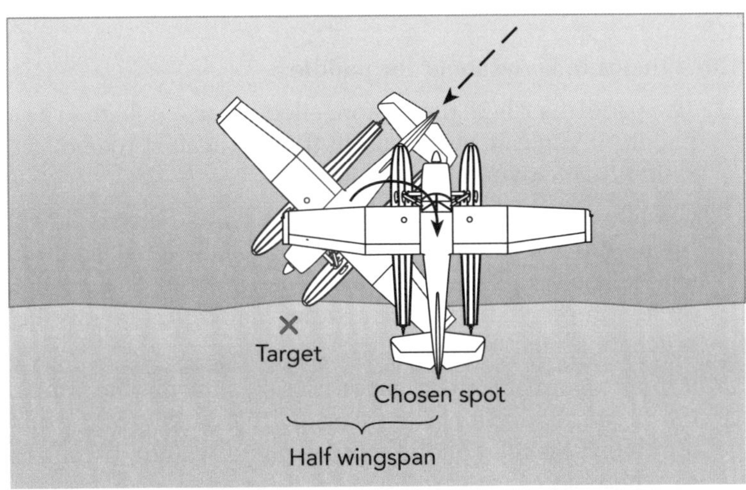

Figure 16-15. Calm winds beaching

get unencumbered and start the approach. Approach the beach at a 45° angle to the beach so the left float (or the float from which you wish to step ashore) touches gently at a point that is a half wingspan to the right of the chosen spot (Figure 16-15). Before leaving the cockpit, be sure all switches are off and water rudders are up! Very shortly after touching, you should be standing on the front deck of the float so your weight serves to hold the float in place. Here, take a moment to assess the situation. If the left wingtip is over the beach, step ashore, lift the wingtip up to loosen the left float's hold in the sand. Then walk the wingtip toward the seaplane a foot or so to put the float in deeper water then to your left along the beach, rotating the floatplane until the tail surface comes to the beach. Then grab the tail and, caring for the water rudders, heel up on the beach.

If you bump the beach a bit too hard, the other float will come to shore, straightening the seaplane so the left wingtip is no longer over the beach. If this happens, you will need the line attached to the stern cleat. Take it ashore and rotate the floatplane by pushing the bow back out into the water and then pulling on the line.

Alternate Method

If the wind is very calm and there is no current, kill the engine so the floatplane stops just short of the beach. Get out on the float and, using the paddle, turn the floatplane stern to the beach and back it onto the beach. If there is foliage or high ground near the beach, heads up! Be sure the opposite wingtip doesn't find that foliage or obstruction. Remember the cautions about using the paddle listed below when you do this.

Three things to know about the **paddle**:

1. The paddle is 20–30 times more effective as a pole than as a paddle. If you can, always use it to push against the bottom rather than move water with it.
2. If, while pushing with the paddle, the handle breaks, it will break with a very sharp end. And, if you fall off-balance, you will "fall on your sword." Always, when pushing on a paddle, do it with only one hand. The other hand ***must*** be pushing opposite against the airframe.
3. If there is any breeze or current at all, you won't be able to move the seaplane against it using the paddle. You probably won't be able to rotate the seaplane, which will tend to weathercock.

Beaching if There is a Breeze or Wind

Most important, remember rule number one: **When docking, beaching or buoying, always do it into the wind. If you can't do it into the wind, expect trouble**.

When beaching, it is likely that you won't be able to do it exactly into the wind, but do it as much into the wind as possible. Use the same 45° approach described above, from whichever side is most into the wind. A wind blowing from the beach toward the water will require a line on the stern cleat, and a firm beaching with you out on the bow of the float quickly to keep the offshore wind from moving you back away from the beach. A wind blowing onto the shore will simplify things as you won't need the line on the aft cleat. The wind will weathercock your floatplane until it is facing into the wind. What can you do, at this point, with air rudder and ailerons to help point the tail more toward the beach? If you have to get out and use the paddle, ask your passenger to maintain pressure on rudder and ailerons.

Worst case scenario is if the wind direction is parallel to the beach, in which case you will need to hop out onto the shoreside float, grab the paddle, step aft, point the paddle at the opposite water rudder, and put it into the sand. Apply a steady pressure (one hand on the paddle, the other on the fuselage) until the tail swings inshore enough for you to hop ashore and grab the tail to heel up.

If the wind is not weathercocking the airplane, it is because the leeward float is stuck tightly enough in the sand to resist the weathercocking force. Two things you can do: one, be patient as

Figure 16-16. Two floatplanes moored out of the water on rail carts after beaching.

the wave action and the wind will eventually get the job done; or two, do what you can to lighten up the stuck float. If you are standing on it, get back in the cabin or walk around to the windward float or, if the big hole in your boot is higher than the water level, step off and walk ashore, waiting there for your floatplane to come to you. You will not always be able to engineer a dry-foot beaching.

Securing the Floatplane on the Beach

How your floatplane is tied down on the beach depends on current, wave action, how long you will be there, and whether you will be out of sight of your airplane during the stay. Most important is that the elements not be allowed to turn the floatplane sideways on the beach where it will be seriously damaged in waves of only a foot or so.

One taught line, at least 3/8-inch diameter, from the tail tiedown point to a stout tiepoint ashore (tail-tie), will work for awhile but is inadequate, even in a sheltered cove, for an overnight stay. Wave action can move the bird several inches further ashore, loosening the tail line and allowing the elements to start the process of turning sideways. So, for stays longer than just a lunch stop, use a tail-tie and at least two lines running ashore at a 45° angle from both

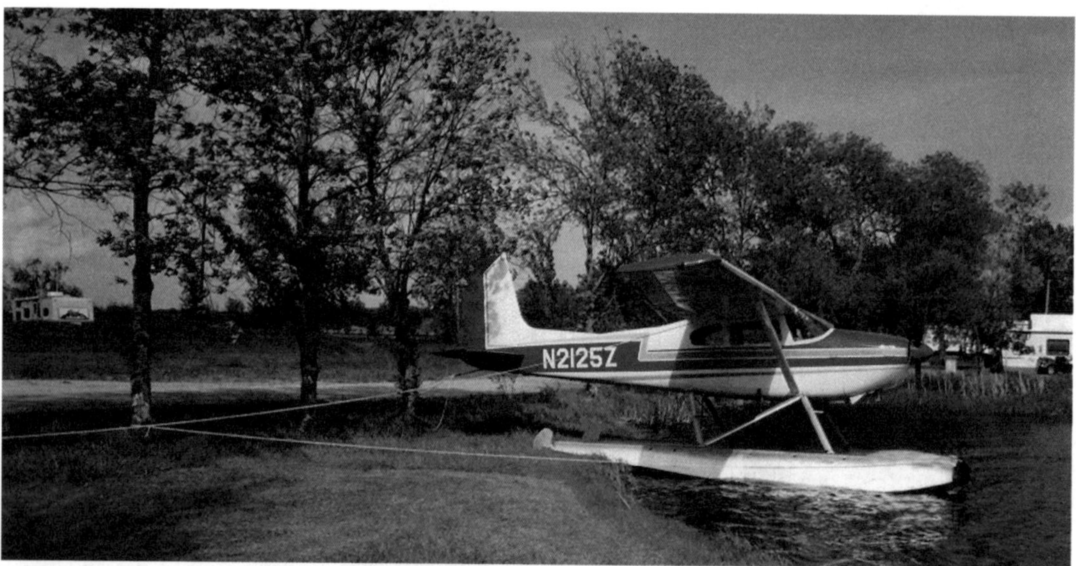

Figure 16-17. Securely moored with two bow lines, two wing lines and two tail lines in a sheltered cove in anticipation of an arriving thunderstorm. One 100-foot line secured from wing lift strut to tree and back to bowline was possible because the tree line was close to the water.

of the wing tiedown points. These lines may also be attached to the bow cleat or the bow line. Caution: the Cessna retractable wing tiedowns are not designed for loads in any direction but down. They will bend and no longer retract if used in this manner. You may use them to "keep" the line up at the top of the lift struts, but the line must also go around the lift strut itself. The line will stay up at the top of the lift strut if tied in a direction 45° away from the tail. Using the tiedown rings isn't necessary unless you are concerned with damaging the plastic fairings.

Departing the Beach

The floatplane is heeled up on the beach and you are ready to load and go. The problem is, if you load passengers, baggage and fuel aboard, the floatplane will be anchored down by that added weight and you will not be able to push off.

So, before loading anything, push the floatplane into the water until it floats, then bring it back until it is just touching the beach. Load some items and push off again, load a passenger and push off again, etc. When everything is loaded but you, hold onto the tail and check that there are no spectators behind the airplane who can get sand in their eyes from the propwash, and no apparent crossing water traffic in front of the airplane. Then push off and bring the airplane back until it is just touching, then quickly get in, start the engine and taxi into safe water. Your added weight on the float will probably hold you until the engine starts. Don't take time to adjust your seat, seatbelt, or anything else. Instead, assume the "half in, half out" position, clear the area, start the engine and guide the seaplane into safe water (don't forget to put the water rudders down when in water that is deep enough). Then do the rest of your tasks. Until you get away from the beach, you need to be able to exit quickly. Once in awhile, one float will stick causing the airplane to turn around and face the beach when the engine starts. Be alert for this. If a turn starts, full opposite rudder and a burst of power may save the moment! If that doesn't work, the turn will continue. Shut down and start over.

A final word of caution about beaching: when you fly out to that pristine lake with the beautiful sandy beach, keep in mind what made that beach…probably big waves, rubbing rocks together until they became sand! So, ten or twelve hours after your arrival, it is possible that weather could move in and recreate that same big wave scene. While doing your landing area assessment, give some thought to a plan B. Is there another beach

Don't ever lose sight of what made that beautiful beach you plan to enjoy!

nearby that is facing a different direction? It would be good to know about it, so you could move in the morning if necessary.

To be properly equipped for anchoring and tiedown away from home base, three lines, each 100 feet long (one on the anchor, two for the 45° ties), and three 40 footers are needed—all 3/8-inch for seaplanes up to 4,000 pounds. The 40 footers are handy for docklines and short ties and can be tied together for longer runs. Seaplane pilots who have cared for their birds during a serious blow will tell you that you never have enough line. See additional comments below about lines and knots so you know the best way to secure your floatplane.

PTS Section XII
◆ D ◆

Ramping

Ramping is the process of putting the floatplane onto a wooden ramp that is sloping down into the water. This is done at displacement taxi speed, with elevator up, and with an application of power at the moment before contact with the ramp. Power continues long enough to move the floatplane well onto the ramp so it will stay, once power is decreased. Only wood ramps are suitable for ramping a floatplane with straight floats, and the pilot needs be assured ahead of time that the ramp is in good condition. Such wood ramps are often put together with large spikes that tend to work loose with age and wave action. A protruding spike can do major damage to a float.

Ramping with a Crosswind

Sometimes, the ramp is oriented such that the pilot is faced with ramping in a direction other than into the wind, so the last part of the ever-pervading rule number one applies: expect trouble. With a crosswind, if wind velocity allows crosswind taxi, such a ramping can be accomplished. The danger is the possibility of a gust weathervaning the floatplane at a critical moment just before contact with the ramp, causing the seaplane to partially or fully miss the ramp. The pilot needs to understand and have practiced the "throttle as a rudder" technique to prevent such an occurrence.

The Throttle as a Rudder

Picture taxiing crosswind with a wind from the left. The wind is just strong enough that you can't hold the course. With elevator fully up, add a little power. This causes the nose to rise somewhat, shifting the center of buoyancy slightly aft. Now the

Seaplanes ramped in Ketchikan, Alaska.

weathercocking force decreases because the arm (the horizontal distance from the center of buoyancy to the center of pressure on the seaplane's side area aft of the center of buoyancy) is less and the arm lengthens to the forward center of pressure, which opposes weathercocking into the wind. *See* Figure 16-18. The nose then will come back to the right. In effect, additions and reductions of power cause the floatplane to turn into or away from the wind, thus "the throttle becomes a rudder." Knowledge of this effect is especially useful when ramping in a crosswind. A review of "Using the Throttle as a Rudder," Chapter 7, Page 65 should help if you are still a little fuzzy about how this works. This is the same characteristic that helps the pilot turn downwind in a strong breeze, using a plowing turn.

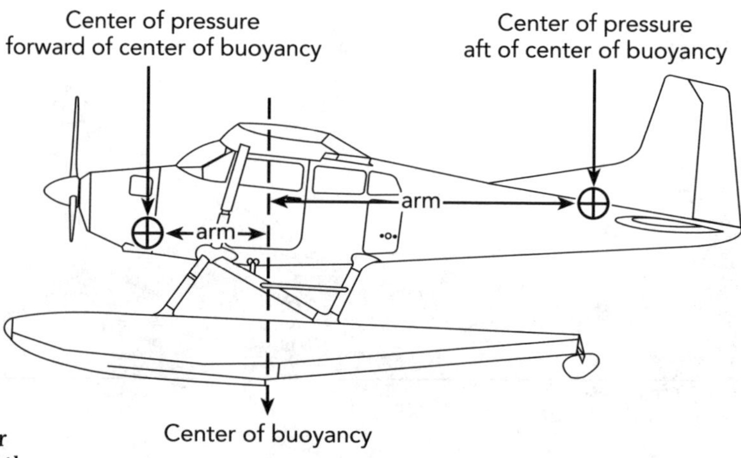

Figure 16-18. The weathercocking moment is the sum of the wind force on the side surface aft of the center of buoyancy times the length of the arm from the center of buoyancy to the center of the side surface area. When the nose rises, the center of buoyancy moves aft, decreasing the side surface area aft and also decreasing the length of the arm. The opposite is happening forward of the center of buoyancy, which increases the downwind weathercocking tendency.

Lines and a Few Important Knots

Lines

As a seaplane pilot you have some serious decisions to make about the kind of line and how much of it to carry aboard. Line choices of materials are nylon, polypropylene and polyester (Dacron) in synthetics, and manila and sisal in natural fibers. Their characteristics are listed in Figure 16-19 and strengths in Figure 16-20.

Shock load is inversely proportional to the line's ability to stretch under load (elasticity). The floating polypropylene line has limited application because it floats and gets easily tangled in passing boat propellers. It is good for lifesaving purposes if attached to a throwing object. It is very difficult to throw by itself because it is so light weight. It is often used in applications that are inappropriate because it is cheap and readily available in stores.

Dacron is the line of choice when you want resistance to sun rotting and a line that doesn't stretch. It doesn't have much application in seaplane operations.

Nylon is the material of choice for seaplane applications, but you have one more choice to make. Nylon rope comes in two styles: twisted and braided. Unfortunately, merchants carry the braided more often because it sells well. Why does it sell well? Because it is pretty, I guess. The twisted line is far superior in seaplane operations because it doesn't slip through your hands like the braided does, and it holds knots much better for the same reason.

There is a recommendation about how much line to carry at the end of the discussion about beaching.

	nylon	polypropylene	polyester	manila	sisal
Shock load	1	2	3	3	4
Rot resistance	1	1	1	4	4
Mildew resistance	1	1	1	4	4
Sunlight resistance	3	4	1	1	1
Handling	1	2	1	3	4
Heat: weakens at, °F	350°	150°	350°	>600°	>600°
Can store	wet	wet	wet	dry	dry
Oil and gas resistance	1	1	1	3	3
Acid resistance	2	1	1	4	4
Abrasion resistance	1	3	1	2	4
Floats	No	Yes	No	No	No

Figure 16-19. Characteristics of line. (Rating: 1 is best, 4 is poor)

Size	Nylon		Polypropylene	
	Working	*Breaking*	*Working*	*Breaking*
1/4"	124	1,125	113	1,025
3/8"	278	2,500	244	2,200
1/2"	525	4,750	420	3,800

Note 1. Nylon line ages, loosing strength and elasticity. It should be replaced when it is abraded or has lost its form, or "life."

Note 2. Working strength computed at 11% of breaking strength — a very conservative approach.

Figure 16-20. Strength of new line, pounds

Knots

As a seaplane pilot you really need to know the first four knots listed: bowline, half hitch and half hitch on a bight, fisherman's knot, and cleat hitch. Once you learn them, practice them every day for two weeks so they become second nature. The fifth (slip knot on a bight) is optional. The slippery knot is sure nice to know when needed, but will probably not be needed for the checkride. The anchor bend is shown so you can use it to attach a rode to your anchor, but you won't use it often enough to memorize it. The airport knot is not shown. Most pilots already know how to tie it, and its applications with seaplanes are few because it won't hold if the angle between the two lines is more than 2 or 3 degrees. So it won't work if the tiedown line is around a tree or any object of significant diameter.

Strength of Knots

Knot	*Relative Strength*
Line	100%
Anchor bend	76%
Double half hitch	65–70%
Bowline	60%
Fisherman's knot	55–60%
Square knot	45%
Eye splice on thimble	90–95%
Splice	85–87%

Bowline

This is probably my favorite knot because I use it in so many applications. It is dependable, won't slip, and is easy to untie after it has been wet and had a heavy load on it. It is useful when you need any kind of a loop, whether a big loop around your chest to haul you out of the water or to tie around a strut or through a tiedown ring. It is sometimes taught using the silly story of the elephant and the mouse (*see* Figure 16-21). The critical part is selecting the right "tree" for the elephant to go behind. If you select the wrong one, the knot will fall apart when you tug on it. The knot releases easily when you slide the part that's around the "tree" up the tree a ways.

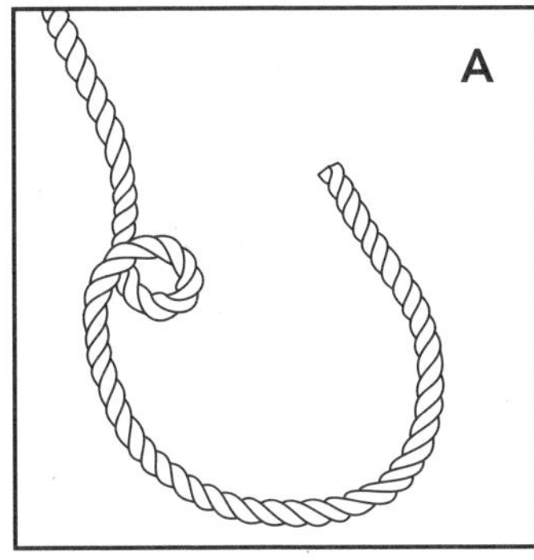

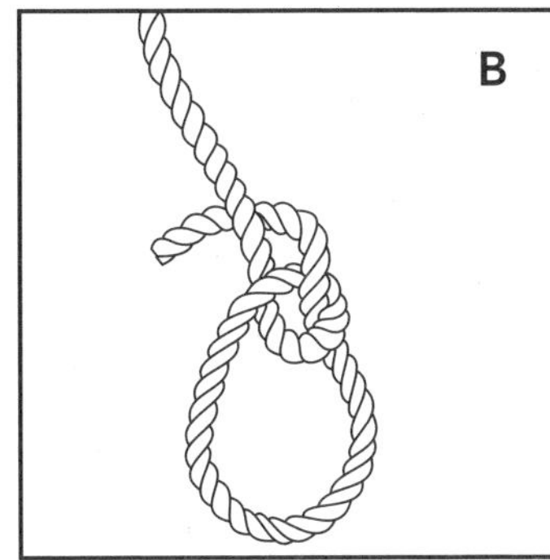

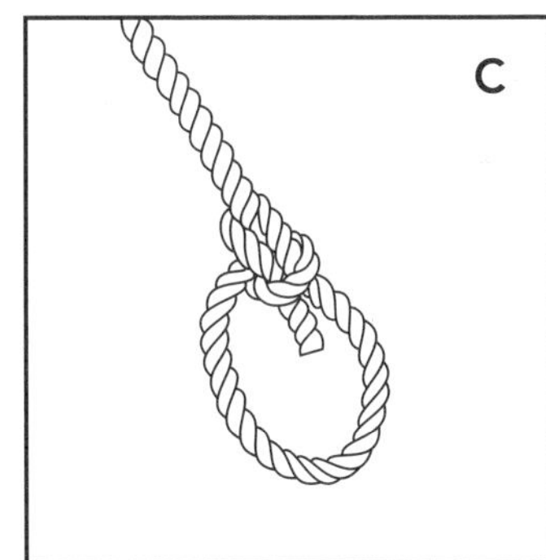

Figure 16-21. Tying the bowline

A. The story begins with making the elephant's hole.
B. The elephant (end of the line) comes up out of his hole and goes around behind the tree (the "tree" is the line crossing, to complete the hole, farthest from your eye).
C. He sees a mouse, gets scared and goes back in his hole.

Half Hitch and Half Hitch on a Bight

The half hitch is actually a double half hitch, because a single half hitch is not a useful knot. But the "double" part is often dropped in common usage. This simple knot can be used to finish a loop, but will slide to close or open the loop. It can be tied with a strain on the loaded end of the line. It is most useful for the seaplane pilot when tying the seaplane to a tree, stump or rock. The critical part of mooring your seaplane to a tree is not the knot, but rather that you take the line around the tree twice, making sure that the second time around crosses over the first circle. Like the cleat hitch, strength comes from the friction of the crossover. When you tie off with a half hitch, make sure that the free end crosses the end-under-load at a 90° angle so the knot won't slip and loosen the loaded line. If you have used a long line and don't want to pull all of it around the tree twice, use the half hitch on a bight. A bight is just a loop, making two lines tied as if they were one. The bight is useful as a quick release with many knots, like the slipknot on a bight and with the cleat hitch.

The half hitch is illustrated on the next page.

Fisherman's Knot

This easy knot is most useful for tying two lines together and is the knot of choice when tying together lines of different diameter. One side (the last one tied) can be done on a bight for easier release because this knot is hard to untie after it has been under strain. It consists simply of an overhand knot (the simplest of knots) in each

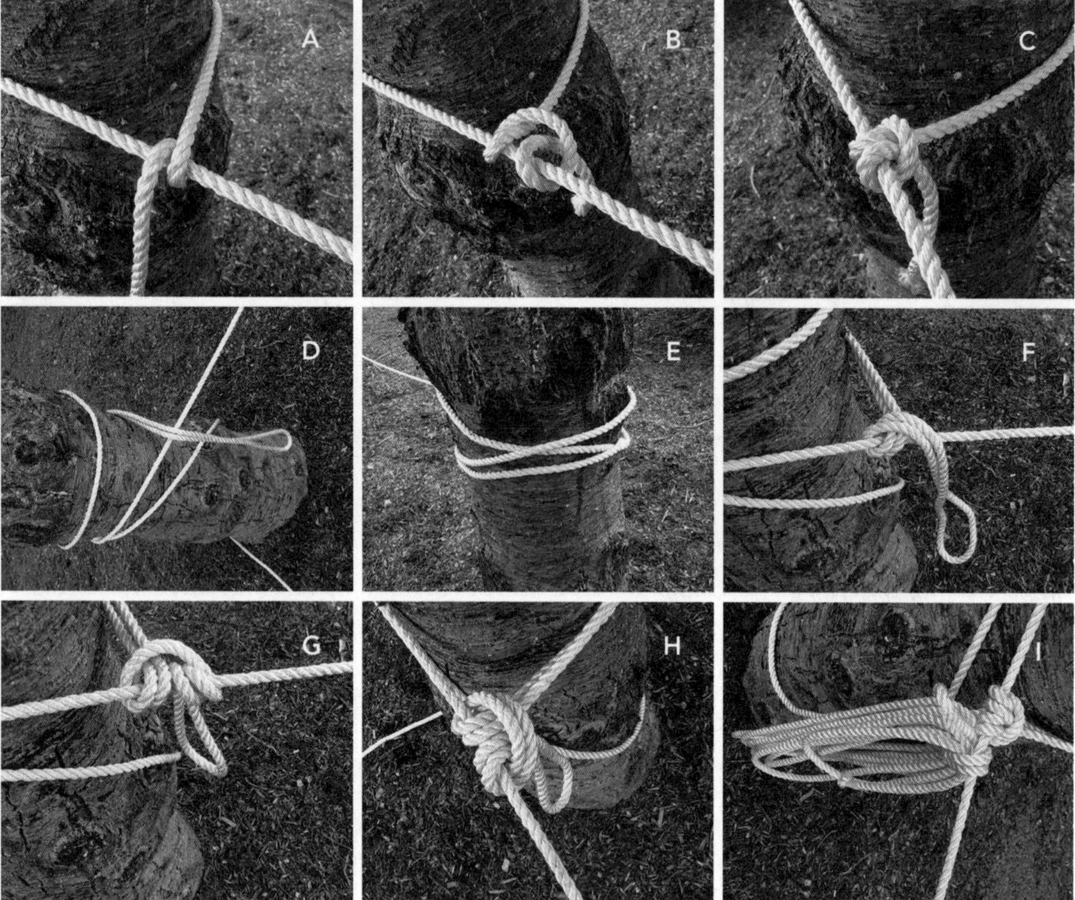

Figure 16-22. The half hitch

A. Single half hitch—not yet a knot
B. Double half hitch before tightening
C. Finished double half hitch. Note that the line that forms the knot makes a 90° angle to the working line. This knot would be more secure if the line was passed around the tree, and over itself, once more.
D. The beginning of the double half hitch on a bight.
E. The important crossover (the real strength of the knot).
F. Single half hitch on a bight (loop)—not yet a real knot.
G. The double half hitch on a bight before tightening.
H. The finished double half hitch on a bight. The bight (loop) should be about 12–18 inches long (next photo shows why).
I. Extra line is coiled neatly and secured off the ground with another half hitch. Note the angle of the line forming the knot to the working line is about 90°.

line with the other line passing through the center of the knot. It is quick to tie when you are hurrying to get tied down before a storm and need to mate two lines together (*See* Figure 16-23.).

Cleat Hitch

This quick and simple hitch used to tie to a cleat is often badly or incorrectly tied. The most important part of this knot is that the line must first pass around the base of the cleat at least one-and-a-half times, because therein lies its strength. After that, one lay on each fluke of the cleat is enough. More than that belies a land-lubber who really doesn't understand the knot. If you are not in a hurry and are a neat person, the free end after the cleat hitch can be coiled on the deck of the dock.

Cleat hitch: *see* Figure 16-24.

Slipknot on a Bight

Simple and quick, but temporary. Don't trust it too much as it can slip, especially with braided and polypropylene lines. (*See* Figure 16-25 on the next page.)

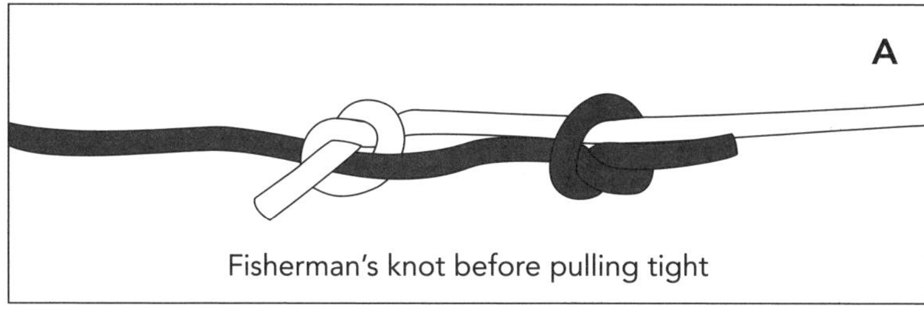

Figure 16-23.
The Fisherman's knot
A. Fisherman's knot before pulling tight
B. Fisherman's knot, pulled tight
C. Fisherman's knot with a bight quick release

Slippery Knot

This knot is a little more complex but wonderful when you need to get away from a dock (*see* the discussion of its use on Page 212). The secret to tying this knot is the first loop tuck is made from the standing line (line to airframe), the second from the trigger line, the third from the "standing," or working line, and the fourth in the trigger line. Note in the first photo how little line has to come back around the dock structure when the knot is released.

Anchor Bend

This knot is the only one to use when tying your rode to your anchor. Of all the knots, it decreases the strength of the line the least.

Cleat Hitch

Cleat hitch on a bight

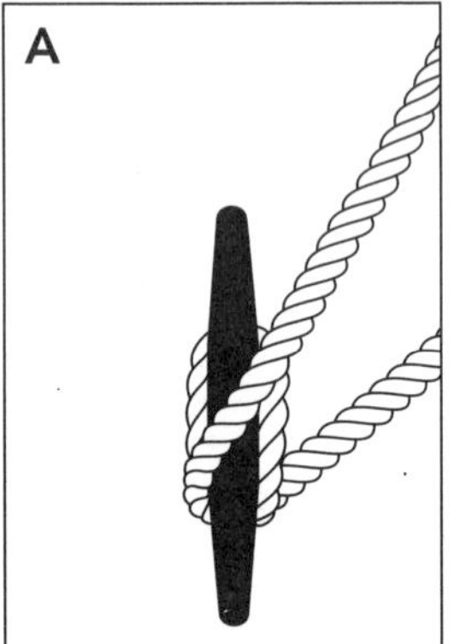

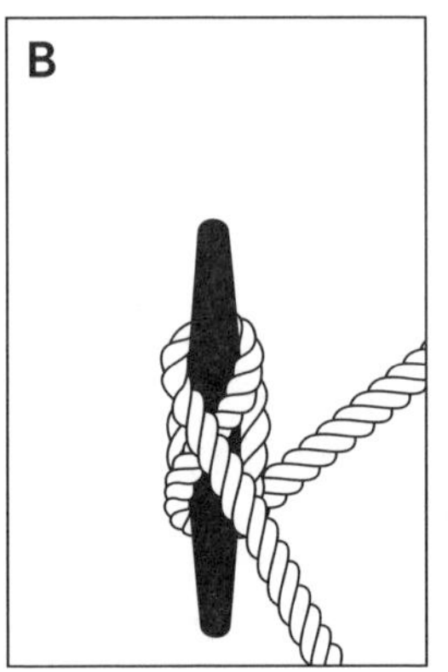

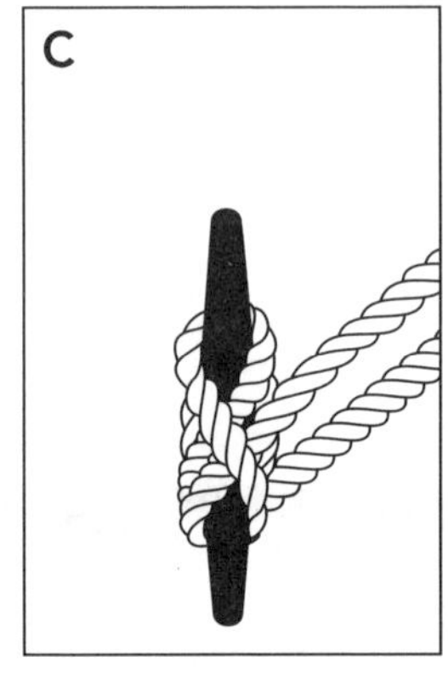

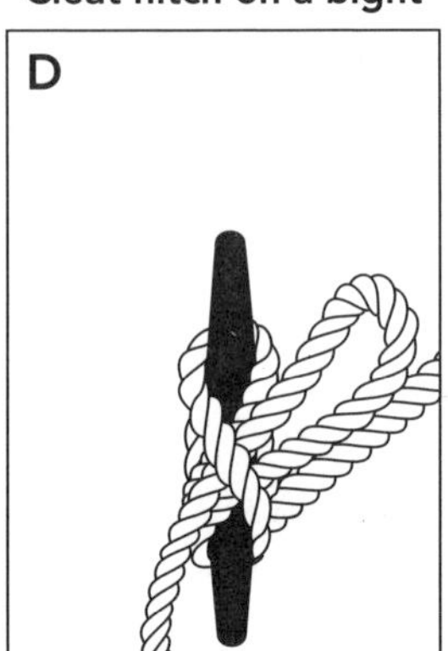

Figure 16-24. Cleat hitch and cleat hitch on a bight.

A. One and a half times around the base of the cleat.
B. First lay around the fluke.
C. The properly finished cleat hitch.
D. Cleat hitch on a bight (quick release).

Figure 16-25. Slipknot on a bight.

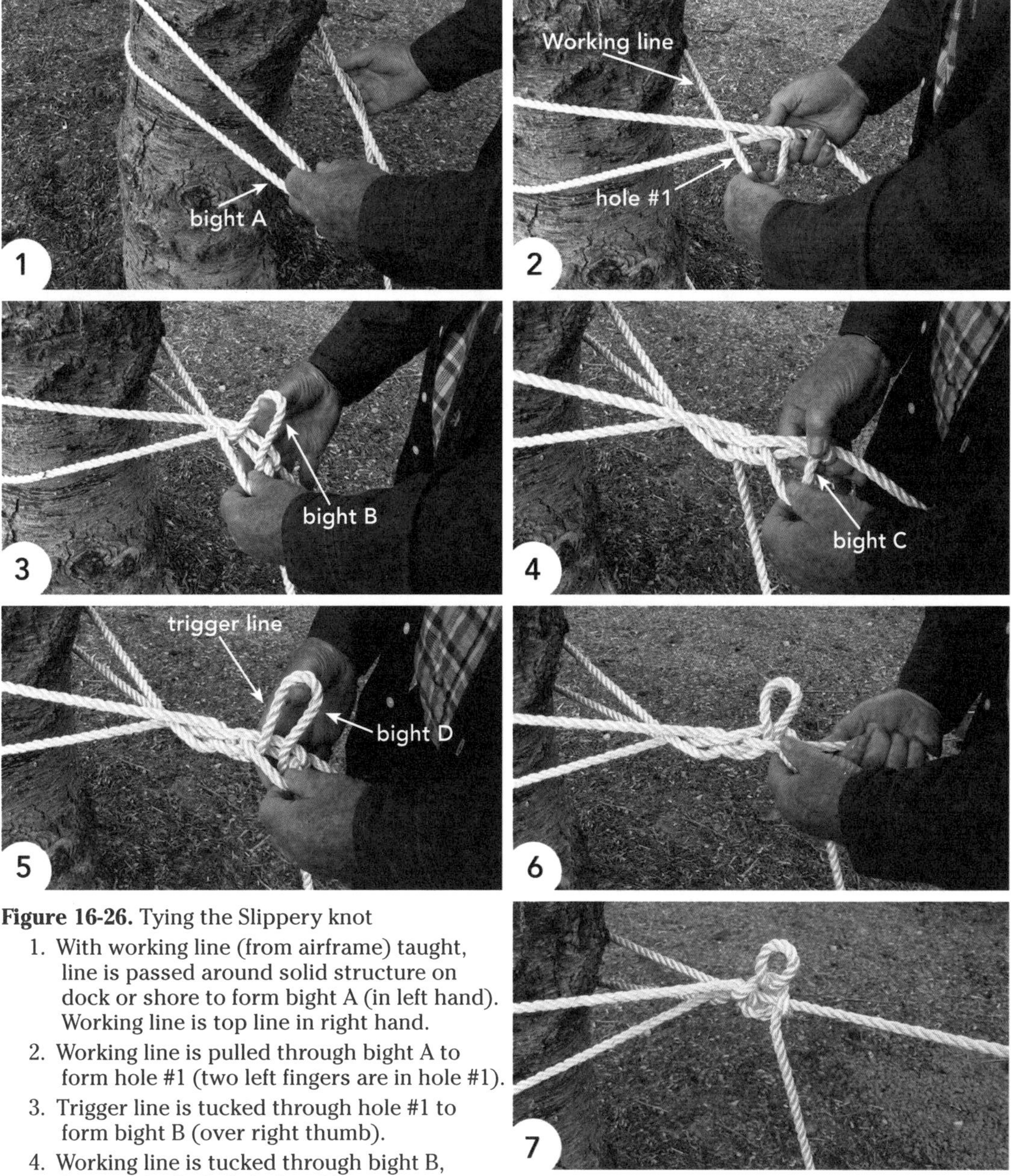

Figure 16-26. Tying the Slippery knot

1. With working line (from airframe) taught, line is passed around solid structure on dock or shore to form bight A (in left hand). Working line is top line in right hand.
2. Working line is pulled through bight A to form hole #1 (two left fingers are in hole #1).
3. Trigger line is tucked through hole #1 to form bight B (over right thumb).
4. Working line is tucked through bight B, forming bight C (left thumb).
5. The last loop is fashioned by pulling the trigger line through bight C to form bight D.
6. Then the knot is pulled tight and tested by tugging on the working line.
7. The finished slippery knot. Line to right is the working line. It is attached to the airframe and is under load with the floatplane tugging on it. Line going to bottom of photo is the trigger line that the pilot takes into the cockpit.

Figure 16-27. The anchor bend. Finish the loose end with twine, or by passing the free end under one strand of the standing line. In this modern age, a cable tie or zip tie is functional to replace the twine binding.

Review

After Landing

- Confirm you are on the water.
- Then throttle back, rudders, flaps and checklist.

In mariner's lingo, the correct terms are:

- line
- rode
- bow line
- stern line
- spring line
- standing, or working line

Anchoring

Considered a temporary means of mooring and is used in emergencies. It is an important skill because it is the seaplane pilot's last defense against engine failure on the water. Should be practiced periodically as it is a multi-faceted task in which you need to develop some skills. The anchor must be stored within easy reach of the pilot, ready for immediate use. Ground tackle includes anchors, rode and associated fittings.

Some things to remember when anchoring:

- You need two hands for handling the rode. How do you do this?
- Uncoiling a 100-foot bundle of line quickly without tangles is an acquired skill.
- You can throw some of the individual loops in the water—why?
- Most anchors will not set if the bottom is weedy or if the rode is around one of the flukes of the anchor.
- Scope (ratio of length of rode to depth of water) should be at least 6:1 if the anchor is fitted with chain, and 10:1 without chain.
- Swing: area of the circle whose radius is the length of rode. If the wind or current changes, the anchored seaplane can go anywhere within this circle.

Docking

Follow the two pervading rules of docking:

1. When docking, beaching or buoying, always do it into the wind. If you can't do it into the wind, expect trouble.
2. If at all possible, plan a straight-in final approach to the dock for the last 50 to 100 feet. This second rule applies primarily to parallel docking.

If it is necessary to dock with the dock on the starboard (right) side, and you are flying a side-by-side floatplane, don't guess where the dock is—move over to the right seat.

Docking Technique

1. Scrutinize the dock thoroughly from the air.
2. Make a close pass on the water.
3. Taxi back out to begin your final approach.
4. Brief your passengers.
5. Get yourself unencumbered.
6. Question if you need a short line for the initial tie-up.
7. Assume the "half-in-half-out" position.
8. Kill the engine.
9. Stay with the rudder pedals until the last possible moment.
10. Go to the dock with BOTH feet.
11. Slow forward motion with the float parallel to and against the dock.

The critical float is the windward float in a bow-to docking (see definition in text above) which must be secured first to prevent dents in the opposite wing. Heavy weather mooring at the dock is serious business because waves washing across the floats will eventually sink them.

Departing the Dock

Be certain both you and the dock handler know exactly what steps will transpire. Don't dawdle at getting the engine started. If you are departing from a dock with no help, the wind is blowing, and there is an unfriendly shore downwind,

1. Use the braking effect of a lee dock.
2. Use the slippery knot.

Buoying

These are some of the points covered in the process of taxiing up to and securing the floatplane to a buoy:

- The buoy ***must*** be approached from exactly downwind.
- The "half in, half out" technique will greatly decrease the time it takes you to get out and acquire the buoy.
- Continue to steer until the last possible moment.
- Wait for the buoy to come to you (describe why this is so).

Beaching

The floatplane can be beached either bow-to or heeled up. Heeling up on the beach is the preferred method to go ashore in unimproved areas for several reasons. Describe at least three.

Sailing back to the beach or into a slip in winds less than 13–15 MPH may be done using accuracy sailing. If the wind is greater than 15, power sail back.

Describe how to protect the water rudders during the process called "heeling up." Keep in mind that:

- The wind direction near shore is often quite different than that out on the lake.
- The wind streaks on the water close to shore do not indicate the true wind direction.
- Light winds along the shoreline tend to have a direction more parallel to the shoreline.

Three Paddle Rules:

1. The paddle is 20 to 30 times more effective as a pole than as a paddle, so you should whenever possible use it to push against the bottom rather than to move water.
2. Describe how to avoid "falling on your sword" if the paddle handle breaks and you lose your balance.
3. In any breeze at all, you won't be able to move the seaplane against it, using the paddle. You probably will not be able to rotate the seaplane, which will tend to weathercock.

Departing the Beach:

- Before loading anything, push the floatplane into the water until it floats then bring it back until it is just touching the beach.
- Load some stuff and push off again, load a passenger and push off again, etc.
- When everything is loaded but you, hold onto the tail while making sure there are no spectators behind the airplane and water traffic won't be a problem.
- Then push off and bring it back until it is just touching; quickly get in, start the engine and taxi into safe water.
- Be alert that once in awhile, one float will stick causing the airplane to turn around and face the beach when the engine starts.
- Keep in mind that big waves probably made that beach!

Ramping:

- The process of putting the floatplane onto a wooden ramp that slopes down into the water.
- Done at displacement taxi speed, elevator up, and with an application of power at the moment before contact with the ramp.
- The power continues as long as it takes to move the floatplane well onto the ramp so that it will stay, once power is decreased.
- Only wood ramps are suitable for ramping a straight float floatplane.
- Make sure ahead of time that the ramp is in good condition.

Describe ramping with a crosswind and "the throttle as a rudder." Check your answers in the text above.

Check the text above in this chapter to refresh on the advantages and disadvantages of each.

Lines

Lines are made of several materials: nylon, polypropylene and polyester (Dacron) in synthetics, and manila and sisal in natural fibers.

Nylon is the material of choice for seaplane applications. Nylon rope comes in two styles: twisted and braided. The twisted line is far superior because it doesn't slip through your hands like the braided does, and it holds knots much better for the same reason.

Knots

As a seaplane pilot you really need to know the first four knots listed below. Once you learn them, practice them every day until you know them well:

- Bowline—dependable, won't slip, easy to untie after it has been wet and had a heavy load on it.
- Half hitch and half hitch on a bight—can be used to finish a loop but will slide to close or open the loop. It can be tied with a strain on the loaded end of the line.
- Fisherman's knot—for tying two lines together; knot of choice when tying together lines of different diameter.
- Cleat hitch—quick and simple hitch used to tie to a cleat, often badly or incorrectly tied; most important about it is that the line must first pass around the base of the cleat at least 1½ times because therein lies its strength.
- Slippery knot—a little more complex but wonderful when you need to get away from a dock.
- Anchor bend—the only knot to use when tying your rode to your anchor; it decreases the strength of the line the least of all the knots.

Burke Mees

An HU-16 Grumman Albatross topping the Chugach Mountains, Alaska.

Chapter 17
Multi-Engine Operations

PTS
FAA-S-8081-14AM*
Airplane Multi-Engine
Land and Sea

* The multi-engine PTS is not reprinted in the appendix; it can be found on the FAA's website at http://afs600.faa.gov

More than 90% of multi-engine seaplane ratings are acquired by pilots who are already single-engine seaplane pilots and hold the multi-engine land rating. Consequently, that expertise is assumed. If you are preparing for the practical test for multi-engine sea, please refer to the PTS before reading each section so you will know what will be expected of you. The appropriate PTS section appears in the sidebar opposite the beginning of each topic.

If you are already a multi-engine sea-rated pilot and are ready for a review, read on or should we say wade right on in!

First things first—"Where can I find an experienced MES instructor?"

The number of active multi-engine sea (MES) instructors are few. A good source for identifying active MES instructors is your local FAA FSDO. A listing of operators providing MES instruction is also available in the *Water Flying Annual* or on the Seaplane Pilots Association's (SPA) website at **www.seaplanes.org**.

V-Speeds and Definitions Table

A Multi-Engine Flying Refresher

Airspeed management is critical when flying multi-engine seaplanes, so let's start with a review of the important airspeeds. Write the actual airspeeds in the margin for the multi-engine seaplane you are flying. Figures 17-1 and 17-2 (next page) show examples of multi-engine airspeed indicators from a Twin Beech and a Twin Otter.

V_{XSE} *Best angle-of-climb speed (single-engine).* At this speed, the seaplane will gain the greatest height for a given distance of forward travel. This speed is used for obstacle clearance with one engine inoperative. Unless the POH states otherwise, gear and flaps are up for best performance.

V_{YSE} *Best rate-of-climb speed (single-engine).* This speed will provide the maximum altitude gain (or minimum altitude loss) for a given period of time with one engine inoperative. Again, gear and flaps up unless the POH says otherwise. Blue line on the airspeed indicator indicates this speed.

V_{SSE} *Intentional one-engine-inoperative speed or otherwise known as "safe single-engine speed."* The speed above both V_{MC} and stall speed selected by the aircraft manufacturer to provide a margin of lateral and directional control when one engine is suddenly intentionally rendered inoperative. Intentional failing of one engine below this speed is not recommended.

V_{MC} *Minimum control speed.* V_{MC} is the calibrated airspeed at which when the critical engine is suddenly made inoperative, it is possible to maintain control of the aircraft with that engine still inoperative and thereafter maintain straight flight at the same speed with an angle of bank not more than five degrees (into the good engine). When determining this speed, it is assumed that the engine has failed in the most critical mode for controllability, i.e., the prop may be unfeathered etc. For those who like details, or if it is a cold winter night and the lake is frozen solid, further reading can be found in 14 CFR §23.149.

V_{MCG} *Minimum control speed with one engine inoperative while on the water.* The minimum airspeed on the water at which directional control can be maintained, when one engine is suddenly made inoperative, using only aerodynamic controls. V_{MCG} is a function of the amount of engine thrust, but also varies with altitude and temperature.

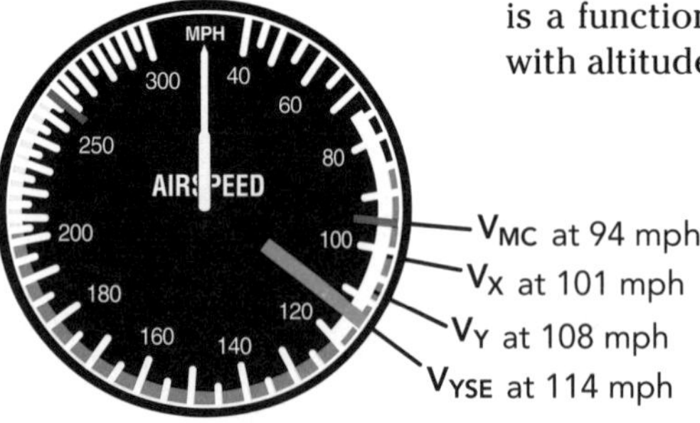

Figure 17-1. Airspeed indicator for Twin Beech on floats

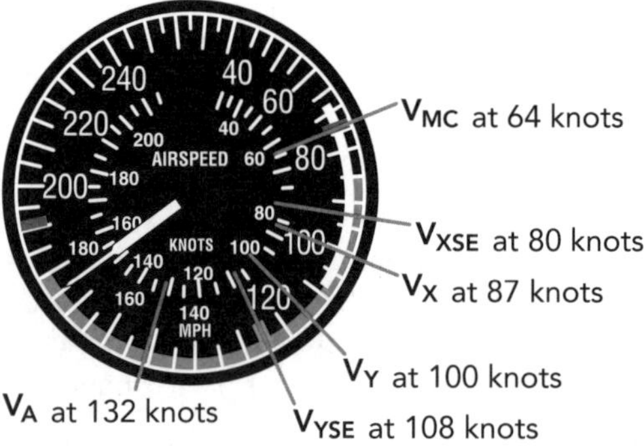

Figure 17-2. Airspeed indicator for Twin Otter on floats

The following are some other important terms you should be familiar with:

Calibrated airspeed

Flight manual airspeed numbers, unless airspeed values are marked as "indicated airspeed" are calibrated airspeed and can be corrected to indicated by using the correction table in the flight manual. The difference between the two airspeeds is due primarily to errors in the static and dynamic pressure sensing systems on that model airplane. Have a look at the CAS vs. IAS values in the flight manual. Probably, the differences are so small as to be insignificant. If not, correct the CAS values to IAS so you can read them right off the airspeed indicator. Then, remember to calibrate your airspeed indicator periodically while you practice stalls (*see* the discussion of stalls and airspeed calibration in Chapter 14).

See Chapter 14 starting at the bottom of Page 168, and continuing through Page 170.

Critical engine

The engine whose failure would most adversely affect the performance or handling qualities of the seaplane.

Normally aspirated engine

Also known as "naturally aspirated." An engine that is not turbocharged or supercharged, which leads to loss of power at higher altitudes due to the reduced density of the air entering the engine.

Boosted engine

General term for a turbocharged or supercharged engine. A **turbocharged** engine uses an exhaust-driven turbine blower or compressor to increase manifold pressure up to 30 inches Hg, or more, at altitude. A **supercharged** engine uses a similar process except the compressor is driven directly by the engine to increase manifold pressure to a level, typically in excess of 30 inches Hg.

Blue line

A blue radial line on the airspeed indicator that denotes the best rate-of-climb airspeed when one engine is inoperative (V_{YSE}).

Red line

There are two red radial lines on the airspeed indicator: the usual one at the top of the operational airspeed arc which denotes V_{NE}, and the other below the blue line, which indicates minimum controllable airspeed (V_{MC}).

It is time to take a look at the items that apply to the multi-engine seaplane. Note that the multi-engine sea pilot applicant is assumed to be knowledgeable in all the other seaplane operations contained in other chapters in this book. So, to prepare for the multi-engine sea rating, study this chapter ***and*** all the others. The PTS items listed are the areas that must be tested for a pilot who holds AMEL and ASES ratings.

MES Section I
F ◆ G

Preflight Preparation

The PTS MES task table says that if you hold the single-engine sea and multi-engine land ratings, you shall be tested on topics F and G but, at the examiner's discretion, any or all of the topics (from A to K) may come up. So review each of them in Chapters 18 through 23 before both the oral and flight portions of the practical test.

MES Section I
◆ F ◆

Performance and Limitations

Multi-engine seaplanes are typically poorer performers than their landplane counterparts. Be sure you are able to access and interpret the performance data from the seaplane portion of the aircraft's POH, and have reviewed thoroughly the systems operations such as the propeller, fuel and electrical systems. A parting thought to keep in mind as we leave the topic of multi-engine performance is that there is nothing in 14 CFR Part 23 that requires a multi-engine seaplane to climb *or maintain altitude* in the takeoff configuration with one engine inoperative. In fact, many multi-engine seaplanes were barely able to do this in any configuration with one engine inoperative when brand new in the hands of a skilled test pilot. This fact is easier to accept when one realizes that the performance of a seaplane can decrease by as much as 80% with the loss of one engine. While you are resting easy in your favorite armchair, it would be a good time to take another look at the single-engine performance numbers in your favorite seaplane's POH! With many multi-engine seaplanes, you can only expect the good engine to provide a flatter glide angle providing you are using good techniques.

MES Section I
◆ G ◆

Operation of Systems

As the holder of a multi-engine land rating, you already understand multi-engine systems. Go over them with your flight instructor before the practical test, just to be sure. Also read Chapter 19 about systems in the seaplane portion of the aircraft you will use for your practical test.

Preflight Procedures

MES Section II
◆ E ◆

If you hold multi-engine land and single-engine sea ratings, only task E is required to be tested, but any tasks may come up at the discretion of the examiner.

Preflight Inspection and Cockpit Management

MES Section II
A ◆ B

These topics are covered in Chapters 4 and 5 and should be reviewed before the oral and checkride.

Engine Starting

MES Section II
◆ C ◆

Please review Chapter 6 regarding engine start. In addition, as you know from your MES landplane experience, typically the engine that is electrically closest to the battery is started first. With the seaplane there may be reasons to start the other engine first. For example, if the right engine is normally started first, but you are at the dock with the left float near the dock, starting the left engine first will start to move you away from the dock. The same would apply if the aircraft is heeled up and the left float is aground harder than the right float.

Taxiing

MES Section II
◆ E ◆

For this section, *see* Chapter 7 (which starts on Page 59). In addition to rudders and ailerons, you can use differential power to assist with directional control.

Sailing

(same as above)

Review Chapter 8 for information and tips about sailing. In addition, remember that you have the use of differential power as well as the air rudder and ailerons to change the angle of the nose relative to the wind when power sailing.

Before Takeoff Check

MES Section II
◆ F ◆

Chapter 9 (Page 85), "The Pretakeoff Check" should be reviewed. The multi-engine seaplane is more complex than the single, so procedure and use of the checklist is a must. A second check of the "things that can kill ya" (*see* Page 90) should be done just before starting the takeoff run. An additional checklist for these items may be necessary if there are too many to remember.

MES Section III

Airport and Seaplane Base Operations

If you hold multi-engine land and single-engine sea ratings, none of the tasks in this PTS section are required. However, they may come up during the practical test. You can always review them by reading Chapter 10 again.

MES Section IV
A • B • C • D • E
F • G • H

Takeoffs, Landings, and Go-Arounds

If you hold multi-engine land and single-engine sea ratings, all tasks except "I" from the PTS are required to be tested. Seaplane takeoffs, landings and go-arounds are covered in Chapters 11, 12, and 13. The principles covered therein apply to multi-engine seaplane operations as well, with some small differences:

1. Starting the takeoff run may involve the use of differential power, either to protect the propeller on the windward side and/or to assist in establishing a crosswind heading.
2. After liftoff, rather than striving for "V_Y and clean before 50" as we do with single-engine seaplanes, the multi-engine philosophies apply. The pilot strives for V_Y but, in getting there, V_{YSE} and V_{MC} are important milestones. Keep in mind that all three of those V-speeds are flaps-up speeds, so in reality, "V_Y and clean" are still the goal with each takeoff, but there are some modifications needed for the glassy water takeoff. Read again about those in Chapter 11. As with the single-engine floatplane, putting it all together with a constant climb angle while the aircraft is accelerating to reach V_Y at about obstacle height makes a smooth, safe takeoff that passengers appreciate. In combination with the above, awareness of traffic, using a safe climb path and use of the checklist at appropriate times makes the examiner smile!
3. By all means, if the manufacturer's recommendations differ from the above, you should follow them.

MES Section V

Performance Maneuver

Steep Turns

Steep turns are discussed in Chapter 14. Please review and practice. It will help you to know your airplane. Plus, they are basic to doing emergency descents.

MES Sections
VI and VII

Ground Reference Maneuvers and Navigation

Task areas VI and VII are not required to be tested for the multi-engine sea unless the applicant is not airplane-rated at the private level or better.

Slow Flight and Stalls

MES Section VIII

Task area VIII is not required for testing if you hold both multi-engine land and single-engine sea ratings. It is a task area common to all multi-engine aircraft, not specific to multi-engine seaplanes, so is not discussed here, except to say that pilots must be mindful that the multi-engine seaplane is a poor performer compared to its land counterparts. Therefore, statistically, stalls are more common and the approach to the stall is more rapid in the seaplane. It is a skill area that requires mastery and continued practice.

Basic Instrument Maneuvers

MES Section IX

Task area IX is not required to be tested for the multi-engine sea rating unless the applicant is not airplane-rated at the private level or better.

Emergency Operations

MES Section X
A • B • C • D • E • F

Since multi-engine emergency operations are a significant part of the multi-engine pilot's training, you will find that much of the *Airplane Flying Handbook*'s multi-engine chapter is included here, with additions, corrections and deletions made as necessary to adapt the information to seaplane training. If any of the procedures found herein differ from the manufacturer's recommendations, the manufacturer's recommendations must be followed. All tasks in this section are required to be tested.

The *Airplane Flight Manual* (AFM) and/or *Pilot's Operating Handbook* (POH) for each seaplane contains information pertinent to most emergency procedures and the safe operation of the seaplane. Manufacturers also provide the checklists that complement the procedures. The owner/operator is responsible for keeping the checklist and the latest information **in the seaplane within easy reach of the crew** for quick reference in case of an emergency. Some emergency procedures for engine failure on takeoff or inflight fire should be memorized and practiced so that response is timely and accurate. Talk with your flight instructor about which of these procedures should be committed to memory.

MES Section X
◆ A ◆

Emergency Descent

First, you should review Chapter 15. When it is necessary to descend rapidly, as in the case of an inflight fire, follow the manufacturer's recommended procedures. When specific procedures are not published, the following may be used and modified, as required:

1. Throttles and props—Closed, then max RPM
2. Airspeed—Here, the multi-engine pilot has some choices to make. Talk the subject over with a flight instructor you trust and plan what airspeed you will use. Different speeds may be appropriate for the emergency descent. If amphibious, max gear down speed is appropriate if extended landing gear provide a significant drag. Remember the discussion about critical altitude, however, in Chapter 15. Don't get caught up in the moment if your ship is amphibious and you plan to land where there is lots of water. The seaplane is so "draggy" that descent rates will be quite good with wheels up and a speed in the V_A to V_{NO} range. It is also possible that max gear down speed and V_A speeds are similar, so only one speed needs to be remembered. Generally, flaps are not recommended for use during emergency descent, as 45° to 60° angles of bank impose load factors that are too close to design load limit with flaps extended. Flaps are appropriate for the emergency approach portion of the descent.
3. Landing gear—Water: up
   Land: down
4. Flaps—For the approach phase

If your twin is an amphibian, remember about **critical altitude** from Page 191 (Chapter 15).

During practice emergency descents, careful consideration should be given to the operating temperature of the engines.

MES Section X
◆ B ◆

Engine Failure During Takeoff Before V_{MC} (Simulated)

When an engine fails during the water run before becoming airborne, close both throttles immediately and employ safe deceleration procedures. The pilot should be able to demonstrate maximum deceleration procedures while maintaining directional control (see the section on takeoff aborts in Chapter 11).

In training, the recommended procedure to simulate an engine failure on takeoff is to close the throttle on one engine before 50 percent V_{MC}. This provides a safety factor for the instructor pilot and more time for the training pilot to make a proper decision. If the training pilot fails to recognize the emergency promptly, the instructor pilot can close the throttle or mixture on the running engine and bring the seaplane safely to a stop.

Engine Failure After Lift-Off (Simulated)

MES Section X
◆ C ◆

If, after becoming airborne, an engine should fail prior to having reached the single-engine best rate-of-climb speed (V_{YSE}), follow the same procedure you use for engine failure before lift-off except that power reduction on the good engine should be reduced more slowly to prevent loss of control or high rates of descent back to the water. This is recommended because an immediate landing is usually inevitable due to the altitude loss required to increase the speed to V_{YSE}.

The pilot must determine **before takeoff** what altitude, airspeed, and seaplane configuration is needed to permit the flight to continue in the event of an engine failure. It is appropriate to brief the crew (or flight instructor) before the throttles come up on takeoff as to what procedure the pilot intends to use. If you are flying solo, it is good practice to verbally brief yourself.

Departing from Water

The pilot should also be aware that if engine failure occurs before these required factors are established, both throttles must be closed (slowly and smoothly) and the situation treated the same as an engine failure on a single-engine seaplane. If it has been predetermined that the single-engine rate of climb under existing circumstances will be at least 50 fpm at 1,000 feet above the airport/water run area, and that at least the single-engine best angle-of-climb speed has been attained, the pilot may decide to continue the takeoff.

Water Departure With/Without Obstacle

If the single-engine best angle-of-climb speed (V_{XSE}) has been obtained and an obstacle is ahead, the pilot should climb at the single-engine best angle-of-climb speed (V_{XSE}) or V_{MC} +5, whichever is higher, to clear the obstruction. The pilot should hold 3° to 5° of bank into the operating engine and after the obstacle, stabilize the airspeed at the single-engine best rate-of-climb speed (V_{YSE}) while identifying, verifying, and (simulate) feathering the inoperative engine propeller. Then, he or she should retract the flaps.

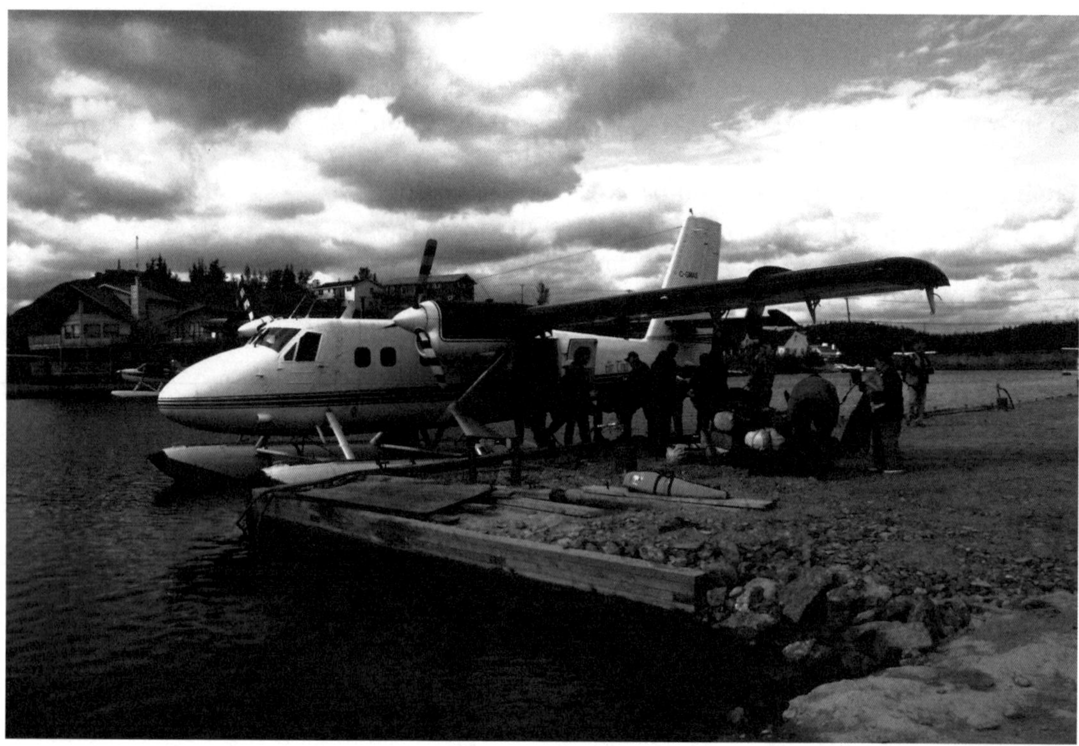
Robert Grant

Loading a "Twotter" (DeHavilland Twin Otter) for a trip into the bush from Yellowknife, Northwest Territories.

When an engine fails after becoming airborne, and an obstacle is not a problem, the pilot should hold the heading with the rudder and simultaneously roll into a bank of 5° to 8° toward the operating engine. The more bank used initially will lower V_{MC} and help maintain control with no or very little climb performance. Once the seaplane is under control and the proper airspeed is attained for climb, the bank angle can be reduced to establish zero slip to increase climb performance. Without a yaw indicator, 2° to 3° of bank and one-half ball deflection is recommended for maximum performance.

Again, if the above differs from the manufacturer's recommendations, the manufacturer's recommendations must be followed.

Glassy Water

The above practice assumes the pilot has a water surface that will allow him to judge the correct flare height. This will not be the case if the water is glassy at takeoff. Therefore, even if V_{MC}

has not been achieved but the seaplane is airborne, reduction of throttle slowly and smoothly until directional control returns will allow the aircraft to settle back into the water without a high rate of sink.

If you know you are faced with a glassy water takeoff, you may wish to stay on the water until higher than normal airspeeds are attained. A thorough discussion and plan should be developed with your flight instructor to cover this situation, which is part of any glassy water takeoff in a multi-engine seaplane.

Departing from Land (Amphibian)

If the airspeed is below the single-engine best angle-of-climb speed (V_{XSE}) and the landing gear has not been retracted, the takeoff should be aborted immediately.

If the single-engine best angle-of-climb speed (V_{XSE}) has been obtained and, if the landing gear is in the retract cycle, the pilot should climb at the single-engine best angle-of-climb speed (V_{XSE}) or V_{MC} +5, whichever is higher, to clear any obstructions. The pilot should hold 5° to 8° of bank into the operating engine and stabilize the airspeed at the single-engine best rate-of-climb speed (V_{YSE}) while identifying, verifying, and (simulate) feathering the inoperative engine propeller. Then he or she should retract the flaps.

When an engine fails after becoming airborne, the pilot should hold the heading with the rudder and simultaneously roll into a bank of 5° to 8° toward the operating engine. The more bank used initially will lower V_{MC} and help maintain control with zero or very little climb performance. Once the seaplane is under control and the proper airspeed is attained for climb, the bank angle can be reduced to establish zero slip to increase climb performance. Without a yaw indicator, 2° to 3° of bank and one-half ball deflection is recommended for maximum performance.

Both engines working fine? Then critical altitude affects landing gear management (Page 191).

When the decision is made to continue the flight, the single-engine best rate-of-climb speed should be attained and maintained with the inoperative engine feathered (simulated). Even if altitude cannot be maintained, it is best to hold that speed because it results in the slowest rate of descent and provides the most time for executing an emergency landing. In the amphibian departing land, once the decision is made to continue flight and a positive rate of climb is attained, the landing gear should be retracted as soon as practical.

If the seaplane is barely able to maintain altitude and airspeed, do not attempt a turn requiring a bank greater than 15°. When such a turn is made under these conditions, both lift and airspeed will decrease. It is advisable to continue straight ahead whenever possible, until reaching a safe maneuvering altitude and V_{YSE}. At that time, a steeper bank may be made safely in either direction. There is nothing wrong with banking toward an "inoperative" engine if a safe speed and zero sideslip (ball centered) are maintained.

One way to identify the inoperative engine is to note the direction of yaw and the rudder pressure required to maintain heading. To counteract the asymmetrical thrust, extra rudder pressure will have to be exerted on the operating engine side. To identify the failed engine, some pilots use the expression "Dead Foot, Dead Engine." Never rely on tachometer or manifold pressure readings to determine which engine has failed. After power has been lost on an engine, the tachometer will often indicate significant rpm, and the manifold pressure gauge will fall (boosted engine) or increase (normally aspirated engine) to indicate the approximate atmospheric pressure, which can be misleading.

Training experience has shown that the biggest problem is not in identifying the inoperative engine, but rather in the pilot's actions after the inoperative engine has been identified. A pilot may identify the inoperative engine and then attempt to shut down the wrong one, resulting in things getting very quiet (no power at all). To avoid this mistake, the pilot should verify the inoperative engine by retarding the throttle of that engine before shutting it down.

When demonstrating or practicing procedures for engine failure on takeoff (near the ground), the feathering of the propeller and securing of the engine should be simulated rather than actually performed, so that the engine may be available for immediate use if needed. All other settings should be made just as in an actual power failure. While actual shutdowns and restarts can and should be practiced at a safe altitude, care should be taken not to rapidly shut down an engine right after developing full power, due to the chance that shock cooling may result in a cracked cylinder on air cooled engines.

Approach and Landing with an Inoperative Engine (Simulated)

MES Section X
◆ D ◆

Essentially, a single-engine approach and landing is the same as a normal approach and landing. Avoid long, flat approaches with high-power output on the operating engine and/or excessive threshold speed that results in floating and unnecessary waterway use. Due to variations in the performance and limitations of many multi-engine seaplanes, a specific flightpath or procedure can not be proposed that would be adequate in all single-engine approaches. In most multi-engine seaplanes, a single-engine approach can be accomplished with the flightpath and procedures almost identical to a normal approach and landing. Many multi-engine manufacturers include a recommended single-engine landing procedure in the AFM/POH.

During the checkout, the transitioning pilot should perform approaches and landings with the power of one engine set to simulate the drag of a feathered propeller (zero thrust), or if feathering propellers are not installed, the throttle of the simulated failed engine set to idle. With the inoperative engine feathered or set to zero thrust, normal drag is reduced considerably, resulting in a longer landing roll. Allowances should be made accordingly for the final approach and landing.

The final approach speed should not be less than V_{YSE} until the landing is assured; thereafter, it should be at the speed commensurate with the flap position until beginning the roundout for landing. Under normal conditions, the approach should be made with full flaps; however, neither full flaps nor the landing gear (amphibian landing at airport) should be extended until landing is assured. When more drag is required, the landing gear should be the first option if it does not conflict with the manufacturer's recommended procedure. With full flaps, the approach speed should be 1.3 V_{SO} or as recommended by the manufacturer.

The pilot should be particularly judicious in lowering the flaps. Once they have been extended, it may not be possible to retract them in time to initiate a go-around. Most of the multi-engine seaplanes are not capable of making a single-engine go-around with full flaps. Each make and model of seaplane must be operated in accordance with the manufacturer's recommended procedures.

MES Section X
◆ E ◆

Systems and Equipment Malfunctions

See Chapter 19 for the discussion of systems and equipment malfunctions.

MES Section X
◆ F ◆

Emergency Equipment and Survival Gear

See Chapter 15 for the discussion of emergency equipment and survival gear.

MES Section XI

Operation of Multi-Engine Systems

Multi-engine operations, including performance and limitations, operation of systems, and engine inoperative principles of flight, is not a required test area for applicants who hold a multi-engine land rating. However, at the discretion of the examiner, the topic may come up. It is suggested that you review these principles found in the *Airplane Flying Handbook* (FAA-H-8083-3) or equivalent.

Multi-engine seaplanes are typically poorer performers than their landplane counterparts.

Multi-engine seaplanes are typically poorer performers than their landplane counterparts. Be sure you are able to access and interpret the performance data from the seaplane portion of the aircraft's POH, and have reviewed systems operation and principles of flight for the multi-engine aircraft operating on one engine.

MES Section XI
◆ A ◆

Maneuvering with One Engine Inoperative

The following procedures are recommended for developing and practicing proficiency in coping with an inoperative engine.

At safe altitude (minimum 3,000 feet above terrain or manufacturer's recommendation, whichever is higher) and within landing distance of a suitable water landing site or airport, an engine may be shut down (after appropriate cooling) with the mixture control or fuel selector. At lower altitudes, however, shut down should be simulated by reducing power, which is done by adjusting the throttle to the zero thrust setting. The following procedures should then be followed:

1. Fly the seaplane .... Maintain control, V_{YSE}, heading, bank into operating engine. Remember, *airspeed is life itself!*
2. Power .... Increase or leave as set for takeoff.
3. Drag (reduce) .... Props, gear, or flaps; pilot's choice based on condition of the aircraft.

4. Identify .... Idle foot = inoperative engine.
5. Verify .... With throttle or other means.
6. Feather .... Inoperative engine.
7. Checklist .... Start from the top.

In all cases, the seaplane manufacturer's recommended procedure for single-engine operation should be followed. The general procedures listed above are not intended to replace or conflict with those established by the manufacturer. The correct procedure can be used effectively for general training purposes to emphasize the importance of maintaining aircraft control and reducing drag.

The FAA expects the pilot to be proficient in the control of heading, airspeed, and altitude; in the prompt identification of a power failure; and in the accuracy of shutdown and restart procedures as prescribed in the AFM/POH.

There is no better way to develop skill in single-engine emergencies than by continued practice. The fact that procedures of single-engine operation of a multi-engine aircraft are mastered thoroughly at one time during a pilot's career is no assurance for coping successfully with a single-engine emergency unless review and practice are continued. Some engine inoperative emergencies are so critical that there is no safety margin for lack of skill or knowledge. Therefore, it is essential that the multi-engine pilot take proficiency training periodically from a competent flight instructor.

The key to good emergency management skills is practice.

The pilot should practice and demonstrate the effects (on single-engine performance) of various configurations of gear and flaps; the use of carburetor heat; and the failure to feather the propeller on an inoperative engine. Each configuration should be maintained at single-engine best rate-of-climb speed long enough to determine its effect on the climb (or sink) achieved. Prolonged use of carburetor heat at high power settings should be avoided. Write down the performance figures you determine for future reference, or if taking a practical test, to show your examiner.

In the event a propeller cannot be unfeathered during a practical test, it shall be treated as an emergency.

MES Section XI
◆ B ◆

Engine Inoperative— Loss of Directional Control (V_{MC}) Demonstration

Every multi-engine seaplane checkout should include a demonstration of the seaplane's single-engine minimum control speed. The single-engine minimum control speed given in the AFM/POH or other manufacturer's published limitations is determined during the original airplane certification under conditions specified in the CFRs. These conditions are usually not duplicated during the pilot training or test because they consist of the most adverse situations for airplane-type certification purposes. Prior to a pilot checkout, a thorough discussion of factors affecting single-engine minimum control speed is essential.

V_{MC} varies with several factors: changes in density altitude (normally aspirated engines), CG location (forward CG provides a greater arm for the air rudder, thus lowering V_{MC} slightly), landing gear position (which affects both CG location and the aircraft's center of drag), whether the prop is feathered or windmilling (amount of asymmetrical drag), critical engine, and possibly some other more minor factors such as cowl flap position, etc.

The FAA describes the proper procedures for a V_{MC} demonstration as follows: The V_{MC} demonstrations should be performed at an altitude that will allow the maneuver to be completed no lower than 3,000 feet above ground level (AGL) or the manufacturer's recommended altitude, whichever is higher. One demonstration should be made while holding the wings level and the ball centered, and another demonstration should be made while banking the seaplane at least 3° to 8° toward the operating engine to establish zero sideslip*. These maneuvers will demonstrate the single-engine minimum control speed for the existing conditions and will emphasize the necessity of banking into the operative engine. An attempt should not be made to duplicate V_{MC}, as determined for aircraft certification. Hint from the author: Write down the differences in performance from these two techniques for future reference and to show your examiner. You might not need to demonstrate it on the practical test if he or she knows you have successfully completed it. Also, if the airspeed you determine differs much from the manufacturer's values, suspect the airspeed indictor or pitot static system. Are you enjoying being a test pilot yet?

*See the discussion of bank angles in the section "Engine failure after liftoff from water, with and without obstacle."

After the propellers are set to high revolutions per minute (rpm), the landing gear is retracted (if an amphibian) and the flaps are in the takeoff position, the seaplane should be placed in a climb attitude and at an airspeed at or above the intentional one-engine inoperative speed (V_{SSE}). With both engines developing as near rated takeoff power as possible, power on the critical engine (usually the left) should then be reduced to idle (windmilling, not shut down). After this is accomplished, the airspeed should be reduced at approximately 1 knot per second using the elevators, until directional control can no longer be maintained. At this point, recovery should be initiated by simultaneously reducing power on the operating engine and reducing the angle of attack, lowering the nose of the seaplane to accelerate to V_{SSE}. Under no circumstances should an attempt be made to fly at a speed below V_{MC} with only one engine operating. Should a stall occur prior to reaching this point, recovery should be initiated immediately by reducing the angle of attack and power on the operating engine to control roll and increase airspeed to V_{SSE}. The demonstration should then be accomplished with the rudder travel limited so V_{MC} occurs at a higher airspeed.

Seaplanes with normally aspirated engines will lose power as altitude increases because of reduced density of the air entering the engine's induction system. This loss of power will result in a V_{MC} lower than the stall speed at higher altitudes. Also, some seaplanes have such an effective rudder that even at sea level V_{MC} is lower than the stall speed. For these seaplanes, the loss of directional control may be safely demonstrated by limiting travel of the rudder pedal to simulate maximum available rudder. Limiting travel of the rudder pedal should be accomplished at a speed well above the power-off stall speed (approximately 20 knots). This will avoid the hazards of stalling one wing with maximum allowable power applied to the engine on the other wing. If you sense any indication of stall prior to loss of directional control, recover to the entry airspeed. The demonstration should then be accomplished with the rudder pedal blocked at a higher airspeed.

Do not perform this maneuver by increasing the pitch attitude to a high angle with both engines operating and then reducing power on the critical engine. This technique is hazardous and may result in loss of seaplane control.

Night Operations

MES Section XII

Night operations is not a required test area for applicants who hold a multi-engine land rating. However, at the discretion of the examiner, the topic may come up. I suggest you review these principles from Chapter 10, especially the section on seaplane base lighting, and also the *Airplane Flying Handbook* (FAA-H-8083-3).

MES Section XIII

Postflight Procedures

The postflight procedures for multi-engine seaplanes differ little from those for the single-engine seaplane. Therefore, I have covered the topics of after landing procedures, anchoring, docking and mooring, beaching, ramping, parking and securing in Chapter 16.

Docking engine shutdown procedures vary. Since the multi-engine propeller extends beyond the outside limits of the floats, a danger exists that is not present with single-engine floatplanes. For this reason, pilots try to have the dockside propeller stopped before arriving at the dock, but this is not always possible, so dock crew need to be aware of this danger and how to avoid it.

The pilot is responsible for the safety of passengers (including the practical test examiner) when those passengers leave the cabin. Work out a safe procedure for the type of seaplane you fly with your flight instructor and always utilize it when loading and offloading passengers (including the examiner, even if you know he's an "old salt").

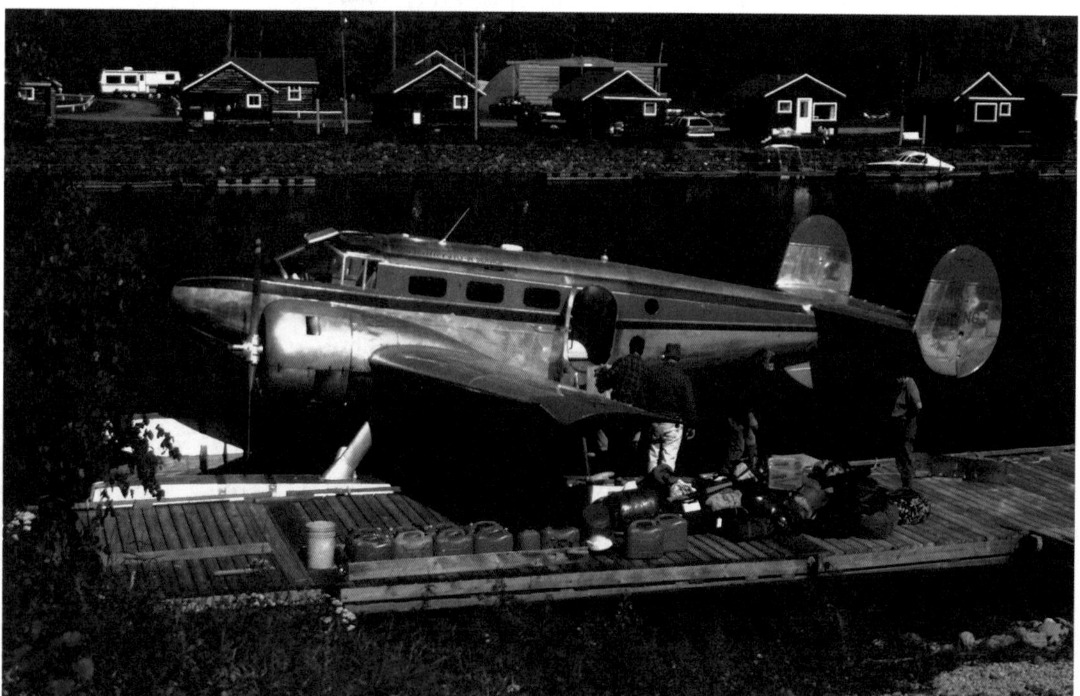

Robert Grant

The Twin Beech floatplane is a workhorse in the north because it is fast and carries a good load.

Learning from Other's Mistakes

We can learn from other's mistakes. According to the accident statistics, the top 10 causes of accidents in multi-engine seaplanes are:

1. Engine failure/malfunction—usually caused by fuel mismanagement.
2. Loss of control in flight/mush/stall—by selecting an unsuitable takeoff or landing area or improper loading and overloading, which causes the pilot to attempt flight at airspeeds that are too low.
3. Dragged wing/float/pod—because of unfavorable wind or water conditions the pilot could not handle.
4. Nose over—glassy water and/or attitude too flat/airspeed too high near the water contribute to the water loop accident.
5. Loss of control ground/water—due to rough water and/or crosswinds that the pilot/seaplane could not handle.
6. Hard landings—caused by an improper landing flare, crosswind or glassy water.
7. Collision—with deadheads, sandbars or other obstacles during takeoff, landing or step taxiing.
8. Overrun—due to excessive airspeed and not enough landing area or poor choice of touchdown point.
9. Wheels down on the water—this occurs with amphibious aircraft (where's the checklist?).
10. Injuries—prop contact, usually due to inattentive passenger handling or improper briefings.

Stall-spin accidents again: No. 2 cause of accidents, but No. 1 cause of **fatal** accidents!

All of these relate directly to the pilot, and most happen during takeoff or landing.

Review

If you have read this chapter and are now skimming in preparation for your practical test, or if the previous section on common pilot errors helped to clear the hazy/glossy eyes that may have been developing, welcome back.

Know the V-speeds for the seaplane that you will be flying and be able to convey to an examiner how they relate to the aircraft's performance. Which ones are related to single-engine operations? Which ones are constant? Which ones change? If they do change, does a pilot have control over the variables? In other words, can *you* change V_{MC}?

Differential power can be a useful tool when conducting operations on the water. How can a pilot use this tool to his or her benefit during taxi and sailing operations? Are there times that differential power and engine locations create complications for water operations? If so, how?

Emergency operations are a significant part of the multi-engine pilot's training. Have you discussed with your instructor which procedures to commit to memory? Are they committed to memory? You *knew* that question was coming! Identify four factors that affect or influence aircraft performance during a V_{MC} demonstration.

Performance can change dramatically for a multi-engine seaplane when an engine quits or is shut down. A thorough review of the performance section of the POH is important. Familiarity with the operation of systems installed in the aircraft is paramount to addressing engine or equipment failures and is just plain handy for every day operations.

Other areas such as preflight preparation/procedures, seaplane base and airport operations, performance maneuvers, night operations and postflight procedures are all important and are covered in the summaries for the respective chapters that discuss these topics in greater detail.

Fly safe and keep those engines synchronized!

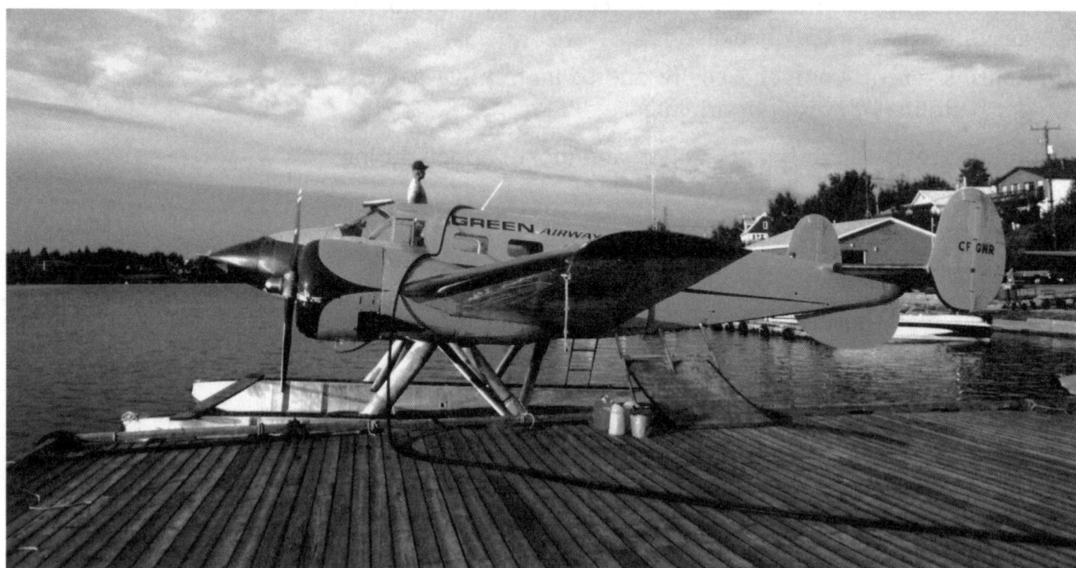

Robert Grant

Fueling a Twin Beech on the water at Red Lake, Ontario.

Section IV
Preflight and Checkride Preparation

Figure 18-1. A weight and balance determination in progress during loading.

Chapter 18
Performance and Limitations

If you are going for your seaplane rating oral and checkride, I suggest you read the PTS section indicated at right. For those of you who are already seaplane pilots, a review of this section and discussion below will help you understand your seaplane better and fly it safer.

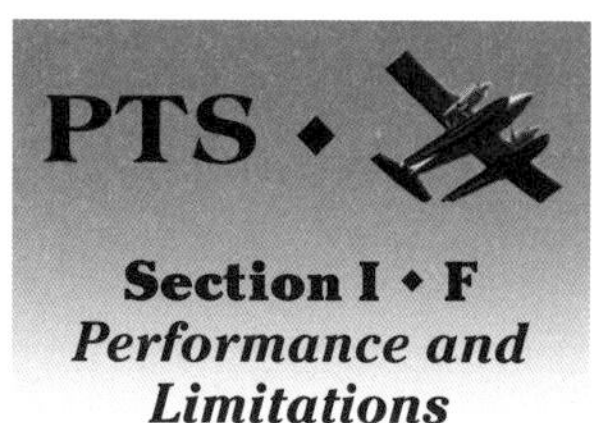

Performance and Limitations

Since the seaplane is an airplane, what you already know about aircraft performance and aircraft limitations applies. Check the seaplane POH for changes in V_A speed, stall speeds (might be lower because the floats provide some lift), and other speed limitations such as V_{NO}, V_{NE} and flap speeds. All performance parameters will be degraded from the landplane charts, so be sure you consult the seaplane portion of the POH. Some older aircraft that have been converted to floatplanes have little or no performance information. Most of that information you can generate yourself in simple flight tests, but that is an advanced topic. See the text *Water Flying Concepts* for how to do that, if you are interested.

As the floatplane flies faster, the floats' angle of attack decreases until the floats may be developing lift downward, which adds loading to the wings. But unless you are in a power dive, this is not a likely scenario. There may be no published limitations regarding high speed, but keep the above idea in mind, and don't try to set any airspeed records (achieved only in a power dive in a floatplane).

Seaplanes are Often Hybrids

Since many seaplanes not originally type certified with floats installed are hybrids (one manufacturer's airframe, another's floats, another's wingtip extensions, another's STOL kit, etc.), the pilot's job of sorting out what book values are appropriate is sometimes complex. For example, a Cessna 185F on Wipline 3730 amphibious floats may be certified to 3,350 pounds, according to the Wipline STC. But the Cessna Seaplane Supplement only gives performance data for EDO 2790 amphibious floats at an allowable gross weight of several hundred pounds less. Common sense tells us that takeoff performance for the Wipline floated aircraft must be much less than for the lighter EDO floated aircraft. No takeoff data is available for the Wipline floated airplane. All it says in the Wipline STC (which legally becomes part of the aircraft's POH) is to use information in the aircraft POH. For pilots who are used to specific numbers, this is a real quandary! What to do? Use good judgment...that is what the examiner is looking for! The Cessna Floatplane POH lists takeoff performance data for the same airplane equipped with EDO 2960 straight floats, with allowable gross weight much closer to the Wipline equipped airplane. Probably that would provide better data. But, keep in mind that takeoff performance of an amphibious aircraft will never match that of a straight-floated aircraft at the same weight because of that big hole in the bottom of the float occupied by the main gear wheel.

Not everything in float flying is black and white, so be careful. Don't take chances with takeoff performance. Determining whether a particular airplane on a particular day will be able to get out of a short lake is an advanced topic covered in other books like *Water Flying Concepts*.

Weight and Balance

This discussion assumes a good, operational understanding of landplane weight and balance (W&B). If you are a little rusty on this subject, I recommend you read the weight and balance chapter in *Aircraft Systems for Pilots*, which carefully covers the subject of weight and balance starting with a simple teeter-totter up to and including the multi-rowed commuter aircraft. For advanced learning, Chapter 15 in the book *Seaplane Operations* has a good discussion of advanced topics about weight and balance that deal directly with seaplanes. If you are not quick and confident with W&B calculations, do ten problems with the aircraft you are going to use for the checkride or with your own airplane, using different loading scenarios. Hint: save those ten scenarios in your flight bag or tuck them in the POH (which must always be on board). If you ever get ramp checked (or dock checked) and are asked if you did a W&B before the flight, you can pull out the one that matches your load for that flight. An occasional review of those scenarios will prepare you for the flight load you are about to take.

Why do a Weight and Balance Calculation for the Flight?

Here are some really good reasons!

1. To find out how heavy the aircraft is, so performance can be predicted. It appears there are many reasons, all boiling down to this: *it allows the pilot to make informed decisions.*
2. To find out where the CG is so the pilot can predict how the aircraft will fly and perform, how the controls will feel, and if there are any dangerous modes of flight.
3. To determine if the insurance policy is any good. Most policies do not pay if the aircraft is overloaded or out of CG limits. Or, as one old bush pilot said, "if there's an accident, to know how much weight to hide in the bush before the investigators get there."
4. To find out if the flight is legal.
5. It is required by law.

The correct order of importance of the above list is up to you to decide.

Weight and Weight Effects on Performance

Most floatplanes, when converted from wheels to floats, accept (or struggle with) an increased allowable gross weight. For example, the Cessna 180F on wheels has 2,650 pounds gross. On floats it is 2,820 pounds on EDO 2870 floats and 2,950 pounds on EDO 2960 floats. So, performance-wise, the airplane is a sports car on wheels and more like a Mack truck on floats. It is the pilot's responsibility to know the airplane and its limitations.

Takeoff and other aircraft performance figures (except maximum power-off glide distance) are affected approximately by the square of the weight change. So, an *approximate* performance multiplier can be determined by:

Weight affects performance.

$$[\text{actual weight/gross certificated weight}]^2 = \text{multiplier}$$

For example, an aircraft loaded so it weighs 90% of gross certificated weight will have a multiplier of $[0.9]^2 = .81$. Takeoff distance will be approximately 81% of that required if the aircraft is loaded to gross weight. CAUTION: This method becomes inaccurate the more the aircraft is loaded over gross weight.

Figure 18-2. We will need a good weight and balance determination when loading all this aboard!

Overloading

It may be possible to obtain authorization to operate at a greater maximum weight than normal, usually around 10%. Waivers are granted by the FAA for experimental, flight test and other special situations. Remember, when operating with such a waiver, your insurance is probably worthless without a document from the insurer granting coverage under the waiver. Commercial operators in Alaska may apply to the FAA for authorization to operate at up to 15% over the certified gross weight for some aircraft and with certain other FAA requirements met, including a high level of pilot expertise.

Water in Floats

A gallon of water weighs over 8 pounds, so water in the floats adds to the gross weight and may adversely effect the CG location, either forward or aft, depending on which compartment contains the water. If my airplane is in the water when I drive up, the first check I make, done upon first sighting, is to see if the wings are level. If not, there is probably water in one float. This visual check complements the pumping of the floats, which must be done. Float pumping is an absolute water check except for one thing: if one of the hoses that extend from the pumpout funnel where the pump attaches to the bilge is missing or has a crack, water cannot be pumped out. When I finish pumping, I check again to see if the wings are level. If not, I investigate further.

Ballast

Amphibious floatplanes usually suffer from a very forward CG, and amphibious hull aircraft tend to suffer from a CG problem that is out of limits either forward or aft. Both are easily loaded out of CG limits, so both are often ballasted. Since the best ballast is the smallest weight (least reduction of payload) placed at the greatest arm (distance from the CG), ballast is often found attached to the tail stinger (tailwheel spring) on the float-amphibian. The seaplane pilot needs to be familiar with the use of ballast and how it enters into the weight and balance calculations. (Figure 18-3 shows ballast attached to the tail stinger (landing wheel spring) of a Cessna 185.) If ballast is permanent, the mechanic considers that when developing the aircraft's weight and balance documentation, so the pilot does not have to consider it

Figure 18-3. Twenty-nine pounds of ballast on the tail stinger of a Cessna 185.

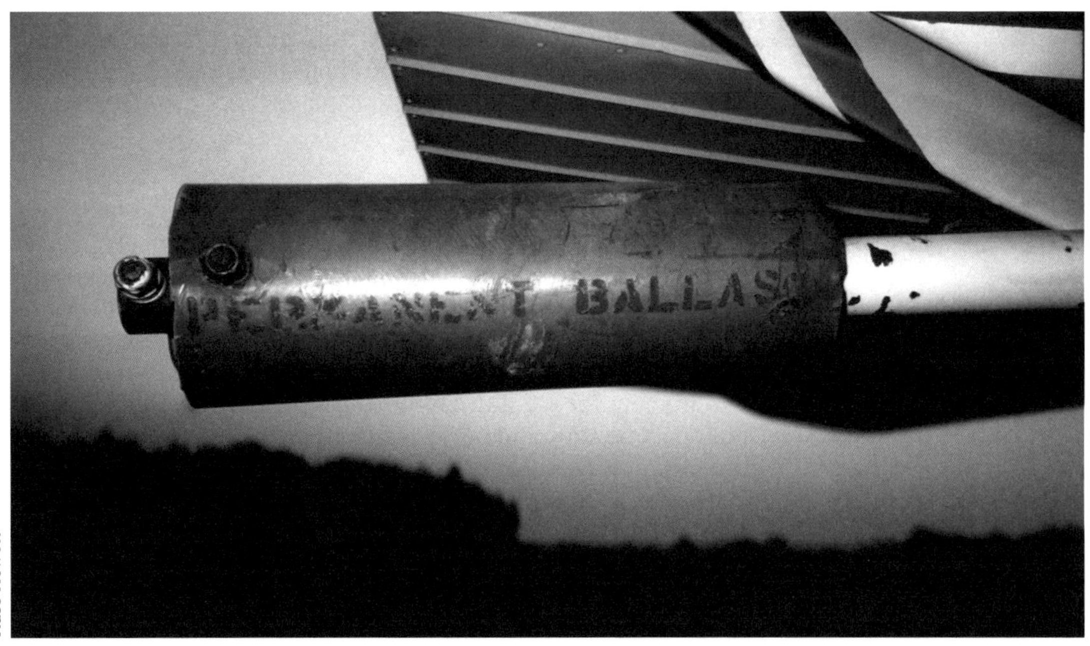

Russ Hewett

in the daily W&B calculations. If the ballast is movable by the crew, it must be considered in daily calculations.

CG—The Need for Balance

Remember that the center of gravity of the aircraft is the point from which the force of weight acts, directed downward toward the center of the earth. The center of gravity is also the point from which the aircraft rotates as it rolls, pitches and yaws. The position of the center of gravity varies according to where the load aboard is placed. When the aircraft is loaded, fueled and manned, it must be within precise limits, called center of gravity limits, established in the flight manual. If the aircraft is not within those limits, it is not guaranteed to be stable or controllable, and the pilot flying such an aircraft is a test pilot, probably without a parachute!

CG location affects how the seaplane handles and whether it has dangerous characteristics in certain parts of the flight envelope.

Weight and balance calculation reason #2 listed above was: to find out where the CG is so the pilot can predict how the aircraft will fly, how the controls will feel, how the aircraft will perform, and if there are any dangerous modes of flight. So, lets talk about that.

CG Effects

CG effects described below may be with the CG within the envelope but near the limits and become more severe as CG moves out of the permitted envelope. If CG is within limits, the aircraft has tested as controllable in all normal modes of flight. Be aware that it is quite easy to load many seaplanes outside the envelope.

If the CG is Forward

Forward CG performance (in the air) will not be as good if compared to an aft CG because the aircraft will be effectively heavier due to the need for additional tail-down force. Control pressures will be heavier, and the aircraft will be pitch stable and very responsive to (steady on) pitch trim settings. The dangerous mode of flight will be the flare to land because the aircraft has a high requirement for tail-down force. During the flare to land, the aircraft may be slow and powerless so there is less air flowing over the elevator. Elevator effectiveness decreases as ground effect increases so there is a greater need for up-elevator as the aircraft enters ground effect. Knowing this and that the CG is forward, the informed pilot can take the proper actions to carry some power until touchdown and use a higher final approach speed and/or a flatter approach.

If the CG is Aft

Many of the characteristics described above are reversed if the CG is aft. Speed and climb performance is better, control pressures are lighter, pitch stability and trim response is decreased, and the dangerous mode of flight is operating at low speeds because a stall might progress to a spin. With an aft CG out of limits, there is the possibility that the spin will develop into a flat spin, which tends to be terminal. Knowing this, the informed pilot will avoid flight at slow speeds and expect the aircraft to be less pitch stable, requiring complete attention to the controls.

Datum

The position of the center of gravity is given in the form of distance from a vertical plane, or datum, arbitrarily chosen by the builder to simplify the calculations and measurements. (For example the tip of the propeller spinner or the leading edge of the wing at the fuselage.) For many single engine Cessnas, the datum coincides with the lower part of the front side of the firewall. For one model of the Cessna 172 floatplane, at a weight of 2,220 pounds, the center of gravity must be between 39.8 and 44.5 inches behind the datum. Thus, the center of gravity limits are defined. *See* Figure 18-4. Can you go mark on the side of your aircraft where the CG limits are? Hint: you will need a tape measure. Why do this? So you can visualize the loading scenario. What you put behind this location will move the CG aft, etc.

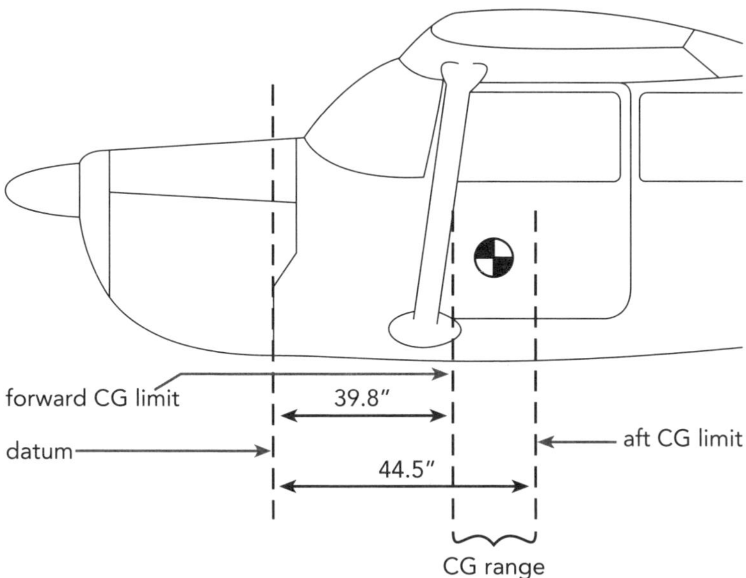

Figure 18-4. Datum and center of gravity limits

Float Compartment Arm and Load

Since seaplane pilots sometimes load strange things in strange places, you need to be able to find the weight and arm (distance from the datum) of anything you put in or on the airplane. You can find the arm of any loaded item by knowing the location of the datum. Just measure the horizontal distance from the datum to the center of the load. Some aircraft manufacturers give you more easily located datum references. For instance, Cessna tells the "station" (distance from the datum) of the front of the rear doorpost in many of the single engine models, which makes figuring the arms of loaded cargo much easier.

OK, let's say you have just had a very successful fishing excursion and want to load 50 pounds of fish in the float compartment. Those 50 pounds are going to increase your aircraft's gross weight by 50 pounds, but how will it affect the CG? First, lets have a look inside the float compartment for a placard showing the load limit of the compartment and the arm. Not there?

Look in the STC for the float installation or for the hatch compartment modification. Not there? Call the float manufacturer. Or, you can easily determine the arm with plumb bob hung from the datum point to a string running laterally from float to float and tape measure measuring the distance from the string to the center of the float compartment. But only the STC will tell you the load limit for the compartment. Added note: don't put anything in a float compartment if it doesn't have a floor, supported by the keel and sister keelsons, because a rough water takeoff or landing will loosen the rivets holding the bottom skins.

Now, just treat the fish load like any other load, such as rear seat passengers, since you know the weight and arm of the item. A good question the examiner might ask, to see if you understand weight and balance is: Will something loaded in the float compartment move the CG forward or aft? If the value of the float compartment arm is less than the value of the existing CG, then CG will be moved forward.

Effect of Atmospheric Conditions

Every good seaplane pilot understands the effect of wind, temperature and humidity on performance, particularly takeoff performance. Lets review:

Wind Effects

As we all know, a headwind aids takeoff performance. A strong wind makes takeoff more difficult because it roughens the water surface. If we don't consider the effect of rough surface, we can get a good sense of the effect of wind by considering the simple relationship called the wind speed correction factor (WSCF) which is:

The WSCF gives you a good sense of wind effects on take-off performance.

WSCF = 0.9 – (headwind component / calm wind liftoff speed)

For example, the POH says the calm wind takeoff distance is 1500 feet and liftoff speed is 45 knots. With a 15 knot headwind on takeoff, we can expect takeoff distance to be reduced to:

WSCF = .9 – (15/45) = .9 – .33 = .57 then

Takeoff distance is reduced to .57 × 1,500 feet = 855 feet

Do seaplanes ever take off downwind? Sure. In very light winds, on waters known to be clear of debris, faced with a long back-taxi to takeoff into a light wind, it is ok to attempt a takeoff down-wind. But remember, the takeoff run will be much longer. Keep an eye on the cylinder head temperature as that may be the limiting factor. If the downwind takeoff is not successful, when your seaplane falls off the step because you reduced power, you are in position for a takeoff into the wind. It is possible the examiner will have you do a landing down a long lake where you may end up with not enough room to takeoff into the wind, then ask you to take off. The examiner is testing your judgement. Tell him or her you are not sure if you have enough room to take off into the wind and you feel you can safely try a downwind takeoff. He or she will get a chance to see your piloting technique on a much longer takeoff run where you must get every bit of performance out of the airplane. The downwind takeoff (in light wind) will be very much like a high density altitude takeoff.

Note: If your POH takeoff performance data show values for various head-winds, use that information. If not, the above is a good approximation. Moreover, while out flying, it will give you a good sense of what the wind is going to do to your next takeoff run.

Downwind takeoffs: Maybe.

Downwind landings? Not a good idea, especially with quartering tailwinds, even if they are light, because as your speed decreases, the aircraft will want to turn into the wind. This is a maneuver for the highly experienced pilot (who probably won't attempt it).

Downwind landings? Don't.

Temperature Effects

As temperature increases, the air becomes less dense (density altitude increases). Lift from the wing and propeller decrease (assuming the same speed) and engine power decreases because there are less oxygen molecules in each cylinder of air available to unite with fuel to make power. So, higher temperature means poorer performance.

The relationship is fairly straightforward. For each 15°F or 8.5°C increase in temperature, density altitude increases about 1,000 feet and takeoff distance increases about 12%. So, for example, if takeoff distance is 1,500 feet at 59°F in the early morning, at 3 o'clock in the afternoon when the temperature has risen to 89°, takeoff distance will increase by:

Warmer temperature increases density altitude and decreases takeoff performance.

89 – 59 = 30° increase/15° per 12% increase = 24%, so takeoff distance can be expected to be 1.24 × 1,500 = 1,860 feet. Density altitude has increased by 2,000 feet!

Again, if temperature effects on takeoff distance is considered in the performance tables in your POH, that should be your first source of information. The 12% rule of thumb is not accurate for turbocharged or supercharged seaplanes. And, it becomes less reliable as the density altitude increases. For example, many seaplanes at gross weight simply won't get on the step at altitudes above 4,000–6,000 feet. *The idea of a 12% distance increase for every 15°F warmer gives you a reasonable approximation of temperature's effect on performance.*

A 12% distance increase for every 15°F warmer is a reasonable approximation of temperature's effect on performance.

Humidity Effects

We seaplane pilots operate on and near water, which means operating in higher humidity than our landplane counterparts. But, humidity varies from day to day. When humidity is higher, there are more water molecules in a volume of air. This means that since the same total number of molecules are in that volume of air at the same temperature and pressure, the water molecules have displaced some oxygen and nitrogen molecules (which make up almost all of the gas we call air). That's not good for us pilots for two reasons:

1. A water molecule weighs a lot less than an oxygen or nitrogen molecule, so air is less dense when humid. (I know, humid air feels heavier and more oppressive to us, but it really is not heavier.)
2. Since water molecules have displaced some oxygen, there are less oxygen molecules to unite with fuel in the engine cylinder, thus producing less power (this effect is minimal in turbine engine aircraft but significant if you are flying pistons).

I don't know of any seaplane POHs that consider humidity as a variable in their takeoff performance charts, so what's a seaplane pilot to do? *The bottom line is that we can expect takeoff run to increase by up to 10% on days when humidity is near 100% (a really humid day in Florida) as compared to when the air is dry (takeoff from the Colorado River).* The only detailed treatise on humidity I know of is in *Seaplane Operations*, Chapter 9. It is only one page long, but provides a nomograph of the effect of humidity on density altitude.

Performance Limitations

The seaplane pilot is expected to determine the seaplane's capabilities by reference to the POH. If the POH does not contain the needed performance data, the pilot is expected to utilize other proper sources, such as applying the principles above. It is the pilot's responsibility to be certain that the aircraft is capable of performing the maneuver and that the maneuver is within the aircraft's limitations.

Review

Know the differences in limitations and performance characteristics of the seaplane as compared to the landplane, and where to find the appropriate performance charts, fuel quantities, etc. Be able to calculate takeoff and landing distance, range, cruising speed and endurance. Know the airspeed limitations and V-speeds (at least have them on a cheatsheet on your checklist). Be able to accomplish an accurate (and speedy) weight and balance for any loading condition. Know how to move people and baggage around in the aircraft to achieve the desired CG. Know the effect of weight and atmospheric conditions on aircraft performance, especially takeoff distance.

Weight: Takeoff and other aircraft performance figures (except maximum power-off glide distance) are affected by the square of the weight change.

Wind: WSCF = 0.9 – (headwind component/calm wind liftoff speed)

Temperature: For each 15°F or 8.5°C increase in temperature, density altitude increases about 1,000 feet and takeoff distance increases about 12%.

Humidity: expect takeoff run to increase by up to 10% on days when humidity is near 100% compared to when the air is dry.

The POH is primary to computing aircraft performance and knowing the aircraft's limitations.

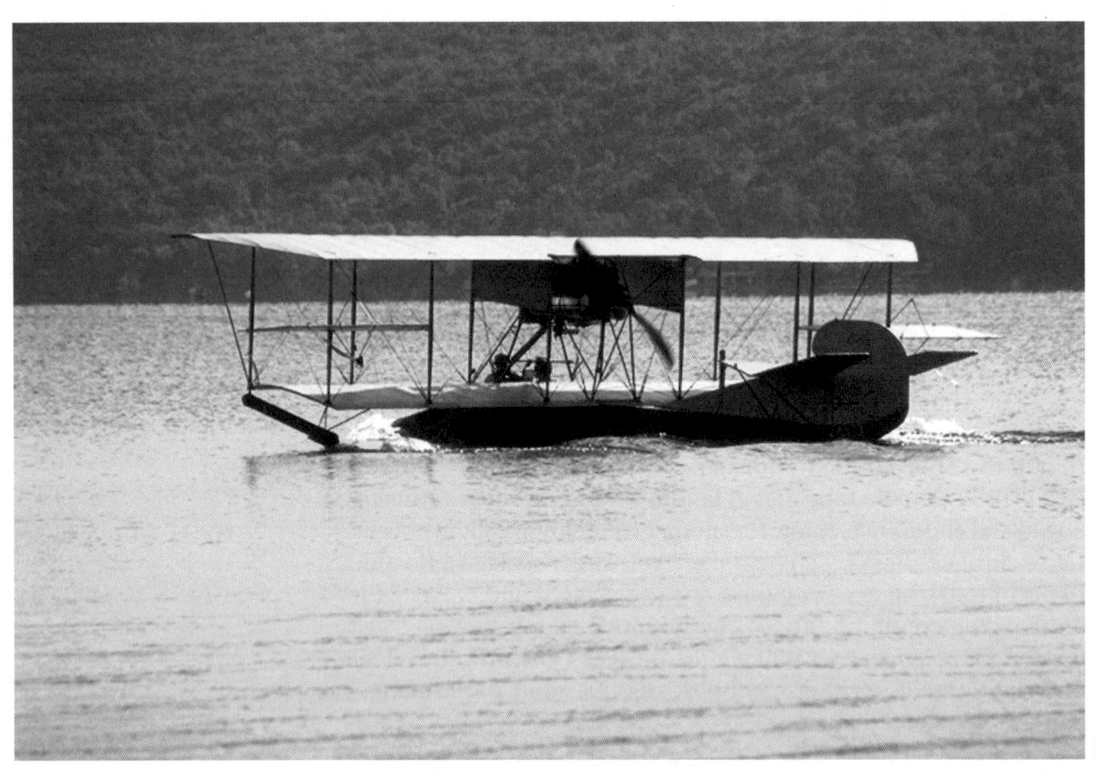

SPA

A replica of a 1913 Curtiss Model E flying boat taxiing on Keuka Lake, NY, in 1999.

Chapter 19
Operation of Systems

If you are going for your seaplane rating oral and checkride, read the PTS section indicated at right. For those who are already seaplane pilots, a review of this section and discussion below will help you understand your seaplane's systems better and fly it safer.

With the exception of items 3, 5, and 6 in Section I • G of the PTS, all of the systems listed are common to all aircraft. For a review of those common systems I refer you to *Aircraft Systems for Pilots* by DeRemer, a Jeppesen Publication, or to any other suitable study guide for aircraft systems.

Water Rudders

Section I • G
Item 3

Water Rudder Movement

Left-Right

On most floatplanes, water rudder left/right control is accomplished with three cables. Two of these cables come from the air rudder tiller bar or mechanism. The cable to the right rudder pulls when the air rudder moves left, the left cable pulls when the air rudder moves right. (*See* Figures 19-1 and 19-2 on the next page.) The balance cable connects to both rudders, pulling the left rudder to the left when the air rudder moves left, etc. Keep in mind that cables can only pull, they can't push. Proper tensioning of these cables is important, as is proper rigging of the water rudders so they are working together rather than fighting each other. When the seaplane is out of the water, the pilot should include an inspection of the rudders, in the down position, to see that they are properly rigged. Do this by positioning the air rudder by hand in the centered position, then looking to see if both water rudders appear to be aligned (when they are down) with the longitudinal axis of their respective floats.

As you taxi different floatplanes on the water, check to see if the floatplane turns more quickly to the left or right. If attempting a turn from into the wind to downwind in a brisk breeze, you find the seaplane won't make the turn in one direction, try turning the other direction. Different airplanes may turn better to the

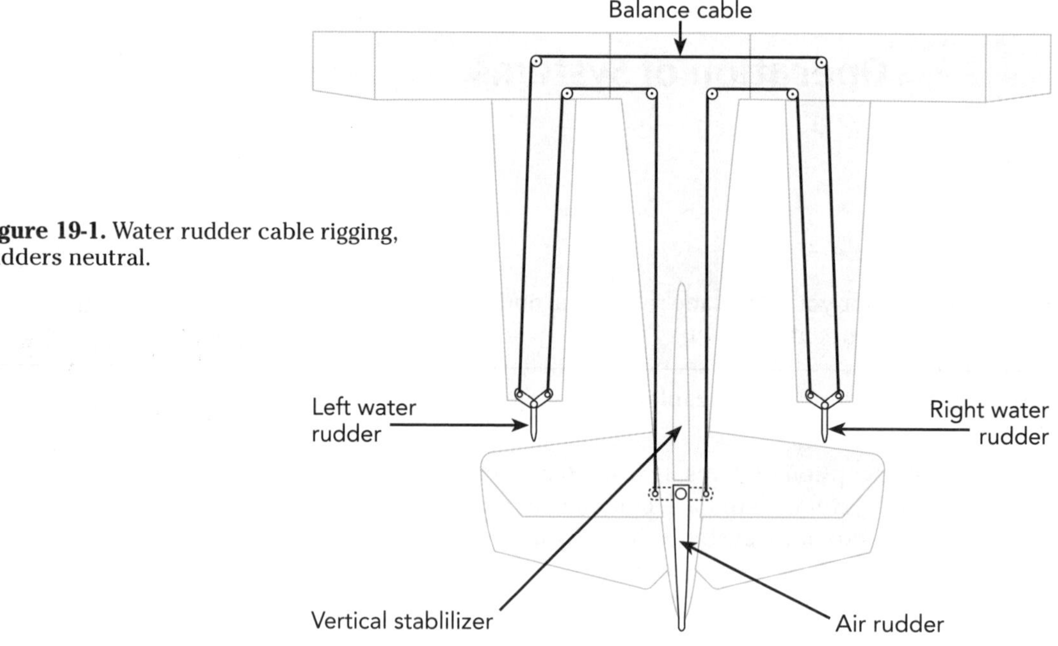

Figure 19-1. Water rudder cable rigging, rudders neutral.

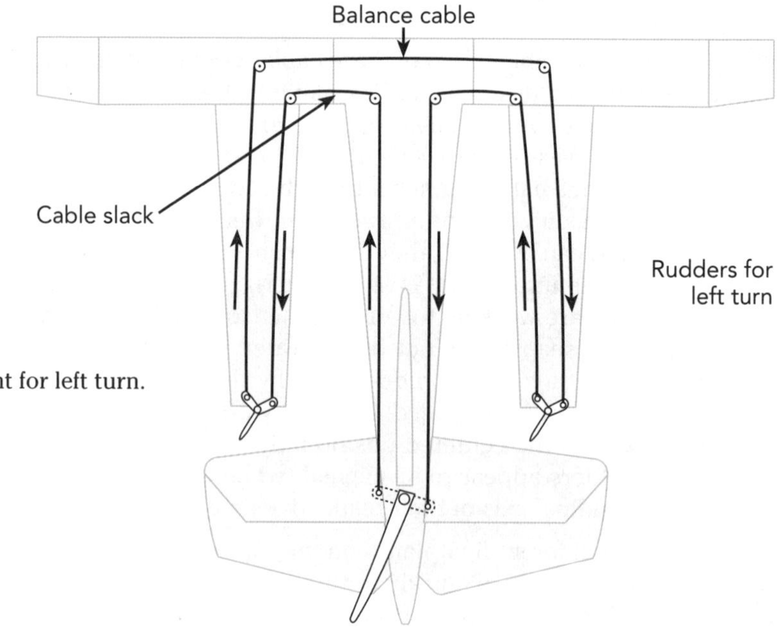

Figure 19-2. Cable movement for left turn.

left or right, depending on how their rudders are rigged. If you encounter a seaplane that doesn't seem to turn well in either direction, especially against a stiff breeze, the cause is probably a balance cable that is rigged to tight or too loose, weak downsprings, or rudders that are too small for the airplane. (Yes, its possible. I have seen more than one airplane whose owner trimmed the leading edge of the rudders to provide more clearance when the rudder was in the up position to facilitate beaching, only to find that his airplane no longer turned as well.)

Up-Down

Water rudders are raised and lowered usually with a control cable that runs through a series of pulleys from the cockpit to the rudders attached to the back of the floats. The pilot either pulls up a handle attached to this cable or, if the airplane (and water rudder) is large, he or she rotates a lever in the cockpit, which pulls the cable to raise the water rudders. The rudders are lowered by gravity and downsprings that hold the rudders in the down position against the force of flowing water but allow them to rotate up out of the water if they encounter an obstacle.

Water Rudder Use

The seaplane pilot must remember the following with respect to water rudder use:

1. Water rudders are only effective if there is water flowing past them. The faster the seaplane is moving through the water, the more authority the water rudders have, up to the point where water pressure is sufficient to overcome downspring force, causing the rudders to lift up and out of the water. So, if the seaplane won't turn downwind, try another hundred rpm, then wait a moment for the forward speed through the water to increase and try the turn again.
2. If the seaplane isn't responding to water rudder input, check to be sure the rudders are down! (Oops! Happens to all of us).
3. Up or down? Remember, there are only three maneuvers when water rudders are down. If you don't remember those three, review them on Page 43.

Review the use of water rudders in Chapter 6 on Page 43.

Landing Gear — Amphibious Systems

Section I • G
Item 5

If you are going to use an amphibian for your flight test, I suggest that you and your flight instructor go over the systems description in the aircraft pilot operating handbook. Be sure you know

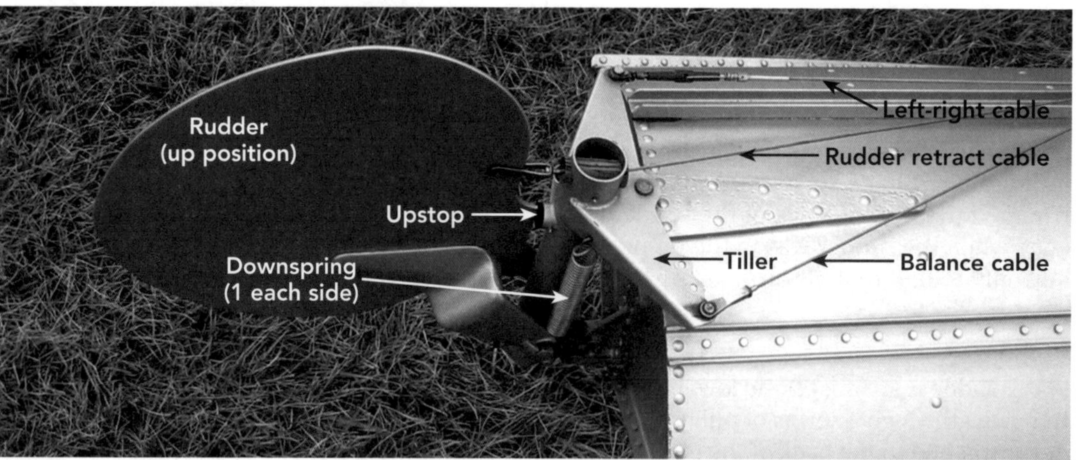

Figure 19-3. Typical water rudder showing retract and control cables, downspring and upstop.

how the system works and understand the emergency procedures appropriate to the aircraft you will use for the test. Some questions you might be asked include:

1. Is the landing gear retract system electric, hydraulic or both?
2. What is an easy way to check for hydraulic leaks inside the floats? (When pumping the floats, watch for red colored liquid being pumped out.)
3. What is the location of the power pak, and what preflight inspection must be done on it?
4. Are there two or four hydraulic cylinders actuating the four gear?
5. If there are only two cylinders and four wheels, how are the other two wheels lowered/retracted?
6. Describe the system of emergency gear extension. How many strokes of the manual pump does it require? How long does that take? In case of engine failure, how many feet of altitude will the aircraft lose before you get the gear down electrically/manually? That becomes an important altitude! If you don't have that much altitude, you don't have the option of putting the gear down if the engine fails.
7. Where can you ***not*** land if one or more gear won't retract/extend?

8. What is the procedure if you get no light indicating the gear is up/down? (Don't forget to describe what to do to eliminate the possibility of a burned out bulb.)
9. What are airspeed limitations for gear extension/retraction?
10. How do you check for landing gear position before landing? (A visual check is mandatory.)

Fuel Systems

Section I • G
Item 6

This is the same as for landplanes, but I feel compelled to mention one item because seaplanes operate in a water and humid air scenario and sometimes are fueled from non-certified fuel delivery systems.

The item is sumping. It is vitally important! Never go flying without *properly* sumping the fuel tanks to check for water and other contaminants. Sumping **must** be done before the first flight of the day and after every fueling. Note I said "proper sumping" because I see it done improperly, and some factory-made preflight checklists actually promote improper sumping. Be sure you know how many sumping points there are on your aircraft (there are six on the Cessna 185 yet many pilots know of only five). ALWAYS sump starting with the fuel tanks on both sides, then work your way toward the engine. If you start with the gascolator sumping point first, or any other sump before the tanks are sumped, you may pull water into the fuel lines. This makes it much harder to remove the water from the system, because we never sump any point enough to get it all out. It is likely that water will remain in the lines until it reaches the engine, probably at 200 feet in the air on takeoff, with my luck! Read more about fuel sumping starting on Page 21.

Sumping ***must*** be done before the first flight of the day and after every fueling.

Review

If you are flying an amphibian, review the ten questions above and be sure you understand the landing gear system completely. Review all the systems in the aircraft with your flight instructor and refer to a good systems book, like the one mentioned above.

The seaplane pilot must remember the following with respect to water rudder use:

Water rudders are only effective if there is water flowing past them. The faster the seaplane is moving through the water, the more authority the water rudders have, up to the point where water pressure is sufficient enough to overcome downspring force, causing the rudders to lift up and out of the water. So, if the seaplane won't turn downwind, try another hundred RPM, then wait a moment for the forward speed through the water to increase and try the turn again.

If the seaplane isn't responding to water rudder input, check to be sure the rudders are down.

Remember, there are only three maneuvers when water rudders are down. If you don't remember those three, review them on Page 43.

Sump before first flight of the day and after every fueling. Sump in the correct sequence. Know and understand your aircraft's fuel system.

A handsome Cessna 180 on EDO 2870 floats heeled up on a tranquil lake near Ketchikan, AK.

Chapter 20
The Minimum Equipment List

Dealing with Failed Instruments and Systems

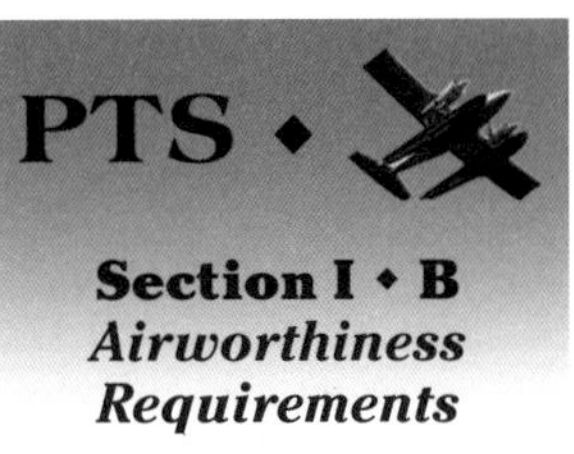

You are expected, as pilot in command, to know when you can and cannot fly an aircraft if it has an equipment deficiency, how to make such a decision, and what you must do to be eligible for further flight.

If you are going for your seaplane rating oral and checkride, I suggest you go to the appendix and read Section I.B of the PTS. If you are landplane rated, this task is not required for the checkride because you are supposed to know it already. If you, like me, forget things you don't use regularly, you will need to read this chapter. It is easier to understand than the regulations.

For those of you who are already seaplane pilots, this section will further your understanding of your seaplane's systems, review the rules for when you can keep flying, and serve as a reminder of what you need to do before you fly if faced with a failed system or component.

The Pilot's Problem

Can you fly legally with:

- A burned-out wingtip light bulb?
- A stuck VSI?
- An inoperative oil gauge?

§91.213 Inoperative instruments and equipment, is the source of the decision-making problem you have. It says:

> (a) Except as provided in paragraph (d) of this section, no person may takeoff an aircraft with inoperative instruments or equipment installed unless...

Does this mean that if you have a burned out lightbulb at the wingtip or a stuck vertical speed indicator or an inoperative oil pressure gauge, you can't fly your seaplane? The answer to this question is complex because of the words "except" and "unless," so read on. **Hint:** if you find yourself getting bored, lost or sleepy reading the regulatory stuff below, read the Summary at the end of the chapter, then go back into the text to pick up the rest of the story.

Paragraph (d) suggests one or more ways you may be able to fly with something inoperative. They are:

1. **If the aircraft has an approved minimum equipment list and the list permits operation without that item being operational.** (91.213 a. 1-5). Note: Unless your seaplane has a turbine engine, it is not likely to have a minimum equipment list, so lets go directly to the other alternatives mentioned below. If your aircraft has a minimum equipment list, please review 91.213 (a) through (c).
2. **If the aircraft has no approved minimum equipment list, and the defective part is not:**
   - Part of the VFR-day type certification instruments and equipment prescribed in the applicable airworthiness regulations under which the aircraft was type certificated (see the day VFR required equipment list below); or
   - Indicated as required on the aircraft's equipment list, or on the Kinds of Operations Equipment List for the kind of flight operation being conducted; or
   - Required for the specific kind of flight operation being conducted (such as night VFR or IFR, etc.); or
   - Required to be operational by an airworthiness directive.

And the inoperative instruments and equipment are either:

- Removed from the aircraft, the cockpit control placarded, and the maintenance recorded in accordance with 14 CFR §43.9; or
- Deactivated and placarded "Inoperative." If deactivation of the inoperative instrument or equipment involves maintenance, it must be accomplished and recorded in accordance with 14 CFR Part 43;

...and a pilot or mechanic determines that the inoperative instrument or equipment does not constitute a hazard to the aircraft. If the above is accomplished, an aircraft with inoperative instruments or equipment is considered to be in a properly altered condition acceptable to the FAA for flight (legally airworthy).

If the defective part is required for flight, there is one option left:

3. An aircraft with required but inoperable instruments or equipment may be operated under a special flight permit issued in accordance with 14 CFR §§21.197 and 21.199.

The process for obtaining a special flight permit is described below in the required instruments listing.

Required Instruments for Day and Night VFR

These requirements are listed in 14 CFR §91.205. The pertinent parts are listed below.

For powered civil aircraft with standard category U.S. airworthiness certificates, instrument and equipment requirements are:

General. Except as provided in paragraphs (c)(3) and (e) of this section, no person may operate a powered civil aircraft with a standard category U.S. airworthiness certificate in any operation described in paragraphs (b) through (f) of this section, unless that aircraft contains the instruments and equipment specified in those paragraphs (or FAA-approved equivalents) for that type of operation, and those instruments and items of equipment are in operable condition.

Day

Visual flight rules (day). For VFR flight during the day, the following instruments and equipment are required:

1. Airspeed indicator.
2. Altimeter.
3. Magnetic direction indicator.
4. Tachometer for each engine.
5. Oil pressure gauge for each engine using pressure system.
6. Temperature gauge for each liquid-cooled engine.
7. Oil temperature gauge for each air-cooled engine.
8. Manifold pressure gauge for each altitude engine.
9. Fuel gauge indicating the quantity of fuel in each tank.
10. Landing gear position indicator, if the aircraft has a retractable landing gear.
11. Approved aviation red or white anticollision light system for small civil airplanes certificated after March 11, 1996, in accordance with Part 23. If a light in the anticollision light system fails, operation of the aircraft may continue to a location where repairs or replacement can be made.
12. Approved flotation gear readily available to each occupant and at least one pyrotechnic signaling device, if the aircraft is operated for hire over water and beyond power-off gliding distance from shore. "Shore" means that area of the land adjacent to the water which is above the high water mark and excludes land areas that are intermittently under water.
13. An approved safety belt with an approved metal-to-metal latching device for each occupant 2 years of age or older.

14. An approved shoulder harness for each front seat for small civil airplanes manufactured after July 18, 1978. The shoulder harness must be designed to protect the occupant from serious head injury when the occupant experiences the ultimate inertia forces specified in §23.561(b)(2). Each shoulder harness installed at a flight crewmember station must permit the crewmember, when seated and with the safety belt and shoulder harness fastened, to perform all flight operation functions.
15. An emergency locator transmitter.

Night

Note: In Canada, a seaplane may not take off or land more than 30 minutes after sunset or 30 minutes before sunrise. In the United States, there is no law restricting seaplane night operations. There are very few seaplane landing areas that are lighted. Those that are, are equipped with a rotating beacon that flashes yellow and white. Night operations at other than lighted landing areas, although not illegal in the U.S. are considered to be dangerous and imprudent because the pilot cannot see what is in front of the aircraft. If a night landing becomes necessary, use glassy water landing technique and...good luck! Listed below is the additional equipment needed for night VFR flight.

Visual flight rules (night). For VFR flight at night, the following instruments and equipment are required:

1. Instruments and equipment specified in paragraph (b).
2. Approved position lights.
3. An approved aviation red or white anticollision light system on all U.S.-registered civil aircraft. Anticollision light systems initially installed after August 11, 1971, on aircraft for which a type certificate was issued or applied for before August 11, 1971, must at least meet the anticollision light standards of Parts 23, 25, 27, or 29, as applicable, that were in effect on August 10, 1971, except that the color may be either aviation red or aviation white. If any light in the anticollision light system fails, operations with the aircraft may be continued to a stop where repairs or replacement can be made.
4. One electric landing light if the aircraft is operated for hire.
5. An adequate source of electrical energy for all installed electrical and radio equipment.

6. One spare set of fuses, or three spare fuses of each kind required, accessible to the pilot in flight.

Obtaining a Special Flight Permit

14 CFR Sections 21.197 and 21.199 describe the process of acquiring a special flight permit, sometimes called a ferry permit or flight operations waiver. It should be noted that most general aviation insurance policies do ***not*** provide coverage while operating under such a permit. An additional endorsement to the policy is required in order to have coverage. Only pertinent parts of §§21.197 and 21.199 are copied here.

§21.197 Special flight permits.

(a) A special flight permit may be issued for an aircraft that may not currently meet applicable airworthiness requirements but is capable of safe flight, for the following purposes:

Flying the aircraft to a base where repairs, alterations, or maintenance are to be performed, or to a point of storage.

---

§21.199 Issue of special flight permits.

(a) Except as provided in §21.197(c), an applicant for a special flight permit must submit a statement in a form and manner prescribed by the Administrator, indicating—

(1) The purpose of the flight.

(2) The proposed itinerary.

(3) The crew required to operate the aircraft and its equipment, e.g., pilot, copilot, navigator, etc.

(4) The ways, if any, in which the aircraft does not comply with the applicable airworthiness requirements.

(5) Any restriction the applicant considers necessary for safe operation of the aircraft.

(6) Any other information considered necessary by the Administrator for the purpose of prescribing operating limitations.

(b) The Administrator may make, or require the applicant to make appropriate inspections or tests necessary for safety.

The application is submitted to your local FAA Flight Standards District Office (FSDO). They will assist you with the application and getting it approved. Remember, having a ferry permit does NOT mean your insurance will be in effect during any flights conducted under a ferry permit.

Review

Unless your seaplane has a turbine engine, or for some other reason has its own minimum equipment list, or a piece of equipment or instrument becomes inoperative and isn't part of the day VFR required list above, you may remove it or otherwise make it no longer a part of your aircraft system (deactivate it) and placard it "inoperative." *And* if you, as pilot, determine that it is not needed for safe flight, you may continue to fly the airplane. The removal or deactivation may need to be done by a mechanic, and whoever does it needs to make an entry in the logbook.

It is obvious why the FAA wants you to know what equipment is required for day VFR flight (night, too, since it is not illegal to fly a seaplane at night in the U.S.A.)! What if the failed device is part of the required items? You have two choices. One, fix it before further flight or, two, get a special flight permit or waiver to fly it where it can be repaired.

Frankly, I see no reason to memorize the list of required equipment for day and night, but you should know where to find it and, if you are flying in the boondocks, it is a good idea to have a copy of the list in your aircraft.

Now you are an expert on this topic, so what about the (1) inoperative light bulb, (2) stuck vertical speed indicator, and (3) inoperative oil pressure gauge...can you still fly? Check yourself on these answers:

1. **Nav light bulb.** Okay to fly day VFR as it's not on that list. But only after deactivation and labeling the switch INOP. Seems a little silly, but you could remove the bulb and label the switch if it was just a burned out bulb (the other bulbs work). Pulling the circuit breaker and labeling it might work but not on most Cessnas because Cessna likes to put the engine starter solenoid on that circuit.
2. **Vertical speed indicator (VSI).** The VSI isn't required for anything, not even IFR flight. Something you should know about the VSI is that it does not require a check during the biennial airspeed and static system check, so it is often in error! NEVER

rely on this instrument for flying activity near the surface. It should never be used as a reference for glassy water approaches or for establishing power settings for glassy water approaches before starting the approach. Use the altimeter and clock at altitude to determine the correct power setting for current loading and density altitude, then use correct glassy approach procedures. It is amazing, but some instructors are still teaching the glassy approach using the VSI, which is somewhat akin to a death wish!

3. **Oil pressure gauge.** According to the regulations, you gotta have it! The only legal way to fly without it is with a waiver. You will have a real dilemma if that gauge goes INOP in the wilderness. The legal issue will be secondary to whether the problem is with the gauge or the oil pump, etc., in which case it would be better to take your chances in the bush than to take off and risk catastrophic engine failure.

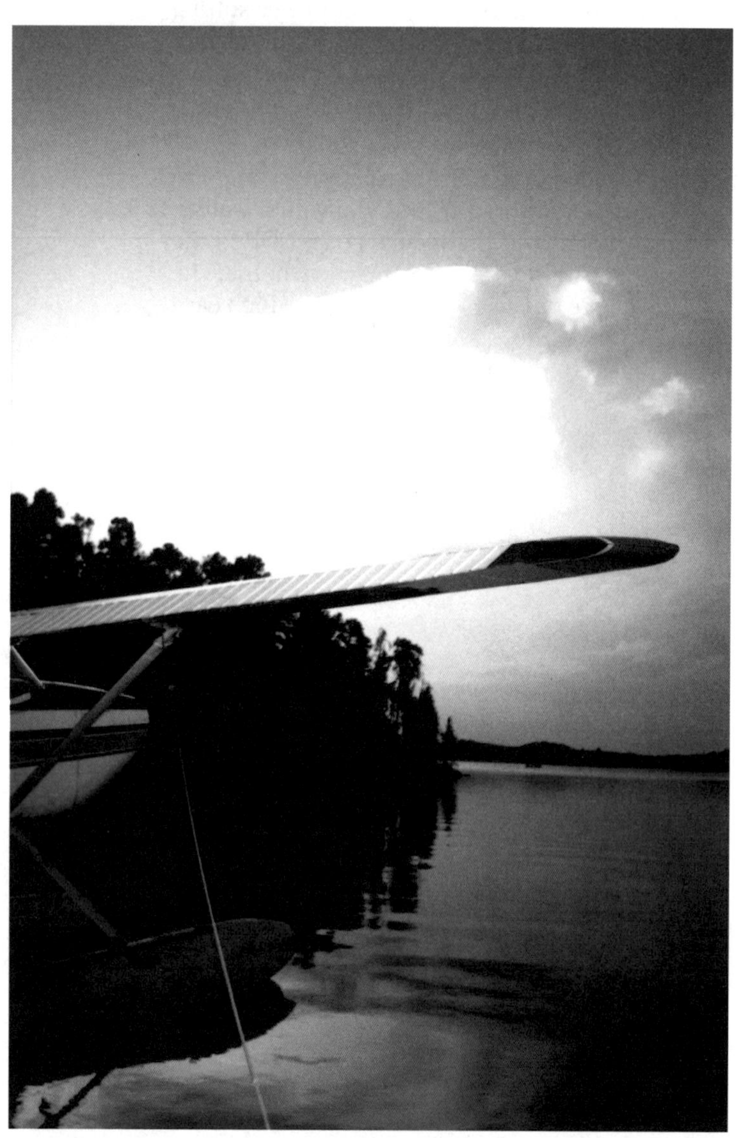

Seaplane flying gives many wonderful opportunities to enjoy nature, such as this gorgeous evening, heeled up in Seduction Cove on a lake in Ontario.

Chapter 21
Water and Seaplane Characteristics

For those of you who are already seaplane pilots, a review of this section and discussion below will help refresh your knowledge of the water and your seaplane's characteristics. Before we begin the discussion and review of water and seaplane characteristics, please review the terms and definitions below as many of them are used in the explanations that follow.

Terms and Definitions

Pilots who fly landplanes may already be familiar with some of the nomenclature associated with operating seaplanes. However, there are several important float, hull and nautical terms that the seaplane pilot should know. They are listed here and some are shown in Figures 21-1 and 21-2.

afterbody length. Length from step, to stern of float or hull.

amphibian. Seaplane that can be operated from both land and water.

beam. Width of the float or hull, at its widest point.

bilge. Lowest point or area inside a float or hull where water collects.

bow. Front end of the floats or hull.

bracing wires. Steel wires with threaded ends to stabilize and rig floats. Often called "flying wires." May be aerodynamically shaped.

bulkhead. Structural upright partitions separating the compartments of the floats or hull.

bumper. Rubber bumper installed on the bow of float or hull.

center of buoyancy. Average point of floatation support on the float or hull.

chine. The intersection of the bottom and the side of a float or hull.

deadrise angle. Angle of rise in "V" design of the float or hull bottom.

displacement. The weight of fresh water displaced by the float when it is pushed down to the design load water line. Like a ship, this is a line on the float that goes from just under the nose bumper to about mid point of the transom.

downwind. The direction the wind blows from an object. The downwind side of an island will have relatively calm water at its shore. Not to be confused with "leeward" (*see* leeward).

fetch. The length of the water surface area that the wind can work on while generating waves. Up to a point, the greater the fetch, the higher will be the wave height, at a given wind velocity.

forebody length. Length from step to bow of the float or hull.

heel. Rear portion of the float.

heel up. To place the floatplane on the beach with the heels on the beach.

keel. Structural member extending from below the bumper, along the length of the bottom of the float or hull to the step.

leeward. *See also* windward. Pronounced "loo-ard" A direction generally downwind *from the observer*. This is a nautical term, often misused. It is therefore not correct to say "on the leeward side of the island" or "on the leeward side of the dock." The so-called leeward side of the island is the side where calm water is found, but the mariner will say he fears the leeward shore (the shore downwind of him where the waves are crashing ashore). The windward shore is the mariner's friend. Confusing? Not if the term is properly used, referring to direction *from the observer*, mariner or seaplane pilot when he's on the water. When referring to wind direction with respect to objects like a dock or island, use the terms "upwind" and "downwind" (upwind side of the island, downwind side of the dock).

Figure 21-1. Float components

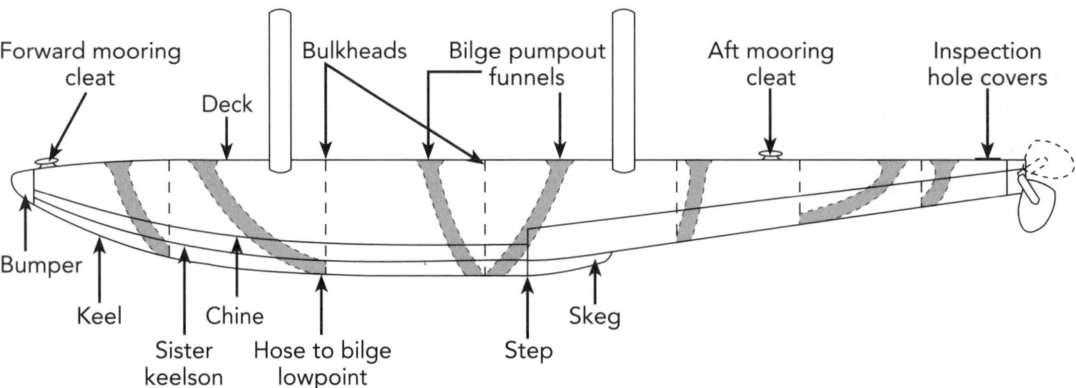

line. Nautical term for rope. Rope may be bought at the store but when it comes aboard a vessel (your seaplane) it becomes line.

mooring cleat. Metal fitting with projecting ends on which a line (rope) can be fastened with a cleat hitch or splice (*see* "Knots," Page 226).

seaplane. An airplane that can take off from, and land on, water.

sister keelson. Additional longitudinal structural members at the bottom of the forebody of the float, to which the outside skin is fastened for additional strength and form.

skeg. Terminal extension of the keel that provides additional stability when the floatplane is resting on a hard surface ashore.

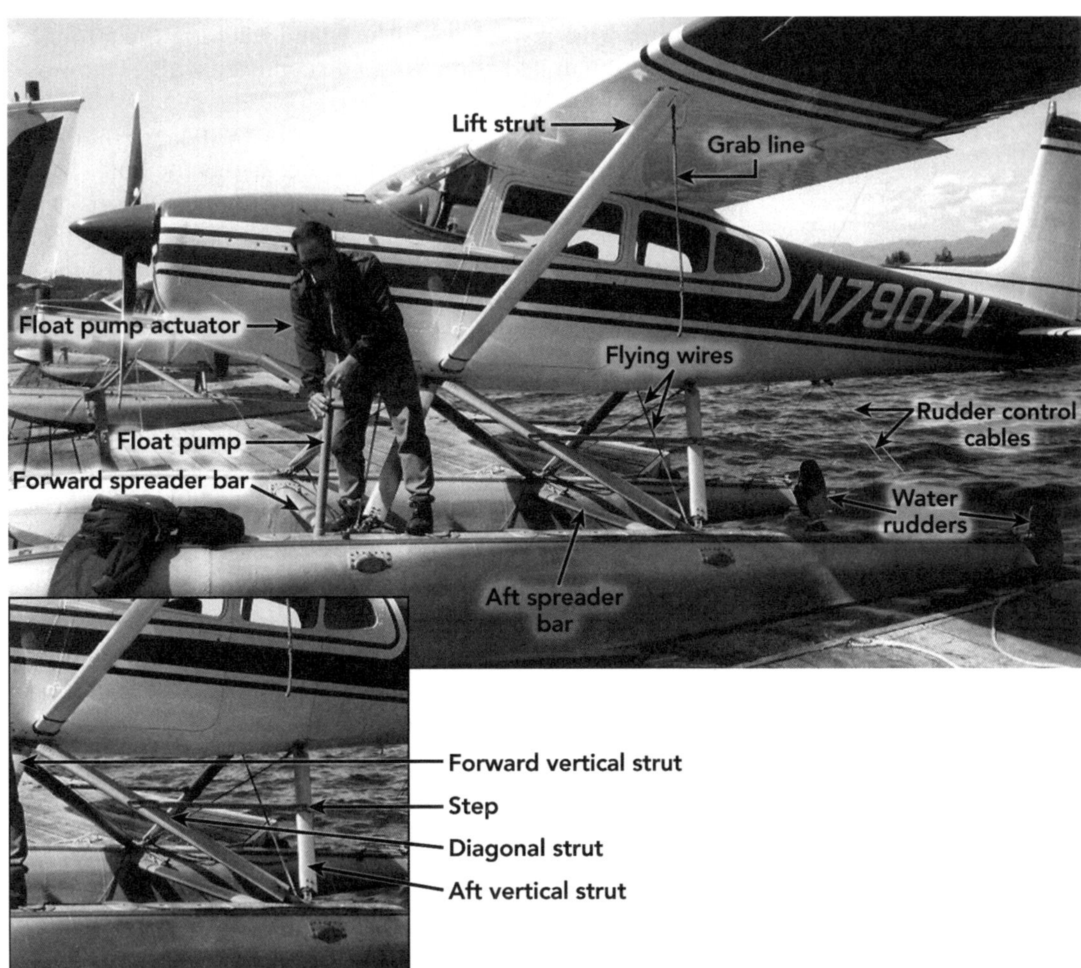

Figure 21-2. Floatplane components

spray strip or rail. An extrusion or surface extending from the chine, to minimize water spray into the propeller.

spreader bars. Aerodynamic structural members attached to the inner portion of each float to establish a predetermined distance between the floats and to keep the floats from rotating about their longitudinal axis.

step. A longitudinal break in the keel line approximately midway down the float or hull.

stern. Aft (back) end of the float or hull.

transom. Rear bulkhead of the float, upon which the water rudder is often mounted.

upwind. The direction from an object to where the wind is coming from. The upwind side of an island will have the strongest wave action at its shore. Not to be confused with "windward" (*see* windward).

water line. Longitudinal line or position on the float or hull when the seaplane is at rest where the water meets the hull.

windward. *See also* leeward. A direction essentially into the wind *from the observer.* This is a nautical term, often misused. It is therefore not correct to say "on the windward side of the island" or "on the windward side of the dock." The so-called windward side of the island is the side the waves are crashing up on—the shore the mariner (and seaplane pilot) fears. Yet, the mariner will say he fears the leeward shore (the shore where the waves are). The windward shore is the mariner's friend. Confusing? Not if the term is properly used, referring to direction *from the observer*, mariner or seaplane pilot when he's on the water.

Characteristics of Water

Operating an airplane on water is somewhat different than operating one on land. This is because of the widely varying and constantly changing conditions of the water surface as well as the beach, dock or buoy where the seaplane will start and end its flight. However, operating a seaplane should not be more difficult than operating a landplane if the pilot has the necessary knowledge and skills for safe water flying.

The competent seaplane pilot must know the characteristics of water to understand its effects on the seaplane. Water is a fluid, and although much heavier than air, it behaves in a manner similar to air.

Since it is a heavy fluid, water seeks its own level and, if not disturbed, lies flat with a glass-like surface. That glassy surface will change if disturbed by wind, current or objects such as boats.

Because of its weight, water can exert tremendous force. This force, in the form of resistance, produces drag as the water flows around or under the floats. The force of drag imposed by the water increases as the square of the speed. This means that as the speed of the float traveling on the water is doubled, the force exerted becomes four times as great. As any water skier knows, falling off skis at 35 MPH is a softer fall than at 60 MPH...the water is really hard and unforgiving at that speed.

Forces created when operating an airplane on water are more complex than those created on land. When a landplane's wheels contact the ground, the force of friction or drag acts at a fixed point on the airplane. But, water forces act along the entire length of a seaplane's floats or hull with the center of pressure constantly changing depending upon the pitch attitude, dynamic float or hull motion, and action of the waves.

Since the surface condition of water varies constantly, it is important that the pilot recognize and understand the effects of the various conditions of the water surface.

Wind

Under calm wind conditions, a glassy water surface is perhaps the most dangerous to the seaplane pilot and requires precise piloting techniques. Glassy water presents a uniform mirror-like appearance from above, eliminating visual references pilots use to judge height. Since the pilot cannot judge when to flare for landing, special landing techniques are used and must be practiced regularly by the seaplane pilot to maintain proficiency. Also, if waves are decaying and setting up certain patterns, or if clouds are reflected from the water surface, or a landing into the sun is attempted, the pilot can experience visual distortions that are potentially confusing. Your flight instructor will provide training in this area, but it is your responsibility as a seaplane pilot to maintain and improve your proficiency.

Waves

Wave conditions on the surface of the water are a very important factor in seaplane operations. Wind provides the force that generates waves, and the velocity of the wind is one of the factors that governs the size of the waves and the roughness of the water surface (Figure 21-3). Another primary factor affecting wave height is **fetch**. The wind velocity may be 30 knots but, in a protected area or on a very small lake, wave height will be under three inches. On a large lake, wave height will be very small at the upwind end of the lake while large breakers are crashing on the shore at the opposite end.

Calm water resists wave motion until a wind velocity of about 2 knots is attained. Although patches of ripples form, there will still be areas of glassy water. If the wind velocity reaches 4 knots, the ripples change to small waves that continue for some time even after the wind stops blowing. If this light breeze diminishes, the water viscosity dampens the ripples and the surface promptly returns to a flat and glassy condition.

As the wind velocity increases above 4 knots, the water surface becomes covered with a complicated pattern of waves; the characteristics vary continuously between wide limits. This is referred to as the generating area. This generating area remains disarranged as long as the wind velocity increases. As the wind velocity increases, the waves become larger and travel faster. When the wind reaches a constant velocity, waves develop into a series of equidistant parallel crests of the same height.

An object floating on the water surface, where simple waves are present, will show that the water itself does not actually move along with waves. The floating object will describe a circle in a vertical plane, moving upward as the crest approaches, forward and downward as the crest passes, and backward as the trough between the waves passes. After the passage of each wave, the object stays at almost the same point it started. Consequently, the actual movement of the object is a vertical circle whose diameter is equal to the height of the wave. This theory must be slightly modified, because the friction of the wind will cause a slow downwind flow of the object and some water, resulting in drift. Therefore, a nearly submerged object, such as a float or hull, will slowly drift with the waves.

When the wind increases to a velocity of 12 knots, waves will no longer maintain smooth curves. They will break at their crest and create foam (whitecaps). When the wind decreases, the whitecaps disappear; however, lines or **streaks** have formed which serve as an accurate indication of the wind path, because the streaks lie parallel to the direction of the wind. Caution: the streaks may persist for a time after a wind shift, and those formed out on the body of water may drift in close to the beach. When they are near the beach, they no longer tell the wind direction,

Near shore, the wind often takes a direction more parallel to the beach.

Terms used by U.S. Weather Service	Velocity mph	Estimating velocities on land	Estimating velocities on sea	Notes
Calm	**Less than 1**	Smoke rises vertically	**Sea like a mirror**	Check your glassy water technique before water flying under these conditions.
Light air	**1 – 3**	Smoke drifts; wind vanes unmoved.	**Ripples with the appearance of scales** are formed but without foam crests.	
Light breeze	**4 – 7**	Wind felt on face; leaves rustle; ordinary vane moves by wind.	**Small wavelets,** still short but more pronounced; crests have a glassy appearance and do not break.	...Streaks begin to form.
Gentle breeze	**8 – 12**	Leaves and small twigs in constant motion; wind extends light flag.	**Large wavelets;** crests begin to break. Foam of glassy appearance (perhaps scattered whitecaps).	Ideal water flying characteristics in protected water. Streaks become apparent after wind has blown for an hour.
Moderate breeze	**13 – 18**	Dust and loose paper raised; small branches are moved.	**Small waves,** becoming longer; **fairly frequent whitecaps.**	Streaks become readily apparent.
Fresh breeze	**19 – 24**	Small trees in leaf begin to sway; crested wavelets form in inland water.	**Moderate waves;** taking a more pronounced long form; many whitecaps are formed. (Chance of some spray.)	This is considered rough water for seaplanes and small amphibians, especially in open water.
Strong breeze	**25 – 31**	Large branches in motion; whistling heard in telegraph wires; umbrellas used with difficulty.	**Large waves begin to form;** white foam crests are more extensive everywhere. (Probably some spray.)	
Moderate gale	**32 – 38**	Whole trees in motion; inconvenience felt in walking against the wind.	**Sea heaps up and white foam from breaking waves** begins to be blown in streaks along the direction of the wind.	This type of water condition is for emergency only in small aircraft in inland waters and for the expert pilot.

Figure 21-3. Surface wind force table

because the wind often has taken a direction more parallel to the beach.

In general, waves generated by wind velocities up to 10 knots do not reach a height of more than one foot. A great amount of wind energy is needed to produce large waves. When the wind ceases, the energy in the wave persists and is reduced only very slightly by internal friction. As a result, the wave patterns continue for long distances from their source and diminish at a barely perceptible rate. These waves are known as swells, and gradually lengthen, shrink in height, but increase in speed.

If the wind changes direction during the diminishing process, an entirely separate wave pattern will form and superimpose itself on the swell. These patterns are easily detected by the pilot from above, but are difficult to see when on or near the surface.

Islands, shoals, and tidal currents also affect the size of waves. An island with steep shores and sharply pointed extremities allows the water at some distance from the shore to pass with little disturbance or wave motion. Normally, this creates a glassy surface on the downwind side. Wind gusts on water will appear as dark patches. Once reading the water becomes second nature, the seaplane pilot will have prior warning of approaching gusts.

Wind gusts on water appear as dark patches.

If the island has rounded extremities, a shallow slope, and outlying shoals where the water shallows and then becomes deep again, the waves will break and slow down. This breaking will cause a considerable loss of wave height on the downwind side of the shoal.

When waves are generated in nonflowing water and travel into moving water, such as a current, they undergo important changes. If the current is moving in the same direction as the waves, they increase in speed and length but decrease in height. If the current is moving opposite to the waves, they will decrease in speed and length, but will increase in height and steepness. This explains "tidal rips," which form when strong streams run against the waves. A current traveling at 6 MPH will break almost all waves traveling against it. When waves break, a considerable loss in wave height occurs to the downwind side of the breaking.

Another characteristic of water that should be mentioned is buoyancy, which causes some objects to float on the surface. Some of these floating objects can be seen from the air, while others can be mostly submerged and difficult to see. Consequently, seaplane pilots must constantly be alert to the possibility of floating debris and avoid striking these objects during operations on the water. Techniques used to accomplish this include intense scrutiny from above during landing area assessment and back-taxiing along the planned takeoff path.

THE Question!

One of the most often asked questions, and the most difficult to answer is: How big of a wave can I operate in? Answer: Nobody knows, not even experienced pilots, because most of them haven't tried to operate from waves large enough to cause a failed attempt. As a general rule, waves higher than 10% of the length of your floats fall into the dangerous category, even for an experienced pilot. Waves higher than 5–7% of the length of your floats will likely cause some damage, even if it is just stretched rivets creating minor leaks in floats. Proper rough water technique is vitally important. Don't expect to learn all you need to know (to handle really rough water) during the training for your rating. Usually, those kinds of wave conditions are accompanied by high and gusty winds, which can be even more dangerous. In making that go/no-go decision, many factors must be considered, such as friendly shores downwind of the taxi takeoff area? Help available? No downwind or crosswind taxiing required? Wind velocity? (Higher is better to get off the rough water quicker.) After you have considered all factors, throw in two more questions: "Do I really need to do this?" And, "Tomorrow, will I think going was a good idea?"

Characteristics of Seaplanes

The seaplane is often a conventional landplane equipped with floats instead of wheels. On the flying boat type, the hull serves the dual purpose of providing buoyancy in the water and space for the pilot, crew, and passengers. The float type is by far the more common seaplane, particularly those with relatively low horsepower engines. Almost all of these seaplanes are of the twin-float variety.

Though there are considerable differences between handling a floatplane and a hull type on the water, the theory on which the procedures and techniques are based is similar. With few exceptions, the explanations given here for one type may be applied to the other; however, keep in mind that the explanations herein are for the floatplane since the vast majority of seaplanes are floatplanes.

The explanations in this chapter are for floatplanes, since the vast majority of seaplanes are floatplanes.

Replacing wheels with floats increases the airplane's empty weight and decreases its useful load.

Examples of added yaw stability for the float installation are evident in Figure 6-2 (Page 44) and Figure 21-4 at right.

In the air, the seaplane is operated and controlled in much the same manner as the landplane. The only major difference is the installation of floats instead of wheels. Because floats weigh more, replacing wheels with floats increases the airplane's empty weight and decreases its useful load. Floats also increase drag and reduce performance.

On many floatplanes, the **directional (yaw) stability** will be adversely affected by the installation of the floats, causing the floatplane to be less yaw stable than its wheelplane counterpart. This is caused by the larger side surface area of the floats found forward of the center of gravity (CG), which adversely changes the location of the side center-of-pressure in relation to the CG. If the **side center-of-pressure** were moved forward of the CG, the aircraft would try to turn around and fly tail into the wind. This, of course, doesn't happen when floats are installed, but there will be a decrease in yaw stability.

To help restore directional stability, an auxiliary fin(s) is often added somewhere in the tail section of the aircraft. A good example of this can be seen in Figure 6-2 on Page 44. Another great example can be seen in Figure 21-4. Some aircraft don't require this addition because they were designed with enough vertical stabilizer to provide the needed stability. The pilot will also find that less aileron pressure is needed to hold the seaplane in a slip, and holding some rudder pressure during the stabilized portion of inflight turns is usually required. This is due to the water rudder being connected to the air rudder or rudder pedals by cables and pulleys whose friction tend to prevent the air rudder from streamlining in a turn. The additional water rudder surface also adds to the air rudder control surface, changing the rudder characteristics.

So, if you find you are having a little trouble keeping the ball in the middle, these are the reasons. You will quickly learn to pay a little more attention to the ball or to your body, which will lean in the same direction as the ball. Ever wonder how your flight instructor knows the ball isn't centered without reading the instrument? The answer is from "body lean." So, now you know…spend your time looking outside but pay attention to what your body is doing. The cheek you are sitting heaviest on is the side that needs additional rudder pressure!

Wipaire

Figure 21-4. Cessna Caravan on Wipline amphibious floats. Note the large vertical fins mounted on the horizontal stabilizer to improve yaw stability.

Float Design

Research and experience have improved float and hull designs throughout the years, although most float design improvements were accomplished by the 1930s. Many floats designed in that period are still in use today. The primary consideration in float and hull construction is the use of sturdy, lightweight material designed hydrodynamically and aerodynamically for optimum performance.

All floats and hulls being used have multiple watertight compartments. This makes the seaplane virtually unsinkable, and prevents the entire float or hull from filling with water in the event it is ruptured. To be certified, floats must be able to support a fully loaded airplane with two chambers flooded on the same side. To meet certification requirements, a pair of floats must provide floatation that will support 180% of the rated gross weight of the floats and airplane. The formula used is:

$$\text{Gross Weight} = \frac{2 \times \text{displacement of one float}}{1.8}$$

For example, the EDO 2870A floats that are on my Cessna 180 will support a maximum gross weight of 3,188 pounds because the displacement (the maximum amount of weight that will be supported without the float sinking below its design water line) of one float is 2,870 pounds. So,

$$\frac{2 \times 2870}{1.8} = 3188.8 \text{ pounds}$$

However, the aircraft was certified on those floats with a maximum gross weight of 2,820 lbs, so the airplane/float combination is said to be overfloated. Overfloating is an advantage when operating on the water but, since the floats are larger than minimum required, they may provide slightly more aerodynamic drag when flying. Most floatplane pilots prefer the safety of being somewhat overfloated.

Both the lateral and longitudinal lines of a float or hull are designed to achieve a maximum lifting force by diverting the water and the air downward. The forward bottom portion of the float (and hull) is designed very much like the bottom surface of a speedboat. The rearward portion, however, differs significantly from a speedboat.

A speedboat is designed for traveling at an almost constant-pitch angle, and the contour of the entire bottom is constructed in a continuous straight line. A seaplane float or hull must be designed to permit the seaplane to be rotated or pitched up to increase the wing's angle of attack and gain the most lift for take-offs and landings. The underside of the float or hull has a sudden break in its longitudinal lines near the point around which the seaplane rotates into the lift-off attitude. This break, called a **step**, also provides a means of interrupting the capillary or adhesive properties of the water. As the seaplane transitions from the plow to the step phase, the step causes the water to detach from all parts of the float aft of the step, resulting in minimum surface friction so the seaplane can continue to accelerate to a speed where it can lift out of the water.

The step is located slightly behind the airplane's CG, at a point near the main wheels of a tricycle landplane. If the step was located very far aft of this point, it would be difficult to rotate the seaplane into a pitch-up attitude prior to planing (rising partly out of the water while moving at a high speed) and prior to lift-off. If the step was located more forward, it would be difficult to rotate the aircraft onto the step.

Although the step is necessary, the sharp break along the float or hull's underside causes structural stress concentration, and in flight, produces considerable drag because of the eddying turbulence it creates in the airflow. Figure 21-6 shows the underside of the floats on a Piper Aztec.

Float Model Number

The **model number** of most older floats indicates the displacement of the float, although some manufacturers have used the total load as the model number. For instance, Aqua Floats model 1900 has a displacement of 1687#. Some manufacturers do it both ways. Others use the number of rivets on a model or some number created by the marketing department. Therefore, the only way to know for sure the float displacement or the allowable gross weight of a particular model float is to consult the POH or the Supplemental Type Certificate (STC).

SPA

Figure 21-5. Bottom side of floats undergoing maintenance. Can you identify the transom, rudder hinges, skeg, step, keel, sister keelson, and chine? Note the fluted bottoms forward of the step.

Bill McCarrel

Figure 21-6. A Piper Aztec flying by shows us the bottom of the float. Note the fluted bottoms forward (curved areas between the keel, sister keelson and chine) that trap and direct the water.

Float Certification

There are two ways a particular model float is certified for use on a model aircraft. Either the float is listed by the airframe manufacturer as optional equipment in the airplane's Type Certificate, or the float has been certified by an STC for use on one or more specific model aircraft. If the float was originally included as optional equipment on the original Type Certificate, the aircraft's POH should have a section describing the use of the float as optional equipment. If not, then there will be an STC in the floatplane's documentation that becomes part of the POH and therefore must be carried on board at all times, within reach of the crew, because it contains operating information for the float.

Typically, when the floats are installed, a different gross weight applies, so you will usually find two weight and balance documents for the airplane—one for wheels and one for floats.

Go over all parts of the float with your flight instructor to be sure you understand each part's purpose and how to inspect it during preflight. Be sure you know how to do a weight and balance problem for your aircraft.

Porpoising and Skipping

Porpoising in a seaplane is much like the antics of a dolphin or porpoise. It is a rhythmic pitching up and down while taxiing on the step. Porpoising is a dynamic instability of the seaplane and may occur when it is moving across the water, while on the step, during takeoff or landing. It occurs when the angle between the float or hull and the water surface exceeds the upper or lower limit of the seaplane's design pitch angle. Improper use of the elevator, resulting in too high or too low a pitch (trim angle), sets off a cyclic oscillation that may, in some seaplanes, steadily increase in amplitude unless the proper trim angle or pitch attitude is reestablished. It can occur in any seaplane but seems to be most severe in some hull types.

A seaplane will travel smoothly across the water while on the step, as long as the floats or hull remains within a moderately tolerant range of pitch angles. If the pitch angle is held too low during planing, water pressure in the form of a small crest or wall is built up under the bow or forward part of the floats or hull. As the seaplane's forward speed is increased to a certain point, the bow of the floats or hull will no longer remain behind this crest, and is abruptly forced upward as the seaplane rides over the crest. As the crest passes the step and on to the stern or aft portion of the floats or hull, the bow abruptly drops into a low position. This again builds a crest or wall of water in front of the bow resulting in another oscillation. Each oscillation may become increasingly severe, and if not corrected will cause the seaplane to nose into the water, resulting in extensive damage or possible capsizing. Porpoising can also cause a premature lift-off with an extremely high angle of attack, resulting in a stall or being in the region of reverse command and unable to climb over obstructions.

Porpoising will occur during the takeoff run if the trim angle is not properly controlled with the right elevator pressure just after passing through the hump speed, or at the highest trim angle before the planing attitude is attained (if up elevator is held too long and the angle reaches the upper limits). On the other hand, if the seaplane is nosed down too sharply, the lower trim range may be entered, resulting in porpoising. Usually, porpoising does not start until a degree or two after the seaplane has passed into the critical trim angle range, and does not cease until a degree or two after the seaplane has passed out of the critical range.

If porpoising does occur, it can be aggravated by pilot induced elevator movements while attempting to "fly" out of the porpoise. *The porpoising can be stopped in most floatplanes by applying constant light back-elevator pressure*. The back-elevator pressure must be applied and maintained until porpoising is damped. If porpoising is not damped by the time the second oscillation occurs, it is recommended that power be reduced to idle and elevator control held firmly back, so the seaplane will settle into the water with no further instability.

The pilot must learn and practice the correct trim angle for takeoff, planing, and landing for each type of seaplane until there is no doubt about the proper angles for the various maneuvers.

Skipping occurs primarily during the landing run just after touchdown. The combination of the right attitude (slightly too flat) and airspeed (slightly too high) results in the seaplane skipping (without porpoising) across the water just like a thrown rock does. However, skipping can also happen during step taxi or takeoff, particularly when crossing a boat wake. It is not especially dangerous if properly handled by the pilot. Just continue to "fly" the aircraft attitude, add power and go around. Raising the nose to stop skipping without applying power may not be a good idea because it may cause the aircraft to fly again, then stall back onto the water. When landing following the go around, touch down with a little less airspeed and the nose slightly higher so the skip is avoided.

With most float aircraft, there are techniques to deal with skipping that don't require a go around. These are considered advanced techniques. Work with your flight instructor on these techniques after you complete your rating.

In most float aircraft, skipping rarely happens and is hard to make happen, so it is not a maneuver easily produced for training purposes. Consult with your flight instructor as to which solution you should use in the aircraft you are flying and for the oral exam.

Review

Review the terms and definitions. Be sure you can look at a floatplane, or a picture of one in this book, and name all the parts. Why? If someone doesn't know the terminology, how can they communicate with flight instructors, mechanics and other seaplane pilots? I hope you find it fun to learn these terms.

The seaplane pilot acquires a special skill that is useful flying landplanes as well as seaplanes, and useful in other walks of life...he or she can read the water! The water tells exactly what the wind is doing, in a specific location. Gusts, wind direction, and velocity can be "seen" without a windsock. Develop this capability to a high skill level. Relate the information in the surface wind force table to what you see when looking at the water from both water level and from aloft.

Seaplanes have decreased performance because they are draggier and probably heavier than their land counterpart. They are also less yaw stable. It is noticeable but not critical. More activity on the rudder pedals is needed to keep the ball centered. The reason is that the side center of pressure moves forward when floats are installed. Some seaplanes have side surface added in the tail section to counteract this characteristic.

Be sure you can walk around a float and name each part and its purpose, and explain how to check for deficiencies during a preflight inspection. Be able to explain why the step is located where it is. Certified maximum gross weight for floats is determined by multiplying the displacement of one float by 2, then dividing that number by 1.8. If the certified maximum gross weight is considerably higher than the certified gross weight of the floatplane, the combination of float and airplane is said to be overfloated, which increases safety and handling ease on the water, but may cause a small penalty in performance due to added drag of the larger floats.

Be sure you can explain porpoising and skipping, how each is recognized, and what the pilot must do to recover.

Burke Mees

Alaskan floatplanes all ramped up near the end of the day.

Chapter 22
Seaplane Bases, Maritime Rules, and Aids to Marine Navigation

For the pilot preparing for the seaplane oral and checkride, reading the PTS section shown at right will help you become familiar with its requirements. The following pages will prepare you to meet these standards. For those of you who are already seaplane pilots, a review of this section will refresh your knowledge of the rules and aids for operating on water.

Identifying and Locating Seaplane Bases on Charts and in Directories

The location of established seaplane bases/landing areas is symbolized on aeronautical charts by an anchor alone or one inside a standard airport circle. Typically, the exact location of the seaplane base (SPB) is depicted by the eye of the anchor on the chart. If the SPB is lighted, the chart will depict the typical lighted airport symbol above the circle. A seaplane base beacon flashes yellow and white.

FAA and state-approved SPBs are listed in the *Airport/Facility Directory* (in Canada, it's the *Water Aerodrome Supplement*). While seaplanes typically land on water surfaces that are not classified as SPBs, those that are listed in directories provide proof to the pilot that landing there is approved and may provide operating restrictions as well. The facilities provided at seaplane bases/landing areas vary greatly, but may include a hard surface ramp for launching, servicing facilities, and an area for mooring or hangaring seaplanes. Many marinas designed for boats also provide a seaplane facility.

Operating restrictions are found in the remarks section of the listing.

In some cases seaplane operations are conducted in bush country where regular or emergency facilities are limited or nonexistent. The terrain and waterways are often hazardous, and any servicing must be the pilot's responsibility. Prior to operating in the bush, it is recommended that seaplane pilots seek local advice from qualified seaplane pilots familiar with the area. Added and periodic training in wilderness operations are important components to seaplane safety and should be sought before pilots attempt flying into such areas. Probably, the most complete listing of SPBs and water landing areas in the U.S. is the *Water Landing Directory*, published by the Seaplane Pilots Association.

Seaplane Bases/Landing Areas and Operating Restrictions

Seaplane bases are approved by state controlling agencies and/or the FAA. They are facilities for servicing seaplanes and their passengers. Landing areas are designated as usual seaplane operating surfaces but may have no facilities. There are many other water surfaces suitable for seaplane operations, but they are not listed as either bases or landing areas.

Some states and cities have no laws or very liberal laws regarding seaplane operations on their lakes and waterways, while other states and cities may impose restrictions. It is recommended that before operating a seaplane on unknown waters, the pilot consult the *Water Landing Directory*. If the pilot doubts whether a particular body of water is usable, it is his or her responsibility to contact the controlling authority for that body of water. If the controlling agency is not known, the Seaplane Pilots Association, the local field director for SPA, the State Aeronautics Department, or the Flight Standards District Office (FSDOs) nearest the site of the planned operation should be contacted concerning local requirements. In any case, seaplane pilots should always avoid creating a nuisance in any area, particularly in congested marine areas or near swimming or boating facilities.

When there's doubt, it is the pilot's responsibility to determine if seaplane operation is permitted before landing there.

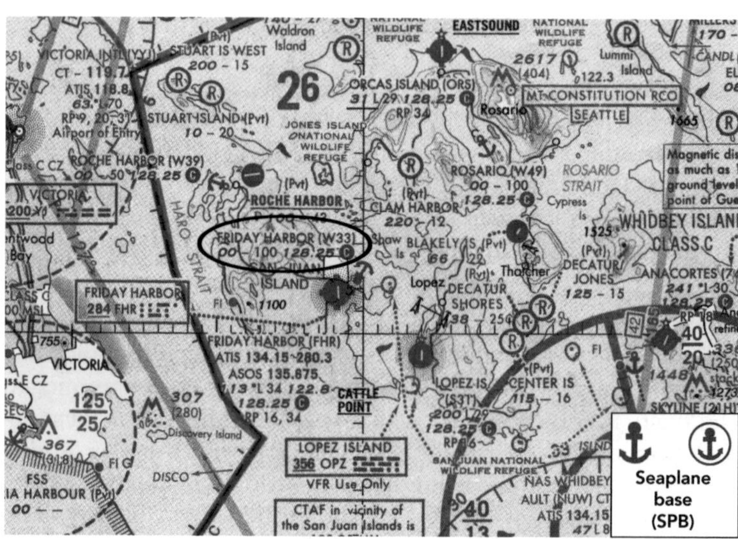

Figure 22-1. Seaplane base symbol and a chart excerpt of Friday Harbor, Washington.

FRIDAY HARBOR SPB (W33) 0 NE UTC–8(–7DT) N48°32.24′ W123°00.58′ **SEATTLE**
00 LRA
WATERWAY 03–21: 10000X2000 (WATER)
WATERWAY 12–30: 6000X1000 (WATER)
SEAPLANE REMARKS: Unattended. All tkfs should be performed N of Browns Island. Seaplanes ops warning lgts in harbor may be activated by keying 5 times on CTAF. US customs user fee arpt. Flight Notification Service (ADCUS) available.
COMMUNICATIONS: CTAF 128.25
SEATTLE FSS (SEA) TF 1–800–WX–BRIEF. NOTAM FILE SEA.

Figure 22-2. Seaplane base listing in the A/FD for Friday Harbor.

FORT NORMAN NWT	**ET7**
REF	N64 54 W125 35 34°E UTC-7(6) Elev 242′ A5035 C-10
OPR	CARS 403-588-3191 Ltd hrs Reg
PF	A-1 C-2,4,5 adj land A/D
FLT PLN FSS CARS	NOTAM FILE CYVQ Norman Wells 403-587-2555 W4 403-588-3191 Ltd hrs
A/D DATA	Open water Jun-Sep. Sheltered in mouth of Great Bear River. Beaches opposite RCMP Post, current 5 kts, mud & gravel bottom. Skiplanes in win.
COMM MF APRT RDO	aprt rdo ltd hrs O/T tfc 122.1 5NM 3300 ASL around Fort Norman land A/D adj 122.1 (V) 16-24Z(DT 15-23Z) Mon-Fri exc hols At land A/D
NAV NDB	ZFN 392 (L) N64 54 24 W125 33 54 adj to A/D
PRO	Land in front of settlement, if river rough land in lake 1.5NM 020° fr settlement.
CAUTION	Choppy in N winds, hi swells in W winds. Shoals at junction of Great Bear & Mackenzie Rivers. Land aprt 1NM N.

Figure 22-3. A seaplane base listing from a Canadian water supplement.

INVER GROVE HEIGHTS—Wipline SPB (09Y) **Location:** Mississippi River, 2 mi SE of city. **Coordinates:** N044-49.0; W093-1.0. **Telephone:** 612/451-1205. **Fax:** 612/451-1786. **Hours:** 24. **Elevation:** 687. **Landing lanes:** 17-35 8,000 X 500, fresh water. **Mooring facilities:** hangar, tie-down, ramp, docking. **Obstructions:** trees. **Frequencies:** CTAF 122.9, FSS Princeton/122.2, 122. **Sectional:** Twin Cities. **Transportation:** Bus, Taxi. **Restaurants:** Peking 1/2 mi, McDonalds 1/2 mi, Kentucky Fried Chicken 1/2 mi. **Lodging:** Golden Steer 3 mi 455-8541, Drover's Inn on site 455-3600, Holiday Inn 2 mi. **Fuel:** Wipaire, Inc 612/451-1205 brand varies 100LL, Jet. **Credit cards:** Exxon, MasterCard, Phillips, Sohio, Visa. **Services:** Repairs. **Notes:** Right tfc lane 35; river channel marked by buoys. Caution required at all times on river for floating debris.

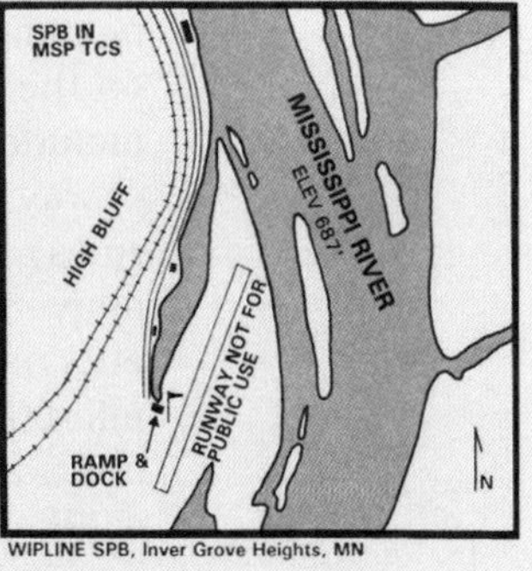

WIPLINE SPB, Inver Grove Heights, MN

Figure 22-4. Example of a seaplane base listing in the SPA *Water Landing Directory*.

Safety Rules for Seaplanes

Title 14 of the Code of Federal Regulations (14 CFR) Part 91 contains the right-of-way rules for operating seaplanes on water. It is brief, clear and to the point:

> §91.115 Right-of-way rules: Water operations.
>
> **(a)** ***General.*** Each person operating an aircraft on the water shall, insofar as possible, keep clear of all vessels and avoid impeding their navigation, and shall give way to any vessel or other aircraft that is given the right-of-way by any rule of this section.
>
> **(b)** ***Crossing.*** When aircraft, or an aircraft and a vessel, are on crossing courses, the aircraft or vessel to the other's right has the right-of-way.
>
> **(c)** ***Approaching head-on.*** When aircraft, or an aircraft and a vessel, are approaching head-on, or nearly so, each shall alter its course to the right to keep well clear.
>
> **(d)** ***Overtaking.*** Each aircraft or vessel that is being overtaken has the right-of-way, and the one overtaking shall alter course to keep well clear.
>
> **(e)** ***Special circumstances.*** When aircraft, or an aircraft and a vessel, approach so as to involve risk of collision, each aircraft or vessel shall proceed with careful regard to existing circumstances, including the limitations of the respective craft.

Burdened Vessel Rule

Despite the above rules, if you are in a seaplane and crossing in front of a 700-foot long tanker that couldn't possibly stop in the next mile, you really do not have the right-of-way even if you are on the vessel's right. The above rules are condensed and don't include anything about the "burdened" vessel having the right-of-way, which is in the Coast Guard rules (you are subject to these rules). A burdened vessel is one that is difficult to stop or maneuver. They have the right-of-way, so large vessels, sailboats, etc., have the right-of-way by virtue of being burdened. Keep in mind that mariners have little knowledge of seaplanes. You may consider yourself burdened because you can't turn out of the wind, etc. They don't know that. They will see your propeller turning and consider you maneuverable, therefore not burdened. So, the best rule is to stay out of everybody's way, always yield right-of-way and don't hit or scare anyone!

Using the burdened vessel concept, an aircraft must give way to all nonpowered vessels while on the surface with an engine running. Since a seaplane in the water may not maneuver as well as one in the air, the aircraft on the water has right-of-way over the one in the air, and one taking off has right-of-way over one landing. That's really different from the way the landplane pilot thinks, isn't it? I hope you can see the wisdom of it, however.

In addition to these operating rules, the U.S. Coast Guard (USCG) manual (M16672.2C) Navigation Rules, International-Inland, applies to all vessels navigating upon the high seas and certain inland waters. The Inland rules apply to all public or private vessels operating upon inland waters of the U.S., high seas, and certain inshore waters. The USCG has jurisdiction over operations on the high seas and certain inland waters. Refer to this document for more information on the subject.

Status of Seaplanes as Vessels

The aircraft on the water has right-of-way over one in the air, and one taking off has right-of-way over one landing.

USCG's Navigation Rules, International-Inland, provides the following definition: "The word 'vessel' includes every description of water craft, including nondisplacement craft and seaplanes, used or capable of being used as a means of transportation on water." Therefore, a seaplane is a vessel once it lands on the water and, as such, is required to comply with the USCG navigation rules applicable to vessels. Adherence to section 91.115 and the paragraph just below it should ensure compliance with the USCG rules.

There is one exception to this: the USCG does not enforce its rules pertaining to personal floatation devices (PFDs) for seaplanes at this time. The SPA has on file a letter from the commander of the Coast Guard to this effect. If the seaplane is flown for hire (including flight instruction), PFDs are required per 14 CFR 91.205. That section requires a pyrotechnic signaling device as well.

The *Aeronautical Information Manual*, Section 7-5-7, entitled "Seaplane Safety" provides a good periodic review for all seaplane pilots. Accordingly, it is reprinted in Appendix 2 of this book.

Safety Equipment for Seaplanes

The safety equipment requirements for seaplanes are included in 14 CFR Part 91. These are minimum requirements only, and are specifically for pilots who operate seaplanes for hire over water and beyond power-off gliding distance from shore. For such operations, approved flotation gear must be readily available to each occupant and at least one pyrotechnic signaling device must be on board. Although this requirement does not apply to seaplane operations not for hire, it is recommended by the FAA. PFDs are required aboard all seaplanes in Canada.

Personal Floatation Devices (PFDs)

There are many different kinds of PFDs. Only the inflatable type are suitable for aircraft use, because a device that provides constant floatation may impede egress from an aircraft, or may pin the wearer at a high point in the aircraft cabin by virtue of its floatation (also inhibiting egress).

Inflatable PFDs can be categorized into those that are USCG approved, those that are FAA approved, and those that are not approved. Any of these may be used in seaplanes that are not flown for hire. Technically, only the FAA approved type (TSOc13f or TSOc726) may be used in seaplanes flown for hire and operated beyond gliding distance of land. (Although, in my mind, a good case could be made for those that are USCG approved.) USCG approved inflatables are new and have been available for only a short period of time.

Additional safety and personal equipment should be reviewed prior to each flight. Equipment requirements should be tailored to meet the needs of potential problems for each type of flight and destination environment. Numerous good checklists exist. See those in the book *Water Flying Concepts*.

A Word to the Wise

Rules, rules, rules! The pilot is inundated with rules. In strange, unfamiliar and sometimes confusing locations, extreme caution is appropriate. Whenever I find myself in this kind of situation, I try to keep in mind that, as long as I am aloft, I can see all, watch what others are doing and then act appropriately. If it appears that things are being done in a manner you wouldn't expect, there is probably a reason for it. Remember, a number of countries drive on the left side of the road. Often those countries also have their navigation aids reversed as well! Stay aloft until you are certain of your plan to operate on the water!

Navigation Aids

In the interest of safety, seaplane pilots should become familiar with navigation aids, such as buoys, day and night beacons, light and sound signals, and steering and sailing rules. You'll never use them, you say? Well, the day may come, as it did for me, when you will need to land on the St. Lawrence Seaway because a fog bank is obscuring the customs destination you are looking for. Sure, your GPS will show you the way, but wouldn't it be nice if you knew what the fog horn you are hearing is telling you? Interesting! You just learned that it may be a good idea, when on the water in fog, to shut off your engine and listen. What are you listening for? Fog horn sound patterns, sound of large engines (important to know the direction from which a large tanker is bearing down on you), waves on the shore, etc. This is not necessary to study as a beginner, but it does illustrate that, when the topic is floatplane flying, you will never stop learning. That is what makes it so much fun and so interesting!

The navigable waterways we fly from or boat on have their own "road signs." The following discussion provides the basic knowledge you need to read most of them. They may take the form of buoys, which are floating aids; daymarkers, which are unlighted fixed structures (posts, pilings, etc.); daybeacons, which are daymarkers with lights; lights, which may be ashore or on fixed structures; fog signals, which may be on ends of jettys or on buoys or posts; and ranges, which give precise visual positioning to mark channel centers.

Buoys

These are floating NAVAIDs, anchored to the bottom. Their shape, color and number all tell something important (*see* Figure 22-5). There are two primary shapes, called nun buoys and can buoys. Nun buoys are a cylinder topped by a cone with its pointy end up.

As shown by the table in Figure 22-6, nun buoys typically are red in color and mark the right side of a channel when returning from sea or from a larger body of water. If they are numbered, the number will be even. Can buoys are typically black, odd numbered and mark the left side of the channel. Hence the old mariner's saying, "Red Right Returning!"

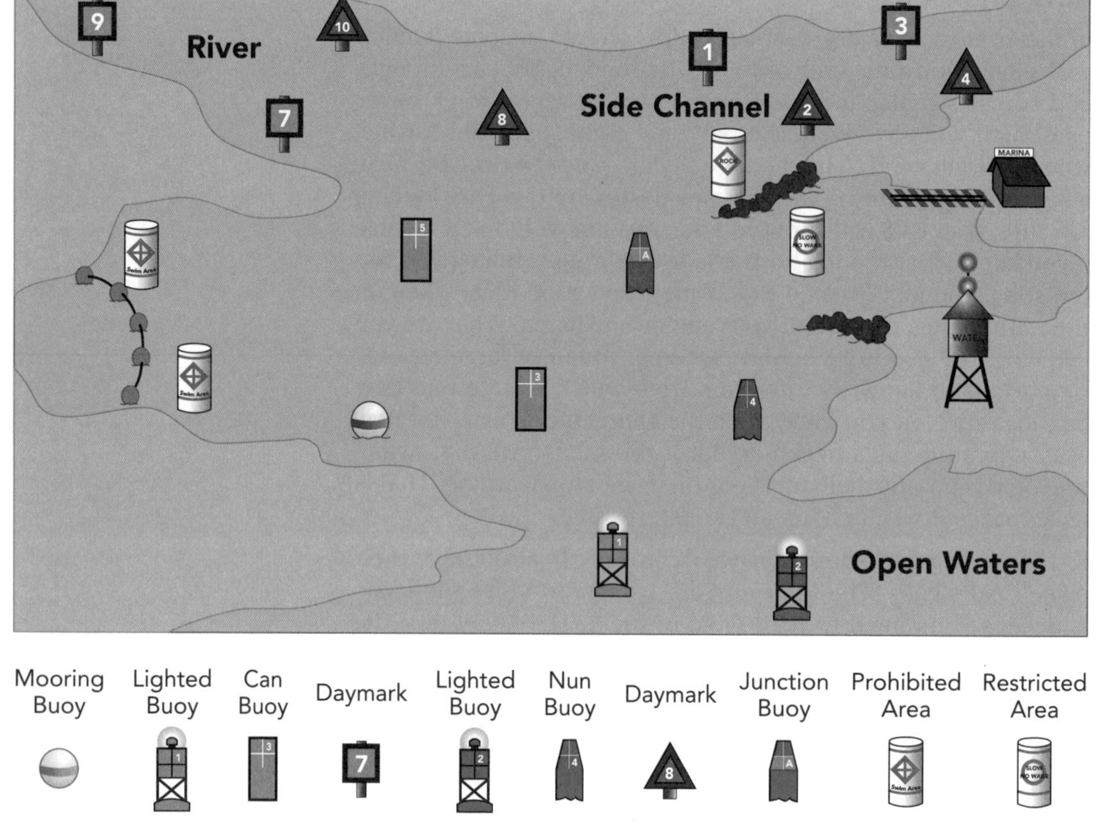

Figure 22-5. Nun buoy, can buoy, daymarker and other NAVAIDs and how they mark the waterway.

Returning from sea*	Color	Number	Unlighted body shape	Light color	Light characteristic	Daymark shape
Right side of channel	Red	Even	Nun	Red or white	Flashing or quick flashing	Triangular
Left side of channel	Black or green	Odd	Can	Green or white	Flashing or quick flashing	Square
*or entering a harbor from a larger body of water						

Figure 22-6. Summary of buoy channel markings

Daymarkers

These are typically shaped as a triangle if on the right side (also even numbered and with red color), and square if on the left side, returning (odd numbered and with some black color).

Sound and Light

Sound (fog horns, whistle buoys, etc.) is only partially useful to the seaplane pilot because the sound (and light) patterns are not published on aeronautical charts. Nautical charts, however, are very useful for depth indications as well as sound and light pattern information.

An Experienced Word

Just when you think you have this system all figured out, you may find a marker system that is confusing, possibly because your idea of "returning" doesn't agree with that of the person who installed the system. Be careful! Do a thorough landing area assessment, flying over and observing before committing to a landing. The above system is used in all of the Americas, but I have had to fly overhead and observe where the boats went, to determine for sure where the channel was. Canada has some wonderful waterways, north of the Great Lakes, that seem to go in many different directions. The seaplane pilot has the wonderful perspective of a bird's-eye view to sort things out. Use it well!

Ranges

As a seaplane pilot, I have found ranges to be very helpful…I know I am landing in the center of the channel. One I use often is at Warroad, MN at the entrance to the Warroad River from Lake of the Woods. Shallow water and sandbars are nearby on both sides of the channel. A range marker or channel marker consists of two fixed structures, ashore or fixed in the water and arranged so that they are aligned when the observer is in the center of the channel. One marker is higher than the other. The higher marker is always the marker farther from the observer. So, if the lower marker is to the left of the higher marker, the observer must move to the left to reach the channel center. *See* Figures 22-7 and 22-8 on the next page.

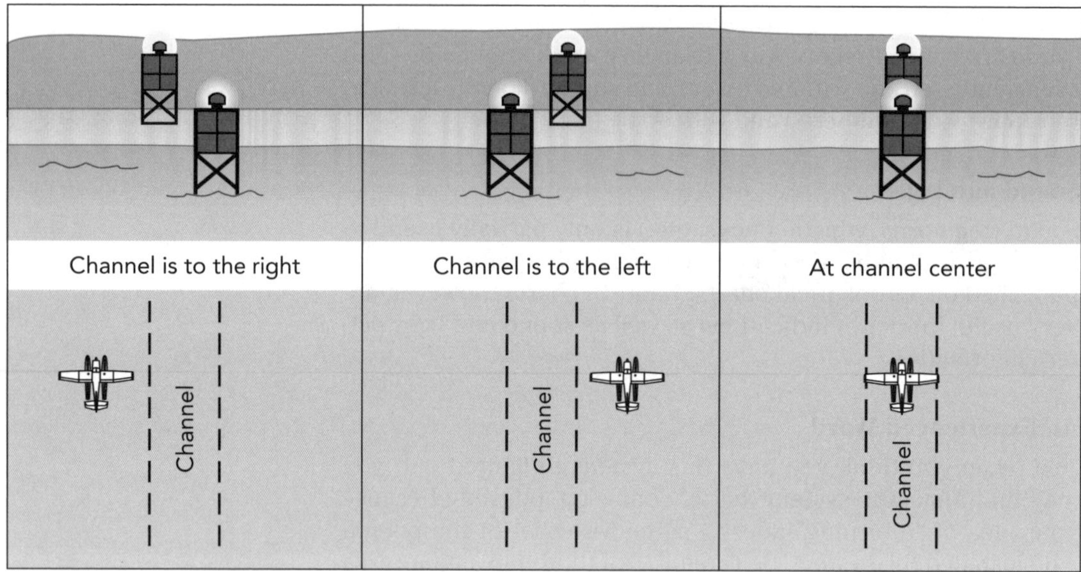

Figure 22-7. Range markers

Figure 22-8. Range markers mark channel centerline for the seaplane pilot on final for the Siuslaw River, OR. Center of channel is to the pilot's left.

Review

Be sure you know how to identify and locate seaplane bases on charts or in directories:

- A seaplane base/landing area is symbolized on aeronautical charts by an anchor alone, or an anchor inside a standard airport circle.
- If a seaplane base is lighted, the chart will depict the typical lighted airport symbol above the circle.
- A seaplane base beacon alternates flashing yellow and white.

Be sure you can explain operating restrictions at various bases. They are found in the remarks section of the listing.

The right-of-way, steering, and sailing rules pertinent to seaplane operation are set forth in 14 CFR §91.115. In addition, "burdened vessels" rules apply. The best rule is to stay out of everybody's way, always yield right-of-way and don't hit or scare anyone. Also, while on the surface with an engine running, an aircraft must give way to all nonpowered vessels. Since a seaplane in the water may not be as maneuverable as one in the air, the aircraft on the water has right-of-way over one in the air, and one taking off has right-of-way over one landing.

Seaplanes, when on the water, are considered vessels and are subject to all the rules that apply to vessels except the one relating to PFDs. PFDs are required aboard seaplanes that fly for hire and must be the FAA-approved kind in the U.S. In Canada, PFDs are required on all flights.

Marine navigation aids such as buoys, beacons, lights, and sound signals should be familiar to the seaplane pilot. Can and nun buoys as well as day beacons and day markers are used as channel markers. "Red Right Returning" should help you remember how channel markers are laid out, but review the channel marker summary table, above, for details. Range markers can be vitally important to seaplane pilots when landing, taxiing or taking off from channels.

Let's see if you understand the maritime aids now: in Figure 22-8 is the pilot landing in the channel toward the ocean or toward the harbor? Hint: consider the green can buoy.

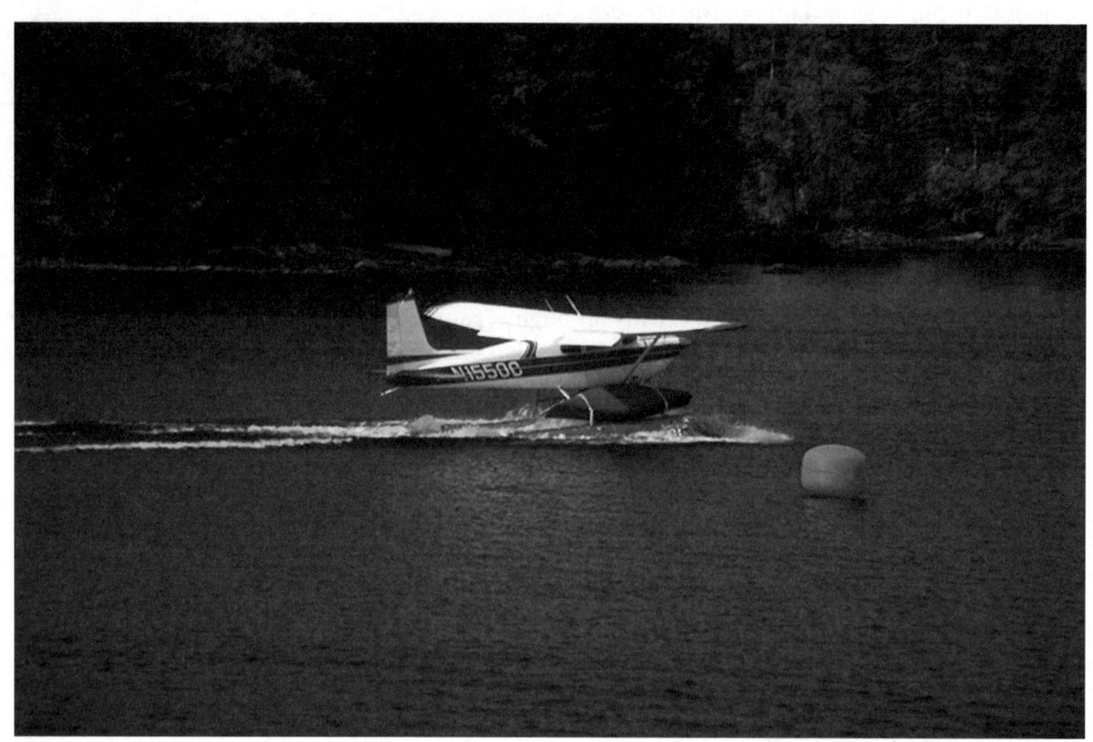

SPA

A Cessna 180 about to depart for remote waters with a canoe aboard. External loads are an advanced topic well covered in Water Flying Concepts, *Chapter 8.*

Chapter 23
Certificates, Documents and Checkride Preparation

If you are going for your seaplane rating "oral and checkride": the PTS task table says that if you hold a private or better landplane certificate, the task area for PTS Section I • A doesn't need to be tested. But the reality is, the examiner is going to want to know the aircraft is airworthy before he or she gets in to fly with you. So, guess what—a paperwork review is in order! Better know your stuff! If you are already a seaplane pilot, I suggest you review this section to make sure you are carrying the required documents when you fly. The second section, "Checkride Preparation" doesn't apply if you are already ASES-rated.

The FAA's newest terminology for this is the "practical test" which encompasses both the oral and flight tests.

For most pilots, paperwork detracts from the fun of flying, but it is an absolute necessity so let's have a look. There are really two parts to this section. First is an understanding of the different pilot and aircraft documents, their purpose, what they look like, and where they should be found (on the pilot's person, in the aircraft or filed at home). Then, we will deal with what needs to be prepared for checkride time.

Pilot Documents

Pilot Certificate

Pertinent regs:

- 14 CFR §61.101
- 14 CFR §61.115
- 14 CFR §61.133
- 14 CFR §61.167

The Recreational, Private, Commercial, and ATP certificates have different privileges and limitations. For example, 14 CFR §61.115 lists the privileges and limitations for pilots holding the Private certificate. Commercial pilots should refer to §61.133, but remember that even though this section allows you to carry passengers or cargo for hire, you may not do so unless you or your employer possess an Air Carrier certificate or a Part 135 (charter) certificate. (There are a few exceptions to this. See the applicability section in 14 CFR Part 135.) Section 61.167 lists the privileges and limitations for the ATP certified pilot, and §61.101 does the same for the recreational pilot. Since you are going to bring a copy of the Federal Aviation Regulations (14 CFR) with you for your oral exam, you may wish to flag the appropriate section to help you find it quickly.

See 14 CFR §61.23

Medical Certificates

Pilots are expected to know what class medical certificate is required for the privileges being exercised. (For example, if you hold a commercial certificate but are not flying for hire, you may fly with a third class medical, since you are exercising the privileges of a private pilot). You should also know when your medical certificate expires. 14 CFR §61.23 explains it all. If you are flying a glider or balloon, a medical is not required. Figure 23-3 is a table that roughly summarizes the medical certificate.

UNITED STATES OF AMERICA
Department of Transportation
Federal Aviation Administration
MEDICAL CERTIFICATE SECOND CLASS
This certifies that (Full name and address):
EDGAR DALE DEREMER
P.O.BOX 126, 315 LINCOLN ST.
TWISP, WA 98856

Date of Birth	Height	Weight	Hair	Eyes	Sex
05/01/1935	71	265	BROWN	BLUE	M

has met the medical standards prescribed in part 67, Federal Aviation Regulations, for this class of Medical Certificate.
Limitations: MUST WEAR CORRECTIVE LENSES FOR NEAR AND DISTANT VISION
Date of Examination 08/28/2001 Examiner's Designation No.
Examiner: Signature / Typed Name WARREN C. JENSEN, M.D.
AIRMAN'S SIGNATURE
FAA Form 8500-9 (3-99) Supersedes Previous Edition

Figure 23-1. Example of a medical certificate

I. UNITED STATES OF AMERICA XI.
DEPARTMENT OF TRANSPORTATION – FEDERAL AVIATION ADMINISTRATION
THIS CERTIFIES THAT IV. EDGAR DALE DEREMER
V. 1323 NOBLE COVE
GRAND FORKS ND 58201

DATE OF BIRTH	HEIGHT	WEIGHT	HAIR	EYES	SEX	NATIONALITY VI.
05-01-35	73 IN	240	BROWN	BLUE	M	USA

IX. HAS BEEN FOUND TO BE PROPERLY QUALIFIED TO EXERCISE THE PRIVILEGES OF
II. AIRLINE TRANSPORT PILOT III. CERT. NO. 1464844
RATINGS AND LIMITATIONS
XII. AIRPLANE SINGLE ENGINE LAND & SEA
COMMERCIAL PRIVILEGES
AIRPLANE MULTIENGINE LAND & SEA
XIII. ROTORCRAFT-HELICOPTER<
VII. SIGNATURE OF HOLDER X.
X. DATE OF ISSUE 01-06-91 VIII. ADMINISTRATOR

Figure 23-2. Example of a pilot's certificate

When exercising the privileges of	Certificate	Medical is good until
Private Pilot	3rd class	End of 24th month after month of exam (36th month if pilot is less than 40 years old at time of issue and medical certificate was issued after September 15, 1996)
Commercial Pilot	2nd class	End of 12th month after month of exam
ATP	1st class	End of 6th month after month of exam

Figure 23-3. Summary of medical certificate duration

Pilot Logbook

Pilots must document and record the following time in a manner acceptable to the FAA:

See 14 CFR §61.51

- Training and aeronautical experience used to meet the requirements for a certificate, rating, or flight review required under the FAA regulations.
- The aeronautical experience required for meeting the recent flight experience requirements of the regulations.

The logbook must show any endorsements by flight instructors, and must be carried on each flight if you are a student or recreational pilot. Details of required entries and how to record them are found in 14 CFR §61.51.

Also, keep in mind that insurance companies base policies on the pilot's documented time, training and attendance of certain seminars such as the SEAWINGS program. Proof of compliance with these policy requirements is usually documented in the pilot logbook.

Photo ID

Pilots must also now have when flying a valid photo ID, such as a driver's license, passport, military ID, etc. This is a new rule, partly the result of 9-11.

Aircraft Documents

An aircraft is not considered airworthy for flight unless it carries several documents aboard at all times. These include: the aircraft registration; airworthiness certificate; pilots operating handbook or manual including copies of all STCs (if the STC states it is part of the POH); aircraft minimum equipment list or list of equipment required for certification; and all documentation needed to compute weight and balance. Aircraft logbooks and pilot logbooks, except for student and recreational pilots, need not be aboard the aircraft for Part 91 operations.

UNITED STATES OF AMERICA
DEPARTMENT OF TRANSPORTATION—FEDERAL AVIATION ADMINISTRATION
STANDARD AIRWORTHINESS CERTIFICATE

1 NATIONALITY AND REGISTRATION MARKS	2 MANUFACTURER AND MODEL	3 AIRCRAFT SERIAL NUMBER	4 CATEGORY
N620FT	American General Aircraft AG-5B	10009	Normal Utility

5 AUTHORITY AND BASIS FOR ISSUANCE
This airworthiness certificate is issued pursuant to the Federal Aviation Act of 1958 and certifies that, as of the date of issuance, the aircraft to which issued has been inspected and found to conform to the type certificate therefor, to be in condition for safe operation, and has been shown to meet the requirements of the applicable comprehensive and detailed airworthiness code as provided by Annex 8 to the Convention on International Civil Aviation, except as noted herein.
Exceptions

None

6 TERMS AND CONDITIONS
Unless sooner surrendered, suspended, revoked, or a termination date is otherwise established by the Administrator, this airworthiness certificate is effective as long as the maintenance, preventative maintenance, and alterations are performed in accordance with Parts 21, 43, and 91 of the Federal Aviation Regulations, as appropriate, and the aircraft is registered in the United States.

DATE OF ISSUANCE	FAA REPRESENTATIVE	DESIGNATION NUMBER
12-20-90	Emil F. Miehlke	CE-51

Any alteration, reproduction, or misuse of this certificate may be punishable by a fine not exceeding $1,000 or imprisonment not exceeding 3 years, or both. THIS CERTIFICATE MUST BE DISPLAYED IN THE AIRCRAFT IN ACCORDANCE WITH APPLICABLE FEDERAL AVIATION REGULATIONS.

FAA Form 8100-2 (8-82) · U.S. GOVERNMENT PRINTING OFFICE: 1988-0-582-105

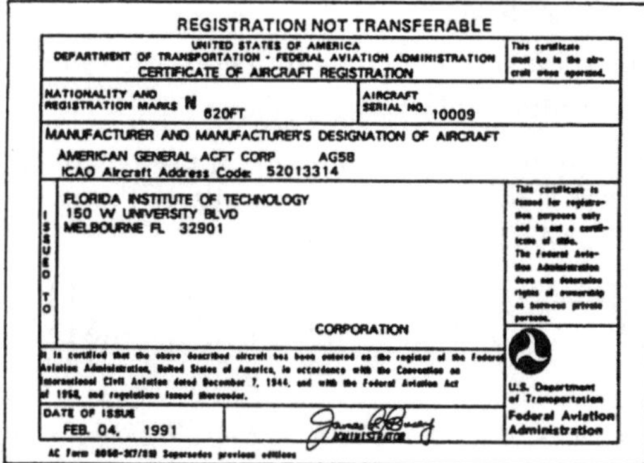

REGISTRATION NOT TRANSFERABLE

UNITED STATES OF AMERICA
DEPARTMENT OF TRANSPORTATION - FEDERAL AVIATION ADMINISTRATION
CERTIFICATE OF AIRCRAFT REGISTRATION

This certificate must be in the aircraft when operated.

NATIONALITY AND REGISTRATION MARKS N 620FT

AIRCRAFT SERIAL NO. 10009

MANUFACTURER AND MANUFACTURER'S DESIGNATION OF AIRCRAFT
AMERICAN GENERAL ACFT CORP AG5B
ICAO Aircraft Address Code: 52013314

ISSUED TO
FLORIDA INSTITUTE OF TECHNOLOGY
150 W UNIVERSITY BLVD
MELBOURNE FL 32901

CORPORATION

This certificate is issued for registration purposes only and is not a certificate of title. The Federal Aviation Administration does not determine rights of ownership as between private persons.

It is certified that the above described aircraft has been entered on the register of the Federal Aviation Administration, United States of America, in accordance with the Convention on International Civil Aviation dated December 7, 1944, and with the Federal Aviation Act of 1958, and regulations issued thereunder.

DATE OF ISSUE
FEB. 04, 1991

ADMINISTRATOR

U.S. Department of Transportation
Federal Aviation Administration

AC Form 8050-3 (7/88) Supersedes previous editions

Figure 23-4. Sample airworthiness certificate, aircraft registration.

Aircraft Registration Certificate

See 14 CFR Part 47

The aircraft registration certificate shows the current registered owner and address. Any address change must be reported to the FAA Aircraft Registration branch by the owner within 30 days.

Airworthiness Certificate

See 14 CFR §21.171

An airworthiness certificate is issued by the FAA and remains with the aircraft as long as it is airworthy (it does not expire). It also remains with the aircraft through transfers of ownership. For details, see 14 CFR Part 21 Subpart H.

Operating Limitations

These are available to the pilot in the POH, on placards on the instrument panel and elsewhere in the cockpit, and on the instruments themselves. It is pretty obvious that the pilot must know and understand the operating limitations. So it becomes his or her responsibility to know where to find the information and to be sure that it is correct.

Placards

Placards may be authorized and required to be in place either by the POH or by the airworthiness directive (AD). If AD and POH-required placards are not in place where they should be in the cockpit, the aircraft is not legally airworthy. Placards may be called for by a service bulletin issued by the manufacturer. While it may be prudent to display such placards, the aircraft's airworthiness is not affected if they are recommended by a service bulletin but are missing.

Whose responsibility is it that required placards be in place? The IA who signs off the aircraft's annual inspection certifies that the placards are in place at that time. The aircraft owner/operator is also held responsible by law. The pilot is responsible for determining the aircraft is airworthy before flight. Placards are important because they notify the crew about aircraft limitations.

Instrument Markings

Instrument markings also display aircraft limitations. The airspeed indicator shows the airspeed limitations of V_S, V_{SO}, V_{FE}, V_{NO} and V_{NE}. I have seen more than one aircraft with an airspeed indicator that was incorrectly marked. As a pilot, you should check these speeds in the POH and be sure they agree with the airspeed indicator! One important speed (limitation) the pilot must know and understand how to use, but is not shown on the airspeed indicator, is V_A (design maneuvering speed or the speed at which the wing will stall before structurally overloading. Sometimes called rough air penetration speed). RPM redline and yellow arcs, cylinder head temperature redlines and operating range, and oil temperature gauge markings are other examples of limitations that must be on panel instruments.

Handbooks and Manuals

This category refers to the document we have been calling the POH (Pilot's Operating Handbook). It is the aircraft owner's manual or aircraft flight handbook. Keep in mind that the "POH" and "owner's manual" are quite different. Aircraft certificated without a POH have their limitations in the form of placards and therefore, do not need to carry the owner's manual in the aircraft.* Only "FAA approved" manuals must be carried on board at all times. Since the POH contains limitations, performance data, operating and emergency procedures it must be available to the flight crew at all times. If there is a separate manual for the seaplane, or seaplane supplement, it also must be on board and available to the crew at all times as it is considered part of the POH when the aircraft is on floats.

* For example, Cessna did not publish a POH for their 172 series until 1979, so any 1956-1978 Cessna 172 would not need to carry the owner's manual, because the aircraft limitations are in the form of placards. Any Cessna 172, 1979 and forward must have the POH in the aircraft, plus the required placards installed.

Weight and Balance Data, and Equipment List

The current weight and balance computation of the aircraft's empty weight and CG arm, signed by a mechanic or IA, must be in the aircraft so that the pilot can accomplish a weight and balance computation at any time. The equipment list is the list of items that were installed in the aircraft at the time of certification. It is a part of the aircraft's records and needs to be carried in the aircraft because you, as pilot, may need to use it to determine whether the aircraft can be legally flown if one of the systems is inoperative.

Airworthiness Directives, Compliance Records, and Maintenance Requirements

An airworthiness directive (AD) is issued by the FAA in response to a corrective need in the interest of safety. It is mandatory that ADs be complied with. ADs may require a one-time treatment, others may require periodic treatment at some time in the future. Some of these are ongoing. Most aircraft have a few ADs that apply, so it is the ultimate responsibility of the pilot to determine the aircraft is airworthy, which includes checking that there are no outstanding ADs that have not been complied with. How is this done?

1. The pilot can refer to the aircraft's logbooks to see if the aircraft's annual is current (complied with within the preceding 12 months). Before the annual inspection can be signed off by the IA, an audit of ADs must be done to ensure compliance and to list any ongoing, repetitive or outstanding ADs. It is the pilot's responsibility to check this list to be certain that there are no repetitive or outstanding ADs that are due.
2. In the aircraft's logbook there should be a record of ADs current and complied with as of the time the annual inspection was accomplished, as well as a list of ADs that have on-going inspection or maintenance requirements.
3. Check with an aircraft mechanic who has access to a current list of ADs if some time has passed since the annual was completed.

Also, remember that ADs cannot be overflown, like the 100-hour can, to go to a place of maintenance.

The aircraft's maintenance records typically consist of an airframe logbook and an engine/propeller logbook. There may or may not be a separate logbook for the propeller and floats.

Maintenance requirements, if not found in the POH, will be found in the aircraft service manual.

Checkride Preparation

Going well prepared to the checkride meeting tells the examiner that the applicant is organized and knowledgeable. Here are most of the ground rules that apply, and then below is a checklist to help you prepare.

Examiner's Role

To administer the practical test, the examiner will evaluate all **Tasks** in each **Area of Operation** as required by the PTS. Any task selected shall be evaluated in its entirety. However, if the elements in one task have already been evaluated in another Task, they need not be repeated.

The terms "Task" and "Area of Operation" refer to the different types of requirements under the various subjects listed in the PTS books.

The examiner may, for any valid reason, elect to evaluate certain tasks orally. Such tasks include those that are impracticable, such as night flying, or glassy water landings on a day when the wind is 15 knots and gusty.

The examiner is not required to follow the precise order in which the Area of Operation and Tasks appear in the PTS. The examiner may change the sequence of tasks or combine them with similar objectives to meet the orderly, efficient flow of a well-run practical test. For example, a glassy water takeoff may be combined with a float-lift takeoff. But, the objectives of all Tasks must be demonstrated and evaluated at some time during the practical test.

Examiners will place special emphasis on those aircraft operations most critical to flight safety. Among these areas are precise aircraft control and sound judgment in making decisions. Although these areas may or may not be covered under each Task, they are essential to flight safety and shall receive careful evaluation throughout the practical test. If these areas are shown in the Objective, additional emphasis will be placed on them. In effect, the examiner will expect you to exhibit good common sense while operating a seaplane.

The FAA expects the examiner to also emphasize stall/spin awareness, spatial disorientation, wake turbulence avoidance, low level wind shear, inflight collision avoidance, landing area incursion avoidance, and checklist usage.

In the performance of emergency procedures, consideration must always be given to local conditions, including weather and terrain. If the procedure being evaluated would jeopardize safety, the examiner shall simulate that portion of the Task.

Flight Test Prerequisites

An applicant for the pilot practical test is required by Federal Aviation Regulations to:

1. Obtain the applicable instruction and aeronautical experience prescribed for the pilot certificate or rating sought;
2. Possess a current medical certificate appropriate to the certificate or rating sought;
3. Meet the age requirement for the issuance of the certificate or rating sought; and
4. Obtain a written statement from an appropriately certificated flight instructor certifying that the applicant was given flight instruction in preparation for the practical test within 60 days preceding the date of application. The statement should also declare the applicant competent to pass the practical test and confirm that he or she has satisfactory knowledge of the subject area(s) in which a deficiency was indicated by the airman knowledge test report.
5. Pass the appropriate pilot knowledge oral test prior to taking the flight test.

Use of Distractions During Practical Tests

Numerous studies show that accidents occur when the pilot is distracted during critical phases of flight. To evaluate the applicant's ability to divide attention, both inside and outside the cockpit, while maintaining safe flight, the examiner will cause realistic distractions during the flight portion of the practical test. Examples of this might include such things as: interruptions during use of the checklist to see if the applicant properly returns to the checklist; interruptions during landing area assessment to see if the applicant returns and completes the assessment; and diverting attention to cows on the ground, or an eagle sighted. The applicant can handle these and other distractions such as discussing boats, fishing, or airplanes during critical phases of flight by invoking the sterile cockpit rule or requesting that a question from the examiner be deferred to a less busy time.

Applicant's Use of Checklists

Throughout the practical test, the applicant is evaluated on using the checklist. Its proper use is dependent on the specific task being evaluated. It is possible that the use of the checklist, while accomplishing the elements of the objective, would be either unsafe or impractical, especially in a single-pilot operation. In this case, a review of the checklist, after the elements have been met, would be more appropriate. However, always remember that use of the checklist must include proper scanning and division of attention at all times while using the checklist.

Positive Exchange of Flight Controls

During flight training, there must always be a clear understanding between student and instructor/examiner about who has control of the aircraft. The PTS recommends a briefing that includes a positive, three-step process in the exchange of flight controls between pilots. When the pilot flying wishes the other pilot to take control of the aircraft, he or she will say, "you have the flight controls." That pilot will acknowledge with "I have the flight controls" at which time the first pilot says, "You have the flight controls." "I have the aircraft" is less desirable terminology because it is also used when a pilot spots other traffic.

Stabilized Approach

The term "stabilized approach" as used in the PTS is not applied in the same context as in large aircraft operation. In the PTS, it means the aircraft is in a position that requires minimum input of all controls to land safely. Excessive control input at any point could be an indication of improper planning. If it appears you may need excessive control input to accomplish the landing, a go-around is appropriate during the checkride. Remember, a go-around is always an appropriate maneuver if you don't like anything about the approach or landing.

Crew Resource Management (CRM)

CRM refers to the effective use of ***all*** available resources: human resources, hardware, and information. Human resources includes all groups routinely working with the cockpit crew (or pilot) who are involved in making decisions to operate a flight safely. These groups include, but are not limited to: dispatchers, cabin crewmembers, maintenance personnel, weather services and air traffic controllers. CRM is not a single Task. It is a set of skill competencies that must be evident in all Tasks in the PTS as applied to either single pilot or a crew operation.

In the seaplane, one or all passengers may be considered crewmembers, if the pilot has briefed them as to their duties before they need to perform the task. Since a preflight briefing of passengers is required, it is up to the pilot to effectively use the passenger-crewmember. For example, if the passenger has been properly briefed on how to notify the pilot if he or she sees other aircraft in the air, or aircraft or vessels on the water, the passenger becomes a crew member with respect to that task.

Metric Conversion Initiative

To assist pilots in understanding and using the metric system, the examiner may ask the pilot to refer to the metric equivalents of temperature or altitude. Since seaplanes often fly into Canada, pilots may be expected to demonstrate proficiency with metric conversions of fuel quantity, temperature and distances.

I fly in both Canada and Mexico where metric is used. I simply remember the following:

Temperature

In Celsius, freezing is 0, boiling water is 100, and I'm comfortable at 20 which is 68°F. At minus 40, both scales read the same. I can wing it from there. If I need a more accurate conversion, I look at the two scales on my outside air temp gauge. You may wish to remember that a 10°C change is equivalent to a 18°F change, or a ratio of 5:9.

Quantity

My Cessna 180 burns 12.2 U.S. gals/hr, which is 10 Imperial gallons or about 45 liters. Using those relationships, I can solve any liquid conversion problem. Develop your own by writing down a conversion relationship that works for you and you will remember. You can use reference documents on the oral, but you are expected to know where to find the information quickly and how to use it!

Distance

A kilometer is about .6 statute miles, so 10 kilometers is 6 statute miles. A nautical mile is 15% greater than a statute mile, or a ratio of 6 NM to 7 statute miles. From there, I can solve the conversion of anything having to do with statute, nautical and kilometers.

Manufacturer's Recommendation

The term "recommended" refers to the manufacturer's recommendation. If the manufacturer's recommendation is not available, the description in AC 61-21 should be used.

Specified by the Examiner

Use of the word "specified" in the PTS means as specified by the examiner.

Examiner Responsibility

The examiner conducting the practical test is responsible for determining that the applicant meets the acceptable standards of knowledge and skill of each Task within the appropriate PTS. Since there is no formal division between the "oral" and "skill" portions of the practical test, oral questioning is an ongoing process throughout the test. Oral questioning, to determine the applicant's knowledge of the Tasks and related safety factors, should be used judiciously at all times, especially during the flight portion of the practical test.

Examiners shall test, to the greatest extent practicable, the applicant's correlative abilities rather than mere rote enumeration of facts. Throughout the flight portion, the examiner shall evaluate the applicant's procedures for visual scanning, inflight collision avoidance, runway incursion avoidance (if an amphibian is used for the flight test*), and positive exchange of flight controls.

*Or if the water landing area has designated operational lanes, such as at Lake Hood on the Anchorage airport.

The word "examiner" denotes either the FAA inspector or FAA-designated pilot examiner who conducts the flight test.

Flight Instructor Responsibility

An appropriately rated flight instructor is responsible for training the student to acceptable standards in all subject matter areas, procedures, and maneuvers included in the task within each pertinent PTS Area of Operation. Flight instructors have great impact in developing safe, proficient pilots, so they should exhibit a high level of knowledge and skill, and the ability to impart that knowledge and skill to students. He or she must certify that the applicant is able to perform safely as a pilot and is competent to pass the required practical test for the certificate or rating sought.

Throughout the applicant's training, the flight instructor is responsible for emphasizing effective visual scanning, collision and runway incursion avoidance, and the positive exchange of flight controls.

Satisfactory Performance

Satisfactory performance is based on the applicant's ability to safely:

1. Perform the Tasks specified in the PTS Area of Operation for the certificate or rating sought within the approved standards;

2. Demonstrate mastery of the aircraft with the successful outcome of each task performed with complete confidence;
3. Demonstrate satisfactory proficiency and competency within the approved standards;
4. Demonstrate sound judgment; and
5. Demonstrate single-pilot competence if the aircraft is type certificated for single-pilot operations.

Unsatisfactory Performance

The tolerances represent the performance expected in good flying conditions. If, in the judgment of the examiner, the applicant does not meet the standards of performance of any Task, the associated Area of Operation is failed and, therefore, the practical test is failed. The examiner or applicant may discontinue the test any time after the failure of an Area of Operation renders the applicant ineligible for the certificate or rating sought. The test will be continued only with the consent of the applicant. If the test is discontinued, the applicant receives credit for only those Areas of Operation and their associated Tasks satisfactorily performed. However, during the retest and at the discretion of the examiner, any Task may be re-evaluated, including those previously passed.

Typical areas of unsatisfactory performance and grounds for disqualification are:

1. Any action or lack of action by the applicant that requires corrective intervention by the examiner to maintain safe flight.
2. Failure to use proper and effective visual scanning techniques to clear the area before and while performing maneuvers.
3. Consistently exceeding tolerances stated in the Objectives.
4. Failure to take prompt corrective action when tolerances are exceeded.

When a disapproval notice is issued, the examiner will record the applicant's unsatisfactory performance in terms of the Area of Operation appropriate to the practical test conducted.

Checklist for the Checkride

Consult with your flight instructor to be sure you are ready for the oral and flight portions of your checkride. Here is a checklist to help you get ready.

The Aircraft

- ☐ Documents showing current annual inspection (and 100-hour inspection if aircraft is used for flight instruction for hire), and AD note compliance (airframe and engine maintenance logbooks).
- ☐ Aircraft is capable of performing all maneuvers and tasks required for the flight test.
- ☐ Aircraft has dual controls (unless exempted by examiner, which is doubtful).
- ☐ Airworthiness, Registration, Weight and balance, Equipment list, Operating limitations.
- ☐ POH (Pilot's Operating Handbook or FAA-Approved Airplane Flight Manual) and all placards in place, including a current compass deviation card.

The Pilot-Applicant

- ☐ Pilot certificate and current medical certificate
- ☐ Current application FAA Form 8710-1, properly and completely filled out with signatures.
- ☐ Airman written test report (not required for adding the seaplane rating to an existing land certificate).
- ☐ Pilot logbook with instructor endorsements (completed within past 60 days)
- ☐ Notice of disapproval (if applicable).
- ☐ Letter of discontinuance (if applicable).
- ☐ Photo ID (driver's license).
- ☐ Current sectional chart.
- ☐ Computer, plotter, flight plan and flight log forms and any other appropriate flight planning tools.
- ☐ Current AIM, FAR and seaplane base facility directory.
- ☐ Current weather information.
- ☐ View limiting device (while it may not be needed, some examiners will issue pink slips if the applicant doesn't come prepared)
- ☐ Examiner's fee (cash).

Good luck with the oral and checkride!

SPA

Floatplanes are sometimes used as skiplanes to land on snow. This one is also being used as a clothes-line (drying line).

Chapter 24
What Now?

You have your seaplane rating.

You have learned everything in this book.

With respect to seaplane flying, now what?

Maintain Proficiency

Practice—don't just go up and fly around. If you have passengers, give them a proper briefing and plan the flight so they will be comfortable and feel they are riding with a professional. Prebrief each thing you do before you do it. Make it a "no excitement" flight. You will be considered a professional by your passengers if you can do that.

Practice some exercises on the water, while either taxiing out or taxiing in, each flight. Practice high wind operations on windy days even if you aren't going flying. Get a flight instructor that you respect to ride with you on that windy day just on the water. A favorite of mine is to taxi out into the wind, set the anchor, use the bridle, then before recovering the anchor, tie a 2.5 gallon plastic jug to the bitter end of the anchor rode and practice the power sailing exercise described on Page 80–81. Then sail back to the mooring area.

If you haven't done that in the past year, you aren't ready for high wind operations. I promise, the above described practice will boost your confidence when that windy day catches you up flying.

Go through the table of contents of this book and list all the seaplane operations you haven't performed in the last year. Use that list to plan what practice exercises you are going to do on the next flight. Then, read about them before you go out to fly or practice high wind maneuvers on the water. Unlike the landplane pilot, much of the seaplane pilot's expertise is in handling the floatplane on the water. You may log all the time that the seaplane is moving, so unlike your unfortunate landplane pilot buddies, you can log time when the propeller isn't even turning!

Recurrent Training

Recurrent training is called "SEAWINGS." The SEAWINGS curriculum is the seaplane pilot's version of the FAA Wings program. After looking at seaplane accident statistics, the curriculum was designed to cover areas of expertise through dual instruction that pilots need in order to avoid typical seaplane accidents. Requirements to meet the SEAWINGS certification are found in Appendix 2 at the back of this book. Don't choose a "santa claus" type flight instructor for this training. You need to learn as much as you can during the time you spend with the instructor. Pick the most knowledgeable flight instructor you can find and be sure he or she knows you really want to learn during the SEAWINGS instruction. Then, go prepared and with questions! SEAWINGS has some real valuable bonuses: when you complete your SEAWINGS training, you have met the requirements for the biennial flight review (BFR). Also, most insurance companies give whopping premium discounts if you have done a SEAWINGS phase within the past year. Some insurance companies insist you do SEAWINGS each year.

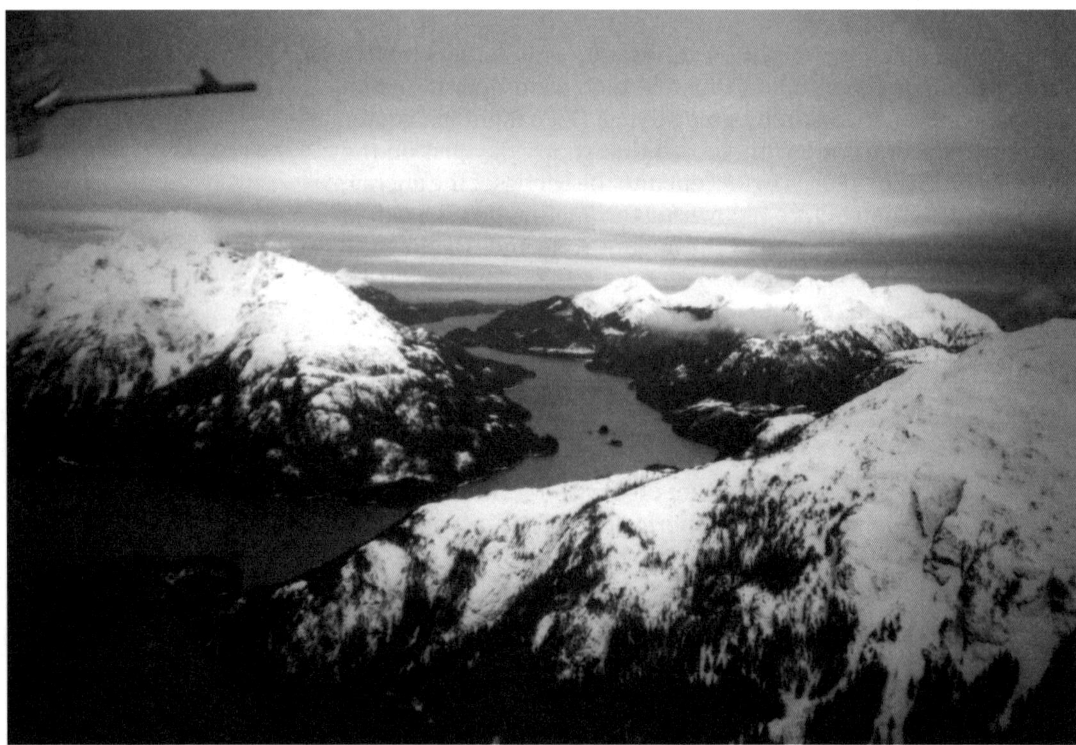

Burke Mees

A seaplane pilot's view of the world: Looking down on Lisianski Inlet, Alaska.

Advanced Training

Advanced Training

This is fun learning. Bush flying courses like the ones I used to teach, provide learning opportunities and challenges in beautiful, remote country.

Advanced Ratings

This can be fun, too. Plus you have the pride that comes from getting that "next ticket." There are very few ATP Single-Engine Sea rated pilots in the world. Why shouldn't you join those ranks?

Regional Learning

I have discovered regional learning is fascinating because operations in different parts of the continent are different. Go to Louisiana and learn how to dock bow-to, land in narrow bayous, and eat real Cajun food. Go to Maine and see how it is done there. Go to British Columbia or Alaska and fly the Fiords and mountain lakes and, while up there, don't fail to visit beautiful Victoria and do the underwater egress course. That particular lifesaving activity is inexpensive and eye-opening. When you have "been there yourself" you give a better passenger briefing (**www.dunk-you.com**). Besides, strolling hand-in-hand with your significant other through the Butchart Gardens and their beautiful old hotel is a nice activity after you both have been dunked!

Advanced Learning

When it comes to seaplane flying, the learning never stops unless you stop it. There are now a number of good books that will advance your learning, such as *Seaplane Operations* and *Water Flying Concepts* and hopefully, by the time you are ready, *Water Flying Concepts II*. Some of the older books, written before 1970, are fascinating reading with some good hints that seem to have become lost on today's water flyers. Check the bibliography for books that, although out of print, may be available through your library.

Sailors have a saying that is all wisdom, which says, "if you wait until your ship is perfectly ready to sail, you will never cast off the lines." It is time to cast off the lines on *Seaplane Pilot*, so I leave you with the wish that you have as much fun and enjoyment from water flying as I have. Good luck and be careful !

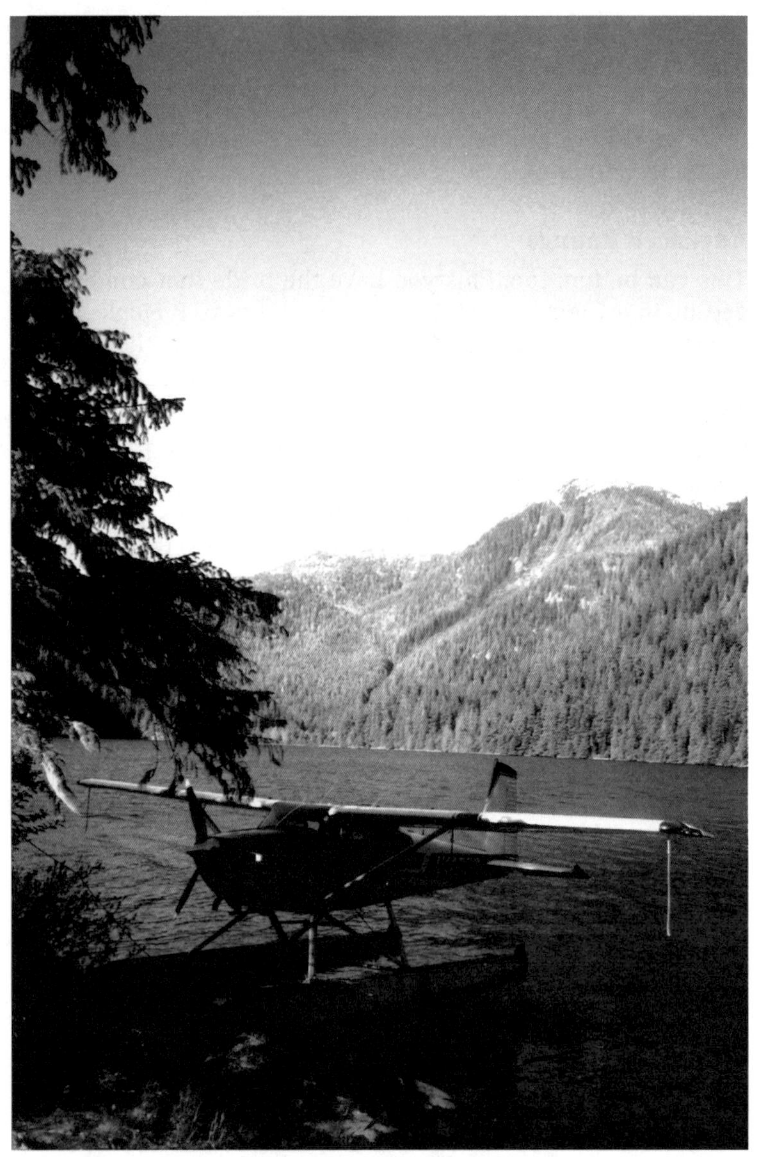

Moored bow-to on a rock ledge in a beachless lake in Ontario. Do you remember the hazards of doing this? If not, check Chapter 16.

Appendix 1

Private Pilot Practical Test Standards for Airplane Single-Engine Sea

FAA-S-8081-14AS

Areas of Operation I – XII for ASES • Pages 340 – 353
PTS Task Table for ASES • Page 354

About this excerpted reprint of FAA-S-8081-14AS:

Only the tasks that apply to ASES (Airplane Single-Engine Sea) have been reprinted as excerpts for this Appendix, according to the Task Table (see Page 354 for a reprint of the PTS Task Table for ASES). For the individual tasks that apply only to ASEL (Airplane Single-Engine Land), please see the complete FAA-S-8081-14AS on the FAA's website (http://afs600.faa.gov/) or ASA's reprint booklet (order number ASA-8081-14AS).

Note: For the Rating Task Table for ASES, see Page 354.

I. Area of Operation: Preflight Preparation

Note: The examiner shall develop a scenario based on real time weather to evaluate TASKs C and D.

A. Task: Certificates and Documents (ASEL and ASES)

References: 14 CFR Parts 43, 61, 91; FAA-H-8083-3, AC 61-23/FAA-H-8083-25; POH/AFM

Objective. To determine that the applicant exhibits knowledge of the elements related to certificates and documents by:

1. Explaining—
   a. private pilot certificate privileges, limitations, and recent flight experience requirements.
   b. medical certificate class and duration.
   c. pilot logbook or flight records.
2. Locating and explaining—
   a. airworthiness and registration certificates.
   b. operating limitations, placards, instrument markings, and POH/AFM.
   c. weight and balance data and equipment list.

B. Task: Airworthiness Requirements (ASEL and ASES)

References: 14 CFR part 91; AC 61-23/FAA-H-8083-25

Objective. To determine that the applicant exhibits knowledge of the elements related to airworthiness requirements by:

1. Explaining—
   a. required instruments and equipment for day/night VFR.
   b. procedures and limitations for determining airworthiness of the airplane with inoperative instruments and equipment with and without an MEL.
   c. requirements and procedures for obtaining a special flight permit.
2. Locating and explaining—
   a. airworthiness directives.
   b. compliance records.
   c. maintenance/inspection requirements.
   d. appropriate record keeping.

C. Task: Weather Information (ASEL and ASES)

References: 14 CFR part 91; AC 00-6, AC 00-45, AC 61-23/FAA-H-8083-25, AC 61-84; AIM

Objective. To determine that the applicant:

1. Exhibits knowledge of the elements related to weather information by analyzing weather reports, charts, and forecasts from various sources with emphasis on—
   a. METAR, TAF, and FA.
   b. surface analysis chart.
   c. radar summary chart.
   d. winds and temperature aloft chart.
   e. significant weather prognostic charts.
   f. convective outlook chart.
   g. AWOS, ASOS, and ATIS reports.
2. Makes a competent "go/no-go" decision based on available weather information.

D. Task: Cross-Country Flight Planning (ASEL and ASES)

References: 14 CFR part 91; AC 61-23/FAA-H-8083-25, AC 61-84; Navigation Charts; A/FD; AIM

Objective. To determine that the applicant:

1. Exhibits knowledge of the elements related to cross-country flight planning by presenting and explaining a pre-planned VFR cross-country flight, as previously assigned by the examiner. On the day of the practical test, the final flight plan shall be to the first fuel stop, based on maximum allowable passengers, baggage, and/or cargo loads using real-time weather.
2. Uses appropriate and current aeronautical charts.
3. Properly identifies airspace, obstructions, and terrain features.
4. Selects easily identifiable en route checkpoints.
5. Selects most favorable altitudes considering weather conditions and equipment capabilities.
6. Computes headings, flight time, and fuel requirements.
7. Selects appropriate navigation system/facilities and communication frequencies.
8. Applies pertinent information from NOTAMs, AF/D, and other flight publications.
9. Completes a navigation log and simulates filing a VFR flight plan.

E. Task: National Airspace System (ASEL and ASES)

References: 14 CFR parts 71, 91; Navigation Charts; AIM

Objective. To determine that the applicant exhibits knowledge of the elements related to the National Airspace System by explaining:

1. Basic VFR weather minimums—for all classes of airspace.
2. Airspace classes—their operating rules, pilot certification, and airplane equipment requirements for the following—
   a. Class A.
   b. Class B.
   c. Class C.
   d. Class D.
   e. Class E.
   f. Class G.
3. Special use and other airspace areas.

F. Task: Performance and Limitations (ASEL and ASES)

References: AC 61-23/FAA-H-8083-25, FAA-H-8083-1, AC 61-84, POH/AFM

Objective. To determine that the applicant:

1. Exhibits knowledge of the elements related to performance and limitations by explaining the use of charts, tables, and data to determine performance and the adverse effects of exceeding limitations.
2. Computes weight and balance. Determines the computed weight and center of gravity is within the airplane's operating limitations and if the weight and center of gravity will remain within limits during all phases of flight.
3. Demonstrates use of the appropriate performance charts, tables, and data.
4. Describes the effects of atmospheric conditions on the airplane's performance.

G. Task: Operation of Systems (ASEL and ASES)

References: AC 61-23/FAA-H-8083-25; POH/AFM

Objective. To determine that the applicant exhibits knowledge of the elements related to the operation of systems on the airplane provided for the flight test by explaining at least three (3) of the following systems.

1. Primary flight controls and trim.
2. Flaps, leading edge devices, and spoilers.
3. Water rudders (ASES).
4. Powerplant and propeller.

5. Landing gear.
6. Fuel, oil, and hydraulic.
7. Electrical.
8. Avionics
9. Pitot-static vacuum/pressure and associated flight instruments.
10. Environmental.
11. Deicing and anti-icing.

H. Task: Water and Seaplane Characteristics (ASES)

Reference: FAA-H-8083-3

Objective. To determine that the applicant exhibits knowledge of the elements related to water and seaplane characteristics by explaining:

1. The characteristics of a water surface as affected by features, such as—
   a. size and location.
   b. protected and unprotected areas.
   c. surface wind.
   d. direction and strength of water current.
   e. floating and partially submerged debris.
   f. sandbars, islands, and shoals.
   g. vessel traffic and wakes.
   h. other features peculiar to the area.
2. Float and hull construction, and their effect on seaplane performance.
3. Causes of porpoising and skipping, and the pilot action required to prevent or correct these occurrences.

I. Task: Seaplane Bases, Maritime Rules, and Aids to Marine Navigation (ASES)

References: FAA-H-8083-3; AIM

Objective. To determine that the applicant exhibits knowledge of the elements related to seaplane bases, maritime rules, and aids to marine navigation by explaining:

1. How to locate and identify seaplane bases on charts or in directories.
2. Operating restrictions at various bases.
3. Right-of-way, steering, and sailing rules pertinent to seaplane operation.
4. Marine navigation aids such as buoys, beacons, lights, and sound signals.

J. Task: Aeromedical Factors (ASEL and ASES)

References: AC 61-23/FAA-H-8083-25; AIM

Objective. To determine that the applicant exhibits knowledge of the elements related to aeromedical factors by explaining:

1. The symptoms, causes, effects, and corrective actions of at least three (3) of the following—
   a. hypoxia.
   b. hyperventilation.
   c. middle ear and sinus problems.
   d. spatial disorientation.
   e. motion sickness.
   f. carbon monoxide poisoning.
   g. stress and fatigue.
   h. dehydration.
2. The effects of alcohol, drugs, and over-the-counter medications.
3. The effects of excesses nitrogen during scuba dives upon a pilot or passenger in flight.

II. Area of Operation: Preflight Procedures

A. Task: Preflight Inspection (ASEL and ASES)

References: FAA-H-8083-3; POH/AFM

Objective. To determine that the applicant:

1. Exhibits knowledge of the elements related to preflight inspection. This shall include which items must be inspected, the reasons for checking each item, and how to detect possible defects.
2. Inspects the airplane with reference to an appropriate checklist.
3. Verifies the airplane is in condition for safe flight.

B. Task: Cockpit Management (ASEL and ASES)

References: FAA-H-8083-3; POH/AFM

Objective. To determine that the applicant:

1. Exhibits knowledge of the elements related to cockpit management procedures.
2. Ensures all loose items in the cockpit and cabin are secured.
3. Organizes material and equipment in an efficient manner so they are readily available.
4. Briefs occupants on the use of safety belts, shoulder harnesses, doors, and emergency procedures.

C. Task: Engine Starting (ASEL and ASES)

References: FAA-H-8083-3, AC 61-23/FAA-H-8083-25, AC 91-13, AC 91-55; POH/AFM

Objective. To determine that the applicant:

1. Exhibits knowledge of the elements related to recommended engine starting procedures. This shall include the use of an external power source, hand propping safety, and starting under various atmospheric conditions.
2. Positions the airplane properly considering structures, surface conditions, other aircraft, and the safety of nearby persons and property.
3. Utilizes the appropriate checklist for starting procedure.

E. Task: Taxiing and Sailing (ASES)

References: FAA-H-8083-3; USCG Navigation Rules, International–Inland; POH/AFM

Objective. To determine that the applicant:

1. Exhibits knowledge of the elements related to water taxi and sailing procedures.
2. Positions the flight controls properly for the existing wind conditions.
3. Plans and follows the most favorable course while taxi or sailing considering wind, water current, water conditions and maritime regulations.
4. Uses the appropriate idle, plow, or step taxi technique.
5. Uses flight controls, flaps, doors, water rudder, and power correctly so as to follow the desired course while sailing.
6. Prevents and corrects for porpoising and skipping.
7. Avoids other aircraft, vessels, and hazards.
8. Complies with seaplane base signs, signals, and clearances.

F. Task: Before Takeoff Check (ASEL and ASES)

References: FAA-H-8083-3; POH/AFM

Objective. To determine that the applicant:

1. Exhibits knowledge of the elements related to the before takeoff check. This shall include the reasons for checking each item and how to detect malfunctions.
2. Positions the airplane properly considering other aircraft/vessels, wind and surface conditions.
3. Divides attention inside and outside the cockpit.
4. Ensures that engine temperature and pressure are suitable for run-up and takeoff.

5. Accomplishes the before takeoff checklist and ensures the airplane is in safe operating condition.
6. Reviews takeoff performance airspeeds, takeoff distances, departure, and emergency procedures.
7. Avoids runway incursions and/or ensures no conflict with traffic prior to taxiing into takeoff position.

III. Area of Operation: Airport and Seaplane Base Operations

A. Task: Radio Communications and ATC Light Signals (ASEL and ASES)

References: 14 CFR part 91; AC 61-23/FAA-H-8083-25; AIM

Objective. To determine that the applicant:

1. Exhibits knowledge of the elements related to radio communications and ATC light signals.
2. Selects appropriate frequencies.
3. Transmits using recommended phraseology.
4. Acknowledges radio communications and complies with instructions.

B. Task: Traffic Patterns (ASEL and ASES)

References: FAA-H-8083-3, AC 61-23/FAA-H-8083-25, AC 90-66; AIM

Objective. To determine that the applicant:

1. Exhibits knowledge of the elements related to traffic patterns. This shall include procedures at airports with and without operating control towers, prevention of runway incursions, collision avoidance, wake turbulence avoidance, and wind shear.
2. Complies with proper traffic pattern procedures.
3. Maintains proper spacing from other aircraft.
4. Corrects for wind drift to maintain the proper ground track.
5. Maintains orientation with the runway/landing area in use.
6. Maintains traffic pattern altitude, ±100 feet (30 meters), and the appropriate airspeed, ±10 knots.

C. Task: Airport/Seaplane Base, Runway, and Taxiway Signs, Markings, and Lighting (ASEL and ASES)

References: AC 61-23/FAA-H-8083-25; AIM

Objective. To determine that the applicant:

1. Exhibits knowledge of the elements related to airport/seaplane base, runway, and taxiway operations with emphasis on runway incursion avoidance.
2. Properly identifies and interprets airport/seaplane base, runway, and taxiway signs, markings, and lighting.

IV. Area of Operation: Takeoffs, Landings, and Go Arounds

A. Task: Normal and Crosswind Takeoff and Climb (ASEL and ASES)

Note: If a crosswind condition does not exist, the applicant's knowledge of crosswind elements shall be evaluated through oral testing.

References: FAA-H-8083-3; POH/AFM

Objective. To determine that the applicant:

1. Exhibits knowledge of the elements related to a normal and crosswind takeoff, climb operations, and rejected takeoff procedures.
2. Positions the flight controls for the existing wind conditions.
3. Clears the area; taxies into the takeoff position and aligns the airplane on the runway center/takeoff path.
4. Retracts the water rudders, as appropriate, (ASES) and advances the throttle smoothly to takeoff power.

5. Establishes and maintains the most efficient planing/lift-off attitude and corrects for porpoising and skipping (ASES).
6. Lifts off at the recommended airspeed and accelerates to V_Y.
7. Establishes a pitch attitude that will maintain V_Y +10/-5 knots.
8. Retracts the landing gear, if appropriate, and flaps after a positive rate of climb is established.
9. Maintains takeoff power and V_Y +10/-5 knots to a safe maneuvering altitude.
10. Maintains directional control and proper wind-drift correction throughout the takeoff and climb.
11. Complies with noise abatement procedures.
12. Completes the appropriate checklist.

B. Task: **Normal and Crosswind Approach and Landing** (ASEL and ASES)

Note: If a crosswind condition does not exist, the applicant's knowledge of crosswind elements shall be evaluated through oral testing.

References: FAA-H-8083-3; POH/AFM

Objective. To determine that the applicant:

1. Exhibits knowledge of the elements related to a normal and crosswind approach and landing.
2. Adequately surveys the intended landing area (ASES).
3. Considers the wind conditions, landing surface, obstructions, and selects a suitable touchdown point.
4. Establishes the recommended approach and landing configuration and airspeed, and adjusts pitch attitude and power as required.
5. Maintains a stabilized approach and recommended airspeed, or in its absence, not more than 1.3 V_{SO}, +10/-5 knots, with wind gust factor applied.
6. Makes smooth, timely, and correct control application during the roundout and touchdown.
7. Contacts the water at the proper pitch attitude (ASES).
8. Touches down smoothly at approximate stalling speed (ASEL).
9. Touches down at or within 400 feet (120 meters) beyond a specified point, with no drift, and with the airplane's longitudinal axis aligned with and over the runway center/landing path.
10. Maintains crosswind correction and directional control throughout the approach and landing sequence.
11. Completes the appropriate checklist.

E. Task: **Short-Field Takeoff** (Confined Area—ASES) **and Maximum Performance Climb** (ASEL and ASES)

References: FAA-H-8083-3; POH/AFM

Objective. To determine that the applicant:

1. Exhibits knowledge of the elements related to a short-field (confined area ASES) takeoff and maximum performance climb.
2. Positions the flight controls for the existing wind conditions; sets the flaps as recommended.
3. Clears the area; taxies into takeoff position utilizing maximum available takeoff area and aligns the airplane on the runway center/takeoff path.
4. Selects an appropriate take off path for the existing conditions (ASES).
5. Applies brakes (if appropriate), while advancing the throttle smoothly to takeoff power.
6. Establishes and maintains the most efficient planing/lift-off attitude and corrects for porpoising and skipping (ASES).
7. Lifts off at the recommended airspeed, and accelerates to the recommended obstacle clearance airspeed or V_X.
8. Establishes a pitch attitude that will maintain the recommended obstacle clearance airspeed, or V_X, +10/-5 knots, until the obstacle is cleared, or until the airplane is 50 feet (20 meters) above the surface.
9. After clearing the obstacle, establishes the pitch attitude for V_Y, accelerates to V_Y, and maintains V_Y, +10/-5 knots, during the climb.

10. Retracts the landing gear, if appropriate, and flaps after clear of any obstacles or as recommended by manufacturer.
11. Maintains takeoff power and V_Y, +10/-5 to a safe maneuvering altitude.
12. Maintains directional control and proper wind-drift correction throughout the takeoff and climb.
13. Completes the appropriate checklist.

F. Task: **Short-Field Approach** (Confined Area—ASES) **and Landing** (ASEL and ASES)

References: FAA-H-8083-3; POH/AFM

Objective. To determine that the applicant:

1. Exhibits knowledge of the elements related to a short-field (confined area ASES) approach and landing.
2. Adequately surveys the intended landing area (ASES).
3. Considers the wind conditions, landing surface, obstructions, and selects the most suitable touchdown point.
4. Establishes the recommended approach and landing configuration and airspeed; adjusts pitch attitude and power as required.
5. Maintains a stabilized approach and recommended approach airspeed, or in its absence not more than 1.3 V_{SO}, +10/-5 knots, with wind gust factor applied.
6. Makes smooth, timely, and correct control application during the roundout and touchdown.
7. Selects the proper landing path, contacts the water at the minimum safe airspeed with the proper pitch attitude for the surface conditions (ASES).
8. Touches down smoothly at minimum control airspeed (ASEL).
9. Touches down at or within 200 feet (60 meters) beyond a specified point, with no side drift, minimum float and with the airplane's longitudinal axis aligned with and over the runway center/landing path.
10. Maintains crosswind correction and directional control throughout the approach and landing sequence.
11. Applies brakes, (ASEL) or elevator control (ASES), as necessary, to stop in the shortest distance consistent with safety.
12. Completes the appropriate checklist.

G. Task: **Glassy Water Takeoff and Climb** (ASES)

Note: If a glassy water condition does not exist, the applicant shall be evaluated by simulating the TASK.

References: FAA-H-8083-3; POH/AFM

Objective. To determine that the applicant:

1. Exhibits knowledge of the elements related to glassy water takeoff and climb.
2. Positions the flight controls and flaps for the existing conditions.
3. Clears the area; selects an appropriate takeoff path considering surface hazards and/or vessels and surface conditions.
4. Retracts the water rudders as appropriate; advances the throttle smoothly to takeoff power.
5. Establishes and maintains an appropriate planing attitude, directional control, and corrects for porpoising, skipping, and increases in water drag.
6. Utilizes appropriate techniques to lift seaplane from the water considering surface conditions.
7. Establishes proper attitude/airspeed, and accelerates to V_Y, +10/-5 knots during the climb.
8. Retracts the landing gear, if appropriate, and flaps after a positive rate of climb is established.
9. Maintains takeoff power V_Y, +10/-5 to a safe maneuvering altitude.
10. Maintains directional control and proper wind-drift correction throughout takeoff and climb.
11. Completes the appropriate checklist.

H. Task: Glassy Water Approach and Landing (ASES)

Note: If a glassy water condition does not exist, the applicant shall be evaluated by simulating the TASK.

References: FAA-H-8083-3; POH/AFM

Objective. To determine that the applicant:

1. Exhibits knowledge of the elements related to glassy water approach and landing.
2. Adequately surveys the intended landing area.
3. Considers the wind conditions, water depth, hazards, surrounding terrain, and other watercraft.
4. Selects the most suitable approach path, and touchdown area.
5. Establishes the recommended approach and landing configuration and airspeed, and adjusts pitch attitude and power as required.
6. Maintains a stabilized approach and the recommended approach airspeed, +10/-5 knots and maintains a touchdown pitch attitude and descent rate from the last altitude reference until touchdown.
7. Makes smooth, timely, and correct power and control adjustments to maintain proper pitch attitude and rate of descent to touchdown.
8. Contacts the water in the proper pitch attitude, and slows to idle taxi speed.
9. Maintains crosswind correction and directional control throughout the approach and landing sequence.
10. Completes the appropriate checklist.

I. Task: Rough Water Takeoff and Climb (ASES)

Note: If a rough water condition does not exist, the applicant shall be evaluated by simulating the TASK.

References: FAA-H-8083-3; POH/AFM

Objective. To determine that the applicant:

1. Exhibits knowledge of the elements related to rough water takeoff and climb.
2. Positions the flight controls and flaps for the existing conditions.
3. Clears the area; selects an appropriate takeoff path considering wind, swells surface hazards and/or vessels.
4. Retracts the water rudders as appropriate; advances the throttle smoothly to takeoff power.
5. Establishes and maintains an appropriate planing attitude, directional control, and corrects for porpoising, skipping, or excessive bouncing.
6. Lifts off at minimum airspeed and accelerates to V_Y, +10/-5 knots before leaving ground effect.
7. Retracts the landing gear, if appropriate, and flaps after a positive rate of climb is established.
8. Maintains takeoff power V_Y, +10/-5 to a safe maneuvering altitude.
9. Maintains directional control and proper wind-drift correction throughout takeoff and climb.
10. Completes the appropriate checklist.

J. Task: Rough Water Approach and Landing (ASES)

Note: If a rough water condition does not exist, the applicant shall be evaluated by simulating the TASK.

References: FAA-H-8083-3; POH/AFM

Objective. To determine that the applicant:

1. Exhibits knowledge of the elements related to rough water approach and landing.
2. Adequately surveys the intended landing area.
3. Considers the wind conditions, water, depth, hazards, surrounding terrain, and other watercraft.
4. Selects the most suitable approach path, and touchdown area.
5. Establishes the recommended approach and landing configuration and airspeed, and adjusts pitch attitude and power as required.

6. Maintains a stabilized approach and the recommended approach airspeed, or in its absence not more than 1.3 V_{SO}, +10/-5 knots with wind gust factor applied.
7. Makes smooth, timely, and correct power and control application during the roundout and touch down.
8. Contacts the water in the proper pitch attitude, and at the proper airspeed, considering the type of rough water.
9. Maintains crosswind correction and directional control throughout the approach and landing sequence.
10. Completes the appropriate checklist.

K. Task: Forward Slip to a Landing (ASEL and ASES)

References: FAA-H-8083-3; POH/AFM

Objective. To determine that the applicant:

1. Exhibits knowledge of the elements related to forward slip to a landing.
2. Considers the wind conditions, landing surface and obstructions, and selects the most suitable touchdown point.
3. Establishes the slipping attitude at the point from which a landing can be made using the recommended approach and landing configuration and airspeed; adjusts pitch attitude and power as required.
4. Maintains a ground track aligned with the runway center/landing path and an airspeed, which results in minimum float during the roundout.
5. Makes smooth, timely, and correct control application during the recovery from the slip, the roundout, and the touchdown.
6. Touches down smoothly at the approximate stalling speed, at or within 400 feet (120 meters) beyond a specified point, with no side drift, and with the airplane's longitudinal axis aligned with and over the runway center/landing path.
7. Maintains crosswind correction and directional control throughout the approach and landing sequence.
8. Completes the appropriate checklist.

L. Task: Go-Around/Rejected Landing (ASEL and ASES)

References: FAA-H-8083-3; POH/AFM

Objective. To determine that the applicant:

1. Exhibits knowledge of the elements related to a go-around/rejected landing.
2. Makes a timely decision to discontinue the approach to landing.
3. Applies takeoff power immediately and transitions to climb pitch attitude for V_Y, and maintains V_Y, +10/-5 knots.
4. Retracts the flaps as appropriate.
5. Retracts the landing gear, if appropriate, after a positive rate of climb is established.
6. Maneuvers to the side of the runway/landing area to clear and avoid conflicting traffic.
7. Maintains takeoff power V_Y, +10/-5 to a safe maneuvering altitude.
8. Maintains directional control and proper wind-drift correction throughout the climb.
9. Completes the appropriate checklist.

V. Area of Operation: Performance Maneuver

Task: Steep Turns (ASEL and ASES)

References: FAA-H-8083-3; POH/AFM

Objective. To determine that the applicant:

1. Exhibits knowledge of the elements related to steep turns.
2. Establishes the manufacturer's recommended airspeed or if one is not stated, a safe airspeed not to exceed V_A.
3. Rolls into a coordinated 360° turn; maintains a 45° bank.
4. Performs the task in the opposite direction, as specified by the examiner.
5. Divides attention between airplane control and orientation.
6. Maintains the entry altitude, ±100 feet (30 meters), airspeed, ±10 knots, bank, ±5°; and rolls out on the entry heading, ±10°.

VI. Area of Operation: Ground Reference Maneuvers

Note: The examiner shall select at least one TASK.

A. Task: Rectangular Course (ASEL and ASES)

Reference: FAA-H-8083-3

Objective. To determine that the applicant:

1. Exhibits knowledge of the elements related to a rectangular course.
2. Selects a suitable reference area.
3. Plans the maneuver so as to enter a left or right pattern, 600 to 1,000 feet AGL (180 to 300 meters) at an appropriate distance from the selected reference area, 45° to the downwind leg.
4. Applies adequate wind-drift correction during straight-and-turning flight to maintain a constant ground track around the rectangular reference area.
5. Divides attention between airplane control and the ground track while maintaining coordinated flight.
6. Maintains altitude, ±100 feet (30 meters); maintains airspeed, ±10 knots.

B. Task: S-Turns (ASEL and ASES)

Reference: FAA-H-8083-3

Objective. To determine that the applicant:

1. Exhibits knowledge of the elements related to S-turns.
2. Selects a suitable ground reference line.
3. Plans the maneuver so as to enter at 600 to 1,000 feet (180 to 300 meters) AGL, perpendicular to the selected reference line.
4. Applies adequate wind-drift correction to track a constant radius turn on each side of the selected reference line.
5. Reverses the direction of turn directly over the selected reference line.
6. Divides attention between airplane control and the ground track while maintaining coordinated flight.
7. Maintains altitude, ±100 feet (30 meters); maintains airspeed, ±10 knots.

C. Task: Turns Around a Point (ASEL and ASES)

Reference: FAA-H-8083-3

Objective. To determine that the applicant:

1. Exhibits knowledge of the elements related to turns around a point.
2. Selects a suitable ground reference point.
3. Plans the maneuver so as to enter left or right at 600 to 1,000 feet (180 to 300 meters) AGL, at an appropriate distance from the reference point.
4. Applies adequate wind-drift correction to track a constant radius turn around the selected reference point.
5. Divides attention between airplane control and the ground track while maintaining coordinated flight.
6. Maintains altitude, ±100 feet (30 meters); maintains airspeed, ±10 knots.

VII. Area of Operation: Navigation

A. Task: Pilotage and Dead Reckoning (ASEL and ASES)

References: AC 61-23/FAA-H-8083-25

Objective. To determine that the applicant:

1. Exhibits knowledge of the elements related to pilotage and dead reckoning.
2. Follows the preplanned course by reference to landmarks.
3. Identifies landmarks by relating surface features to chart symbols.
4. Navigates by means of precomputed headings, groundspeeds, and elapsed time.
5. Corrects for and records the differences between preflight groundspeed and heading calculations and those determined en route.
6. Verifies the airplane's position within three (3) nautical miles of the flight-planned route.
7. Arrives at the en route checkpoints within five (5) minutes of the initial or revised ETA and provides a destination estimate.
8. Maintains the appropriate altitude, ±200 feet (60 meters) and headings, ±15°.

B. Task: Navigation Systems and Radar Services (ASEL and ASES)

References: FAA-H-8083-3, AC 61-23/FAA-H-8083-25; Navigation Equipment Operation Manuals, AIM

Objective. To determine that the applicant:

1. Exhibits knowledge of the elements related to navigation systems and radar services.
2. Demonstrates the ability to use an airborne electronic navigation system.
3. Locates the airplane's position using the navigation system.
4. Intercepts and tracks a given course, radial or bearing, as appropriate.
5. Recognizes and describes the indication of station passage, if appropriate.
6. Recognizes signal loss and takes appropriate action.
7. Uses proper communication procedures when utilizing radar services.
8. Maintains the appropriate altitude, ±200 feet (60 meters) and headings ±15°.

C. Task: Diversion (ASEL and ASES)

References: AC 61-23/FAA-H-8083-25; AIM

Objective. To determine that the applicant:

1. Exhibits knowledge of the elements related to diversion.
2. Selects an appropriate alternate airport and route.
3. Makes an accurate estimate of heading, groundspeed, arrival time, and fuel consumption to the alternate airport.
4. Maintains the appropriate altitude, ±200 feet (60 meters) and heading, ±15°.

D. Task: Lost Procedures (ASEL and ASES)

References: AC 61-23/FAA-H-8083-25; AIM

Objective. To determine that the applicant:

1. Exhibits knowledge of the elements related to lost procedures.
2. Selects an appropriate course of action.
3. Maintains an appropriate heading and climbs, if necessary.
4. Identifies prominent landmarks.
5. Uses navigation systems/facilities and/or contacts an ATC facility for assistance, as appropriate.

VIII. Area of Operation: Slow Flight and Stalls

A. Task: Maneuvering During Slow Flight (ASEL and ASES)

References: FAA-H-8083-3; POH/AFM

Objective. To determine that the applicant:

1. Exhibits knowledge of the elements related to maneuvering during slow flight.
2. Selects an entry altitude that will allow the task to be completed no lower than 1,500 feet (460 meters) AGL.
3. Establishes and maintains an airspeed at which any further increase in angle of attack, increase in load factor, or reduction in power, would result in an immediate stall.
4. Accomplishes coordinated straight-and-level flight, turns, climbs, and descents with landing gear and flap configurations specified by the examiner.
5. Divides attention between airplane control and orientation.
6. Maintains the specified altitude, ±100 feet (30 meters); specified heading, ±10°; airspeed, +10/-0 knots; and specified angle of bank, ±10°.

B. Task: Power-Off Stalls (ASEL and ASES)

References: FAA-H-8083-3, AC 61-67; POH/AFM

Objective. To determine that the applicant:

1. Exhibits knowledge of the elements related to power-off stalls.
2. Selects an entry altitude that allows the task to be completed no lower than 1,500 feet (460 meters) AGL.
3. Establishes a stabilized descent in the approach or landing configuration, as specified by the examiner.
4. Transitions smoothly from the approach or landing attitude to a pitch attitude that will induce a stall.
5. Maintains a specified heading, ±10°, in straight flight; maintains a specified angle of bank not to exceed 20°, ±10°; in turning flight, while inducing the stall.
6. Recognizes and recovers promptly after the stall occurs by simultaneously reducing the angle of attack, increasing power to maximum allowable, and leveling the wings to return to a straight-and-level flight attitude with a minimum loss of altitude appropriate for the airplane.
7. Retracts the flaps to the recommended setting; retracts the landing gear, if retractable, after a positive rate of climb is established.
8. Accelerates to V_X or V_Y speed before the final flap retraction; returns to the altitude, heading, and airspeed specified by the examiner.

C. Task: Power-On Stalls (ASEL and ASES)

Note: In some high performance airplanes, the power setting may have to be reduced below the practical test standards guideline power setting to prevent excessively high pitch attitudes (greater than 30° nose up).

References: FAA-H-8083-3, AC 61-67; POH/AFM

Objective. To determine that the applicant:

1. Exhibits knowledge of the elements related to power-on stalls.
2. Selects an entry altitude that allows the task to be completed no lower than 1,500 feet (460 meters) AGL.
3. Establishes the takeoff or departure configuration. Sets power to no less than 65 percent available power.
4. Transitions smoothly from the takeoff or departure attitude to the pitch attitude that will induce a stall.
5. Maintains a specified heading, ±10°, in straight flight; maintains a specified angle of bank not to exceed 20°, ±10°, in turning flight, while inducing the stall.
6. Recognizes and recovers promptly after the stall occurs by simultaneously reducing the angle of attack, increasing power as appropriate, and leveling the wings to return to a straight-and-level flight attitude with a minimum loss of altitude appropriate for the airplane.
7. Retracts the flaps to the recommended setting; retracts the landing gear if retractable, after a positive rate of climb is established.
8. Accelerates to V_X or V_Y speed before the final flap retraction; returns to the altitude, heading, and airspeed specified by the examiner.

D. Task: Spin Awareness (ASEL and ASES)

References: FAA-H-8083-3, AC 61-67; POH/AFM

Objective. To determine that the applicant exhibits knowledge of the elements related to spin awareness by explaining:

1. Aerodynamic factors related to spins.
2. Flight situations where unintentional spins may occur.
3. Procedures for recovery from unintentional spins.

IX. Area of Operation: Basic Instrument Maneuvers

Note: The examiner shall select task E and at least two other TASKs.

A. Task: Straight-and-Level Flight (ASEL and ASES)

References: FAA-H-8083-3, FAA-H-8083-15

Objective. To determine that the applicant:

1. Exhibits knowledge of the elements related to attitude instrument flying during straight-and-level flight.
2. Maintains straight-and-level flight solely by reference to instruments using proper instrument cross-check and interpretation, and coordinated control application.
3. Maintains altitude, ±200 feet (60 meters); heading, ±20°; and airspeed, ±10 knots.

B. Task: Constant Airspeed Climbs (ASEL and ASES)

References: FAA-H-8083-3, FAA-H-8083-15

Objective. To determine that the applicant:

1. Exhibits knowledge of the elements related to attitude instrument flying during constant airspeed climbs.
2. Establishes the climb configuration specified by the examiner.

3. Transitions to the climb pitch attitude and power setting on an assigned heading using proper instrument cross-check and interpretation, and coordinated control application.
4. Demonstrates climbs solely by reference to instruments at a constant airspeed to specific altitudes in straight flight and turns.
5. Levels off at the assigned altitude and maintains that altitude, ±200 feet (60 meters); maintains heading, ±20°; maintains airspeed, ±10 knots.

C. Task: **Constant Airspeed Descents** (ASEL and ASES)

References: FAA-H-8083-3, FAA-H-8083-15

Objective. To determine that the applicant:

1. Exhibits knowledge of the elements related to attitude instrument flying during constant airspeed descents.
2. Establishes the descent configuration specified by the examiner.
3. Transitions to the descent pitch attitude and power setting on an assigned heading using proper instrument cross-check and interpretation, and coordinated control application.
4. Demonstrates descents solely by reference to instruments at a constant airspeed to specific altitudes in straight flight and turns.
5. Levels off at the assigned altitude and maintains that altitude, ±200 feet (60 meters); maintains heading, ±20°; maintains airspeed, ±10 knots.

D. Task: **Turns to Headings** (ASEL and ASES)

References: FAA-H-8083-3, FAA-H-8083-15

Objective. To determine that the applicant:

1. Exhibits knowledge of the elements related to attitude instrument flying during turns to headings.
2. Transitions to the level-turn attitude using proper instrument cross-check and interpretation, and coordinated control application.
3. Demonstrates turns to headings solely by reference to instruments; maintains altitude, ±200 feet (60 meters); maintains a standard rate turn and rolls out on the assigned heading, ±10°; maintains airspeed, ±10 knots.

E. Task: **Recovery from Unusual Flight Attitudes** (ASEL and ASES)

References: FAA-H-8083-3, FAA-H-8083-15

Objective. To determine that the applicant:

1. Exhibits knowledge of the elements related to attitude instrument flying during unusual attitudes.
2. Recognizes unusual flight attitudes solely by reference to instruments; recovers promptly to a stabilized level flight attitude using proper instrument cross-check and interpretation and smooth, coordinated control application in the correct sequence.

F. Task: **Radio Communications, Navigation Systems/Facilities, and Radar Services** (ASEL and ASES)

References: FAA-H-8083-3, FAA-H-8083-15, AC 61-23/FAA-H-8083-25

Objective. To determine that the applicant:

1. Exhibits knowledge of the elements related to radio communications, navigation systems/facilities, and radar services available for use during flight solely by reference to instruments.
2. Selects the proper frequency and identifies the appropriate facility.
3. Follows verbal instructions and/or navigation systems/facilities for guidance.
4. Determines the minimum safe altitude.
5. Maintains altitude, ±200 feet (60 meters); maintains heading, ±20°; maintains airspeed, ±10 knots.

X. Area of Operation: Emergency Operations

A. Task: Emergency Approach and Landing (Simulated) (ASEL and ASES)

References: FAA-H-8083-3; POH/AFM

Objective. To determine that the applicant:

1. Exhibits knowledge of the elements related to emergency approach and landing procedures.
2. Analyzes the situation and selects an appropriate course of action.
3. Establishes and maintains the recommended best-glide airspeed, ±10 knots.
4. Selects a suitable landing area.
5. Plans and follows a flight pattern to the selected landing area considering altitude, wind, terrain, and obstructions.
6. Prepares for landing, or go-around, as specified by the examiner.
7. Follows the appropriate checklist.

B. Task: Systems and Equipment Malfunctions (ASEL and ASES)

References: FAA-H-8083-3; POH/AFM

Objective. To determine that the applicant:

1. Exhibits knowledge of the elements related to system and equipment malfunctions appropriate to the airplane provided for the practical test.
2. Analyzes the situation and takes appropriate action for simulated emergencies appropriate to the airplane provided for the practical test for at least three (3) of the following—
   a. partial or complete power loss.
   b. engine roughness or overheat.
   c. carburetor or induction icing.
   d. loss of oil pressure.
   e. fuel starvation.
   f. electrical malfunction.
   g. vacuum/pressure, and associated flight instruments malfunction.
   h. pitot/static.
   i. landing gear or flap malfunction.
   j. inoperative trim.
   k. inadvertent door or window opening.
   l. structural icing.
   m. smoke/fire/engine compartment fire.
   n. any other emergency appropriate to the airplane.
3. Follows the appropriate checklist or procedure.

C. Task: Emergency Equipment and Survival Gear (ASEL and ASES)

References: FAA-H-8083-3; POH/AFM

Objective. To determine that the applicant:

Exhibits knowledge of the elements related to emergency equipment and survival gear appropriate to the airplane and environment encountered during flight. Identifies appropriate equipment that should be aboard the airplane.

XI. Area of Operation: Night Operation

Task: Night Preparation (ASEL and ASES)

References: FAA-H-8083-3, AC 61-23/FAA-H-8083-25, AC 67-2; AIM, POH/AFM

Objective. To determine that the applicant exhibits knowledge of the elements related to night operations by explaining:

1. Physiological aspects of night flying as it relates to vision.
2. Lighting systems identifying airports, runways, taxiways and obstructions, and pilot controlled lighting.
3. Airplane lighting systems.
4. Personal equipment essential for night flight.
5. Night orientation, navigation, and chart reading techniques.
6. Safety precautions and emergencies unique to night flying.

XII. Area of Operation: Postflight Procedures

Note: The examiner shall select TASK A and for ASES applicants at least one other TASK.

A. Task: After Landing, Parking, and Securing (ASEL and ASES)

References: FAA-H-8083-3; POH/AFM

Objective. To determine that the applicant:

1. Exhibits knowledge of the elements related to after landing, parking and securing procedures.
2. Maintains directional control after touchdown while decelerating to an appropriate speed.
3. Observes runway hold lines and other surface control markings and lighting.
4. Parks in an appropriate area, considering the safety of nearby persons and property.
5. Follows the appropriate procedure for engine shutdown.
6. Completes the appropriate checklist.
7. Conducts an appropriate postflight inspection and secures the aircraft.

B. Task: Anchoring (ASES)

References: FAA-H-8083-3; POH/AFM

Objective. To determine that the applicant:

1. Exhibits knowledge of the elements related to anchoring.
2. Selects a suitable area for anchoring, considering seaplane movement, water depth, tide, wind, and weather changes.
3. Uses an adequate number of anchors and lines of sufficient strength and length to ensure the seaplane's security.

C. Task: Docking and Mooring (ASES)

References: FAA-H-8083-3; POH/AFM

Objective. To determine that the applicant:

1. Exhibits knowledge of the elements related to docking and mooring.
2. Approaches the dock or mooring buoy in the proper direction considering speed, hazards, wind, and water current.
3. Ensures seaplane security.

D. Task: Ramping/Beaching (ASES)

References: FAA-H-8083-3; POH/AFM

Objective. To determine that the applicant:

1. Exhibits knowledge of the elements related to ramping/beaching.
2. Approaches the ramp/beach considering persons and property, in the proper attitude and direction, at a safe speed, considering water depth, tide, current and wind.
3. Ramps/beaches and secures the seaplane in a manner that will protect it from the harmful effect of wind, waves, and changes in water level.

TASK TABLE • Airplane Single-Engine Sea

Addition of an Airplane Single-Engine Sea Rating to an existing Private Pilot Certificate								
Required TASKs are indicated by either the TASK letter(s) that apply(s) or an indication that all or none of the TASKs must be tested based on the notes in each AREA OF OPERATION.								
PRIVATE PILOT RATING(S) HELD								
Areas of Operation	**ASEL**	**AMEL**	**AMES**	**RH**	**RG**	**Glider**	**Balloon**	**Airship**
I	F,G,H,I	F,G,H,I	F,G	F,G,H,I	F,G,H,I	F,G,H,I	F,G,H,I	F,G,H,I
II	E	E	E	A,B,C,E,F	A,B,E,F	A,B,C,E,F	A,B,C,E,F	A,B,C,E,F
III	C	C	NONE	B,C	C	B,C	B,C	B,C
IV	A,B,E,F, G,H,I,J	A,B,E,F, G,H,I,J	A,B,E,F, G,H,I,J	A,B,E,F,G, H,I,J,K,L	A,B,E,F,G, H,I,J,K,L	A,B,E,F,G, H,I,J,K,L	A,B,E,F,G, H,I,J,K,L	A,B,E,F,G, H,I,J,K,L
V	NONE	NONE	NONE	ALL	ALL	ALL	ALL	ALL
VI	NONE	NONE	NONE	ALL	NONE	ALL	ALL	ALL
VII	NONE	NONE	NONE	NONE	NONE	ALL	ALL	NONE
VIII	NONE	NONE	NONE	ALL	ALL	ALL	ALL	ALL
IX	NONE	NONE	NONE	ALL	ALL	ALL	ALL	ALL
X	A,B	A,B	A,B	ALL	ALL	ALL	ALL	ALL
XI	NONE	NONE	NONE	NONE	NONE	ALL	ALL	ALL
XII	B,C,D	B,C,D	NONE	B,C,D	B,C,D	B,C,D	B,C,D	B,C,D

Appendix 2

Seaplane Safety and Proficiency

AIM and Advisory Circular Excerpts

SEAWINGS: AC 61-91H
Pilot Proficiency Award Program

Who May Participate

All pilots holding a recreational pilot certificate or higher and a current medical certificate, when required, may participate.

Incentive Awards—Pilot Wings and Certificate

The Pilot Proficiency Award Program is now a 20-phase program. Upon completion of each of the first 10 phases, pilots become eligible to wear and are presented with a distinctive lapel or tie pin (wings) and a certificate of completion.

> **Note:** Seaplane-rated pilots who specify "seawings" on their proficiency record/wings application form and complete the requirements listed below for seaplanes and amphibians will receive a distinctive seawings pin.

SEAWINGS Substitutes for the BFR Requirement

Participation in the Pilot Proficiency Award Program in Lieu of a Flight Review

A pilot need not accomplish the flight review requirements of 14 CFR part 61, §61.56 if, since the beginning of the 24th calendar month before the month in which that pilot acts as pilot in command, he or she has satisfactorily completed one or more phases of an FAA-sponsored Pilot Proficiency Award Program in an aircraft.

Training Requirements

Seaplanes and Amphibians

(1) One hour of flight training in a seaplane or amphibian to include a demonstration by the applicant of a complete seaplane or amphibian passenger safety briefing, a weight and balance computation and interpretation for the actual flight, a review and evaluation of the current and forecast weather, and on-the-water training in docking, beaching and anchoring, and maneuvering in confined areas.

(2) One hour of flight training in a seaplane or amphibian to include landing area assessment, safe approaches and departures, takeoffs, and landings, including crosswind, rough water, and glassy water techniques. (Conditions may be simulated.)

(3) One hour of flight training in a seaplane or amphibian to include power-on and power-off stalls in various configurations with minimum altitude loss, power-off emergency landings, step taxi, step turns, rapid decelerations from the step, and emergency procedures. In addition to the I hour of flight time (not included in the I hour), there must be a discussion of stall avoidance and prevention techniques.

> **Note:** If the applicant is not qualified and current in accordance with §61.57 for instrument flight, 1 additional hour of basic instrument training with emphasis on partial panel approaches, inadvertent penetration into instrument meteorological conditions (180° turn), descent into visual meteorological conditions, and safe operations shall be accomplished in an airplane, seaplane, FAA-approved aircraft simulator, or training device for each odd-numbered award phase (Phase 1, III, V, etc.).

Continued

Safety Meetings

(1) All applicants must attend at least one FAA-sponsored or FAA-sanctioned aviation safety seminar or industry-conducted recurrent training program.

(2) Attendance at an Aviation Safety Program aviation safety seminar must be verified in the pilot's logbook or other proficiency record. This verification must be signed by an FAA SPM, other FAA inspector, or an ASC involved in conducting the seminar.

A Summary of SEAWINGS

The complete rules for SEAWINGS are found in Advisory Circular 61-91H. To summarize, to participate requires only that you fly three (or possibly four) hours with your favorite flight instructor and attend a safety seminar. The benefits are many and long lasting!

Aeronautical Information Manual
Chapter 7 • Safety of Flight

Section 5 • Potential Flight Hazards

7–5–7 Seaplane Safety

a. Acquiring a seaplane class rating affords access to many areas not available to landplane pilots. Adding a seaplane class rating to your pilot certificate can be relatively uncomplicated and inexpensive. However, more effort is required to become a safe, efficient, competent "bush" pilot. The natural hazards of the backwoods have given way to modern man-made hazards. Except for the far north, the available bodies of water are no longer the exclusive domain of the airman. Seaplane pilots must be vigilant for hazards such as electric power lines, power, sail and rowboats, rafts, mooring lines, water skiers, swimmers, etc.

b. Seaplane pilots must have a thorough understanding of the right-of-way rules as they apply to aircraft versus other vessels. Seaplane pilots are expected to know and adhere to both the U.S. Coast Guard's (USCG) Navigation Rules, International—Inland, and 14 CFR Section 91.115, Right-of-Way Rules; Water Operations. The navigation rules of the road are a set of collision avoidance rules as they apply to aircraft on the water. A seaplane is considered a vessel when on the water for the purposes of these collision avoidance rules. In general, a seaplane on the water shall keep well clear of all vessels and avoid impeding their navigation. The CFR requires, in part, that aircraft operating on the water "...shall, insofar as possible, keep clear of all vessels and avoid impeding their navigation, and shall give way to any vessel or other aircraft that is given the right-of-way..." This means that a seaplane should avoid boats and commercial shipping when on the water. If on a collision course, the seaplane should slow, stop, or maneuver to the right, away from the bow of the oncoming vessel. Also, while on the surface with an engine running, an aircraft must give way to all nonpowered vessels. Since a seaplane in the water may not be as maneuverable as one in the air, the aircraft on the water has right-of-way over one in the air, and one taking off has right-of-way over one landing. A seaplane is exempt from the USCG safety equipment requirements, including the requirements for Personal Flotation Devices (PFD). Requiring seaplanes on the water to comply with USCG equipment requirements in addition to the FAA equipment requirements would be an unnecessary burden on seaplane owners and operators.

c. Unless they are under Federal jurisdiction, navigable bodies of water are under the jurisdiction of the state, or in a few cases, privately owned. Unless they are specifically restricted, aircraft have as much right to operate on these bodies of water as other vessels. To avoid problems, check with Federal or local officials in advance of operating on unfamiliar waters. In addition to the agencies listed in Table 7-5-1, the nearest Flight Standards District Office can usually offer some practical suggestions as well as regulatory information. If you land on a restricted body of water because of an inflight emergency, or in ignorance of the restrictions you have violated, report as quickly as practical to the nearest local official having jurisdiction and explain your situation.

d. When operating a seaplane over or into remote areas, appropriate attention should be given to survival gear. Minimum kits are recommended for summer and winter, and are required by law for flight into sparsely settled areas of Canada and Alaska. Alaska State Department of Transportation and Canadian Ministry of Transport officials can provide specific information on survival gear requirements. The kit should be assembled in one container and be easily reachable and preferably floatable.

e. The FAA recommends that each seaplane owner or operator provide flotation gear for occupants any time a seaplane operates on or near water. 14 CFR Section 91.205(b)(12) requires approved flotation gear for aircraft operated for hire over water and beyond power-off gliding distance from shore. FAA-approved gear differs from that required for navigable waterways under USCG rules. FAA-approved life vests are inflatable designs as compared to the USCG's noninflatable PFDs that may consist of solid, bulky material. Such USCG PFDs are impractical for seaplanes and other aircraft because they may block passage through the relatively narrow exits available to pilots and passengers. Life vests approved under Technical Standard Order (TSO) C13E contain fully inflatable compartments. The wearer inflates the compartments (AFTER exiting the aircraft) primarily by independent CO2 cartridges, with an oral inflation tube as a backup. The flotation gear also contains a water-activated, self-illuminating signal light. The fact that pilots and passengers can easily don and wear inflatable life vests (when not inflated) provides maximum effectiveness and allows for unrestricted movement. It is imperative that passengers are briefed on the location and proper use of available PFDs prior to leaving the dock.

f. The FAA recommends that seaplane owners and operators obtain Advisory Circular (AC) 91-69, Seaplane Safety for 14 CFR Part 91 Operations, free from the U.S. Department of Transportation, Subsequent Distribution Office, SVC-121.23, Ardmore East Business Center, 3341 Q 75th Avenue, Landover, MD 20785; fax: (301) 386-5394. The USCG Navigation Rules International-Inland (COMDTINSTM 16672.2B) is available for a fee from the Government Printing Office by facsimile request to (202) 512-2250, and can be ordered using Mastercard or Visa.

Jurisdictions Controlling Navigable Bodies of Water (Table 7-5-1)

Authority to Consult For Use of a Body of Water

Location	Authority	Contact
Wilderness Area	U.S. Department of Agriculture, Forest Service	Local forest ranger
National Forest	USDA Forest Service	Local forest ranger
National Park	U.S. Department of the Interior, National Park Service	Local park ranger
Indian Reservation	USDI, Bureau of Indian Affairs	Local Bureau office
State Park	State government or state forestry or park service	Local state aviation office for further information
Canadian National and Provincial Parks	Supervised and restricted on an individual basis from province to province and by different departments of the Canadian government; consult Canadian Flight Information Manual and/or Water Aerodrome Supplement	Park Superintendent in an emergency

Advisory Circular 91-69A
Seaplane Safety for 14 CFR Part 91 Operators

Background

a. For-Hire Operations. For-hire operations are subject to additional regulatory requirements, even if they are permitted to be conducted only under part 91. While most for-hire operations will be covered by both part 91 and part 135, some operations may be permitted to operate only under part 91 pursuant to an exception provided in 14 CFR part 119, section 119.1(e). In any event, section 91.205(b)(12) also applies to an aircraft operating in a for-hire capacity when it is over water and beyond power-off gliding distance from shore. Each person operating a civil aircraft for-hire must provide at least one pyrotechnic signaling device and have FAA-approved flotation gear readily available to each occupant (section 91.205(b)(12)). Aircraft operations subject to part 135 also require a preflight briefing on the use of flotation gear and exiting the aircraft in an emergency (section 135.117(a)(4)). As indicated above, the FAA recommends that seaplane operators engaged in not-for-hire operations under part 91 also conduct such preflight briefings.

b. Status of Seaplanes as Vessels. USCG's Navigation Rules, International-Inland, provides the following definition: "The word 'vessel' includes every description of water craft, including nondisplacement craft and seaplanes, used or capable of being used as a means of transportation on water." Therefore, a seaplane is a vessel once it lands on the water and, as such, is required to comply with the USCG navigation rules applicable to vessels. Adherence to section 91.115 should ensure compliance with the USCG rules.

Seaplane Preflight

All PICs, including those operating within the territorial waters of the U.S. coast, are responsible for taking preflight action consistent with section 91.103. Additionally, in order to comply with the requirements in section 91.7 (Civil aircraft airworthiness), the PIC is responsible for determining whether the aircraft is in a condition for safe flight. One means of assuring compliance with section 91.7 is for the PIC to make sure a thorough preflight inspection of the aircraft is conducted. With some exceptions, the preflight inspection of a seaplane is similar to that for a landplane. The major difference is checking the floats or hull. The airplane flight manual (AFM), pilot's operating handbook (POH), or manufacturer's recommendations will contain procedures for doing this in addition to the usual preflight actions, such as fuel sumping, fuel quantity, engine oil quantity, control checks, etc.

a. Some operators haul seaplanes out of the water for dry land storage on a trailer or raft, making preflight more convenient for the pilot. However, the pilot should not conduct an abbreviated inspection just because a seaplane is preflighted while in the water.

b. The pilot should first note how the seaplane rides in the water. If the stern of the floats or hull is very low in the water, i.e., float stern submerged or, in a flying boat, tail in the water, the seaplane could be loaded incorrectly, or there could be a leak in a float compartment or in the hull. This is why manufacturers recommend that floats and hulls be inspected and bilge-pumped before each flight.

(1) The pilot should first inspect floats and hulls for obvious or apparent defects or damage, such as dents, cracks, deep scratches, loose rivets, corrosion, separation of seams, punctures, and general condition of the skin. This might also be a good time to inspect the fuselage for damage. Ensure that the airframe/float combination and attachments are approved for use on the seaplane.

(2) Because of the rigidity of float installations, the pilot should check fittings, wire or tubular bracing, and adjacent structures for cracks, defective welds, proper attachment, alignment, and safety wires and nuts.

(3) Pilots should check all hinge points for wear and corrosion, particularly if the seaplane operates on salt water.

(4) The pilot should inspect the water rudders, if installed, and their cables and springs for free and proper movement. Special attention should be paid to the area where cables go over pulleys, and the pilot should inspect the cable for fraying.

(5) The pilot should pump out each bilge or compartment of a float or the hull to remove water. A small amount of water, e.g., a cupful, is not unusual and can occur from condensation or normal seepage. (If the bilge pumps out no water, it is more likely that the pump itself, or the tube leading to the bilge, is defective.) All water should be removed before flight by pumping or with a sponge because the water may critically affect the seaplane's weight and its center of gravity. Finding an excessive amount of water should cue the pilot to look for the source of the leak. If drain plugs and inspection plates are installed, the pilot should use a systematic method (refer to manufacturer's recommendations) to remove the plugs and plates and examine the compartments thoroughly. Of course, it is equally important to reinstall the plugs and plates systematically before a water takeoff.

(a) Some floats are equipped with a bilge funnel which does not require the removal of a cover to pump the bilge. However, if the funnel becomes disconnected from the hose that goes to the bottom of the float, the pump will not pump any water, and there may still be water in the float. The answer is to be suspicious if no water emerges when bilging after the seaplane has spent an extended time on the water or in storage.

(b) Floats stored in freezing climates should be inspected particularly closely because water in the floats expands upon freezing. Frozen water in compartment seams can cause severe leakage problems. Many operators who store the floats off the airplane for a season put them away upside down with compartment covers off to allow drainage. It might also be a good idea to look for any creatures that might have made a home in the floats.

(6) The pilot should ensure that nothing is stored in compartments of floats not approved for storage. For those floats approved for storage of items, the pilot must ensure that the contents and their placement allow the seaplane to remain within its weight and balance limitations. Another consideration is that floats are certificated to continue to float after two compartments per float have been flooded. The potential for capsizing or sinking is increased where compartments are at their limit for storage and other compartments become filled with water after accident damage. Pilots should be aware that float compartments have no ventilation. It is extremely dangerous and illegal to carry a container of fuel anywhere fuel vapors could accumulate. Title 49 CFR section 175.310 specifies the manner in which fuel must be transported by air. It permits limited amounts of flammable liquid fuel to be carried on board airplanes for use in remote areas, provided it is carried in closed metal containers that meet the specifications prescribed in section 175.310.

Note: Pilots transporting flammable liquids under this section must assure that their operation is not-for-hire; otherwise, they would be required to complete the training specified in 49 CFR sections 172.700–704.

(7) Pilots should be careful when carrying external cargo and should follow the manufacturer's recommendations regarding such carriage. If the manufacturer does not permit it, then the pilot should not either. Because of their bulk or size, certain items may not be able to be loaded in the cabin of small aircraft. Floats, because of their size, make a useful platform for carrying items that are too large to fit into the cabin. However, certain precautions must be taken to ensure safety of flight. Items must be placed to ensure compliance with weight and balance limitations. The weight should be equally distributed on both floats, items should be aft of the propeller arc, and the weight of any external cargo should be included during the weight and balance calculations. Finally, external loads must be properly secured to the aircraft in a manner that does not block the emergency exits.

Passenger Briefings

a. Background. From the standpoint of passenger survival in seaplanes, an upset or capsizing from accidental water contact—whether it is a float or a wingtip or an encounter with a large wave or landing gear down on amphibious floats—is the most critical type of occurrence. This is because of the lack of time to prepare for evacuation and the likelihood of major cabin structural damage from impact with the water. During such a crisis, the pilot may be too busy coping with the problem to give instructions beyond the order to evacuate. Furthermore, if the pilot becomes incapacitated in an emergency, it is important for the passengers to know what to do and how to do it without additional prompting from the pilot. Since seaplanes tend to come to rest inverted in water accidents or incidents but can remain afloat for long periods if the floats are not breached, ***the FAA cannot stress enough the importance of a thorough preflight passenger briefing, even when one is not required.*** (Although this AC suggests topics to cover in such a preflight briefing, the pilot should also consult the POH or AFM for any special evacuation procedures.) Evacuation of a seaplane creates a few problems not associated with a landplane; therefore, passengers need to know the location and operation of normal and emergency exits, flotation gear, seatbelts, and shoulder harnesses, etc. The PIC is directly responsible for and is the final authority for the safe operation of an aircraft. Being "directly responsible" may also include responsibility for passengers carried in that aircraft in the event of an accident or incident.

b. Presentation. The pilot should present the pretakeoff oral briefing preferably before engine start so passengers can easily hear it and easily see the actual or simulated demonstrations. Pilots should speak clearly and distinctly and physically point out and explain the operation of both normal and emergency exits and any safety equipment on board. Whenever possible, pilots should demonstrate the use of safety equipment and both normal and emergency exits. When a demonstration is impractical, such as demonstrating the actual inflation of flotation gear, the pilot should simulate the actions involved as closely as possible. The FAA Aviation Safety Program has produced an excellent series of videotapes including one that addresses passenger briefings for seaplane operators. Please contact the Aviation Safety Program Manager at your local Flight Standards District Office (FSDO) to view a copy of this videotape.

c. Pretakeoff Briefing. Before each takeoff, the pilot should orally brief all passengers on each of the following:

(1) When, where, and under what conditions passengers may smoke and when smoking materials must be extinguished.

(2) How to fasten, tighten, and unfasten the safety belt and shoulder harness (if installed) without looking at the mechanism, and how to stow the loose end of the seatbelt so that the loose end does not hinder opening the seatbelt in the event of capsizing.

(3) How to recognize, by feel, seatbelt rollover and that the buckle, in this condition, must be righted so it can be opened.

(4) How to operate seats, forward and backward, to enhance egress.

(5) That the seat back should be upright for takeoff and landing.

(6) The location of each normal and emergency exit.

(7) The operation of each normal and emergency exit by explanation and demonstration, if practical.

(8) To leave carry-on items behind in the event of an evacuation in the water.

(9) To establish "situational awareness." During the preflight briefing, the pilot should help passengers establish a definite frame of reference, such as left hand on the left knee or left armrest or right hand toward the direction of the exit. Once they have established situational awareness, passengers can use a "hand-over-hand" technique to make their way to an exit when the pilot gives the evacuation order; e.g., "Exit through the left rear door," or "Exit right side." Using positional and situational awareness and the "hand-over-hand" technique decreases the possibility of becoming disoriented. The pilot should stress the point that whether a passenger is upright or inverted, left and right are still the same; i.e., if the exit is on the passenger's right while upright, it will still be on the passenger's right if inverted. The pilot should also be sure to make all directional references to the passenger's right or left, **not** the pilot's. Pilots should advise passengers if the door handle on the inside of the airplane will work in reverse when they are upside down and that, when the door is closed and locked as in flight, the door may not be able to be opened from the outside.

(10) The following various aspects of flotation gear:

(a) If using flotation cushions, the pilot should brief on the type, location, and how to use in the water, including a physical demonstration, if possible; e.g., how to insert arms through the straps and rest the torso on the cushion once in the water and not to wear the cushion on one's back.

(b) If using some form of PFD, the pilot should brief on the type, location, and use of the available PFD, including a demonstration of how to don the device and a simulated demonstration of how to inflate an inflatable device either by carbon dioxide (CO_2) or by oral or manual methods **after** entering the water. ***The pilot must emphasize that an inflatable PFD should NOT be inflated until clear of the wreckage after exiting the aircraft since these devices can easily get hung up on wreckage, block an exit, or prevent a passenger from exiting an inverted seaplane***. An inflated PFD that becomes damaged because of punctures caused by contact with the wreckage or snagged on debris, may be rendered useless.

Note: The FAA suggests that operators consider establishing a policy where all occupants wear an inflatable PFD anytime the seaplane operates on or near the water.

(11) The use and operation of any fire extinguishers on board, location of survival gear—including the Emergency Locator Transmitter (ELT) and pyrotechnic signaling device (flares)—an appropriate brace position, and the proper location for carry-on items.

(12) Seaplanes are dangerous at both ends. Exercise extreme caution when around the propeller and the elevator. Serious injuries, amputations, and death have resulted from propeller strikes and the horizontal stabilizer when unwary passengers attempt to help in the launching or docking of a seaplane. The elevator balance weight on many seaplanes is an effective finger guillotine. In the preflight briefing ***pilots should instruct passengers not to assist unless specifically requested to do so by the pilot.*** If the pilot anticipates needing passenger assistance, the pilot should provide specific instructions on the passenger's duties, including a precaution about avoiding the spinning propeller, and how to properly handle the horizontal stabilizer.

d. Passengers Needing Assistance. The pilot should individually brief a passenger who may need assistance in exiting. The briefing should include all of the above information and who will be assisting the passenger to exit. If the passenger is accompanied by an attendant, the pilot should brief both the passenger and the attendant on the above information, including the most appropriate route to an exit, when to move toward the exit, and the most appropriate manner of assisting the passenger.

e. Prelanding Briefing. At a minimum before each landing, the pilot should ensure that all passengers have been briefed to fasten seatbelts and shoulder harnesses (if installed), place seat backs in the upright position, and stow carry-on items.

Use of Seatbelts and Shoulder Harnesses in Seaplanes

a. Seaplanes are subject to the seatbelt and shoulder harness requirements of section 91.107. Unfortunately, takeoff and landing are the phases of flight where improper pilot technique or water or wind conditions could result in a capsized seaplane. The shock of entering cold water and being inverted while strapped into a seat can cause panic in passengers. That is why the preflight briefing on seatbelt operations is very important. The FAA is aware that some operators have passengers leave seatbelts unfastened or loosened during any type of water taxiing to position for takeoff or after landing. Both of these practices are prohibited under FAA regulations.

b. Pilots are reminded that section 91.105(a) requires them to keep their seatbelt fastened during takeoff, landing, and while en route when at the crewmember station unless an absence is necessary to perform duties in connection with the operation of the aircraft. Section 91.105(b) requires pilots to keep their shoulder harness, if installed, fastened during takeoff and landing. However, section 91.107(a)(3) provides that the person pushing off the seaplane from the dock and the person mooring the seaplane are excepted from the requirement to be seated in an approved seat and secured with a seatbelt.

Escape/Egress in the Event of an Upset in the Water

a. Accident History. A review of past seaplane accidents on the water indicates that the pilots and passengers in inverted aircraft often survived the impact but were unable to evacuate the aircraft under water and subsequently drowned. In some cases, passengers were unable to unfasten their seatbelts, and, consequently, their bodies were discovered with little or no impact injuries still strapped to the seats. In other cases, passengers were able to get out of their seatbelts but were unable to find an exit and/or open the exit because of impact damage or ambient water pressure. Those who did survive generally spoke of the extreme disorientation and that they did not exit in what may be considered a normal procedure; i.e., they did whatever they had to in order to get out of the aircraft.

(1) Opening a door under water can be extremely difficult, and some operators adopt the practice of water taxiing with one door open at all times to permit easier egress. However, operators should check the POH or AFM for evacuation procedures since, in the event of capsizing, this practice could lead to the cockpit and cabin flooding sooner and sinking the seaplane faster.

(2) In many cases, pilots exited relatively easily through a smashed cockpit windshield or the cockpit door and seemed to have less difficulty evacuating the seaplane because of their familiarity with it. Passengers, on the other hand, often do not have a thorough knowledge of their surroundings. Investigations of evacuations of air carrier aircraft have shown that passengers tend to want to exit through the door where they entered. It is likely this would hold true even for a small seaplane because where the passenger entered might be the only familiar frame of reference in an emergency.

(3) In some of the accidents where pilots survived and passengers did not, investigation revealed that pilots had met the requirements of section 91.107 but did not go beyond that; i.e., did not brief passengers on how to exit in an emergency, on the location, donning, and inflation of a PFD, and on the procedures for an underwater exit of the aircraft. There were accidents where the pilot was injured or killed and could not assist passengers in an underwater evacuation. Therefore, ***a comprehensive preflight briefing, although not a regulatory requirement, can provide critical information to passengers so that they can help themselves***. The information in that preflight briefing could make the difference between a successful evacuation and being trapped inside a submerged seaplane.

b. Evacuation. The pilot should **never** take for granted that people already know how to exit the seaplane. After an accident, and especially while submerged inverted in water, the passengers are likely to panic, but they will usually defer to what the pilot instructs. In their eyes, the pilot knows what to do.

(1) The pilot should keep commands simple and concise, since it is likely that passengers will cease to listen much beyond the initial order to evacuate. Passengers respond to very short instructions, i.e., "stop," "leave it," and "come here." Pilots should issue commands and make decisions in a positive, confident, and expeditious manner.

(2) Being upside down can cause orientation problems. Once the turbulence of the upset has subsided, even though the pilot may have briefed passengers on situational awareness before takeoff, the pilot may still need to help passengers establish positive situational awareness so that they can determine left from right.

(3) Maneuvering while holding flotation devices can also be disorienting because it occupies the hands, making swimming or treading water difficult. This adds to the argument for wearing an inflatable PFD. However, it is important to remember ***not to inflate the PFD until after exiting the seaplane***. It is virtually impossible to swim downward to an exit (from an inverted position) with an inflated PFD. Any preflight briefing on the use of inflatable PFDs should include this vital point.

(4) Impact forces may jam normal or emergency exits and prevent them from operating. Pilots should be prepared to, and have briefed passengers to be prepared to, break out or kick out windows in order to escape. In many instances, this may be the only option for evacuation and everyone on board should plan to use this technique if necessary.

Water Survival

Successful egress from an inverted seaplane into the water is only the beginning of the survival process. The pilot may be the only person who understands the effects of cold water, even water only a few degrees cooler than normal body temperature, on the human body. Seaplane accidents that occur even on small bodies of water may mean a wait for rescue, especially if the location is remote. Furthermore, even if the evacuees make it to shore fairly quickly after submersion, they may still be at risk for hypothermia if the outside temperatures are cold and the evacuees do not have access to dry clothing or shelter. Especially for seaplanes operating into remote areas, operators should consider stocking the seaplane with survival gear appropriate for the operation. The survival kit should be assembled in one container that is leak proof, easily accessible, and floatable. Some Alaskan and Canadian operators attach a rope and a float to the survival kit to allow for easier recovery once everyone has exited the aircraft. This has proved quite successful in emergency situations in some of North America's harshest terrain. Pilots are advised that some states and other countries require survival equipment appropriate for the geographical area, the season of the year, and anticipated seasonal climatic variations. Pilots should familiarize themselves and comply with these requirements before flight. Seaplane operators should include provisions for shelter, water, fire, and signaling when considering what equipment to include in a survival kit. They should also emphasize the need for passengers to wear appropriate survival gear, e.g., good shoes and clothing. Also, if the weather is cool enough to wear a coat, it should be a coat that will still maintain insulating properties after being submerged. Also, anything you wear on board the seaplane should not be bulky enough to hinder escape through an aircraft window. Section 91.509 specifies the operations for survival equipment for overwater operations for large and turbine-powered multiengine airplanes.

a. Hypothermia. Cold water (less than 70°F) lowers body temperature rapidly, creating a condition called ***hypothermia***. Hypothermia means that the body's inner core temperature has begun to descend significantly below the body's norm of 98.6°F. A drop of only 3° or 4° in body temperature could overload the heart, impair circulation, and lead to irreversible brain damage. (Hypothermic persons still in the water generally lose consciousness and drown before these effects can occur.)

(1) Even though a person may be wearing a life jacket-type PFD, the body cools down about 25 times faster in cold water than in cold air. Water temperature, body size, amount of body fat, and movement in the water are all factors that play a part in how quickly a person becomes hypothermic and, therefore, in that person's survival. Generally, small people cool down faster than larger people; children cool down faster than adults.

(2) Flotation gear can help a person stay alive longer in cold water because it allows the person to float without expenditure of energy; i.e., the person's movement in the water can be used exclusively for moving toward shore rather than trying to stay afloat. Flotation gear also protects the upper torso somewhat from the effects of cold water. For example, a snug-fitting life vest would be more effective in keeping the upper torso warm than a loose-fitting one or a seat cushion used as flotation gear.

(3) Because any activity not necessary for survival will quicken the body's heat loss, before takeoff pilots should instruct their passengers that in the event of an accident, they should assume the "Heat Escape Lessening Position" while awaiting rescue. This position may be used in the water or land and reportedly will reduce the body's heat loss by 50 percent. The position is assumed by holding your arms tightly to the sides of the chest, crossing the forearms over the chest, and drawing up the legs and crossing them at the ankles. This position closes off most major heat loss areas. If there are several people involved, huddling close, side to side in a circle, will also help preserve body heat.

b. Effects of Hypothermia. The exact nature of the hypothermic process is not yet fully understood. The following table provides some indication of onset of unconsciousness and the expected time of survival in water of specific temperatures.*

Water Temperature in °F	Exhaustion or Unconsciousness	Expected Time of Survival
Up to 32.5°	Under 15 minutes	15 to 45 minutes
32.5° to 40°	15 to 30 minutes	30 to 90 minutes
40° to 50°	30 to 60 minutes	1 to 3 hours
50° to 60°	1 to 2 hours	1 to 6 hours
60° to 70°	2 to 7 hours	2 to 40 hours
70° to 80°	2 to 12 hours	3 hours to indefinitely
Over 80°	Deferred indefinitely	Indefinitely

Information from Underwriters Laboratory, Inc.

c. Handling Victims of Hypothermia. A hypothermic person requires special attention, and rescue personnel (this could be the operator's personnel who have no medical training) should be aware of the following guidelines on how to handle victims of hypothermia.

(1) Lack of movement does not mean dead. Rescue personnel should make no assumptions based only on the victim's appearance, touch, or absence of a discernible pulse or breathing. In deep hypothermia, it is not always possible to make an onsite determination whether a person is still alive. Some medical experts believe that deep hypothermia places the body in a state similar to hibernation, where brain and other organ functions become depressed, therefore requiring less oxygen from a reduced blood flow. Some victims have been revived, but the extent of injury or damage from the hypothermia has varied.

(2) Rescuers should **not** warm the victim externally, such as by immersion in warm water or by applying heat directly to the body. Rescuers should cover exposed skin with a blanket and provide shelter but should avoid abrupt temperature changes in the victim's immediate environment. The rescuers should arrange for transport to a medical facility as soon as possible.

Flotation Gear for Seaplanes

As stated above, one of the purposes of this AC is to suggest that seaplane operators who are not engaged in for-hire operations provide flotation gear for occupants any time a seaplane operates on or near water. The following paragraphs will discuss the various requirements of the FAA and the USCG for the types of flotation gear. Operators must bear in mind that seaplane operations pose unique ingress/egress situations in which a non-inflatable, USCG-approved PFD, because of its bulkiness, could restrict or impair exiting the seaplane. For this reason, the FAA recommends the use of FAA or USCG-approved, inflatable PFD in not-for-hire operations. For-hire operators must use FAA-approved PFD.

a. USCG Requirements. Title 33 CFR part 175, section 175.15 (USCG regulation), requires a PFD for each occupant on all vessels, but this does not include seaplanes. A seaplane is exempt from the USCG safety equipment requirements, including the requirements for USCG-approved PFDs. Requiring seaplanes on the water to comply with USCG equipment requirements in addition to the FAA equipment requirements would be an unnecessary burden on seaplane owners and operators. However, many states have statutes requiring PFDs to be carried on board vessels operating on any inland body of water for which the USCG has no jurisdiction. Navigable bodies of water may come under Federal, State, or local jurisdiction or, in a few cases, may be privately owned.

b. FAA Requirements. Section 91.205(b)(12) requires approved flotation gear for aircraft operated for-hire over water and beyond power-off gliding distance from shore. FAA approves life preservers under Technical Standard Order (TSO) C13f and individual flotation devices under TSO C726. In addition, section 91.509 specifies the requirements for survival equipment for overwater operations for large and turbine-powered multiengine airplanes.

(1) At one time, FAA-approved gear differed substantially from that required for navigable waterways under USCG rules. FAA-approved life preservers are inflatable designs as compared to the USCG's inherently buoyant PFDs that may consist of solid, bulky material. Such USCG PFDs are impractical for seaplanes and other aircraft because they may block passage through the relatively narrow exits available to pilots and passengers. In 1995, the USCG adopted structural and performance standards for inflatable PFDs used on recreational boats. These PFDs are intended for general boating activities by adults and on inland waters, or where there is a good chance of a fast rescue. However, USCG-approved inflatable PFDs are **not** for use by **children** younger than 16 years of age or by persons weighing less than 80 pounds, not recommended for nonswimmers or weak swimmers (unless worn **inflated**), and not for water sports like skiing or for personal water craft use. Therefore, the FAA recommends that seaplane operators who are not engaged in for-hire operations use the FAA's TSO life preservers or individual PFDs.

(2) Life preservers approved under TSO C13f contain fully inflatable compartments. The wearer inflates the compartments primarily by independent CO_2 cartridges with an oral inflation tube as a backup. This flotation gear also contains a water-activated, self-illuminating signal light. The fact that pilots and passengers can easily don and wear inflatable life preservers (when not inflated) provides maximum effectiveness and features an uncluttered exterior surface that protects the working components and allows for unrestricted movement.

c. Buoyancy. The buoyancy in a flotation device must be distributed so that if the wearer is unconscious or disoriented in the water, the device will "self-right" the wearer; i.e., if the wearer is face down in the water, the distribution of the buoyant material in the device will "turn" the wearer face up. This is another important reason why pilots should demonstrate or supervise the proper donning of the device so that wearers will not put the device on improperly and defeat this self-righting ability. The TSO C13f life preservers have excellent self-righting capabilities.

d. Flotation Gear Maintenance. Lifesaving equipment must be maintained in serviceable condition in accordance with the manufacturer's recommendations. Any FAA-approved flotation gear used in operations for compensation or hire must be inspected at least every 12 months by persons authorized by 14 CFR part 43. This inspection would be included in the annual or 100-hour inspection for the aircraft or under any other inspection program that the operator is authorized to use.

e. Wearing of Flotation Gear During all Phases of Flight. When a standard marine life jacket or FAA-approved life preserver stored in a pouch is tucked unrestrained under a seat, it could be thrown or tossed from the seaplane with other debris in the event of an accident or capsizing. In this case, the flotation gear becomes ineffective for swimmer and nonswimmer alike. Furthermore, life jackets in sealed pouches can be awkward to remove and don in a flooded aircraft. When a survivor attempts to put on a jacket in the water, it may be difficult to find and fasten its straps and hooks. It would take considerable effort to accomplish the combined maneuver of pulling a life jacket over one's head while in the water trying to stay afloat. If a life preserver is not worn before flight, it is practically impossible for a survivor with an injured arm, for example, to don the life preserver in time for it to be effective for survival. Wearing an ***uninflated*** TSO C13f life preserver at all times in the seaplane and inflating it only ***after exiting the seaplane*** would seem to be the best protection.

f. Types of PFDs. There are various types of inherently buoyant and inflatable, USCG-approved PFDs categorized by type and intended use. The USCG has indicated the advantages and disadvantages of each. To obtain information, go to the following URL: http://www.uscg.mil/hq/g%2dm/mse4/pfd.htm. If you do not have Internet access, contact your local FAA FSDO, which can print the information out for you, or contact the USCG Auxiliary.

g. The USCG regulations allow for the approval of PFDs that inflate automatically when the inflation mechanism contacts water. Please keep the following in mind regarding USCG-approved inflatable PFDs:

(1) Type I and Type II inflatable PFDs have a higher minimum buoyancy than a Type III PFD. They will out perform a Type III PFD that does not exceed the USCG minimum requirements.

(2) Some automatics will allow the user to disarm the automatic portion of the inflation mechanism.

(3) If the user improperly disarms the automatic portion of the inflatable PFD, he/she might also disarm the manual portion.

(4) Wearing a PFD with the automatic portion armed would most certainly put passengers at risk of being trapped in the airplane or damaging the PFD, rendering it unusable.

(5) If the device is to be used in both a seaplane and a boat, then the device must be rearmed for boating.

h. Other Water Survival Equipment. Dive shops and marine equipment retailers offer many types of supplemental water survival equipment. Among these are buoyancy compensatory belts and small, compact alternate air source containers used by scuba divers as a backup to their regular air tanks. These containers were originally developed for military helicopter crews, can hold up to 4 minutes of air, and are relatively lightweight and easy to stow. Four minutes of breathable air could provide pilots and passengers with some extra time to don lifejackets and exit an overturned seaplane that has flooded. Although these alternate air source containers may meet or exceed USCG requirements, they are not FAA-approved.

Summary

The best time to know emergency procedures and the worst time to learn them is during an actual emergency. Inherently buoyant USCG-approved PFDs are usually impractical for most seaplanes and other aircraft because they may prevent people from exiting through doors or windows. The best protection is afforded when wearing inflatable life preservers. When wearing inflatable life preservers, pilots and passengers should always wait until clear of the seaplane before inflating. Finally, the best safety devices are useless without the proper preflight briefings and safety demonstrations.

Appendix

Sample Passenger Preflight Briefing Checklist

Note: This "checklist" is a guideline for pilots to use in conducting an oral preflight briefing of passengers. This list should not be used as a substitute for the briefing itself.

1. Smoking considerations: Where, when, and under what conditions.
2. Seatbelts/Shoulder harnesses: How to fasten, tighten, and unfasten; how to stow the loose end of the belt.
3. Seats: Operation forward and rearward; seat backs upright for takeoff and landing.
4. Exits: Location and operation (by demonstration) of each normal and, if applicable, emergency exit.
5. Carry-on items: Stowed properly and left on board during evacuation.
6. Situational awareness: Establish a frame of reference for left and right in relation to the aircraft exits; remind left and right are the same whether right side up or upside down. Bubbles always travel up.
7. Flotation gear:
   - Cushions: Type, location, use, and demonstration of use.
   - PFDs: Type, location, use, donning, and simulated demonstration of inflation.
8. Fire extinguishers: Location and how to operate.
9. Survival equipment: Location and how to retrieve.
10. ELT or Emergency Position Indicating Radio Beacon: Location and how to turn on.

11. Pyrotechnic signaling device: Location and how to use.
12. Brace position: Demonstration.
13. Heat Escape Lessening Position: Demonstration.
14. Propeller cautions: No assistance in docking/launching by passengers unless requested by pilot; if passenger assistance is required, specific instructions on duties, placement, and caution about propellers.
15. Passengers needing assistance: Briefed individually on all above topics including who will be assisting the passenger to exit; if passenger is accompanied by an attendant, brief both.

Be Safe—Wear Your PFD

Most drownings occur way out at sea, right? Wrong! Fact is, the USCG reports that 9 out of 10 drownings occur in inland waters, most within a few feet of safety. Most of the victims owned PFDs, but they died without them. A wearable PFD can save your life—if you wear it.

If you or your passengers haven't been wearing your PFD because of the way it makes you look or feel, there's good news. Today's PFDs fit better, look better, and allow easy movement. A brightly colored PFD can increase your chances of rescue.

One more thing: Before you take off, make sure all on board are wearing PFDs. To work best, a PFD must be worn with all straps, zippers, and ties fastened. Tuck in any loose strap ends to avoid getting hung up.

When you don't wear your PFD, the odds are against you. You're taking a chance on your life.

Bibliography

Allward, Maurice, (1982). *Illustrated History of Seaplanes and Flying Boats.* Aztex Corporation. ISBN 0861900111

Brimm, Daniel J., Jr. (1937). *Seaplanes: Maneuvering, Maintaining, Operating.* New York, NY: Pitman Publishing Corporation. LC # 37005263

Bruder, Gerry. (1988). *Northern Flights.* Boulder, CO: Pruett Publishing Company.

Casey, Louis and Batchelor, John. (1980). *The Illustrated History of Seaplanes and Flying Boats.* Phoebus Publishing Company.

Causley, Dick. (1981). *Fly, Float and Flounder: How to Fly a Lake Amphibian.* Published by author.

Chapman, C.F. and Maloney, E.S. (1983). *Piloting: Seamanship and Small Boat Handling.* New York, NY: Hearst Corporation. ISBN 0-87851-814-2

Craig, Paul A. (1997). *Multiengine Flying.* (2nd ed.). McGraw-Hill. ISBN 0-07-013452-9

DeRemer, Dale. (1997). *Water Flying Concepts—An Advanced Text on Wilderness Water Flying* (second edition). Newcastle, WA: Aviation Supplies & Academics, Inc. ISBN 1-56027-484-0

DeRemer, Dale. (1991). *Aircraft Systems for Pilots.* Englewood, CO: Jeppesen Co.

DeRemer, Dale and Baj, Cesare. (1998). *Seaplane Operations.* Como, Italy: Edizioni New Press. (distributed by ASA, Inc.) ISBN 1-56027-485-9

DeRemer, Dale and McLean, Don. (1998). *Global Navigation for Pilots: International Flight Techniques and Procedures.* (2nd ed.). Newcastle, WA: Aviation Supplies & Academics, Inc. ISBN 1-56027-312-7

DeRemer, Dale and Gallagher, Ron. (1993). *Human Factors and Crew Resource Management for Flight Instructors: The New Student Involvement.* Grand Forks, ND: Eastern Dakota Publishers.

EDO Corporation. (1995). *The EDO Guide to Straight and Amphibious Floats.* (2nd ed.). College Point, NY: EDO Corporation.

Faure, C. Marin. (1996). *Flying a Floatplane.* (3rd ed.). New York, NY: McGraw-Hill. ISBN 0-07-021304-6

Fisk, William D. (1964). *Fundamentals of Float Flying, Seaplanes in the Mountain Lakes, and Glacier Flying.* Kenmore, WA: Published by author.

Fogg, Robert S. and Strohmeier, William D. and Brimm, Daniel J., Jr. (1949). *Seaplane Flying and Operations.* New York, NY: Pitman Publishing Corporation. LC # 49008587

Frey, Jay J. (1988). *How to Fly Floats*. College Point, NY: Aviation Book Company. ISBN 0911721711

Nav Canada. (1999). *Water Aerodrome Supplement*. Ottawa, ON, Canada: Geomatics Canada, Department of Natural Resources.

Newstrom, Gordon K. (1983). *Fly a Seaplane*. Grand Rapids, MN: Published by author.

Grant, Robert S. (1995). *Bush Flying, The Romance of the North*. Surrey, BC, Canada: Hancock House Publishers. ISBN 0888393504

Grant, Robert S. (1997). *Great Northern Bushplanes*. Surrey, BC, Canada: Hancock House Publishers. ISBN 0888394004

Green, William. (1962). *Floatplanes*. MacDonald.

Green, William. (1962). *Flying Boats*. MacDonald.

Hoffsommer, Alan. (1966). *Flying with Floats*. North Hollywood, CA: Pan American Navigation Service, Inc. LCC# 66016261

Jablonski, Edward. (1972). *Sea Wings: The Romance of the Flying Boats*. Doubleday. ISBN 0385069464

Kurt, Franklin T. (1974). *Water Flying*. New York, NY: Macmillan Publishing Co, Inc. ISBN 0-02-567130-8

Nicolaou, Stephane. (1998). *Flying Boats & Seaplanes*. Bideford, Devon: Bay View Books Ltd. ISBN 1-901432-20-3

Oliver, David. (1996). *Flying Boats & Amphibians since 1945*. Naval Institute Press. ISBN 0870218980

Reep, Steve. (1996). *Go to Hull*. Grand Forks, ND: Eastern Dakota Publishers. ISBN 0-9639984-5-5

Rivest, Pierre. (1988). *Bush Pilot*. Montreal, PQ, Canada: Publications Aeroscope.

Seaplane Pilots Association. *Water Flying*. Lakeland, FL: Published by author. Phone number 863-701-7979

Seaplane Pilots Association. (2000). *Water Landing Directory* (6th ed.). Frederick, MD: Published by author. ISSN 0894-5667

Thurston, David B. (1994). *Design for Flying*. (2nd ed.). McGraw-Hill. ISBN 0070645574

Wigton, Don C. (1973). *Those Fabulous Amphibians*. Detroit, MI: Harlo Press. ISBN 0-8187-0012-2

U.S. Department of Commerce. (1949). *Seaplane Facilities*.

U.S. Department of Transportation, Federal Aviation Administration. (1999). *Airplane Flying Handbook* (FAA-H-8083-3). Washington, DC: U.S. Government Printing Office.

U.S. Department of Transportation, Federal Aviation Administration. (1999). *Seaplane Safety for 14 CFR and Part 91 Operators* (AC 91-69A). Published by author.

Index

Boldface page numbers refer to figures.

A

B

C

D

E

F

G

H

I

J

K

L

M

N

O

P

R

S

T

U

V

W

Y